DATE DUE

OCT 2 3 2013

BRODART, CO.   Cat. No. 23-221

2,000+ Essential English Verbs

2,000+
ESSENTIAL
ENGLISH
VERBS

WRITTEN BY
Louise Stracke

EDITED BY
Suzanne McQuade

LIVING LANGUAGE®

Published in the United States by Living Language, an imprint of Random House, Inc.

www.livinglanguage.com

ISBN: 978-1-4000-0655-7

Library of Congress Cataloging-in-Publication Data available upon request.

This book is available at special discounts for bulk purchases for sales promotions or premiums. Special editions, including personalized covers, excerpts of existing books, and corporate imprints, can be created in large quantities for special needs. For more information, write to Special Markets/Premium Sales, 1745 Broadway, MD 6-2, New York, New York 10019 or e-mail specialmarkets@randomhouse.com.

PRINTED IN THE UNITED STATES OF AMERICA

10 9 8 7 6 5 4 3 2 1

ACKNOWLEDGMENTS

I'd like to thank Ian Case and Elise Catera for grammar expertise; Michael, Milena, and Lisa Solo for creative word combinations; Jane and Bill Bradbury for being quick with the idiom; and Bob, Maria, and Ben Stracke for providing the best workplace ever and the perfect company.

Thanks also to the Living Language team: Tom Russell, Nicole Benhabib, Christopher Warnasch, Suzanne McQuade, Shaina Malkin, Elham Shabahat, Linda K. Schmidt, Alison Skrabek, Carolyn Roth, Tom Marshall, and Sophie Ye Chin. Without their dedication and hard work, this book would not have been possible.

CONTENTS

Appendixes

INTRODUCTION

Welcome to *2,000+ Essential English Verbs: The Easiest Way to Master Verbs and Speak Fluently.* Whether you are more-or-less fluent in English, have already mastered the basics of English grammar and usage, or are just embarking on a learning adventure in English, *2,000+ Essential English Verbs* is the right book for you. It is an essential reference manual about English verbs, developed by native speakers and experts in teaching English as a second language. Keep this simple and practical guide on your desk, and consult it whenever you're not sure about a form of an English verb or are wondering about when and how to use an English tense! With repeated use, you'll quickly acquire a complete knowledge of English verbs—their forms, tenses, and current, everyday usage in conversation.

2,000+ Essential English Verbs consists of an elaborate reference section, followed by a large practice section. The reference part of the book, All About English Verbs, contains an alphabetical index of more than 2,000 English verbs, listed with their past tense and participle; a pronunciation guide; and alphabetically ordered conjugation charts of 125 English verbs. The second part of the book, English Verbs in Action, lays out the nitty-gritty details of formation and usage for all major English tenses, using numerous examples. And so you can put your knowledge to use (and to the test!) right away, we've also included 80 exercises for practice.

The appendices offer more useful information on English verbs: lists of verbs followed by the gerund, verbs followed by the infinitive, and even adjectives followed by verbs in the infinitive.

This versatile book can be used in many different ways. For example: Look up an English verb you have a question about in the Index. Right away you will see its past tense and participle, and then you can go to the Verb Chart indicated in the Index to find the full conjugation of the verb itself (all verbs in the Index that are fully conjugated in the Verb Charts are in bold-face) or its model. In addition to the conjugations in each verb chart, you'll also find examples of usage, important forms of usage, phrasal verbs, idioms, and related words. If you're wondering about how the pronunciation of a verb alters in its various tenses, refer to the guide to pronunciation. Or go to a section in the English Verbs in Action part of the book if you'd like to concentrate further on a particular tense, and get more examples of English verb usage. Complete the exercises that follow the explanations and examples to reinforce what you've learned.

Remember that whichever way you decide to proceed, your fluency in and understanding of English will grow with each use! Have fun!

Part I

ALL ABOUT ENGLISH VERBS

Pronunciation Guide

The following rules should serve as guidelines for the pronunciation of verb endings in the third person singular and past tense.

Third Person Singular
1. Voiced consonants + *s* = "z" sound; voiceless consonants + *s* = "s" sound
   blogs, bobs, lives
   walks, sleeps, laughs

2. A pronounced -*es* is always "iz"
   releases, pleases, watches, judges, washes, massages

3. Vowel sounds are always followed by "z" sound
   plays, rows, flies

Past Tense
1. Voiced consonants + *ed* = "d" sound; voiceless consonants + *ed* = "t" sound
   sneezed, blogged, bobbed, lived
   released, walked, slept, laughed

2. After *t* and *d*, full syllable pronounced as "id"
   dedicated, constructed, dated
   raided, resided, downloaded

3. Vowel sounds are always followed by "d" sound
   laid, stayed, gnawed

Guide to Chart Numbers

1 verbs in which *-ed* is added, no vowel change (example: *act*)

7 *i* to *a* to *u* vowel change (example: *begin*)

13 final *d* changes to *t* in past tense (example: *build*)

15 "eye" to "awe" sound shift (example: *buy*)

17 verbs ending in *y* that change to *-ie* before adding *-d* or *-s* (example: *carry*)

21 verbs that end in an *-e* and add only *-d* in past tense (example: *close*)

23 verbs ending in *-ss, -x, -ch,* etc., that add an *-es* in third person present (example: *cross*)

25 no change (example: *cut*)

27 *-ive* to *-ove* to *-ived* (example: *dive*)

30 *-ise/-ive* to *-ose/-ove* to *-isen/-iven* (example: *drive*)

31 verbs in which the last consonant is doubled before adding *-ed* or *-ing* (example: *drop*)

37 long vowel + *l/m/n/p* to short vowel shift + *lt/mt/nt/pt* (example: *feel*)

40 *-ind* to *-ound* (example: *find*)

43 *-id* to *-ade* to *-idden* (example: *forbid*)

63 long vowel to short vowel shift, no consonant change (example: *lead*)

66 *-ie* to *-ay* to *-aid* (example: *lie*)

74 *-ic* changes to *-ick* before adding *-ed* or *-ing* (example: *panic*)

78 verbs ending in *y* that don't change to *-ie* and add *-ed* (example: *play*)

81 consonant doubled and *-es* added in third person singular (example: *quiz*)

89 *-end* to *-ent* (example: *send*)

91 *-ake* to *-ook* to *-aken* (example: *shake*)

98 *-eak* to *-oke* to *-oken* (example: *speak*)

99 no vowel change, consonant ending alternate *ll* to *lt* in past tense and participle (example: *spell*)

101 *i* to *u* vowel shift (example: *spin*)

110 *-each* to *-aught, -eek* to *-ought* (example: *teach*)

116 *-ead* to *-od* to *-odden* (example: *tread*)

125 *-ide/-ite* to *-ode/-ote* to *-idden/-itten* (example: *write*)

INDEX OF 2,000+
ESSENTIAL ENGLISH VERBS

A

assign (assigned, assigned) 1

assimilate (assimilated, assimilated) 21

associate (associated, associated) 21

assume (assumed, assumed) 21

atrophy (atrophied, atrophied) 17

attach (attached, attached) 23

attack (attacked, attacked) 1

attempt (attempted, attempted) 1

attend (attended, attended) 1

attract (attracted, attracted) 1

attribute (attributed, attributed) 21

audit (audited, audited) 1

audition (auditioned, auditioned) 1

augment (augmented, augmented) 1

automate (automated, automated) 21

avenge (avenged, avenged) 21

avert (averted, averted) 1

avoid (avoided, avoided) 1

award (awarded, awarded) 1

awe (awed, awed) 21

axe (axed, axed) .21

B

babble (babbled, babbled) 21

back (backed, backed) 3

bail (bailed, bailed) 1

balance (balanced, balanced) 21

balk (balked, balked) 1

bang (banged, banged) 1

bargain (bargained, bargained) 1

bark (barked, barked) 1

barter (bartered, bartered) 1

base (based, based) 21

bat (batted, batted) 1

bathe (bathed, bathed) 21

battle (battled, battled) 21

be (was/were, been) 4

bear (bore, borne/born) 5

beat (beat, beaten/beat) 6

beautify (beautified, beautified) 17

become (became, become) 22

beg (begged, begged) 31

begin (began, begun) 7

behave (behaved, behaved) 21

belch (belched, belched) 23

believe (believed, believed) 21

belong (belonged, belonged) 1

bend (bent, bent) 89

benefit (benefited, benefited) 1

best (bested, bested) 1

bet (bet, bet) 25

betray (betrayed, betrayed) 78

bid (bid, bid) 25

bid (bade/bid, bidden/bid/bade) 43

bide (bode/bided, bided) 21

bill (billed, billed) .1

bind (bound, bound) 40

binge (binged, binged) 21

bite (bit, bitten/bit*) 8

blab (blabbed, blabbed) 31

blacklist (blacklisted, blacklisted) 1

blade (bladed, bladed) 21

blame (blamed, blamed) 21

blaze (blazed, blazed) 21

bleed (bled, bled) 63

blend (blended/blent*, blended/
blent*) 1/89

blink (blinked, blinked) 1

block (blocked, blocked) 1

blog (blogged, blogged) 31

blot (blotted, blotted) 31

blow (blew, blown) 9

blush (blushed, blushed) 23

boast (boasted, boasted) 1

bogart (bogarted, bogarted) 1

boil (boiled, boiled) 1

bombard (bombarded, bombarded) 1

book (booked, booked) 1

bookmark (bookmarked,
bookmarked) 21

boot (booted, booted) 1

bootleg (bootlegged, bootlegged) 31

borrow (borrowed, borrowed) 1

boss (bossed, bossed) 23

bother (bothered, bothered) 1

Verb List

*Forms marked by an asterisk (*) are typically more British in usage.

*Forms marked by an asterisk (*) are typically more British in usage.

*Forms marked by an asterisk (*) are typically more British in usage.

*Forms marked by an asterisk (*) are typically more British in usage.

e-mail (e-mailed, e-mailed) 1

emanate (emanated, emanated) 21

emancipate (emancipated,
   emancipated) .21

embark (embarked, embarked) 1

embarrass (embarrassed,
   embarrassed) .23

embed (embedded, embedded) 31

embolden (emboldened, emboldened) 1

emerge (emerged, emerged) 21

empathize (empathized, empathized) . . .21

employ (employed, employed) 78

enable (enabled, enabled) 21

enact (enacted, enacted) 1

enchant (enchanted, enchanted) 1

end (ended, ended) 34

endeavor (endeavored, endeavored) 1

endorse (endorsed, endorsed) 21

endure (endured, endured) 21

engross (engrossed, engrossed) 23

enhance (enhanced, enhanced) 21

enjoy (enjoyed, enjoyed) 78

enlarge (enlarged, enlarged) 21

enlist (enlisted, enlisted) 1

enliven (enlivened, enlivened) 1

enrage (enraged, enraged) 21

ensnare (ensnared, ensnared) 21

entangle (entangled, entangled) 21

enter (entered, entered) 1

entertain (entertained, entertained) 1

enthuse (enthused, enthused) 21

entrap (entrapped, entrapped) 31

equal (equaled/equalled*,
   equaled/equalled*) 1/31

equate (equated, equated) 21

erect (erected, erected) 1

establish (established, established) 23

esteem (esteemed, esteemed) 1

etch (etched, etched) 23

evade (evaded, evaded) 21

evaluate (evaluated, evaluated) 21

exacerbate (exacerbated, exacerbated) . . .21

exaggerate (exaggerated,
   exaggerated) .21

examine (examined, examined) 21

excel (excelled, excelled) 31

excite (excited, excited) 21

excrete (excreted, excreted) 21

excuse (excused, excused) 21

execute (executed, executed) 21

exercise (exercised, exercised) 21

exert (exerted, exerted) 1

exhale (exhaled, exhaled) 21

exhaust (exhausted, exhausted) 1

exhilarate (exhilarated, exhilarated) 21

exist (existed, existed) 1

expand (expanded, expanded) 1

expect (expected, expected) 1

expel (expelled, expelled) 31

experience (experienced,
   experienced) .21

explain (explained, explained) 1

explode (exploded, exploded) 21

expose (exposed, exposed) 21

express (expressed, expressed) 23

exude (exuded, exuded) 21

F

face (faced, faced) 35

facilitate (facilitated, facilitated) 21

fail (failed, failed) .1

faint (fainted, fainted) 1

fake (faked, faked) 21

fall (fell, fallen) .36

falsify (falsified, falsified) 78

falter (faltered, faltered) 1

fantasize (fantasized, fantasized) 21

fashion (fashioned, fashioned) 1

father (fathered, fathered) 1

fatten (fattened, fattened) 1

fault (faulted, faulted) 1

fawn (fawned, fawned) 1

fax (faxed, faxed) .1

fear (feared, feared) 1

feature (featured, featured) 21

feed (fed, fed) 63

feel (felt, felt) 37

*Forms marked by an asterisk (*) are typically more British in usage.

ferment (fermented, fermented) 1

fester (festered, festered) 1

fetch (fetched, fetched) 23

field (fielded, fielded) 1

fight (fought, fought) 15

figure (figured, figured) 38

fill (filled, filled) 39

film (filmed, filmed) 1

filter (filtered, filtered) 1

finance (financed, financed) 21

find (found, found) 40

finger (fingered, fingered) 1

finish (finished, finished) 23

fish (fished, fished) 23

fit (fit/fitted*, fit/fitted*) 25/31

fixate (fixated, fixated) 21

fizzle (fizzled, fizzled) 21

flag (flagged, flagged) 31

flank (flanked, flanked) 1

flash (flashed, flashed) 23

flatter (flattered, flattered) 1

flaunt (flaunted, flaunted) 1

flavor (flavored, flavored) 1

flee (fled, fled) .63

flesh (fleshed, fleshed) 23

flex (flexed, flexed) 23

flick (flicked, flicked) 1

flicker (flickered, flickered) 1

fling (flung, flung) 101

flip (flipped, flipped) 31

flirt (flirted, flirted) 1

flit (flitted, flitted) 31

flounder (floundered, floundered) 1

flourish (flourished, flourished) 23

flout (flouted, flouted) 1

flow (flowed, flowed) 1

flower (flowered, flowered) 1

flub (flubbed, flubbed) 31

flunk (flunked, flunked) 1

flush (flushed, flushed) 23

fluster (flustered, flustered) 1

flutter (fluttered, fluttered) 1

fly (flew, flown) 41

follow (followed, followed) 42

fondle (fondled, fondled) 21

forage (foraged, foraged) 21

forbid (forbade, forbidden) 43

force (forced, forced) 21

forecast (forecast/forecasted*, forecast/
forecasted*) 25/1

foreshadow (foreshadowed,
foreshadowed) 1

forfeit (forfeited, forfeited) 1

forget (forgot, forgotten) 42

forgive (forgave, forgiven) 45

forgo (forwent, forgone) 46

form (formed, formed) 1

forsake (forsook, forsaken) 91

fortify (fortified, fortified) 17

forward (forwarded, forwarded) 1

foster (fostered, fostered) 1

foul (fouled, fouled) 1

found (founded, founded) 1

fractionalize (fractionalized,
fractionalized) 21

fracture (fractured, fractured) 21

fragment (fragmented, fragmented) 1

frame (framed, framed) 21

fray (frayed, frayed) 78

freak out (freaked out, freaked
out) 1

free (freed, freed) 21

freeze (froze, frozen) 98

frequent (frequented, frequented) 1

freshen (freshened, freshened) 1

frighten (frightened, frightened) 1

frisk (frisked, frisked) 1

fritter (frittered, frittered) 1

frolic (frolicked, frolicked) 74

front (fronted, fronted) 1

froth (frothed, frothed) 1

frustrate (frustrated, frustrated) 21

fuel (fueled, fueled) 1

fulfill (fulfilled, fulfilled) 1

fumigate (fumigated, fumigated) 21

function (functioned, functioned) 1

fund (funded, funded) 1

Verb List

*Forms marked by an asterisk (*) are typically more British in usage.

furnish (furnished, furnished) 23

further (furthered, furthered) 1

fuss (fussed, fussed) 23

G

gain (gained, gained) 1

galvanize (galvanized, galvanized) 21

gamble (gambled, gambled) 21

gang up (ganged up, ganged up) 1

gargle (gargled, gargled) 21

garner (garnered, garnered) 1

gas (gassed, gassed) 23

gather (gathered, gathered) 1

gauge (gauged, gauged) 21

gawk (gawked, gawked) 1

gaze (gazed, gazed) 21

gentrify (gentrified, gentrified) 17

gesticulate (gesticulated, gesticulated) . . .21

gesture (gestured, gestured) 21

get (got, gotten/got*) 44

giggle (giggled, giggled) 21

give (gave, given) 45

glance (glanced, glanced) 21

glaze (glazed, glazed) 21

glide (glided, glided) 21

glimpse (glimpsed, glimpsed) 21

glisten (glistened, glistened) 1

gloat (gloated, gloated) 1

globalize (globalized, globalized) 21

go (went, gone) .46

Google (Googled, Googled) 21

gossip (gossiped, gossiped) 1

gouge (gouged, gouged) 21

govern (governed, governed) 1

grab (grabbed, grabbed) 31

grade (graded, graded) 21

graduate (graduated, graduated) 21

grant (granted, granted) 1

graph (graphed, graphed) 1

grapple (grappled, grappled) 21

grasp (grasped, grasped) 1

grate (grated, grated) 21

gratify (gratified, gratified) 17

gravitate (gravitated, gravitated) 21

graze (grazed, grazed) 21

grease (greased, greased) 21

greet (greeted, greeted) 1

grieve (grieved, grieved) 21

grill (grilled, grilled) 1

grimace (grimaced, grimaced) 21

grin (grinned, grinned) 31

grind (ground, ground) 40

grip (gripped, gripped) 31

grit (gritted, gritted) 31

grovel (groveled/grovelled*, groveled/
grovelled*) 1/31

grow (grew, grown) 47

grunt (grunted, grunted) 1

guarantee (guaranteed, guaranteed) 21

guess (guessed, guessed) 23

guffaw (guffawed, guffawed) 1

gulp (gulped, gulped) 1

gun (gunned, gunned) 31

gush (gushed, gushed) 23

guzzle (guzzled, guzzled) 21

gyrate (gyrated, gyrated) 21

H

hack (hacked, hacked) 1

haggle (haggled, haggled) 21

hail (hailed, hailed) 1

halt (halted, halted) 1

halve (halved, halved) 21

ham (hammed, hammed) 31

hammer (hammered, hammered) 1

hamper (hampered, hampered) 1

hand (handed, handed) 48

handcuff (handcuffed, handcuffed) 1

handicap (handicapped,
handicapped) .31

handle (handled, handled) 21

hang (hung, hung) 49

hang (hanged, hanged) 1

hanker (hankered, hankered) 1

happen (happened, happened) 1

*Forms marked by an asterisk (*) are typically more British in usage.

harangue (harangued, harangued) 21

harass (harassed, harassed) 23

harbor (harbored, harbored) 1

harden (hardened, harden) 1

harm (harmed, harmed) 1

harmonize (harmonized, harmonized) . . .21

harp (harped, harped) 1

hash out (hashed out, hashed out) 23

hassle (hassled, hassled) 21

hasten (hastened, hastened) 1

hatch (hatched, hatched) 23

hate (hated, hated) 21

haul (hauled, hauled) 1

haunt (haunted, haunted) 1

have (had, had) .50

head (headed, headed) 51

headhunt (headhunted, headhunted) 1

headline (headlined, headlined) 21

heal (healed, healed) 1

heap (heaped, heaped) 1

hear (heard, heard) 52

hearken (hearkened, hearkened) 1

hearten (heartened, heartened) 1

heave (heaved, heaved) 21

hedge (hedged, hedged) 21

heighten (heightened, heightened) 1

helm (helmed, helmed) 1

help (helped, helped) 53

hem (hemmed, hemmed) 31

herd (herded, herded) 1

hesitate (hesitated, hesitated) 21

hex (hexed, hexed) 23

hide (hid, hidden) 54

hijack (hijacked, hijacked) 1

hike (hiked, hiked) 21

hinder (hindered, hindered) 1

hint (hinted, hinted) 1

hire (hired, hired) 21

hiss (hissed, hissed) 23

hit (hit, hit) 55

hitch (hitched, hitched) 23

hobble (hobbled, hobbled) 21

hog (hogged, hogged) 31

hoist (hoisted, hoisted) 1

hold (held, held) 56

homeschool (homeschooled,
  homeschooled) 1

hoof (hoofed, hoofed) 1

hook (hooked, hooked) 1

hoot (hooted, hooted) 1

hop (hopped, hopped) 31

hope (hoped, hoped) 21

horrify (horrified, horrified) 17

host (hosted, hosted) 1

hound (hounded, hounded) 1

house (housed, housed) 21

hover (hovered, hovered) 1

howl (howled, howled) 1

huff (huffed, huffed) 1

hug (hugged, hugged) 31

humble (humbled, humbled) 21

humiliate (humiliated, humiliated) 21

hunch (hunched, hunched) 23

hunker down (hunkered down,
  hunkered down) 1

hunt (hunted, hunted) 1

hurry (hurried, hurried) 17

hurt (hurt, hurt) .25

hurtled (hurtled, hurtled) 21

hush (hushed, hushed) 23

hydrate (hydrated, hydrated) 21

hype (hyped, hyped) 21

I

ID (IDed, IDed) 1

idealize (idealized, idealized) 21

identify (identified, identified) 17

idle (idled, idled) 21

idolize (idolized, idolized) 21

ignite (ignited, ignited) 21

ignore (ignored, ignored) 21

illuminate (illuminated, illuminated) 21

illustrate (illustrated, illustrated) 21

imagine (imagined, imagined) 21

Verb List

imbibe (imbibed, imbibed) 21

imbrue (imbrued, imbrued) 21

imbue (imbued, imbued) 21

imitate (imitated, imitated) 21

immerse (immersed, immersed) 21

immigrate (immigrated, immigrated) 21

immobilize (immobilized, immobilized) 21

immolate (immolated, immolated) 21

immortalize (immortalized, immortalized)

impale (impaled, impaled) 21

impede (impeded, impeded) 21

import (imported, imported) 1

impress (impressed, impressed) 23

imprison (imprisoned, imprisoned) 1

improve (improved, improved) 1

incense (incensed, incensed) 21

inch (inched, inched) 23

include (included, included) 21

incorporate (incorporated, incorporated) 21

increase (increased, increased) 21

incubate (incubated, incubated) 21

indent (indented, indented) 1

index (indexed, indexed) 23

indicate (indicated, indicated) 21

indict (indicted, indicted) 1

induce (induced, induced) 21

indulge (indulged, indulged) 21

infect (infected, infected) 1

infer (inferred, inferred) 31

inform (informed, informed) 1

initiate (initiated, initiated) 21

inject (injected, injected) 1

inquire (inquired, inquired) 21

insert (inserted, inserted) 1

install (installed, installed) 1

instruct (instructed, instructed) 1

intend (intended, intended) 1

inter (interred, interred) 31

interact (interacted, interacted) 1

interest (interested, interested) 1

interfere (interfered, interfered) 21

interpret (interpreted, interpreted) 1

interrogate (interrogated, interrogated) ..21

intervene (intervened, intervened) 21

interview (interviewed, interviewed) 1

inundate (inundated, inundated) 21

invent (invented, invented) 1

involve (involved, involved) 21

iron (ironed, ironed) 1

irritate (irritated, irritated) 21

itch (itched, itched) 23

iterate (iterated, iterated) 21

J

jab (jabbed, jabbed) 31

jack (jacked, jacked) 1

jail (jailed, jailed) 1

jazz (jazzed, jazzed) 23

jeopardize (jeopardized, jeopardized) 21

jerk (jerked, jerked) 1

jet (jetted, jetted) 31

jiggle (jiggled, jiggled) 21

jingle (jingled, jingled) 21

jinx (jinxed, jinxed) 23

jockey (jockeyed, jockeyed) 78

jog (jogged, jogged) 31

join (joined, joined) 1

joke (joked, joked) 21

jolt (jolted, jolted) 1

journal (journaled, journaled) 1

journey (journeyed, journeyed) 78

judge (judged, judged) 21

juggle (juggled, juggled) 21

jump (jumped, jumped) 57

jump-start (jump-started, jump-started) 1

junk (junked, junked) 1

jut (jutted, jutted) 31

juxtapose (juxtaposed, juxtaposed) 21

K

kayo (kayoed, kayoed) 1

keep (kept, kept) 58

key (keyed, keyed) 78

kick (kicked, kicked) 59

kid (kidded, kidded) 31

kidnap (kidnapped, kidnapped) 31

kill (killed, killed) .1

kindle (kindled, kindled) 21

kiss (kissed, kissed) 23

knead (kneaded, kneaded) 1

knee (kneed, kneed) 21

kneel (knelt/kneeled, knelt/kneeled) . . .37/1

knight (knighted, knighted) 1

knit (knit/knitted*, knit/knitted*) 31/1

knock (knocked, knocked) 60

knot (knotted, knotted) 31

know (knew, known) 61

kowtow (kowtowed, kowtowed) 1

kvetch (kvetched, kvetched) 23

L

labor (labored, labored) 1

lace (laced, laced) 21

lack (lacked, lacked) 1

ladle (ladled, ladled) 21

lag (lagged, lagged) 31

lament (lamented, lamented) 1

laminate (laminated, laminated) 21

land (landed, landed) 1

landscape (landscaped, landscaped) 21

languish (languished, languished) 23

lap (lapped, lapped) 31

lapse (lapsed, lapsed) 21

lash (lashed, lashed) 23

last (lasted, lasted) 1

latch (latched, latched) 23

lather (lathered, lathered) 1

laud (lauded, lauded) 1

laugh (laughed, laughed) 1

launch (launched, launched) 23

lay (laid, laid) .62

leach (leached, leached) 23

lead (led, led) .63

leak (leaked, leaked) 1

lean (leaned/leant*, leaned/leant*) 1/37

leap (leaped/leapt*, leaped/leapt*) 1/37

learn (learned/learnt*, learned/
learnt*) 1/37

lease (leased, leased) 21

leave (left, left) 64

lecture (lectured, lectured) 21

legalize (legalized, legalized) 21

legislate (legislated, legislated) 21

legitimate (legitimated, legitimated) 21

legitimize (legitimized, legitimized) 21

lend (lent, lent) .13

lessen (lessened, lessened) 23

let (let, let) 65

level (leveled/levelled*, leveled/
levelled*) 1/31

libel (libeled/libelled*, libel/
libelled*) 1/31

liberate (liberated, liberated) 21

lick (licked, licked) 1

lie (lay, lain) 66

lie (lied, lied) 21

lift (lifted, lifted) .1

light (lit/lighted*, lit/lighted*) 67

like (liked, liked) 21

limit (limited, limited) 1

linger (lingered, lingered) 1

liquidate (liquidated, liquidated) 21

lisp (lisped, lisped) 1

list (listed, listed) 1

listen (listened, listened) 1

litigate (litigated, litigated) 21

litter (littered, littered) 1

live (lived, lived) 68

liven (livened, livened) 1

load (loaded, loaded) 1

loathe (loathed, loathed) 21

lob (lobbed, lobbed) 31

localize (localized, localized) 21

lock (locked, locked) 69

lodge (lodged, lodged) 21

log (logged, logged) 31

loiter (loitered, loitered) 1

*Forms marked by an asterisk (*) are typically more British in usage.

Verb List

misinterpret (misinterpreted,
  misinterpreted) 1

misjudge (misjudged, misjudged) 21

mislay (mislaid, mislaid) 62

mislead (misled, misled) 63

mismanage (mismanaged,
  mismanaged) 21

misplace (misplaced, misplaced) 21

miss (missed, missed) 23

misspeak (misspoke, misspoken) 98

misspell (misspelled/misspelt*,
  misspelled/misspelt*) 99

mistake (mistook, mistaken) 108

misunderstand (misunderstood,
  misunderstood) 102

mix (mixed, mixed) 23

mob (mobbed, mobbed) 31

mobilize (mobilized, mobilized) 21

model (modeled/modelled*, modeled,
  modelled*) 1/31

moderate (moderated, moderated) 21

modernize (modernized, modernized) . . .21

modulate (modulated, modulated) 21

mollify (mollified, mollified) 17

molt (molted, molted) 1

monitor (monitored, monitored) 1

mooch (mooched, mooched) 23

moor (moored, moored) 1

mortgage (mortgaged, mortgaged) 21

mother (mothered, mothered) 1

motivate (motivated, motivated) 21

mount (mounted, mounted) 1

move (moved, moved) 21

mow (mowed, mowed/mown) 93

mulch (mulched, mulched) 23

multiply (multiplied, multiplied) 17

murder (murdered, murdered) 1

murmur (murmured, murmured) 1

muscle (muscled, muscled) 21

muster (mustered, mustered) 1

mutate (mutated, mutated) 21

mute (muted, muted) 21

muzzle (muzzled, muzzled) 21

mystify (mystified, mystified) 17

nab (nabbed, nabbed) 31

nag (nagged, nagged) 31

nail (nailed, nailed) 1

nap (napped, napped) 31

narrate (narrated, narrated) 21

narrow (narrowed, narrowed) 1

naturalize (naturalized, naturalized) 21

navigate (navigated, navigated) 21

near (neared, neared) 1

need (needed, needed) 1

needle (needled, needled) 21

negate (negated, negated) 21

neglect (neglected, neglected) 1

negotiate (negotiated, negotiated) 21

nestle (nestled, nestled) 21

net (netted, netted) 31

neutralize (neutralized, neutralized) 21

nibble (nibbled, nibbled) 21

nick (nicked, nicked) 1

nickname (nicknamed, nicknamed) 21

nip (nipped, nipped) 31

nix (nixed, nixed) 23

nod (nodded, nodded) 31

nominate (nominated, nominated) 21

nonplus (nonplused/nonplussed,
  nonplused/nonplussed) 1/23

normalize (normalized, normalized) 21

note (noted, noted) 21

notice (noticed, noticed) 21

nudge (nudged, nudged) 21

number (numbered, numbered) 1

nurse (nursed, nursed) 21

nurture (nurtured, nurtured) 21

nuzzle (nuzzled, nuzzled) 21

obey (obeyed, obeyed) 78

obfuscate (obfuscated, obfuscated) 21

object (objected, objected) 1

oblige (obliged, obliged) 21

obliterate (obliterated, obliterated) 21

observe (observed, observed) 21

*Forms marked by an asterisk (*) are typically more British in usage.

Verb List

obstruct (obstructed, obstructed) 1
obtain (obtained, obtained) 1
obviate (obviated, obviated) 21
occur (occurred, occurred) 31
offend (offended, offended) 1
offer (offered, offered) 1
offset (offset, offset) 90
ogle (ogled, ogled) 21
oil (oiled, oiled) .1
one-up (one-upped, one-upped) 31
ooze (oozed, oozed) 21
open (opened, opened) 73
operate (operated, operated) 21
opine (opined, opined) 21
oppose (opposed, opposed) 21
oppress (oppressed, oppressed) 23
opt (opted, opted) 1
optimize (optimized, optimized) 21
option (optioned, optioned) 1
orbit (orbited, orbited) 1
ordain (ordained, ordained) 1
order (ordered, ordered) 1
organize (organized, organized) 21
orient (oriented, oriented) 1
ornament (ornamented, ornamented) 1
orphan (orphaned, orphaned) 1
ostracize (ostracized, ostracized) 21
oust (ousted, ousted) 1
out (outed, outed) 1
outdo (outdid, outdone) 27
outfit (outfitted, outfitted) 31
outgrow (outgrew, outgrown) 45
outrage (outraged, outraged) 21
outshoot (outshot, outshot) 92
outsource (outsourced, outsourced) 21
outstay (outstayed, outstayed) 103
overcome (overcame, overcome) 22
overcompensate (overcompensated,
  overcompensated) 21
overdose (overdosed, overdosed) 21
overeat (overate, overeaten) 32
overflow (overflowed, overflowed) 1
overhear (overheard, overheard) 52

overindulge (overindulged,
  overindulged) 21
overlap (overlapped, overlapped) 31
overlay (overlaid, overlaid) 62
overlook (overlooked, overlooked) 70
overrate (overrated, overrated) 21
override (overrode, overridden) 125
overrun (overran, overrun) 85
oversee (oversaw, overseen) 87
overshoot (overshot, overshot) 92
oversleep (overslept, overslept) 96
overtake (overtook, overtaken) 108
overthrow (overthrew, overthrown) 114
overturn (overturned, overturned) 118
owe (owed, owed) 21
own (owned, owned) 1
oxidize (oxidize, oxidize) 21

P

pack (packed, packed) 1
package (packaged, packaged) 21
pad (padded, padded) 31
padlock (padlocked, padlocked) 1
page (paged, paged) 21
pain (pained, pained) 1
paint (painted, painted) 1
pale (paled, paled) 21
palm (palmed, palmed) 1
palpate (palpated, palpated) 21
pamper (pampered, pampered) 1
pan (panned, panned) 31
pander (pandered, pandered) 1
panic (panicked, panicked) 74
pant (panted, panted) 1
paper (papered, papered) 1
parachute (parachuted, parachuted) 21
parade (paraded, paraded) 21
parallel (paralleled, paralleled) 1
paralyze (paralyzed, paralyzed) 21
paraphrase (paraphrased,
  paraphrased) 21
parboil (parboiled, parboiled) 1
pardon (pardoned, pardoned) 1

park (parked, parked) 1

parody (parodied, parodied) 17

part (parted, parted) 1

partake (partook, partaken) 108

participate (participated, participated) . . .21

partner (partnered, partnered) 1

party (partied, partied) 17

pass (passed, passed) 75

pat (patted, patted) 31

patch (patched, patched) 23

patent (patented, patented) 1

patrol (patrolled, patrolled) 31

pattern (patterned, patterned) 1

pause (paused, paused) 21

paw (pawed, pawed) 1

pay (paid, paid) 76

peak (peaked, peaked) 1

peal (pealed, pealed) 1

peck (pecked, pecked) 1

pedal (pedaled/pedalled*, pedaled/
   pedalled*) 1/31

peddle (peddled, peddled) 21

peel (peeled, peeled) 1

peep (peeped, peeped) 1

peer (peered, peered) 1

pen (penned, penned) 31

penalize (penalized, penalized) 21

penetrate (penetrated, penetrated) 21

people (peopled, peopled) 21

people-watch (people-watched,
   people-watched) 122

pepper (peppered, peppered) 1

perceive (perceived, perceived) 21

perfect (perfected, perfected) 1

perform (performed, performed) 1

perish (perished, perished) 23

perm (permed, permed) 1

permeate (permeated, permeated) 21

permit (permitted, permitted) 31

perplex (perplexed, perplexed) 23

persevere (persevered, persevered) 21

persist (persisted, persisted) 1

perspire (perspired, perspired) 21

pertain (pertained, pertained) 1

perturb (perturbed, perturbed) 1

pester (pestered, pestered) 1

pet (petted, petted) 31

petition (petitioned, petitioned) 1

phase (phased, phased) 21

philosophize (philosophized,
   philosophized) 21

phone (phoned, phoned) 21

photocopy (photocopied,
   photocopied) 17

phrase (phrased, phrased) 21

pick (picked, picked) 1

picket (picketed, picketed) 1

picture (pictured, pictured) 21

piece (pieced, pieced) 21

pierce (pierced, pierced) 21

pile (piled, piled) 21

pilot (piloted, piloted) 1

pin (pinned, pinned) 31

pinch (pinched, pinched) 23

pinpoint (pinpointed, pinpointed) 1

pioneer (pioneered, pioneered) 1

pipe (piped, piped) 21

pirate (pirated, pirated) 21

pit (pitted, pitted) 31

pitch (pitched, pitched) 23

pity (pitied, pitied) 17

pivot (pivoted, pivoted) 1

placate (placated, placated) 21

place (placed, placed) 21

plan (planned, planned) 77

plant (planted, planted) 1

plaster (plastered, plastered) 1

play (played, played) 78

plead (pleaded/pled, pleaded/pled) 1/63

please (pleased, pleased) 21

pleasure (pleasured, pleasured) 21

pleat (pleated, pleated) 1

pledge (pledged, pledged) 21

plod (plodded, plodded) 31

plop (plopped, plopped) 31

plug (plugged, plugged) 31

*Forms marked by an asterisk (*) are typically more British in usage.

plunder (plundered, plundered) 1

pocket (pocketed, pocketed) 1

podcast (podcasted, podcasted) 21

poetize (poetized, poetized) 21

point (pointed, pointed) 1

poison (poisoned, poisoned) 1

poke (poked, poked) 21

polarize (polarized, polarized) 21

police (policed, policed) 21

polish (polished, polished) 23

poll (polled, polled) 1

pollute (polluted, polluted) 21

ponder (pondered, pondered) 1

pool (pooled, pooled) 1

pop (popped, popped) 31

popularize (popularized, popularized) . . .21

pose (posed, posed) 21

posit (posited, posited) 1

possess (possessed, possessed) 23

post (posted, posted) 1

posture (postured, postured) 21

pounce (pounced, pounced) 21

pound (pounded, pounded) 1

powder (powdered, powdered) 1

power (powered, powered) 1

practice (practiced, practiced) 21

precede (preceded, preceded) 21

predate (predated, predated) 21

predetermine (predetermined,
  predetermined) 21

preface (prefaced, prefaced) 21

prefer (preferred, preferred) 31

preheat (preheated, preheated) 1

prejudge (prejudged, prejudged) 21

preoccupy (preoccupied, preoccupied) . . .17

prepare (prepared, prepared) 21

prepay (prepaid, prepaid) 72

prescribe (prescribed, prescribed) 21

present (presented, presented) 1

press (pressed, pressed) 23

pressure (pressured, pressured) 21

presume (presumed, presumed) 21

presuppose (presupposed,
  presupposed) .21

pretend (pretended, pretended) 1

prevent (prevented, prevented) 1

price (priced, priced) 21

prick (pricked, pricked) 1

prickle (prickled, prickled) 21

prime (primed, primed) 21

print (printed, printed) 1

prioritize (prioritized, prioritized) 21

privatize (privatized, privatized) 21

prize (prized, prized) 21

probe (probed, probed) 21

proceed (proceeded, proceeded) 1

proclaim (proclaimed, proclaimed) 1

procrastinate (procrastinated,
  procrastinated) 21

prod (prodded, prodded) 31

produce (produced, produced) 21

profess (professed, professed) 23

profile (profiled, profiled) 21

profit (profited, profited) 1

program (programmed/programed,
  programmed/programed) 31/1

progress (progressed, progressed) 23

prohibit (prohibited, prohibited) 1

project (projected, projected) 1

prolong (prolonged, prolonged) 1

promise (promised, promised) 21

promote (promoted, promoted) 21

propel (propelled, propelled) 31

prophesy (prophesied, prophesied) 17

proportion (proportioned,
  proportioned) 1

propose (proposed, proposed) 21

prosecute (prosecuted, prosecuted) 21

protect (protected, protected) 1

prove (proved, proved/proven) 1

provide (provided, provided) 21

provoke (provoked, provoked) 21

psyche (psyched, psyched) 21

psychoanalyze (psychoanalyzed,
  psychoanalyzed) 21

publicize (publicized, publicized) 21

publish (published, published) 23

pucker (puckered, puckered) 1

puff (puffed, puffed) 1

pull (pulled, pulled) 79

pulverize (pulverized, pulverized) 21

pump (pumped, pumped) 1

punish (punished, punished) 23

purge (purged, purged) 21

pursue (pursued, pursued) 21

push (pushed, pushed) 23

put (put, put) 80

puzzle (puzzled, puzzled) 21

Q

quadruple (quadrupled, quadrupled) 21

quake (quaked, quaked) 21

qualify (qualified, qualified) 17

quantify (quantified, quantified) 17

quarrel (quarreled/quarrelled*,
  quarreled/quarrelled*) 1/31

quarter (quartered, quartered) 1

quarterback (quarterbacked,
  quarterbacked) 1

quell (quelled, quelled) 1

quench (quenched, quenched) 23

query (queried, queried) 17

question (questioned, questioned) 1

quibble (quibbled, quibbled) 21

quicken (quickened, quickened) 1

quiet (quieted, quieted) 1

quilt (quilted, quilted) 1

quit (quit/quitted, quit/quitted) 25/31

quiver (quivered, quivered) 1

quiz (quizzed, quizzed) 81

quote (quoted, quoted) 21

R

race (raced, raced) 21

radiate (radiated, radiated) 21

rag (ragged, ragged) 31

rage (raged, raged) 21

raid (raided, raided) 1

railroad (railroaded, railroaded) 1

rain (rained, rained) 1

raise (raised, raised) 21

rake (raked, raked) 21

rally (rallied, rallied) 17

rank (ranked, ranked) 1

rap (rapped, rapped) 31

rape (raped, raped) 21

rappel (rappelled, rappelled) 31

rate (rated, rated) 21

ration (rationed, rationed) 1

rattle (rattled, rattled) 21

rave (raved, raved) 21

ravish (ravished, ravished) 23

reach (reached, reached) 82

react (reacted, reacted) 1

read (read, read) 83

ready (readied, readied) 17

realign (realigned, realigned) 1

realize (realized, realized) 21

reappear (reappeared, reappeared) 1

rearrange (rearrange, rearrange) 21

reason (reasoned, reasoned) 1

reassure (reassured, reassured) 21

rebel (rebelled, rebelled) 31

reboot (rebooted, rebooted) 1

rebuild (rebuilt, rebuilt) 13

recede (receded, receded) 21

receive (received, received) 21

reciprocate (reciprocated,
  reciprocated) .21

recognize (recognized, recognized) 21

recollect (recollected, recollected) 1

recommend (recommended,
  recommended) .1

reconfigure (reconfigured,
  reconfigured) .21

rectify (rectified, rectified) 17

recur (recurred, recurred) 31

recuse (recused, recused) 21

recycle (recycled, recycled) 21

Verb List

*Forms marked by an asterisk (*) are typically more British in usage.

rob (robbed, robbed) 31

rock (rocked, rocked) 1

roll (rolled, rolled) 84

romance (romanced, romanced) 21

room (roomed, roomed) 1

rope (roped, roped) 21

rot (rotted, rotted) 31

roughhouse (roughhoused,
  roughhoused) 21

round (rounded, rounded) 1

route (routed, routed) 21

rove (roved, roved) 21

rub (rubbed, rubbed) 31

rubberneck (rubbernecked,
  rubbernecked) .1

ruin (ruined, ruined) 1

rule (ruled, ruled) 21

rumor (rumored, rumored) 1

run (ran, run) 85

rush (rushed, rushed) 23

rust (rusted, rusted) 1

rustle (rustled, rustled) 21

S

sack (sacked, sacked) 1

sacrifice (sacrificed, sacrificed) 21

safeguard (safeguarded, safeguarded) 1

sag (sagged, sagged) 31

sail (sailed, sailed) 1

salt (salted, salted) 1

sample (sampled, sampled) 21

sand (sanded, sanded) 1

satirize (satirized, satirized) 21

satisfy (satisfied, satisfied) 17

saturate (saturated, saturated) 21

save (saved, saved) 21

savor (savored, savored) 1

saw (sawed, sawed/sawn) 1

say (said, said) .86

scan (scanned, scanned) 31

scar (scarred, scarred) 31

scare (scared, scared) 21

scatter (scattered, scattered) 1

schedule (scheduled, scheduled) 21

scheme (schemed, schemed) 21

schlep (schlepped, schlepped) 31

schmooze (schmoozed, schmoozed) 21

school (schooled, schooled) 1

scoff (scoffed, scoffed) 1

scoop (scooped, scooped) 1

scorch (scorched, scorched) 23

score (scored, scored) 21

scour (scoured, scoured) 1

scrap (scrapped, scrapped) 31

scrape (scraped, scraped) 21

scratch (scratched, scratched) 23

scream (screamed, screamed) 1

scuttle (scuttled, scuttled) 21

seal (sealed, sealed) 1

search (searched, searched) 23

season (seasoned, seasoned) 1

seat (seated, seated) 1

secure (secured, secured) 21

seduce (seduced, seduced) 21

see (saw, seen) .87

seek (sought, sought) 110

seem (seemed, seemed) 1

seize (seized, seized) 21

select (selected, selected) 1

sell (sold, sold) .88

send (sent, sent) 89

separate (separated, separated) 21

sequester (sequestered, sequestered) 1

serve (served, served) 21

service (serviced, serviced) 21

set (set, set) 90

settle (settled, settled) 21

sew (sewed, sewn/sewed) 93

shack (shacked, shacked) 1

shake (shook, shaken) 91

shape (shaped, shaped) 1

share (shared, shared) 21

sharpen (sharpened, sharpened) 1

shave (shaved, shaved) 1

shed (shed, shed) 25

shine (shone/shined, shone/shined) 27

ship (shipped, shipped) 31

shirk (shirked, shirked) 1

shoot (shot, shot) 92

shop (shopped, shopped) 31

shorten (shortened, shortened) 1

shovel (shoveled/shovelled*, shoveled/
shovelled*) 1/31

show (showed, shown/showed) 93

shred (shredded/shred, shredded/
shred) 31/25

shrink (shrank/shrunk, shrunk) 7/101

shrivel (shriveled/shrivelled*,
shriveled/shrivelled*) 1/31

shut (shut, shut) 94

shuttle (shuttled, shuttled) 21

sidetrack (sidetracked, sidetracked) 1

sigh (sighed, sighed) 1

sign (signed, signed) 1

silence (silenced, silenced) 21

simulate (simulated, simulated) 21

sing (sang, sung) .7

sink (sank, sunk) .7

sip (sipped, sipped) 31

sit (sat, sat) 95

situate (situated, situated) 21

size (sized, sized) 21

skate (skated, skated) 21

sketch (sketched, sketched) 23

ski (skied, skied) .1

skip (skipped, skipped) 31

slap (slapped, slapped) 31

slash (slashed, slashed) 23

sleep (slept, slept) 96

slice (sliced, sliced) 21

slide (slid, slid) 8

sling (slung, slung) 101

slink (slunk/slinked, slunk/slinked) . . .101/1

slip (slipped, slipped) 97

slit (slit, slit) 25

slow (slowed, slowed) 1

smack (smacked, smacked) 1

smash (smashed, smashed) 23

smell (smelled/smelt*, smelled/
smelt*) 99

smile (smiled, smiled) 21

smoke (smoked, smoked) 21

smooch (smooched, smooched) 23

snack (snacked, snacked) 1

snap (snapped, snapped) 31

snatch (snatched, snatched) 23

sneak (sneaked/snuck, sneaked/
snuck) 1/101

sniff (sniffed, sniffed) 1

snip (snipped, snipped) 31

snow (snowed, snowed) 1

soap (soaped, soaped) 1

sob (sobbed, sobbed) 31

socialize (socialized, socialized) 21

soften (softened, softened) 1

solicit (solicited, solicited) 1

sound (sounded, sounded) 1

space (spaced, spaced) 21

spam (spammed, spammed) 31

spark (sparked, sparked) 1

spasm (spasmed, spasmed) 1

spaz (spazzed, spazzed) 81

speak (spoke, spoken) 98

specialize (specialized, specialized) 21

specify (specified, specified) 17

speed (sped/speeded, sped/speeded) . . .63/1

spell (spelled/spelt*, spelled/spelt*) 99

spend (spent, spent) 100

spill (spilled/spilt*, spilled/spilt*) 99

spin (spun, spun) 101

spiral (spiraled/spiralled*, spiraled/
spiralled*) 1/31

spit (spit/spat, spit/spat) 25/94

splash (splashed, splashed) 23

split (split, split) 25

splurge (splurged, splurged) 21

spoil (spoiled/spoilt*, spoiled/
spoilt*) 99

spoon (spooned, spooned) 1

spot (spotted, spotted) 31

sprain (sprained, sprained) 1

spray (sprayed, sprayed) 78

spread (spread, spread) 25

*Forms marked by an asterisk (*) are typically more British in usage.

spring (sprang/sprung, sprung) 7/101

sprinkle (sprinkled, sprinkled) 21

spurn (spurned, spurned) 1

squander (squandered, squandered) 1

squeeze (squeezed, squeezed) 21

stabilize (stabilized, stabilized) 21

stack (stacked, stacked) 1

stage (staged, staged) 21

stain (stained, stained) 1

stalk (stalked, stalked) 1

stammer (stammered, stammered) 1

stand (stood, stood) 102

staple (stapled, stapled) 21

star (starred, starred) 31

start (started, started) 1

state (stated, stated) 21

stay (stayed, stayed) 103

steady (steadied, steadied) 17

steal (stole, stolen) 98

step (stepped, stepped) 104

stick (stuck, stuck) 105

stiff (stiffed, stiffed) 1

sting (stung, stung) 101

stink (stank/stunk, stunk) 7/101

stir (stirred, stirred) 31

stock (stocked, stocked) 1

stomach (stomached, stomached) 1

stomp (stomped, stomped) 1

stop (stopped, stopped) 106

stow (stowed, stowed) 1

strap (strapped, strapped) 31

strategize (strategized, strategized) 21

stray (strayed, strayed) 78

streak (streaked, streaked) 1

stretch (stretched, stretched) 23

stride (strode, stridden) 125

strike (struck, struck) 101

string (strung, strung) 101

strive (strove/strived, striven/
striven) 30/1

stroke (stroked, stroked) 21

stroll (strolled, strolled) 1

strum (strummed, strummed) 31

study (studied, studied) 17

stuff (stuffed, stuffed) 1

stutter (stuttered, stuttered) 1

subdivide (subdivided, subdivided) 21

subtitle (subtitled, subtitled) 21

succeed (succeeded, succeeded) 1

sucker (suckered, suckered) 1

suffocate (suffocated, suffocated) 21

sugarcoat (sugarcoated, sugarcoated) 1

suit (suited, suited) 1

summarize (summarized, summarized) ..21

superimpose (superimposed,
superimposed) 21

supersede (superseded, superseded) ...21

supersize (supersized, supersized) 21

supervise (supervised, supervised) 21

supply (supplied, supplied) 17

support (supported, supported) 1

suppose (supposed, supposed) 21

surf (surfed, surfed) 1

surface (surfaced, surfaced) 21

surprise (surprised, surprised) 21

survey (surveyed, surveyed) 78

swagger (swaggered, swaggered) 1

swallow (swallowed, swallowed) 1

swarm (swarmed, swarmed) 1

swat (swatted, swatted) 31

swear (swore, sworn) 107

sweat (sweat/sweated, sweat/
sweated) 25/1

sweep (swept, swept) 37

sweeten (sweetened, sweetened) 1

swim (swam, swum) 7

swindle (swindled, swindled) 21

swing (swung, swung) 101

swipe (swiped, swiped) 21

sympathize (sympathized,
sympathized) 21

synchronize (synchronized,
synchronized) 21

syndicate (syndicated, syndicated) 21

synthesize (synthesized, synthesized) 21

systematize (systematized,
systematized) 21

Verb List

T

tack (tacked, tacked) 1

tackle (tackled, tackled) 21

tag (tagged, tagged) 31

tail (tailed, tailed) 1

tailgate (tailgated, tailgated) 21

take (took, taken) 108

talk (talked, talked) 109

tamper (tampered, tampered) 1

tan (tanned, tanned) 31

tangle (tangled, tangled) 21

tank (tanked, tanked) 1

tantalize (tantalized, tantalized) 21

tap (tapped, tapped) 31

tape (taped, taped) 21

taste (tasted, tasted) 21

tax (taxed, taxed) 23

teach (taught, taught) 110

team (teamed, teamed) 1

tear (tore, torn) 111

tease (teased, teased) 21

telephone (telephoned, telephoned) 21

televise (televised, televised) 21

tell (told, told) 112

temper (tempered, tempered) 1

tempt (tempted, tempted) 1

tend (tended, tended) 1

terrify (terrified, terrified) 17

terrorize (terrorized, terrorized) 21

test (tested, tested) 1

tether (tethered, tethered) 1

text (texted, texted) 1

text message (text messaged, text
    messaged) 21

thank (thanked, thanked) 1

thicken (thickened, thickened) 1

thin (thinned, thinned) 31

think (thought, thought) 113

thirst (thirsted, thirsted) 1

thrash (thrashed, thrashed) 23

threaten (threatened, threatened) 1

thrill (thrilled, thrilled) 1

throng (thronged, thronged) 1

throw (threw, thrown) 114

thrust (thrust, thrust) 25

thumb (thumbed, thumbed) 1

tick (ticked, ticked) 1

tickle (tickled, tickled) 21

tidy (tidied, tidied) 17

tie (tied, tied) .115

tighten (tightened, tightened) 1

tilt (tilted, tilted) .1

tinge (tinged, tinged) 21

tingle (tingled, tingled) 21

tinkle (tinkled, tinkled) 21

toast (toasted, toasted) 1

tolerate (tolerated, tolerated) 21

tone (toned, toned) 21

top (topped, topped) 31

topple (toppled, toppled) 21

torch (torched, torched) 23

torture (tortured, tortured) 21

toss (tossed, tossed) 23

total (totaled/totalled*, totaled/
    totalled*) 1/31

touch (touched, touched) 23

toy (toyed, toyed) 78

trace (traced, traced) 21

track (tracked, tracked) 1

trade (traded, traded) 21

traffic (trafficked, trafficked) 74

trail (trailed, trailed) 1

trample (trampled, trampled) 21

transcend (transcended, transcended) 1

transfer (transferred, transferred) 31

transform (transformed, transformed) 1

transition (transitioned, transitioned) 1

translate (translated, translated) 21

transport (transported, transported) 1

trap (trapped, trapped) 31

trash (trashed, trashed) 23

traumatize (traumatized, traumatized) . . .21

travel (traveled/travelled*, traveled/
    travelled*) .1/31

tread (trod/treaded, trodden/trod) 116

---

*Forms marked by an asterisk (*) are typically more British in usage.

treat (treated, treated) 1
trek (trekked, trekked) 31
trick (tricked, tricked) 1
trickle (trickled, trickled) 21
trifle (trifled, trifled) 21
trigger (triggered, triggered) 1
trip (tripped, tripped) 31
triple (tripled, tripled) 21
triumph (triumphed, triumphed) 1
troll (trolled, trolled) 1
trouble (troubled, troubled) 21
trounce (trounced, trounced) 21
truck (trucked, trucked) 1
trust (trusted, trusted) 1
try (tried, tried) 117
tube (tubed, tubed) 21
tuck (tucked, tucked) 1
tug (tugged, tugged) 31
tumble (tumbled, tumbled) 21
tune (tuned, tuned) 21
turn (turned, turned) 118
tweak (tweaked, tweaked) 1
twinge (twinged, twinged) 21
twinkle (twinkled, twinkled) 21
twist (twisted, twisted) 1
twitch (twitched, twitched) 23
type (typed, typed) 21
typecast (typecast, typecast) 25
typify (typified, typified) 17
tyrannize (tyrannized, tyrannized) 21

U

uglify (uglified, uglified) 17
umpire (umpired, umpired) 21
unarm (unarmed, unarmed) 1
unbend (unbent, unbent) 89
unbuckle (unbuckled, unbuckled) 21
uncork (uncorked, uncorked) 1
uncover (uncovered, uncovered) 1
uncurl (uncurled, uncurled) 1
underfund (underfunded, underfunded) . . .1
undergo (underwent, undergone) 44

underlie (underlay, underlain) 66
underline (underlined, underlined) 21
undermine (undermined, undermined) . . .21
underplay (underplayed, underplayed) . . .78
underscore (underscored, underscored) . .21
undersell (undersold, undersold) 85
understand (understood,
    understood) 102
undertake (undertook, undertaken) 91
undo (undid, undone) 28
undress (undressed, undressed) 23
unearth (unearthed, unearthed) 1
unfold (unfolded, unfolded) 1
unfurl (unfurled, unfurled) 1
unhand (unhanded, unhanded) 1
unify (unified, unified) 17
unionize (unionized, unionized) 21
unite (united, united) 21
unlearn (unlearned, unlearned) 1
unleash (unleashed, unleashed) 23
unplug (unplugged, unplugged) 31
unroll (unrolled, unrolled) 1
unscramble (unscrambled,
    unscrambled) 21
untangle (untangled, untangled) 21
unveil (unveiled, unveiled) 1
unwind (unwound, unwound) 40
unzip (unzipped, unzipped) 31
update (updated, updated) 21
uphold (upheld, upheld) 56
uplift (uplifted, uplifted) 1
upload (uploaded, uploaded) 1
uproot (uprooted, uprooted) 1
upset (upset, upset) 25
upstage (upstaged, upstaged) 21
urge (urged, urged) 21
urinate (urinated, urinated) 21
use (used, used) 21
usher (ushered, ushered) 1
usurp (usurped, usurped) 1
utilize (utilized, utilized) 21
utter (uttered, uttered) 1

Verb List

V

vacate (vacated, vacated) 21

vacation (vacationed, vacationed) 1

vaccinate (vaccinated, vaccinated) 21

vacuum (vacuumed, vacuumed) 1

validate (validated, validated) 21

value (valued, valued) 21

vanish (vanished, vanished) 23

vaporize (vaporized, vaporized) 21

vary (varied, varied) 17

vault (vaulted, vaulted) 1

veer (veered, veered) 1

veg (vegged, vegged) 81

veil (veiled, veiled) 1

vend (vended, vended) 1

vent (vented, vented) 1

venture (ventured, ventured) 21

verbalize (verbalized, verbalized) 21

vest (vested, vested) 1

vibrate (vibrated, vibrated) 21

video (videoed, videoed) 1

videotape (videotaped, videotaped) 21

view (viewed, viewed) 1

vilify (vilified, vilified) 17

vindicated (vindicated, vindicated) 21

violate (violated, violated) 21

visit (visited, visited) 1

vitalize (vitalized, vitalized) 21

vocalize (vocalized, vocalized) 21

voice (voiced, voiced) 21

void (voided, voided) 1

volunteer (volunteered, volunteered) 1

vote (voted, voted) 21

vouch (vouched, vouched) 23

vow (vowed, vowed) 1

W

wack (wacked, wacked) 1

wade (waded, waded) 21

waffle (waffled, waffled) 21

wag (wagged, wagged) 31

wager (wagered, wagered) 1

wail (wailed, wailed) 1

wait (waited, waited) 119

wake (woke/waked, woken/waked) . . .10/1

waken (wakened, wakened) 1

walk (walked, walked) 120

wall (walled, walled) 1

wallow (wallowed, wallowed) 1

wander (wandered, wandered) 1

wane (waned, waned) 21

want (wanted, wanted) 1

warble (warbled, warbled) 21

warm (warmed, warmed) 1

warn (warned, warned) 1

warp (warped, warped) 1

wash (washed, washed) 23

waste (wasted, wasted) 121

watch (watched, watched) 122

water (watered, watered) 1

wave (waved, waved) 21

waver (wavered, wavered) 1

wax (waxed, waxed) 23

weaken (weakened, weakened) 1

wear (wore, worn) 123

weather (weathered, weathered) 1

weave (wove/weaved, woven/
    weaved) 98/1

wed (wed/wedded*, wed/wedded*) . . .25/31

weep (wept, wept) 37

weigh (weighed, weighed) 1

welcome (welcomed, welcomed) 21

wet (wet, wet) .25

whack (whacked, whacked) 1

while (whiled, whiled) 21

whimper (whimpered, whimpered) 1

whine (whined, whined) 21

whip (whipped, whipped) 31

whisk (whisked, whisked) 1

whisper (whispered, whispered) 1

whistle (whistled, whistled) 21

whiten (whitened, whitened) 1

whitewash (whitewashed,
    whitewashed) 23

wield (wielded, wielded) 1

will (willed, willed) 1

---

*Forms marked by an asterisk (*) are typically more British in usage.

wilt (wilted, wilted) 1

win (won, won) 101

wince (winced, winced) 21

wind (winded, winded) 1

wind (wound, wound) 40

windsurf (windsurfed, windsurfed) 1

wing (winged, winged) 1

wink (winked, winked) 1

winter (wintered, wintered) 1

wipe (wiped, wiped) 21

wish (wished, wished) 23

withdraw (withdrew, withdrawn) 29

wither (withered, withered) 1

withhold (withheld, withheld) 54

withstand (withstood, withstood) 102

witness (witnessed, witnessed) 23

wobble (wobbled, wobbled) 21

wolf (wolfed, wolfed) 1

wonder (wondered, wondered) 1

word (worded, worded) 1

work (worked, worked) 124

worm (wormed, wormed) 1

worry (worried, worried) 17

worsen (worsened, worsened) 1

worship (worshiped/worshipped*,
  worshiped/worshipped*) 1/31

wound (wounded, wounded) 1

wrangle (wrangled, wrangled) 21

wrap (wrapped, wrapped) 31

wreak (wreaked, wreaked) 1

wreck (wrecked, wrecked) 1

wrench (wrenched, wrenched) 23

wrestle (wrestled, wrestled) 21

wring (wrung, wrung) 101

wrinkle (wrinkled, wrinkled) 21

write (wrote, written) 125

wrong (wronged, wronged) 1

X

x (x-ed/x'd/xed, x-ed/x'd/xed) 1

Xerox (Xeroxed, Xeroxed) 23

X-ray (X-rayed, X-rayed) 78

Y

yack (yacked, yacked) 1

yank (yanked, yanked) 1

yawn (yawned, yawned) 1

yearn (yearned, yearned) 1

yell (yelled, yelled) 1

yield (yielded, yielded) 1

yoke (yoked, yoked) 21

yuk (yukked, yukked) 31

yuppify (yuppified, yuppified) 17

Z

zap (zapped, zapped) 31

zigzag (zigzagged, zigzagged) 31

zip (zipped, zipped) 31

zombify (zombified, zombified) 17

zone (zoned, zoned) 21

zoom (zoomed, zoomed) 1

Verb List

*Forms marked by an asterisk (*) are typically more British in usage.

125 Verb Conjugation Charts

act

	ACTIVE	PASSIVE
Infinitive	to act	to be acted
Perfect Infinitive	to have acted	to have been acted
Past Participle	acted	been acted
Present Participle	acting	being acted

ACTIVE

I		
you/we/they		
he/she/it		

SIMPLE PRESENT	SIMPLE PAST	SIMPLE FUTURE
act	acted	will act
act	acted	will act
acts	acted	will act

PRESENT PROGRESSIVE	PAST PROGRESSIVE	FUTURE PROGRESSIVE
am acting	was acting	will be acting
are acting	were acting	will be acting
is acting	was acting	will be acting

PRESENT PERFECT	PAST PERFECT	FUTURE PERFECT
have acted	had acted	will have acted
have acted	had acted	will have acted
has acted	had acted	will have acted

PRESENT PERFECT PROGRESSIVE	PAST PERFECT PROGRESSIVE	FUTURE PERFECT PROGRESSIVE
have been acting	had been acting	will have been acting
have been acting	had been acting	will have been acting
has been acting	had been acting	will have been acting

EXAMPLES:

Are you acting in the school play this year?

Stephanie was acting strange and wouldn't speak to me when I asked her what was wrong.

Ian had always acted like he wasn't interested in school.

PASSIVE

SIMPLE PRESENT	SIMPLE PAST	SIMPLE FUTURE
am acted	was acted	will be acted
are acted	were acted	will be acted
is acted	was acted	will be acted

PRESENT PROGRESSIVE	PAST PROGRESSIVE	FUTURE PROGRESSIVE*
am being acted	was being acted	will be being acted*
are being acted	were being acted	will be being acted*
is being acted	was being acted	will be being acted*

PRESENT PERFECT	PAST PERFECT	FUTURE PERFECT
have been acted	had been acted	will have been acted
have been acted	had been acted	will have been acted
has been acted	had been acted	will have been acted

EXAMPLES:

The part of Desdemona was acted by Ms. Graves.

I'm glad that my ideas are being acted on. Something new needs to happen here.

Many roles have been acted by Ralph Fiennes on stage as well as on film.

PRINCIPAL CONDITIONALS

PRESENT	PRESENT PROGRESSIVE	PRESENT PASSIVE
would act	would be acting	would be acted
would act	would be acting	would be acted
would act	would be acting	would be acted

PAST	PAST PROGRESSIVE	PAST PASSIVE
would have acted	would have been acting	would have been acted
would have acted	would have been acting	would have been acted
would have acted	would have been acting	would have been acted

EXAMPLES:

The fire department would act more swiftly if it had more resources available.

Don't you think he would have been acting more strangely if he were guilty of the crime?

act

Important Forms in Use

IF/THEN CONDITIONALS

	IF ...	... THEN	EXAMPLE
Real Present/ Future	act/acts	simple present	*If you <u>act</u> out one more time, young man, you go to your room.*
		will + base form	*If she <u>acts</u> like this all the time, she'll lose her job.*
Unreal Present/ Future	acted	would + base form	*If we <u>acted</u> in a play together, we would be very convincing.*
Unreal Past	had acted	would have + past participle	*If I <u>had acted</u> on the advice of my accountant, I would have made a lot of money.*

SUBJUNCTIVE

ACTIVE	act	*It is important that the kids <u>act</u> in a way that is appropriate to their age.*
PASSIVE	be acted	*It is essential that these scenes <u>be acted</u> out before we end rehearsal today.*

PHRASAL VERBS

act on/upon	to take action after getting advice or suggestions *I would act on his advice now.*
act out	to show your feelings through your actions, especially feelings of anxiety *The kids started to act out after being inside the whole day without a chance to run around or play.*
act up	when a chronic medical condition begins to bother you, it acts up *My rheumatism always acts up when it starts to rain.*

IDIOMS

to act your age	said to a person who is misbehaving or not acting in a serious way *Those jokes are so stupid. Why don't you act your age!*
to act as if/like nothing ever happened	to pretend that an event didn't affect the current situation *If we act like nothing ever happened, maybe he won't notice that we broke his best china.*
to act accordingly	to behave appropriately for the situation *Now that you've turned eighteen, you'll have to act accordingly.*

RELATED WORDS

action (n.)	a movement or the process of doing something
actor/actress (n.)	a person who performs in a play or movie

* Note that the form "will be being acted" is rarely used. To convey a future progressive passive, use the present progressive passive.

ask

	ACTIVE	PASSIVE
Infinitive	to ask	to be asked
Perfect Infinitive	to have asked	to have been asked
Past Participle	asked	been asked
Present Participle	asking	being asked

ACTIVE

I		
you/we/they		
he/she/it		

SIMPLE PRESENT	SIMPLE PAST	SIMPLE FUTURE
ask	asked	will ask
ask	asked	will ask
asks	asked	will ask

PRESENT PROGRESSIVE	PAST PROGRESSIVE	FUTURE PROGRESSIVE
am asking	was asking	will be asking
are asking	were asking	will be asking
is asking	was asking	will be asking

PRESENT PERFECT	PAST PERFECT	FUTURE PERFECT
have asked	had asked	will have asked
have asked	had asked	will have asked
has asked	had asked	will have asked

PRESENT PERFECT PROGRESSIVE	PAST PERFECT PROGRESSIVE	FUTURE PERFECT PROGRESSIVE
have been asking	had been asking	will have been asking
have been asking	had been asking	will have been asking
has been asking	had been asking	will have been asking

EXAMPLES:
Americans usually don't ask others about their salaries. *Who asked me for toothpaste?* *He had been asking too many questions and we had to tell him to give others a chance.*

PASSIVE

SIMPLE PRESENT	SIMPLE PAST	SIMPLE FUTURE
am asked	was asked	will be asked
are asked	were asked	will be asked
is asked	was asked	will be asked

PRESENT PROGRESSIVE	PAST PROGRESSIVE	FUTURE PROGRESSIVE*
am being asked	was being asked	will be being asked*
are being asked	were being asked	will be being asked*
is being asked	was being asked	will be being asked*

PRESENT PERFECT	PAST PERFECT	FUTURE PERFECT
have been asked	had been asked	will have been asked
have been asked	had been asked	will have been asked
has been asked	had been asked	will have been asked

EXAMPLES:
The suspect was being asked some questions by the detective. *Do you think you will be asked to be best man in the wedding?* *I had been asked to cater the event by the vice president of the company.*

PRINCIPAL CONDITIONALS

PRESENT	PRESENT PROGRESSIVE	PRESENT PASSIVE
would ask	would be asking	would be asked
would ask	would be asking	would be asked
would ask	would be asking	would be asked

PAST	PAST PROGRESSIVE	PAST PASSIVE
would have asked	would have been asking	would have been asked
would have asked	would have been asking	would have been asked
would have asked	would have been asking	would have been asked

EXAMPLES:
I would ask him about his new girlfriend, but I don't want to pry. *If they were interested in buying the house, they would be asking more questions.*

ask

PRINCIPAL PARTS: ask, asked, asked

2

Important Forms in Use

IF/THEN CONDITIONALS

	IF . . .	. . . THEN	EXAMPLE
Real Present/ Future	ask/asks	simple present	*If an employer <u>asks</u> about whether you expect to have children or not, that's discrimination.*
		will + base form	*If he <u>asks</u> me how old I am, I'll kill him.*
Unreal Present/ Future	asked	would + base form	*If we <u>asked</u> them about it, they probably wouldn't tell us.*
Unreal Past	had asked	would have + past participle	*If I <u>had asked</u> him to the wedding, he wouldn't have come.*

SUBJUNCTIVE

ACTIVE	ask	*The director proposed that we <u>ask</u> Terry and John to handle the new account.*
PASSIVE	be asked	*It was necessary that the gentlemen <u>be asked</u> to leave the bar.*

PHRASAL VERBS

ask for	to request something *With this warm weather, a lot of customers have been asking for rosé wine. We should order more.*
ask out	to invite on a date *Traditionally, it was men who asked women out, but nowadays a lot of women ask men out.*
ask over	to invite someone to come to your home *Why don't we ask the Ferrys over for drinks?*

IDIOMS

to be asking for it	to be deserving of punishment or retribution *He was asking for it when he kept leaving work half an hour early without permission.*
ask me no questions and I'll tell you no lies	an expression used when someone doesn't want to give any details about something *"Tell us about your new girlfriend." "Ask me no questions and I'll tell you no lies."*
it's yours for the asking	an expression that means that someone is willing to give something away at no cost *The guy wanted to give me fifty bucks for the table but I told him it was his for the asking.*

RELATED WORDS

asking price (n.)	the amount of money that someone wants to receive for something but that is usually negotiable

* Note that the form "will be being asked" is rarely used. To convey a future progressive passive, use the present progressive passive.

Verb Chart

back

	ACTIVE	PASSIVE
Infinitive	to back	to be backed
Past Infinitive	to have backed	to have been backed
Past Participle	backed	been backed
Present Participle	backing	being backed

ACTIVE

I
you/we/they
he/she/it

SIMPLE PRESENT	SIMPLE PAST	SIMPLE FUTURE
back	backed	will back
back	backed	will back
backs	backed	will back

PRESENT PROGRESSIVE	PAST PROGRESSIVE	FUTURE PROGRESSIVE
am backing	was backing	will be backing
are backing	were backing	will be backing
is backing	was backing	will be backing

PRESENT PERFECT	PAST PERFECT	FUTURE PERFECT
have backed	had backed	will have backed
have backed	had backed	will have backed
has backed	had backed	will have backed

PRESENT PERFECT PROGRESSIVE	PAST PERFECT PROGRESSIVE	FUTURE PERFECT PROGRESSIVE
have been backing	had been backing	will have been backing
have been backing	had been backing	will have been backing
has been backing	had been backing	will have been backing

EXAMPLES:

We backed the new company but unfortunately, they closed down last month.

Mom and I back the Chicago Cubs, while Dad and my cousin back the White Sox.

The mayor had been backing the incumbent for governor, until he changed his position on school funding.

PASSIVE

SIMPLE PRESENT	SIMPLE PAST	SIMPLE FUTURE
am backed	was backed	will be backed
are backed	were backed	will be backed
is backed	was backed	will be backed

PRESENT PROGRESSIVE	PAST PROGRESSIVE	FUTURE PROGRESSIVE*
am being backed	was being backed	will be being backed*
are being backed	were being backed	will be being backed*
is being backed	was being backed	will be being backed*

PRESENT PERFECT	PAST PERFECT	FUTURE PERFECT
have been backed	had been backed	will have been backed
have been backed	had been backed	will have been backed
has been backed	had been backed	will have been backed

EXAMPLES:

Our candidate is backed by all of the major unions in the city.

My car was being backed out of the garage when I went to pick it up at the dealership.

Even after the steroids scandal, the cyclist is still being backed by his sponsors.

PRINCIPAL CONDITIONALS

PRESENT	PRESENT PROGRESSIVE	PRESENT PASSIVE
would back	would be backing	would be backed
would back	would be backing	would be backed
would back	would be backing	would be backed

PAST	PAST PROGRESSIVE	PAST PASSIVE
would have backed	would have been backing	would have been backed
would have backed	would have been backing	would have been backed
would have backed	would have been backing	would have been backed

EXAMPLES:

I would be backing the New York Mets, but they don't look like they're going to win this year.

They guaranteed us that our new proposal would be backed by the CEO.

back

Important Forms in Use

IF/THEN CONDITIONALS

	IF ...	...THEN	EXAMPLE
Real Present/ Future	back/backs	simple present	*If I back into a parking space, I always hit the curb.*
		will + base form	*If the governor backs the mayor in his reelection, the mayor will do all he can to support him in the following four years.*
Unreal Present/ Future	backed	would + base form	*If we backed out of the deal now, we would lose the money we put down as a deposit.*
Unreal Past	had backed	would have + past participle	*If I had backed down, he would have taken complete advantage of me.*

SUBJUNCTIVE

ACTIVE	back	*We ask that you back up your work so that it will not be lost.*
PASSIVE	be backed	*It was essential that the candidate be backed by the president if he expected to be reelected.*

PHRASAL VERBS

back away	to move backward away from someone or something that you are afraid of *We backed away slowly from the man with the gun until we were out of the building.*
back down	to give in to someone, to let someone have his or her way *I didn't want to lend John the car, but I finally backed down when he promised to take it to the car wash after he used it.*
back out	to pull out of something that you have committed to doing *The new Web site couldn't be launched, because several investors backed out.*
back up	to move backward, especially in a car or another vehicle; to save your computer work in more than one place *If you want to, you can back up a little bit farther so that you are closer to the car behind you. / Make sure you back up these files. We don't want to lose all of this work.*

IDIOMS

to go back to the drawing board	an expression meaning you must start something over again *The last idea was rejected at the meeting, so I guess we should go back to the drawing board.*

RELATED WORDS

backing (n.)	support
backer (n.)	a person who supports a business venture or political campaign by giving money

* Note that the form "will be being backed" is rarely used. To convey a future progressive passive, use the present progressive passive.

be

	ACTIVE	PASSIVE
Infinitive	to be	–
Past Infinitive	to have been	–
Past Participle	been	–
Present Participle	being	–

ACTIVE

I
you/we/they
he/she/it

SIMPLE PRESENT	SIMPLE PAST	SIMPLE FUTURE
am	was	will be
are	were	will be
is	was	will be

PRESENT PROGRESSIVE	PAST PROGRESSIVE	FUTURE PROGRESSIVE
am being	was being	will be being
are being	were being	will be being
is being	was being	will be being

PRESENT PERFECT	PAST PERFECT	FUTURE PERFECT
have been	had been	will have been
have been	had been	will have been
has been	had been	will have been

PRESENT PERFECT PROGRESSIVE	PAST PERFECT PROGRESSIVE	FUTURE PERFECT PROGRESSIVE
have been being	had been being	will have been being
have been being	had been being	will have been being
has been being	had been being	will have been being

EXAMPLES:

We will be disappointed if the travel arrangements don't work out.

The dogs were being very difficult and we decided to leave them at home.

She will have been through a lot by the time her plane finally lands.

PASSIVE

SIMPLE PRESENT	SIMPLE PAST	SIMPLE FUTURE
-	-	-
-	-	-
-	-	-

PRESENT PROGRESSIVE	PAST PROGRESSIVE	FUTURE PROGRESSIVE
-	-	-
-	-	-
-	-	-

PRESENT PERFECT	PAST PERFECT	FUTURE PERFECT
-	-	-
-	-	-
-	-	-

PRINCIPAL CONDITIONALS

PRESENT	PRESENT PROGRESSIVE	PRESENT PASSIVE
would be	would be being	-
would be	would be being	-
would be	would be being	-

PAST	PAST PROGRESSIVE	PAST PASSIVE
would have been	would have been being	-
would have been	would have been being	-
would have been	would have been being	-

EXAMPLES:

I would be happier in first class.

She would have been surprised if the concert had started on time.

Would it be too forward to ask you if you are married?

be

Important Forms in Use

IF/THEN CONDITIONALS

	IF . . .	. . . THEN	EXAMPLE
Real Present/ Future	am/are/is	simple present	*If I am on time, I make a lot more money than when I show up late.*
		will + base form	*If she is ready, we'll have time to get a bite to eat before the movie.*
Unreal Present/ Future	was/were	would + base form	*If we were younger, we'd think about traveling in a different way.*
Unreal Past	had been	would have + past participle	*If I had been there, I would have told you not to come.*

SUBJUNCTIVE

ACTIVE   be   *It is important that the author be warned about the changes in the schedule.*

PASSIVE   -

PHRASAL VERBS

be after someone	to be searching for someone *The cops were after me, and so I had to leave town.*
be on to someone	to know that someone is doing something wrong or dishonest *His cheating was so obvious, the other players were soon on to him.*
be out of something	to have no more of something *The pharmacy was out of my favorite shampoo.*

IDIOMS

to be all ears	to be anxious to hear something *If you have a better idea of how to fix it, then I'm all ears!*
to be all for something	to give something your full support *I'm all for freedom of expression, but those costumes are ridiculous.*
to be as good as new	to be fully recovered from a mishap or illness *After his third trip to the doctor, he will be as good as new.*
to not be your day	if it's not your day, things are not going well for you *I locked myself out of the house, lost my wallet on the bus to work, and twisted my ankle on a patch of ice. This is not my day!*

RELATED WORDS

the end-all be-all (n.)	the best item of a certain category
human being (n.)	a human

Verb Chart

41

bear

	ACTIVE	PASSIVE
Infinitive	to bear	to be borne
Past Infinitive	to have borne	to have been borne
Past Participle	borne	been borne
Present Participle	bearing	being borne

ACTIVE

I		
you/we/they		
he/she/it		

SIMPLE PRESENT	SIMPLE PAST	SIMPLE FUTURE
bear	bore	will bear
bear	bore	will bear
bears	bore	will bear

PRESENT PROGRESSIVE	PAST PROGRESSIVE	FUTURE PROGRESSIVE
am bearing	was bearing	will be bearing
are bearing	were bearing	will be bearing
is bearing	was bearing	will be bearing

PRESENT PERFECT	PAST PERFECT	FUTURE PERFECT
have borne	had borne	will have borne
have borne	had borne	will have borne
has borne	had borne	will have borne

PRESENT PERFECT PROGRESSIVE	PAST PERFECT PROGRESSIVE	FUTURE PERFECT PROGRESSIVE
have been bearing	had been bearing	will have been bearing
have been bearing	had been bearing	will have been bearing
has been bearing	had been bearing	will have been bearing

EXAMPLES:

How do you bear him? He's such a bore.

"How's the baby-sitting going?" "I don't like kids but I'm bearing it."

Cynthia has borne the brunt of the difficulties that finding a new manager has caused.

PASSIVE

SIMPLE PRESENT	SIMPLE PAST	SIMPLE FUTURE
am borne	was borne	will be borne
are borne	were borne	will be borne
is borne	was borne	will be borne

PRESENT PROGRESSIVE	PAST PROGRESSIVE	FUTURE PROGRESSIVE*
am being borne	was being borne	will be being borne*
are being borne	were being borne	will be being borne*
is being borne	was being borne	will be being borne*

PRESENT PERFECT	PAST PERFECT	FUTURE PERFECT
have been borne	had been borne	will have been borne
have been borne	had been borne	will have been borne
has been borne	had been borne	will have been borne

EXAMPLES:

The takeover has caused a lot of inconveniences, but I believe they are being borne well by the employees.

The casket was being borne by the representatives of the four Spanish kingdoms.

The difficulties were borne with a certain degree of discomfort.

PRINCIPAL CONDITIONALS

PRESENT	PRESENT PROGRESSIVE	PRESENT PASSIVE
would bear	would be bearing	would be borne
would bear	would be bearing	would be borne
would bear	would be bearing	would be borne

PAST	PAST PROGRESSIVE	PAST PASSIVE
would have borne	would have been bearing	would have been borne
would have borne	would have been bearing	would have been borne
would have borne	would have been bearing	would have been borne

EXAMPLES:

I would have borne more of the responsibility if I had known you were so overworked.

The casket would have been borne by his brothers if they were still living.

bear

PRINCIPAL PARTS: bear, bore, borne/born

Important Forms in Use

IF/THEN CONDITIONALS

	IF . . .	. . . THEN	EXAMPLE
Real Present/ Future	bear/bears	simple present	*If you <u>bear</u> to the right at the next turn off, you are on your way to my house.*
		will + base form	*If you <u>bear</u> with me for a few more minutes, I'll have the sound system fixed.*
Unreal Present/ Future	bore	would + base form	*If I <u>bore</u> a grudge, I would miss out on all the benefits of his friendship.*
Unreal Past	had borne	would have + past participle	*If I <u>had borne</u> down on him more, he would have given up.*

SUBJUNCTIVE

ACTIVE	bear	*We ask that you <u>bear</u> with us for a few more minutes until the speaker arrives.*
PASSIVE	be borne	*It is essential that the responsibilities <u>be borne</u> by members of each department equally.*

PHRASAL VERBS

bear down on	to put pressure on someone to do something *I don't want to take on another case, but my boss is bearing down on me.*
bear on	to have an influence on the outcome of something *What you do will bear on the decision that I make.*
bear up	to be strong when things are difficult *We will all have to bear up during the winter months, especially considering that we want to save money on heat.*
bear with (someone)	to be patient with someone while he or she is repairing something or explaining something tedious *Bear with me. I know this part of the story isn't as interesting, but it picks up later on.*

IDIOMS

to bear a grudge	to stay angry with someone for something that he or she did to annoy you *Make sure to return the money to my sister right away. She's the type to bear a grudge.*
to be unable to bear something	to have strong feelings against someone or something *I can't bear to see him suffer.*
to bear the brunt of something	to take most of the responsibility for something that has gone wrong or something difficult *As usual, I am going to bear the brunt of his mistake.*

RELATED WORDS

bearer (n.)	a person who carries something
pallbearer (n.)	one of several people who carry the casket to the grave in a funeral
bearings (n.)	orientation, awareness of one's location

* Note that the form "will be being borne" is rarely used. To convey a future progressive passive, use the present progressive passive.

Verb Chart

beat

	ACTIVE	PASSIVE
Infinitive	to beat	to be beaten
Past Infinitive	to have beaten	to have been beaten
Past Participle	beaten	been beaten
Present Participle	beating	being beaten

ACTIVE

	I	you/we/they	he/she/it

SIMPLE PRESENT	SIMPLE PAST	SIMPLE FUTURE
beat	beat	will beat
beat	beat	will beat
beats	beat	will beat

PRESENT PROGRESSIVE	PAST PROGRESSIVE	FUTURE PROGRESSIVE
am beating	was beating	will being beating
are beating	were beating	will being beating
is beating	was beating	will being beating

PRESENT PERFECT	PAST PERFECT	FUTURE PERFECT
have beaten	had beaten	will have beaten
have beaten	had beaten	will have beaten
has beaten	had beaten	will have beaten

PRESENT PERFECT PROGRESSIVE	PAST PERFECT PROGRESSIVE	FUTURE PERFECT PROGRESSIVE
have been beating	had been beating	will have been beating
have been beating	had been beating	will have been beating
has been beating	had been beating	will have been beating

EXAMPLES:

The chef always beats the mixture until it is smooth and creamy.

I had never beaten my brother in a race before yesterday.

There are a few problem kids in the neighborhood who have been beating up the younger kids.

PASSIVE

SIMPLE PRESENT	SIMPLE PAST	SIMPLE FUTURE
am beaten	was beaten	will be beaten
are beaten	were beaten	will be beaten
is beaten	was beaten	will be beaten

PRESENT PROGRESSIVE	PAST PROGRESSIVE	FUTURE PROGRESSIVE*
am being beaten	was being beaten	will be being beaten*
are being beaten	were being beaten	will be being beaten*
is being beaten	was being beaten	will be being beaten*

PRESENT PERFECT	PAST PERFECT	FUTURE PERFECT
have been beaten	had been beaten	will have been beaten
have been beaten	had been beaten	will have been beaten
has been beaten	had been beaten	will have been beaten

EXAMPLES:

The Blue Jays were beaten by the Cubs in the series.

He had been beaten so many times playing chess that he gave up the game.

I predict that the home team will be beaten by the visiting team.

PRINCIPAL CONDITIONALS

PRESENT	PRESENT PROGRESSIVE	PRESENT PASSIVE
would beat	would be beating	would be beaten
would beat	would be beating	would be beaten
would beat	would be beating	would be beaten

PAST	PAST PROGRESSIVE	PAST PASSIVE
would have beaten	would have been beating	would have been beaten
would have beaten	would have been beating	would have been beaten
would have beaten	would have been beating	would have been beaten

EXAMPLES:

I never thought I would beat my best friend in the cross-country race.

She would have beaten me if she hadn't twisted her ankle in the last mile.

beat

PRINCIPAL PARTS: beat, beat, beaten/beat

Important Forms in Use

IF/THEN CONDITIONALS

	IF ...	... THEN	EXAMPLE
Real Present/ Future	beat/beats	simple present will + base form	*If I <u>beat</u> you in the race, don't be angry.* *If the rookie <u>beats</u> Jim this afternoon, it will be a big upset.*
Unreal Present/ Future	beat	would + base form	*If the boy <u>beat</u> someone up again, we would notify the police.*
Unreal Past	had beaten	would have + past participle	*If I <u>had beaten</u> the butter and the sugar more, the cake would have been less dense.*

SUBJUNCTIVE

ACTIVE	beat	*It is vital that the young player <u>beat</u> her opponent in this match to stay in the tournament.*
PASSIVE	be beaten	*It is essential that the eggs <u>be beaten</u> when they're at room temperature.*

PHRASAL VERBS

beat (someone) out	to compete against someone for something specific, such as a job, and win *John beat me out for the promotion.*
beat (someone) up	to physically harm someone by hitting and punching him or her *He's the school bully. He's always beating kids up on the playground.*

IDIOMS

to beat someone to the draw	to be first in doing something, specifically, before someone else who wanted to be first *I wanted to pay for dinner, but he beat me to the draw when he pulled out his credit card and gave it to the waitress.*
to beat the drum for someone or something	to give strong support to someone or some cause *Which charity is it this time? You're always beating the drum for something.*
to beat around the bush	to take a long time to get to your point *Don't beat around the bush. Just tell me what's on your mind.*

RELATED WORDS

beater (n.)	a device used in the kitchen to mix foods together

* Note that the form "will be being beaten" is rarely used. To convey a future progressive passive, use the present progressive passive.

begin

	ACTIVE	PASSIVE
Infinitive	to begin	to be begun
Past Infinitive	to have begun	to have been begun
Past Participle	begun	been begun
Present Participle	beginning	being begun

ACTIVE

I		
you/we/they		
he/she/it		

SIMPLE PRESENT	SIMPLE PAST	SIMPLE FUTURE
begin	began	will begin
begin	began	will begin
begins	began	will begin

PRESENT PROGRESSIVE	PAST PROGRESSIVE	FUTURE PROGRESSIVE
am beginning	was beginning	will be beginning
are beginning	were beginning	will be beginning
is beginning	was beginning	will be beginning

PRESENT PERFECT	PAST PERFECT	FUTURE PERFECT
have begun	had begun	will have begun
have begun	had begun	will have begun
has begun	had begun	will have begun

PRESENT PERFECT PROGRESSIVE	PAST PERFECT PROGRESSIVE	FUTURE PERFECT PROGRESSIVE
have been beginning	had been beginning	will have been beginning
have been beginning	had been beginning	will have been beginning
has been beginning	had been beginning	will have been beginning

EXAMPLES:
The sun was beginning to come out today after lunch, but then it clouded over again.   *We arrived at the concert after the music had already begun.*   *The class will begin in five minutes.*

PASSIVE

SIMPLE PRESENT	SIMPLE PAST	SIMPLE FUTURE
am begun	was begun	will be begun
are begun	was begun	will be begun
is begun	was begun	will be begun

PRESENT PROGRESSIVE	PAST PROGRESSIVE	FUTURE PROGRESSIVE*
am being begun	was being begun	will be being begun*
are being begun	were being begun	will be being begun*
is being begun	was being begun	will be being begun*

PRESENT PERFECT	PAST PERFECT	FUTURE PERFECT
have been begun	had been begun	will have been begun
have been begun	had been begun	will have been begun
has been begun	had been begun	will have been begun

EXAMPLES:
The quarrel about evolution was begun by two students with completely differing opinions on the matter.   *The yoga class is begun immediately after the kick-boxing class finishes.*

PRINCIPAL CONDITIONALS

PRESENT	PRESENT PROGRESSIVE	PRESENT PASSIVE
would begin	would be beginning	would be begun
would begin	would be beginning	would be begun
would begin	would be beginning	would be begun

PAST	PAST PROGRESSIVE	PAST PASSIVE
would have begun	would have been beginning	would have been begun
would have begun	would have been beginning	would have been begun
would have begun	would have been beginning	would have been begun

EXAMPLES:
You would begin to understand if you would listen to what I'm talking about.   *We would have begun sooner, but we were having engine trouble.*

begin

PRINCIPAL PARTS: begin, began, begun

VERB CHART

7

Important Forms in Use

IF/THEN CONDITIONALS

	IF ...	... THEN	EXAMPLE
Real Present/ Future	begin/begins	simple present	*If you begin to see lightning, get out of the water right away.*
		will + base form	*If my dog begins to bother you, I'll put her outside.*
Unreal Present/ Future	began	would + base form	*If we began class at seven, we would finish in time to see a movie.*
Unreal Past	had begun	would have + past participle	*If I had begun to feel sick, I would have gone home.*

SUBJUNCTIVE

ACTIVE	begin	*I recommend that you begin your tour in the East Village.*
PASSIVE	be begun	*It is important that the job be begun in the spring.*

IDIOMS

to begin to see the light	to start to understand something or come around to a new point of view *I've been telling you about this idea for an hour, and I think you're just beginning to see the light.*
to begin at the beginning	to start at the top of the story *I'm completely lost. Begin at the beginning so I can follow what you're saying.*
to come from humble beginnings	to have been born to a poor or uneducated family *It's amazing how far Seth has progressed, considering he came from such humble beginnings.*

RELATED WORDS

beginner's luck (n.)	early success in a venture
beginning (n.)	the start of something

* Note that the form "will be being begun" is rarely used. To convey a future progressive passive, use the present progressive passive.

Verb Chart

47

bite

	ACTIVE	PASSIVE
Infinitive	to bite	to be bitten
Past Infinitive	to have bitten	to have been bitten
Past Participle	bitten	been bitten
Present Participle	biting	being bitten

ACTIVE

I		
you/we/they		
he/she/it		

SIMPLE PRESENT	SIMPLE PAST	SIMPLE FUTURE
bite	bit	will bite
bite	bit	will bite
bites	bit	will bite

PRESENT PROGRESSIVE	PAST PROGRESSIVE	FUTURE PROGRESSIVE
am biting	was biting	will be biting
are biting	were biting	will be biting
is biting	was biting	will be biting

PRESENT PERFECT	PAST PERFECT	FUTURE PERFECT
have bitten	had bitten	will have bitten
have bitten	had bitten	will have bitten
has bitten	had bitten	will have bitten

PRESENT PERFECT PROGRESSIVE	PAST PERFECT PROGRESSIVE	FUTURE PERFECT PROGRESSIVE
have been biting	had been biting	will have been biting
have been biting	had been biting	will have been biting
has been biting	had been biting	will have been biting

EXAMPLES:
I'm afraid Ellen has bitten off more than she can chew with this new project.   *The mosquitoes had been biting a lot that summer due to the rain.*   *Does your dog bite?*

PASSIVE

SIMPLE PRESENT	SIMPLE PAST	SIMPLE FUTURE
am bitten	was bitten	will be bitten
are bitten	were bitten	will be bitten
is bitten	was bitten	will be bitten

PRESENT PROGRESSIVE	PAST PROGRESSIVE	FUTURE PROGRESSIVE*
am being bitten	was being bitten	will be being bitten*
are being bitten	were being bitten	will be being bitten*
is being bitten	was being bitten	will be being bitten*

PRESENT PERFECT	PAST PERFECT	FUTURE PERFECT
have been bitten	had been bitten	will have been bitten
have been bitten	had been bitten	will have been bitten
has been bitten	had been bitten	will have been bitten

EXAMPLES:
Terry was miles ahead of us on the bike trip, and so we didn't realized that he had been bitten by the snake.   *We were being bitten by horseflies and so we ran into the house.*   *The girl was bitten by a cat when she was younger, and for that reason, never wanted to have one of her own.*

PRINCIPAL CONDITIONALS

PRESENT	PRESENT PROGRESSIVE	PRESENT PASSIVE
would bite	would be biting	would be bitten
would bite	would be biting	would be bitten
would bite	would be biting	would be bitten

PAST	PAST PROGRESSIVE	PAST PASSIVE
would have bitten	would have been biting	would have been bitten
would have bitten	would have been biting	would have been bitten
would have bitten	would have been biting	would have been bitten

EXAMPLES:
The mosquitoes wouldn't bite you if you put on insect repellent.   *The girl wouldn't have been bitten if she had known how to pet the dog.*

bite

PRINCIPAL PARTS: bite, bit, bitten/bit

Important Forms in Use

IF/THEN CONDITIONALS

	IF ...	... THEN	EXAMPLE
Real Present/ Future	bite/bites	simple present will + base form	*If a dog bites someone, it is sent to the pound.* *If you bite down firmly on the mold, the dentist will get a good imprint of your teeth.*
Unreal Present/ Future	bit	would + base form	*If we bit the bullet and finished the work today, we wouldn't need to come to work over the weekend.*
Unreal Past	had bitten	would have + past participle	*If their cat had bitten me, I wouldn't have grown so attached to it.*

SUBJUNCTIVE

ACTIVE	bite	*His teacher recommended that he not bite off more than he could chew.*
PASSIVE	be bitten	*I wondered if it was fair that I be bitten by twenty mosquitoes while by brother got away with nary an itch.*

PHRASAL VERBS

bite back	to attack in response to an attack *Don't bite back just because she hurt your feelings.*

IDIOMS

to bite off more than you can chew	to take on more work or responsibility than you can handle *When I agreed to cook dinner for both their family and my own, I bit off more than I could chew.*
to bite the dust	to die, especially in combat, or to be defeated *The tennis player bit the dust after losing the third set in a row.*
to bite someone's head off	to attack someone verbally *You have to be careful of Uncle Bill. He can be very kind, but you never know when he is going to bite someone's head off.*
to bite the bullet	to do something that needs to be done without hesitation, even though you may not want to do it *I know you don't want to discuss this issue with your boss, but you're just going to have to bite the bullet.*
to bite the hand that feeds you	to damage your relationship with someone who supports you *Annie's boss worked hard to make sure she wasn't laid off in the last batch of firings. If she complains now about her salary, she would be biting the hand that feeds her.*

RELATED WORDS

biting (adj.)	very harsh
bite (n.)	a quick meal

* Note that the form "will be being bitten" is rarely used. To convey a future progressive passive, use the present progressive passive.

Verb Chart

blow

	ACTIVE	PASSIVE
Infinitive	to blow	to be blown
Past Infinitive	to have blown	to have been blown
Past Participle	blown	been blown
Present Participle	blowing	being blown

ACTIVE

I		
you/we/they		
he/she/it		

SIMPLE PRESENT	SIMPLE PAST	SIMPLE FUTURE
blow	blew	will blow
blow	blew	will blow
blows	blew	will blow

PRESENT PROGRESSIVE	PAST PROGRESSIVE	FUTURE PROGRESSIVE
am blowing	was blowing	will be blowing
are blowing	were blowing	will be blowing
is blowing	was blowing	will be blowing

PRESENT PERFECT	PAST PERFECT	FUTURE PERFECT
have blown	had blown	will have blown
have blown	had blown	will have blown
has blown	had blown	will have blown

PRESENT PERFECT PROGRESSIVE	PAST PERFECT PROGRESSIVE	FUTURE PERFECT PROGRESSIVE
have been blowing	had been blowing	will have been blowing
have been blowing	had been blowing	will have been blowing
has been blowing	had been blowing	will have been blowing

EXAMPLES:
The kids are blowing up balloons in preparation for the party this afternoon.

The flag had been blowing in the wind and got wrapped around the pole.

He felt that he had blown his big chance when he failed the test.

PASSIVE

SIMPLE PRESENT	SIMPLE PAST	SIMPLE FUTURE
am blown	was blown	will be blown
are blown	were blown	will be blown
is blown	was blown	will be blown

PRESENT PROGRESSIVE	PAST PROGRESSIVE	FUTURE PROGRESSIVE*
am being blown	was being blown	will be being blown*
are being blown	were being blown	will be being blown*
is being blown	was being blown	will be being blown*

PRESENT PERFECT	PAST PERFECT	FUTURE PERFECT
have been blown	had been blown	will have been blown
have been blown	had been blown	will have been blown
has been blown	had been blown	will have been blown

EXAMPLES:
The sailboat was blown by a strong wind and traveled quickly across the lake.

The plants had all been blown over in the storm.

If we don't take the clothes off the line, they will be blown away.

PRINCIPAL CONDITIONALS

PRESENT	PRESENT PROGRESSIVE	PRESENT PASSIVE
would blow	would be blowing	would be blown
would blow	would be blowing	would be blown
would blow	would be blowing	would be blown

PAST	PAST PROGRESSIVE	PAST PASSIVE
would have blown	would have been blowing	would have been blown
would have blown	would have been blowing	would have been blown
would have blown	would have been blowing	would have been blown

EXAMPLES:
I didn't think he would blow it, but he did.

His knee would have been blown out during the play if he hadn't been wearing the brace.

blow

PRINCIPAL PARTS: blow, blew, blown

Important Forms in Use

IF/THEN CONDITIONALS

	IF ...	... THEN	EXAMPLE
Real Present/ Future	blow/blows	simple present	*If I <u>blow</u> out all the candles on my birthday cake, my wish comes true, right?*
		will + base form	*If she <u>blows</u> him off again, he won't ask her out any more.*
Unreal Present/ Future	blew	would + base form	*If the storm <u>blew</u> over, we wouldn't be stuck here.*
Unreal Past	had blown	would have + past participle	*If the wind <u>had blown</u> in through the open windows we would have felt some relief from the heat.*

SUBJUNCTIVE

ACTIVE	blow	*We ask that he <u>blow</u> out the candles only after everyone gets to the party.*
PASSIVE	be blown	*He asked that the candles <u>be blown</u> out after the dinner.*

PHRASAL VERBS

blow (someone) away	to impress someone greatly *His new artwork blew me away! I had no idea that he was so talented.*
blow (someone or something) off	to not do something that you were supposed to do, or to not keep an appointment with someone *She's completely unreliable. Every time we make plans, she blows me off.*
blow (something) out	to extinguish using your breath; to do serious damage to a joint *The football player blew out his knee in the last game and will be out for the rest of the season.*
blow over	to pass by without causing harm, even though something appeared problematic initially *They predicted the tornado would destroy some houses, but it blew over without causing any damage.*
blow (something) up	to destroy something using explosives *The radical group called the Weathermen accidentally blew up an apartment building in Chicago in the 1960s.*

IDIOMS

to blow something out of proportion	to make something a bigger deal than it really is *I'm sorry that I lost the keys, but I don't think it's such a big deal. You're blowing this way out of proportion.*
to blow your own horn	to show off your talent, skills or accomplishments *I can't stand Tim. I know he's gifted, but does he have to constantly blow his own horn?*
to blow your mind	to impress you greatly or to strike you as odd *That she would do something so rude completely blows my mind.*

RELATED WORDS

whistle-blower (n.)	someone who exposes wrongdoing
blow-by-blow (n.)	a description of something that happened that tells every single detail

---

* Note that the form "will be being blown" is rarely used. To convey a future progressive passive, use the present progressive passive.

break

	ACTIVE	PASSIVE
Infinitive	to break	to be broken
Past Infinitive	to have broken	to have been broken
Past Participle	broken	been broken
Present Participle	breaking	being broken

ACTIVE

I		
you/we/they		
he/she/it		

SIMPLE PRESENT	SIMPLE PAST	SIMPLE FUTURE
break	broke	will break
break	broke	will break
breaks	broke	will break

PRESENT PROGRESSIVE	PAST PROGRESSIVE	FUTURE PROGRESSIVE
am breaking	was breaking	will be breaking
are breaking	were breaking	will be breaking
is breaking	was breaking	will be breaking

PRESENT PERFECT	PAST PERFECT	FUTURE PERFECT
have broken	had broken	will have broken
have broken	had broken	will have broken
has broken	had broken	will have broken

PRESENT PERFECT PROGRESSIVE	PAST PERFECT PROGRESSIVE	FUTURE PERFECT PROGRESSIVE
have been breaking	had been breaking	will have been breaking
have been breaking	had been breaking	will have been breaking
has been breaking	had been breaking	will have been breaking

EXAMPLES:
Do we break at 11:00 or 12:00?   *Who broke the vase that was sitting on the dining room table?*   *The workers were called to repair a support beam that was breaking away from the wall.*

PASSIVE

SIMPLE PRESENT	SIMPLE PAST	SIMPLE FUTURE
am broken	was broken	will be broken
are broken	were broken	will be broken
is broken	was broken	will be broken

PRESENT PROGRESSIVE	PAST PROGRESSIVE	FUTURE PROGRESSIVE*
am being broken	was being broken	will be being broken*
are being broken	were being broken	will be being broken*
is being broken	was being broken	will be being broken*

PRESENT PERFECT	PAST PERFECT	FUTURE PERFECT
have been broken	had been broken	will have been broken
have been broken	had been broken	will have been broken
has been broken	had been broken	will have been broken

EXAMPLES:
The chair had been broken and shoved in a closet.   *His arm was broken again so that it would heal properly.*   *I'm afraid the raft will be broken if the kids play with it so roughly.*

PRINCIPAL CONDITIONALS

PRESENT	PRESENT PROGRESSIVE	PRESENT PASSIVE
would break	would be breaking	would be broken
would break	would be breaking	would be broken
would break	would be breaking	would be broken

PAST	PAST PROGRESSIVE	PAST PASSIVE
would have broken	would have been breaking	would have been broken
would have broken	would have been breaking	would have been broken
would have broken	would have been breaking	would have been broken

EXAMPLES:
We didn't know that the school guards wouldn't break up a fight until the police came.   *Your house would have been broken into if you hadn't gotten that alarm system.*

break

PRINCIPAL PARTS: break, broke, broken

Important Forms in Use

IF/THEN CONDITIONALS

	IF . . .	. . . THEN	EXAMPLE
Real Present/ Future	break/breaks	simple present	If I <u>break</u> something at work, I have to pay for it.
		will + base form	If she <u>breaks</u> up with him, she'll be much happier.
Unreal Present/ Future	broke	would + base form	If war <u>broke</u> out, we would leave our home-land.
Unreal Past	had broken	would have + past participle	If he <u>had broken</u> my guitar, I would have expected him to fix it.

SUBJUNCTIVE

ACTIVE	break	It is required that a politician break off any connections to private firms before he or she takes office.
PASSIVE	be broken	It is essential that the silence <u>be broken</u> by a member of one of the families.

PHRASAL VERBS

break away	to separate from someone or something *The iceberg broke away from the glacier as the temperature began rising.*
break down	when something mechanical stops working; also used to describe an emotional collapse *My car broke down on the highway, and I had to get it towed. / She broke down in tears when she heard the news of the accident.*
break in	to use force to get into a house or building *The burglars broke in by forcing the door open.*
break out	to start suddenly, usually a war or disease *Civil war broke out as soon as the colonizers left the country. / James breaks out in hives when he eats cheese.*
break up	to end a relationship *Hal and Jeanne broke up after being together for ten years.*
break (something) up	to stop two people from fighting *The security guard broke up the fight between the students in the school playground.*

IDIOMS

to break someone's heart	to cause someone to be very sad or to disappoint someone *Tom broke Tanya's heart when he told her had met someone else.*
to break a leg	used to wish someone good luck before a performance or any important event *You're on stage next, Cindy. Break a leg!*
to break your back	to work very hard *I don't know why I'm breaking my back trying to finish this report. My boss probably won't even look at it until next week.*
to break the ice	to make an initially uncomfortable situation become more comfortable *Nobody was talking at the party, so I told a joke and it broke the ice.*

RELATED WORDS

lucky break (n.)	an opportunity that improves your chances for success
heartbreaker (n.)	a person that is often rejecting people and causing them to be unhappy
break-up (n.)	the end of a romantic relationship
broken down (adj.)	old and worn out
nervous breakdown (n.)	a mental collapse

Verb Chart

* Note that the form "will be being broken" is rarely used. To convey a future progressive passive, use the present progressive passive.

53

bring

	ACTIVE	PASSIVE
Infinitive	to bring	to be brought
Past Infinitive	to have brought	to have been brought
Past Participle	brought	been brought
Present Participle	bringing	being brought

ACTIVE

I		
you/we/they		
he/she/it		

SIMPLE PRESENT	SIMPLE PAST	SIMPLE FUTURE
bring	brought	will bring
bring	brought	will bring
brings	brought	will bring

PRESENT PROGRESSIVE	PAST PROGRESSIVE	FUTURE PROGRESSIVE
am bringing	was bringing	will be bringing
are bringing	were bringing	will be bringing
is bringing	was bringing	will be bringing

PRESENT PERFECT	PAST PERFECT	FUTURE PERFECT
have brought	had brought	will have brought
have brought	had brought	will have brought
has brought	had brought	will have brought

PRESENT PERFECT PROGRESSIVE	PAST PERFECT PROGRESSIVE	FUTURE PERFECT PROGRESSIVE
have been bringing	had been bringing	will have been bringing
have been bringing	had been bringing	will have been bringing
has been bringing	had been bringing	will have been bringing

EXAMPLES:
Mary always brings the most delicious desserts.

Charlie will be bringing home his new girlfriend for dinner tonight, so let's make something special.

Gavin had been bringing the guitars and amps to practice, but he's no longer in the band.

PASSIVE

SIMPLE PRESENT	SIMPLE PAST	SIMPLE FUTURE
am brought	was brought	will be brought
are brought	were brought	will be brought
is brought	was brought	will be brought

PRESENT PROGRESSIVE	PAST PROGRESSIVE	FUTURE PROGRESSIVE*
am being brought	was being brought	will be being brought*
are being brought	were being brought	will be being brought*
is being brought	was being brought	will be being brought*

PRESENT PERFECT	PAST PERFECT	FUTURE PERFECT
have been brought	had been brought	will have been brought
have been brought	had been brought	will have been brought
has been brought	had been brought	will have been brought

EXAMPLES:
Some new reporters were brought in to try to change the newspaper's image.

The unrest was brought on by the director's inability to communicate with his staff.

The child had been brought up in an orphanage.

PRINCIPAL CONDITIONALS

PRESENT	PRESENT PROGRESSIVE	PRESENT PASSIVE
would bring	would be bringing	would be brought
would bring	would be bringing	would be brought
would bring	would be bringing	would be brought

PAST	PAST PROGRESSIVE	PAST PASSIVE
would have brought	would have been bringing	would have been brought
would have brought	would have been bringing	would have been brought
would have brought	would have been bringing	would have been brought

EXAMPLES:
We were hoping you would bring your daughter so that we could meet her.

I would have brought the pictures from my last trip if I had thought about it.

bring

PRINCIPAL PARTS: bring, brought, brought

Important Forms in Use

IF/THEN CONDITIONALS

	IF...	...THEN	EXAMPLE
Real Present/ Future	bring/brings	simple present will + base form	*If I <u>bring</u> the wine, he usually brings the snacks. If she <u>brings</u> her mom to the party, we'll be happy to see her.*
Unreal Present/ Future	brought	would + base form	*If we <u>brought</u> up the money they owe us, they would be offended.*
Unreal Past	had brought	would have + past participle	*If the weather <u>had brought</u> on her moodiness, things would have changed when we moved to Florida.*

SUBJUNCTIVE

ACTIVE	bring	*It is essential that each musician <u>bring</u> his or her own stand and music.*
PASSIVE	be brought	*We ask that beach towels <u>be brought</u> to the front desk.*

PHRASAL VERBS

bring (something) about	to cause a change to occur *Her kind words brought about a change in Ellen's attitude.*
bring (something) on	to cause something to happen *What brought on her bad mood?*
bring (something) out	to make something more apparent *The blue in your sweater brings out the color of your eyes.*
bring (someone) up	to raise someone *I was brought up by my grandparents.*

IDIOMS

to bring someone down a peg	to make someone feel that they are less important than they might have thought *John needs to be brought down a peg. He's beginning to get so arrogant.*
to bring someone to his or her knees	to take the power away from someone, especially in a war or competition *The new company soon got all of the business in the tri-state region. They brought the competition to their knees.*
to bring something to someone's attention	to let someone know about something *The memo brought to my attention the need for new computers in the ESL lab.*
to bring out the best/worst in someone	to cause someone to behave well or badly *He really shouldn't drink; alcohol brings out the worst in him.*

* Note that the form "will be being brought" is rarely used. To convey a future progressive passive, use the present progressive passive.

brush

	ACTIVE	PASSIVE
Infinitive	to brush	to be brushed
Past Infinitive	to have brushed	to have been brushed
Past Participle	brushed	been brushed
Present Participle	brushing	being brushed

ACTIVE

I	
you/we/they	
he/she/it	

SIMPLE PRESENT	SIMPLE PAST	SIMPLE FUTURE
brush	brushed	will brush
brush	brushed	will brush
brushes	brushed	will brush

PRESENT PROGRESSIVE	PAST PROGRESSIVE	FUTURE PROGRESSIVE
am brushing	was brushing	will be brushing
are brushing	were brushing	will be brushing
is brushing	was brushing	will be brushing

PRESENT PERFECT	PAST PERFECT	FUTURE PERFECT
have brushed	had brushed	will have brushed
have brushed	had brushed	will have brushed
has brushed	had brushed	will have brushed

PRESENT PERFECT PROGRESSIVE	PAST PERFECT PROGRESSIVE	FUTURE PERFECT PROGRESSIVE
have been brushing	had been brushing	will have been brushing
have been brushing	had been brushing	will have been brushing
has been brushing	had been brushing	will have been brushing

EXAMPLES:

Her mother brushes her long, thick hair every morning. *They were brushing up on their performance until the last moment.* *Did you brush your teeth?*

PASSIVE

SIMPLE PRESENT	SIMPLE PAST	SIMPLE FUTURE
am brushed	was brushed	will be brushed
are brushed	were brushed	will be brushed
is brushed	was brushed	will be brushed

PRESENT PROGRESSIVE	PAST PROGRESSIVE	FUTURE PROGRESSIVE*
am being brushed	was being brushed	will be being brushed*
are being brushed	were being brushed	will be being brushed*
is being brushed	was being brushed	will be being brushed*

PRESENT PERFECT	PAST PERFECT	FUTURE PERFECT
have been brushed	had been brushed	will have been brushed
have been brushed	had been brushed	will have been brushed
has been brushed	had been brushed	will have been brushed

EXAMPLES:

They had been brushed off so many times by the company that they decided to take their concept elsewhere. *The new idea was quickly brushed aside by the board of trustees.* *All of the animals have been washed and brushed by the vet's assistant.*

PRINCIPAL CONDITIONALS

PRESENT	PRESENT PROGRESSIVE	PRESENT PASSIVE
would brush	would be brushing	would be brushed
would brush	would be brushing	would be brushed
would brush	would be brushing	would be brushed

PAST	PAST PROGRESSIVE	PAST PASSIVE
would have brushed	would have been brushing	would have been brushed
would have brushed	would have been brushing	would have been brushed
would have brushed	would have been brushing	would have been brushed

EXAMPLES:

I would brush my teeth more often if I brought a toothbrush to work. *We didn't know that our idea would be brushed aside without any real discussion.*

brush

PRINCIPAL PARTS: brush, brushed, brushed

Important Forms in Use

IF/THEN CONDITIONALS

	IF . . .	. . . THEN	EXAMPLE
Real Present/ Future	brush/brushes	simple present	*If I <u>brush</u> my teeth with that toothbrush, my gums bleed.*
		will + base form	*If the boy <u>brushes</u> his hair before the picture, he'll look much better.*
Unreal Present/ Future	brushed	would + base form	*If we <u>brushed</u> them off, they would be offended.*
Unreal Past	had brushed	would have + past participle	*If I <u>had brushed</u> the cat last night, we would have found the tick sooner.*

SUBJUNCTIVE

ACTIVE	brush	*It is important that you <u>brush</u> up on your Shakespeare before the test.*
PASSIVE	be brushed	*It is essential that the horses <u>be brushed</u> every day.*

PHRASAL VERBS

brush (something) aside	to not consider something, or to disregard it as not feasible or not important *They brushed aside the concerns of members of the community and started to build the new stadium without delay.*
brush (someone or something) off	to dismiss or ignore *I don't know how I offended my manager, but he always brushes me off, even when I have a good idea.*
brush up on (something)	to perfect or to refresh one's knowledge *I had to brush up on my Spanish before the oral test, considering that it had been months since I had spoken the language.*

IDIOMS

to brush it under the carpet	to relegate something to secrecy, to ignore a problem *The corporation tried to solve their tax problem by brushing it under the carpet, but the press found out about it.*

RELATED WORDS

brush (n.)	a tool which is used to clean a variety of things or to keep hair from tangling
brush-off (n.)	a dismissal
brush with greatness (n.)	an experience in which you were close to someone who is successful or famous

* Note that the form "will be being brushed" is rarely used. To convey a future progressive passive, use the present progressive passive.

Verb Chart

build

	ACTIVE	PASSIVE
Infinitive	to build	to be built
Past Infinitive	to have built	to have been built
Past Participle	built	been built
Present Participle	building	being built

ACTIVE

I		
you/we/they		
he/she/it		

SIMPLE PRESENT	SIMPLE PAST	SIMPLE FUTURE
build	built	will build
build	built	will build
builds	built	will build

PRESENT PROGRESSIVE	PAST PROGRESSIVE	FUTURE PROGRESSIVE
am building	was building	will be building
are building	were building	will be building
is building	was building	will be building

PRESENT PERFECT	PAST PERFECT	FUTURE PERFECT
have built	had built	will have built
have built	had built	will have built
has built	had built	will have built

PRESENT PERFECT PROGRESSIVE	PAST PERFECT PROGRESSIVE	FUTURE PERFECT PROGRESSIVE
have been building	had been building	will have been building
have been building	had been building	will have been building
has been building	had been building	will have been building

EXAMPLES:
My architectural firm builds educational institutions.

Frank Lloyd Wright built his home and studio in Oak Park, Illinois.

PASSIVE

SIMPLE PRESENT	SIMPLE PAST	SIMPLE FUTURE
am built	was built	will be built
are built	were built	will be built
is built	was built	will be built

PRESENT PROGRESSIVE	PAST PROGRESSIVE	FUTURE PROGRESSIVE*
am being built	was being built	will be being built*
are being built	were being built	will be being built*
is being built	was being built	will be being built*

PRESENT PERFECT	PAST PERFECT	FUTURE PERFECT
have been built	had been built	will have been built
have been built	had been built	will have been built
has been built	had been built	will have been built

EXAMPLES:
The Brooklyn Bridge was built in the 1860s.

We lived with my mother while our house was being built.

After it had been built at the onset of the Great Depression, the Empire State Building remained empty for years.

PRINCIPAL CONDITIONALS

PRESENT	PRESENT PROGRESSIVE	PRESENT PASSIVE
would build	would be building	would be built
would build	would be building	would be built
would build	would be building	would be built

PAST	PAST PROGRESSIVE	PAST PASSIVE
would have built	would have been building	would have been built
would have built	would have been building	would have been built
would have built	would have been building	would have been built

EXAMPLES:
We would build our own home, but the expense is astronomical.

The neighbors protested when they learned that an expensive housing complex would be built in their neighborhood.

build

Important Forms in Use

IF/THEN CONDITIONALS

	IF ...	... THEN	EXAMPLE
Real Present/ Future	build/builds	simple present	If I <u>build</u> a tree house for the kids, they can play in it.
		will + base form	If the landlord <u>builds</u> another apartment building behind ours, we will lose our sunlight.
Unreal Present/ Future	built	would + base form	If we <u>built</u> the house next to the waterfall, we would see it and hear it all the time.
Unreal Past	had built	would have + past participle	If I <u>had built</u> my home several years ago, I would have saved thousands of dollars.

SUBJUNCTIVE

ACTIVE	build	We ask that he not <u>build</u> a garage next to where the children play.
PASSIVE	be built	It is essential that the house <u>be built</u> according to the specifications of the owner.

PHRASAL VERBS

build into	to add something in where something else already exists *The cabinets were built into all of the rooms on the first floor.*
build on	to use a foundation which you already have to move forward from *Building on his experience as a chef and a waiter, he decided to open a restaurant.*
build (someone) up	to make someone feel like he or she is doing well, to encourage; to place expectations on someone *His manager always has to build him up before he goes on stage. /* *He built me up to be someone I'm not.*
build up to	to lead into, to come before *The argument built up to their ultimate separation.*

IDIOMS

to build bridges	to make connections *He's always building bridges with other people in his field. That's why he's so successful.*

RELATED WORDS

builder (n.)	a person who constructs buildings or homes
building block (n.)	the pieces that are used to construct something
well-built (adj.)	having a good figure (a person), or well-constructed
built-in (adj.)	included in the construction or the price of something

* Note that the form "will be being built" is rarely used. To convey a future progressive passive, use the present progressive passive.

Verb Chart

burn

	ACTIVE	PASSIVE
Infinitive	to burn	to be burned
Past Infinitive	to have burned	to have been burned
Past Participle	burned	been burned
Present Participle	burning	being burned

ACTIVE

I		
you/we/they		
he/she/it		

SIMPLE PRESENT	SIMPLE PAST	SIMPLE FUTURE
burn	burned	will burn
burn	burned	will burn
burns	burned	will burn

PRESENT PROGRESSIVE	PAST PROGRESSIVE	FUTURE PROGRESSIVE
am burning	was burning	will be burning
are burning	were burning	will be burning
is burning	was burning	will be burning

PRESENT PERFECT	PAST PERFECT	FUTURE PERFECT
have burned	had burned	will have burned
have burned	had burned	will have burned
has burned	had burned	will have burned

PRESENT PERFECT PROGRESSIVE	PAST PERFECT PROGRESSIVE	FUTURE PERFECT PROGRESSIVE
have been burning	had been burning	will have been burning
have been burning	had been burning	will have been burning
has been burning	had been burning	will have been burning

EXAMPLES:

We went out to dinner because I burned the lasagna.

The family was burning a candle in honor of their son who had died.

Have you noticed that all the light bulbs have burned out?

PASSIVE

SIMPLE PRESENT	SIMPLE PAST	SIMPLE FUTURE
am burned	was burned	will be burned
are burned	were burned	will be burned
is burned	was burned	will be burned

PRESENT PROGRESSIVE	PAST PROGRESSIVE	FUTURE PROGRESSIVE*
am being burned	was being burned	will be being burned*
are being burned	were being burned	will be being burned*
is being burned	was being burned	will be being burned*

PRESENT PERFECT	PAST PERFECT	FUTURE PERFECT
have been burned	had been burned	will have been burned
have been burned	had been burned	will have been burned
has been burned	had been burned	will have been burned

EXAMPLES:

The leaves were being burned behind the house next door.

I'm afraid the meal will be burned if we don't take it out of the oven right now.

The girl had been burned in the fire and had scars that covered her legs.

PRINCIPAL CONDITIONALS

PRESENT	PRESENT PROGRESSIVE	PRESENT PASSIVE
would burn	would be burning	would be burned
would burn	would be burning	would be burned
would burn	would be burning	would be burned

PAST	PAST PROGRESSIVE	PAST PASSIVE
would have burned	would have been burning	would have been burned
would have burned	would have been burning	would have been burned
would have burned	would have been burning	would have been burned

EXAMPLES:

The gasoline would burn more efficiently if you had a tune-up.

The teacher would have burned out years before if he hadn't taken a sabbatical every few years.

The beach fire would still be burning if it hadn't started to rain.

burn

PRINCIPAL PARTS: burn, burned/burnt, burned/burnt

Important Forms in Use

IF/THEN CONDITIONALS

	IF ...	... THEN	EXAMPLE
Real Present/ Future	burn/burns	simple present will + base form	*If you <u>burn</u> yourself, go to the hospital.* *If the fire <u>burns</u> itself out during the night, you'll have to start it again in the morning.*
Unreal Present/ Future	burned	would + base form	*If the house <u>burned</u> down, we would find temporary housing for the family.*
Unreal Past	had burned	would have + past participle	*If the murderer <u>hadn't burned</u> the evidence, we would've had a much stronger case.*

SUBJUNCTIVE

ACTIVE	burn	*The owner asked that we <u>burn</u> the leaves while he is away.*
PASSIVE	be burned	*We recommend that contaminated clothing <u>be burned</u> in order not to spread infection.*

PHRASAL VERBS

burn down	to be destroyed completely by fire; used for buildings *The abandoned house had burned down by the time the firefighters arrived.*
burn out	to be drained of energy or drive as a result of working too much *Teachers often burn out in this school because of all the discipline problems.*
burn up	to be completely destroyed by fire *The debris from the space shuttle burned up as it reentered the atmosphere.*

IDIOMS

to burn (your) bridges	to destroy relationships that could have been valuable to you in the future *I know that you're very happy about your new job, but don't burn your bridges at your old company. You never know when you might want to go back.*
to burn the candle at both ends	to try to do too much so that you end up completely exhausted *She's burning the candle at both ends, trying to go out every night after working a full-time job.*
to burn a hole in your pocket	to be sitting there eager to be used; used with money or credit cards *Let's go out to dinner— my treat. This money is burning a hole in my pocket.*

RELATED WORDS

burned-out (adj.)	completely exhausted of energy or drive after working too much
burner (n.)	the ring on top of the stove where you cook food or heat liquids

* Note that the form "will be being burned" is rarely used. To convey a future progressive passive, use the present progressive passive.

buy

	ACTIVE	PASSIVE
Infinitive	to buy	to be bought
Past Infinitive	to have bought	to have been bought
Past Participle	bought	been bought
Present Participle	buying	being bought

ACTIVE

I
you/we/they
he/she/it

SIMPLE PRESENT	SIMPLE PAST	SIMPLE FUTURE
buy	bought	will buy
buy	bought	will buy
buys	bought	will buy

PRESENT PROGRESSIVE	PAST PROGRESSIVE	FUTURE PROGRESSIVE
am buying	was buying	will be buying
are buying	were buying	will be buying
is buying	was buying	will be buying

PRESENT PERFECT	PAST PERFECT	FUTURE PERFECT
have bought	had bought	will have bought
have bought	had bought	will have bought
has bought	had bought	will have bought

PRESENT PERFECT PROGRESSIVE	PAST PERFECT PROGRESSIVE	FUTURE PERFECT PROGRESSIVE
have been buying	had been buying	will have been buying
have been buying	had been buying	will have been buying
has been buying	had been buying	will have been buying

EXAMPLES:

We are buying a new house in upstate New York.

The magazine didn't buy my article, but I'm sending it on to other places where it might get published.

The farmers had bought thousands of acres of land before they realized that it had been contaminated.

PASSIVE

SIMPLE PRESENT	SIMPLE PAST	SIMPLE FUTURE
am bought	was bought	will be bought
are bought	were bought	will be bought
is bought	was bought	will be bought

PRESENT PROGRESSIVE	PAST PROGRESSIVE	FUTURE PROGRESSIVE*
am being bought	was being bought	will be being bought*
are being bought	were being bought	will be being bought*
is being bought	was being bought	will be being bought*

PRESENT PERFECT	PAST PERFECT	FUTURE PERFECT
have been bought	had been bought	will have been bought
have been bought	had been bought	will have been bought
has been bought	had been bought	will have been bought

EXAMPLES:

Our family home was bought by some friends of mine from high school.

I'm hoping that this table will be bought by someone before we have to close up.

How many copies of your new book have been bought?

PRINCIPAL CONDITIONALS

PRESENT	PRESENT PROGRESSIVE	PRESENT PASSIVE
would buy	would be buying	would be bought
would buy	would be buying	would be bought
would buy	would be buying	would be bought

PAST	PAST PROGRESSIVE	PAST PASSIVE
would have bought	would have been buying	would have been bought
would have bought	would have been buying	would have been bought
would have bought	would have been buying	would have been bought

EXAMPLES:

We would have bought more stock in your company if more had been available.

I never thought that you would buy your daughter a convertible.

buy

Important Forms in Use

IF/THEN CONDITIONALS

	IF . . .	. . . THEN	EXAMPLE
Real Present/ Future	buy/buys	simple present will + base form	*If I buy lunch, you leave the tip.* *If he buys so many toys for his son, he'll end up having a spoiled child.*
Unreal Present/ Future	bought	would + base form	*If you bought her a gift every once and a while, she would appreciate it.*
Unreal Past	had bought	would have + past participle	*If I had bought up more property in this area when it was cheap, I would have made a lot of money.*

SUBJUNCTIVE

ACTIVE	buy	*We recommend that you buy a three-year warranty to go along with your product.*
PASSIVE	be bought	*We ask that a membership be bought before the first of September.*

PHRASAL VERBS

buy into (something)	to believe in a certain idea *She bought into the idea that girls didn't play basketball.*
buy off	to convince someone (not) to do something by paying him or her money *The article informed us that two members of the jury had been bought off, and therefore had found the defendant not guilty.*
buy out	to purchase all of someone's shares in a business so that he or she no longer has a stake *We bought out Dr. Kramer's share in the company.*
buy up	to buy all of what is available of a certain item *The real estate company bought up all of the land around the hospital to build housing.*

IDIOMS

to buy someone's story	to believe what someone is saying *My parents didn't buy my story about how I got into an accident.*
to buy time	to do something that allows you to delay making a final decision *We bought time by asking the CEO to give us more figures concerning the company's profits from the previous year.*

RELATED WORDS

buyer (n.)	the person who is buying something
buyer's market (n.)	when prices are low, and therefore favorable to someone who is buying
buyout (n.)	a situation in which someone buys all of the shares of a company and thereby takes control of it

* Note that the form "will be being bought" is rarely used. To convey a future progressive passive, use the present progressive passive.

call

	ACTIVE	PASSIVE
Infinitive	to call	to be called
Past Infinitive	to have called	to have been called
Past Participle	called	been called
Present Participle	calling	being called

ACTIVE

	I	you/we/they	he/she/it

SIMPLE PRESENT	SIMPLE PAST	SIMPLE FUTURE
call	called	will call
call	called	will call
calls	called	will call

PRESENT PROGRESSIVE	PAST PROGRESSIVE	FUTURE PROGRESSIVE
am calling	was calling	will be calling
are calling	were calling	will be calling
is calling	was calling	will be calling

PRESENT PERFECT	PAST PERFECT	FUTURE PERFECT
have called	had called	will have called
have called	had called	will have called
has called	had called	will have called

PRESENT PERFECT PROGRESSIVE	PAST PERFECT PROGRESSIVE	FUTURE PERFECT PROGRESSIVE
have been calling	had been calling	will have been calling
have been calling	had been calling	will have been calling
has been calling	had been calling	will have been calling

EXAMPLES:

What happened to Mr. and Ms. Burns? We haven't called them in ages.

The doctor's office has been calling all morning. It must be something important.

You didn't tell me that my mother had called. When did she call?

PASSIVE

SIMPLE PRESENT	SIMPLE PAST	SIMPLE FUTURE
am called	was called	will be called
are called	were called	will be called
is called	was called	will be called

PRESENT PROGRESSIVE	PAST PROGRESSIVE	FUTURE PROGRESSIVE*
am being called	was being called	will be being called*
are being called	were being called	will be being called*
is being called	was being called	will be being called*

PRESENT PERFECT	PAST PERFECT	FUTURE PERFECT
have been called	had been called	will have been called
have been called	had been called	will have been called
has been called	had been called	will have been called

EXAMPLES:

My name is Gabrielle, but I'm called Gabby.

The actors were being called on one by one at the audition.

All of the guests had been called and notified that the location of the reception had been changed.

PRINCIPAL CONDITIONALS

PRESENT	PRESENT PROGRESSIVE	PRESENT PASSIVE
would call	would be calling	would be called
would call	would be calling	would be called
would call	would be calling	would be called

PAST	PAST PROGRESSIVE	PAST PASSIVE
would have called	would have been calling	would have been called
would have called	would have been calling	would have been called
would have called	would have been calling	would have been called

EXAMPLES:

Would you call us and let us know when you're coming?

All of the students would have been called on if there had been more time.

call

PRINCIPAL PARTS: call, called, called

Important Forms in Use

IF/THEN CONDITIONALS

	IF ...	... THEN	EXAMPLE
Real Present/ Future	call/calls	simple present · will + base form	*If he <u>calls</u> me at 10:00, I can be there by 11:00.* *If I <u>call</u> my brother too early, he won't answer the phone.*
Unreal Present/ Future	called	would + base form	*If we <u>called</u> around, we would find a better price.*
Unreal Past	had called	would have + past participle	*If they <u>had called</u> the game because of rain, we would have gotten our money back.*

SUBJUNCTIVE

ACTIVE	call	*We insist that the doctor <u>call</u> as soon as he knows anything.*
PASSIVE	be called	*It is essential that I <u>be called</u> and notified of any changes in the patient's condition.*

PHRASAL VERBS

call back	to return a phone call or to ask somebody to return for a second interview or audition *Did you call Mr. Smith back? / I can't believe they called me back for the second round of auditions.*
call for	to require *This recipe calls for two cups of butter.*
call in	to ask someone to come somewhere, especially to work, or to ask a specialist to become involved in solving a problem *The restaurant was so busy that we had to call in two more waiters. / I don't know how to get rid of this bees' nest. I think we'll have to call in an exterminator.*
call off	to cancel *The outdoor performance of the ballet was called off because of rain.*
call on	to visit *It would be nice if we could call on Mary in the rehabilitation center.*
call out	to focus attention on someone for something that he or she has done wrong *My classmate called me out for not having finished my part of the presentation.*

IDIOMS

to call it a day	to finish working *Let's do one more chapter and then call it a day.*
to call it for what it is	to be honest about something *This is discrimination. We need to call it for what it is.*
to call something into question	to express doubts about something *His theory was called into question after an outside source did further investigations.*
to call the shots	to be in charge of a situation *Who's calling the shots here?*

RELATED WORDS

caller (n.)	a person who is calling someone on the telephone, or a person visiting someone's home
calling card (n.)	a card that is bought and then used to make telephone calls
calling (n.)	a feeling of duty
call-waiting (n.)	a service on your telephone in which you are notified of a second call when you are already on the phone

* Note that the form "will be being called" is rarely used. To convey a future progressive passive, use the present progressive passive.

carry

	ACTIVE	PASSIVE
Infinitive	to carry	to be carried
Past Infinitive	to have carried	to have been carried
Past Participle	carried	been carried
Present Participle	carrying	being carried

ACTIVE

I
you/we/they
he/she/it

SIMPLE PRESENT	SIMPLE PAST	SIMPLE FUTURE
carry	carried	will carry
carry	carried	will carry
carries	carried	will carry

PRESENT PROGRESSIVE	PAST PROGRESSIVE	FUTURE PROGRESSIVE
am carrying	was carrying	will be carrying
are carrying	were carrying	will be carrying
is carrying	was carrying	will be carrying

PRESENT PERFECT	PAST PERFECT	FUTURE PERFECT
have carried	had carried	will have carried
have carried	had carried	will have carried
has carried	had carried	will have carried

PRESENT PERFECT PROGRESSIVE	PAST PERFECT PROGRESSIVE	FUTURE PERFECT PROGRESSIVE
have been carrying	had been carrying	will have been carrying
have been carrying	had been carrying	will have been carrying
has been carrying	had been carrying	will have been carrying

EXAMPLES:

He always carried his father's watch with him.

Will you carry my bag for a while? It's really heavy.

You have been carrying on about this for months!

PASSIVE

SIMPLE PRESENT	SIMPLE PAST	SIMPLE FUTURE
am carried	was carried	will be carried
are carried	were carried	will be carried
is carried	was carried	will be carried

PRESENT PROGRESSIVE	PAST PROGRESSIVE	FUTURE PROGRESSIVE*
am being carried	was being carried	will be being carried*
are being carried	were being carried	will be being carried*
is being carried	was being carried	will be being carried*

PRESENT PERFECT	PAST PERFECT	FUTURE PERFECT
have been carried	had been carried	will have been carried
have been carried	had been carried	will have been carried
has been carried	had been carried	will have been carried

EXAMPLES:

We were carried away and bought the most expensive car we found.

The tent and backpack had been carried by each member of the camping group at different times during the day.

Just as we got home, all of our belongings were being carried off by the burglars.

PRINCIPAL CONDITIONALS

PRESENT	PRESENT PROGRESSIVE	PRESENT PASSIVE
would carry	would be carrying	would be carried
would carry	would be carrying	would be carried
would carry	would be carrying	would be carried

PAST	PAST PROGRESSIVE	PAST PASSIVE
would have carried	would have been carrying	would have been carried
would have carried	would have been carrying	would have been carried
would have carried	would have been carrying	would have been carried

EXAMPLES:

Would you carry the suitcase for a while?

We didn't know whom the Olympic torch would be carried by until the list appeared in the paper.

carry

PRINCIPAL PARTS: carry, carried, carried

Important Forms in Use

IF/THEN CONDITIONALS

	IF . . .	. . . THEN	EXAMPLE
Real Present/ Future	carry/carries	simple present	If I <u>carry</u> on about something, she inevitably gives in.
		will + base form	If she <u>carries</u> that stuffed animal around, I won't go with her on the trip!
Unreal Present/ Future	carried	would + base form	If we <u>carried</u> the project out as planned, John would be more than satisfied.
Unreal Past	had carried	would have + past participle	If the last administration's work <u>had carried</u> over into the new administration, they wouldn't have had the kind of problems they did.

SUBJUNCTIVE

ACTIVE	carry	It is important that we <u>carry</u> on the work of the last director.
PASSIVE	be carried	We ask that the evening's activities <u>be carried</u> out as planned.

PHRASAL VERBS

carry (something) off	to do something successfully *He wanted them to believe that he was over twenty-one, but he couldn't carry it off.*
carry on	to continue *I want to carry on where the last teacher left off.*
carry (something) out	to do something that was planned earlier *The plan for building a new planetarium was finally carried out.*
carry over	when something that had influence continues to have influence under a new set of circumstances, it carries over *We hope that his ideas will carry over into the new curriculum.*

IDIOMS

to carry the show	to be the most successful part of a production, the part that makes it work *Lindsey's acting is great, but you know it's Andy who carries the show.*
to carry your weight	to do what you are responsible for *Some people in the group are not carrying their weight. Otherwise, all of the work would be done.*
to carry a torch for someone	to be in love with someone *Linda is married. I don't know why Bill continues to carry a torch for her.*

RELATED WORDS

carry-all (n.)	a large bag that is large enough to fit everything you need for an outing
carry-on (n.)	a suitcase that doesn't exceed the limit that an airline gives, and can be brought on board

* Note that the form "will be being carried" is rarely used. To convey a future progressive passive, use the present progressive passive.

catch

	ACTIVE	PASSIVE
Infinitive	to catch	to be caught
Past Infinitive	to have caught	to have been caught
Past Participle	caught	been caught
Present Participle	catching	being caught

ACTIVE

SIMPLE PRESENT	SIMPLE PAST	SIMPLE FUTURE
catch	caught	will catch
catch	caught	will catch
catches	caught	will catch

I
you/we/they
he/she/it

PRESENT PROGRESSIVE	PAST PROGRESSIVE	FUTURE PROGRESSIVE
am catching	was catching	will be catching
are catching	were catching	will be catching
is catching	was catching	will be catching

PRESENT PERFECT	PAST PERFECT	FUTURE PERFECT
have caught	had caught	will have caught
have caught	had caught	will have caught
has caught	had caught	will have caught

PRESENT PERFECT PROGRESSIVE	PAST PERFECT PROGRESSIVE	FUTURE PERFECT PROGRESSIVE
have been catching	had been catching	will have been catching
have been catching	had been catching	will have been catching
has been catching	had been catching	will have been catching

EXAMPLES:
We catch the 7:30 bus every morning.   *Will you catch any of that TV show tonight?*   *One of the kids had caught a bad cold that was passed on to several other students.*

PASSIVE

SIMPLE PRESENT	SIMPLE PAST	SIMPLE FUTURE
am caught	was caught	will be caught
are caught	were caught	will be caught
is caught	was caught	will be caught

PRESENT PROGRESSIVE	PAST PROGRESSIVE	FUTURE PROGRESSIVE*
am being caught	was being caught	will be being caught*
are being caught	were being caught	will be being caught*
is being caught	was being caught	will be being caught*

PRESENT PERFECT	PAST PERFECT	FUTURE PERFECT
have been caught	had been caught	will have been caught
have been caught	had been caught	will have been caught
has been caught	had been caught	will have been caught

EXAMPLES:
How were the bank robbers caught?   *The clerk next to me was caught taking money from her drawer.*   *I wouldn't have continued playing those practical jokes if I had been caught.*

PRINCIPAL CONDITIONALS

PRESENT	PRESENT PROGRESSIVE	PRESENT PASSIVE
would catch	would be catching	would be caught
would catch	would be catching	would be caught
would catch	would be catching	would be caught

PAST	PAST PROGRESSIVE	PAST PASSIVE
would have caught	would have been catching	would have been caught
would have caught	would have been catching	would have been caught
would have caught	would have been catching	would have been caught

EXAMPLES:
We wouldn't have caught the show on TV last night if my mother hadn't told us it was on.   *The mouse would have been caught if we had had better mousetraps.*

Important Forms in Use

IF/THEN CONDITIONALS

	IF ...	...THEN	EXAMPLE
Real Present/ Future	catch/catches	simple present	*If I catch the news on TV, I know what the weather is going to be for the following day.*
		will + base form	*If she catches me taking money from her purse, she'll kill me.*
Unreal Present/ Future	caught	would + base form	*If we caught that last train, we would still make it on time.*
Unreal Past	had caught	would have + past participle	*If I had caught him in the act, I would have gone to the police.*

SUBJUNCTIVE

ACTIVE	catch	*They suggested that we catch a show at a theater in the Broadway district.*
PASSIVE	be caught	*It is vital that the perpetrators be caught and brought to justice.*

PHRASAL VERBS

catch on	to begin to gain popularity *I couldn't believe that slogan t-shirts would catch on again thirty-five years later.*
catch up (on)	to work hard to complete work that you missed *When Maddie returned after she was out with the chicken pox, she had a lot of work to catch up on.*
catch up (with)	to work hard to come to the same place where others are *By kilometer 23, I had caught up with the runners that had left me in the dust at the beginning of the race. / When she saw how far the rest of the students were on their physics problems, she thought she would never catch up.*

IDIOMS

to catch someone off guard	to surprise someone *He caught me off guard when he asked me to marry him.*
to catch a few winks	to take a nap *You guys go ahead. I'm going to try to catch a few winks before dinner.*
to catch someone's drift	to understand what someone is saying *Do you catch my drift or should I explain the idea again?*
to not be caught dead (doing something)	to refuse to do something *Issak wouldn't be caught dead wearing a suit and tie, even to his own funeral.*
to catch someone red-handed	to find someone while he or she is in the process of doing something wrong *The thief was caught red-handed taking the silver out of the drawers.*

RELATED WORDS

catch (n.)	a problem
catch-all (adj.)	something that can be used in any situation
catch-as-catch-can (adv.)	by any means or in the best way you know how

---

* Note that the form "will be being caught" is rarely used. To convey a future progressive passive, use the present progressive passive.

Verb Chart

check

	ACTIVE	PASSIVE
Infinitive	to check	to be checked
Past Infinitive	to have checked	to have been checked
Past Participle	checked	been checked
Present Participle	checking	being checked

I
you/we/they
he/she/it

ACTIVE

SIMPLE PRESENT	SIMPLE PAST	SIMPLE FUTURE
check	checked	will check
check	checked	will check
checks	checked	will check

PRESENT PROGRESSIVE	PAST PROGRESSIVE	FUTURE PROGRESSIVE
am checking	was checking	will be checking
are checking	were checking	will be checking
is checking	was checking	will be checking

PRESENT PERFECT	PAST PERFECT	FUTURE PERFECT
have checked	had checked	will have checked
have checked	had checked	will have checked
has checked	had checked	will have checked

PRESENT PERFECT PROGRESSIVE	PAST PERFECT PROGRESSIVE	FUTURE PERFECT PROGRESSIVE
have been checking	had been checking	will have been checking
have been checking	had been checking	will have been checking
has been checking	had been checking	will have been checking

EXAMPLES:
Did you check that the kids were asleep before you left the house? *I haven't checked the oil for months. I'm sure I need to get it changed.* *My husband will check with you later to make sure that you have everything you need.*

PASSIVE

SIMPLE PRESENT	SIMPLE PAST	SIMPLE FUTURE
am checked	was checked	will be checked
are checked	were checked	will be checked
is checked	was checked	will be checked

PRESENT PROGRESSIVE	PAST PROGRESSIVE	FUTURE PROGRESSIVE*
am being checked	was being checked	will be being checked*
are being checked	were being checked	will be being checked*
is being checked	was being checked	will be being checked*

PRESENT PERFECT	PAST PERFECT	FUTURE PERFECT
have been checked	had been checked	will have been checked
have been checked	had been checked	will have been checked
has been checked	had been checked	will have been checked

EXAMPLES:
The customers were checked in and the flight was ready to leave. *Everything on the airplane had been checked and double-checked.*

PRINCIPAL CONDITIONALS

PRESENT	PRESENT PROGRESSIVE	PRESENT PASSIVE
would check	would be checking	would be checked
would check	would be checking	would be checked
would check	would be checking	would be checked

PAST	PAST PROGRESSIVE	PAST PASSIVE
would have checked	would have been checking	would have been checked
would have checked	would have been checking	would have been checked
would have checked	would have been checking	would have been checked

EXAMPLES:
Would you check with me before you leave? *I would have checked the gas but I thought we had plenty.*

check

PRINCIPAL PARTS: check, checked, checked

Important Forms in Use

IF/THEN CONDITIONALS

	IF ...	... THEN	EXAMPLE
Real Present/ Future	check/checks	simple present	If I _check_ the weather before I leave the house, I can figure out if I need to bring a jacket with me.
		will + base form	If she _checks_ out the story, she'll find that there's no truth to it.
Unreal Present/ Future	checked	would + base form	If we _checked_ up on them a couple of times a day, would that be enough?
Unreal Past	had checked	would have + past participle	If I _had checked_ the time before we left, we would have seen that we were running late.

SUBJUNCTIVE

ACTIVE	check	We require that airport personnel _check_ all boarding passes before passengers enter the gates.
PASSIVE	be checked	We ask that any baggage larger than carry-on size _be checked_.

PHRASAL VERBS

check in	to register at a hotel or airport _As soon as we got to the hotel, Harry went to the front desk to check in._
check in with	to let someone know of your presence, to visit _Check in with me every once in a while to report on your progress._
check on (someone or something)	to look at someone or something to see if everything is okay _When I was in vacation, I gave Alphonse the keys so he could check on my house periodically._
check out	to leave a hotel _We checked out at noon in order to avoid paying for an extra day._
check (someone or something) out	to try to find out something; to look at someone or something _Can you check out whether the movie is really playing tonight? / His friend told him to check out the girl standing in the corner._

IDIOMS

to double-check	to look at something again to make sure it's okay _We checked and double-checked, but we couldn't find anything wrong with the car._
to check something off your list	to finish a chore, or to accomplish something that you wanted to do _Well, now that we've been to Niagara Falls, I can check that off my list of places that I want to see._

RELATED WORDS

checks and balances (n.)	a systems that ensures that different branches of the government have equal power
rain check (n.)	a certificate for later purchase of a sale product that was out of stock when you tried to purchase it
check-up (n.)	when a doctor looks at a patient's overall health
checklist (n.)	a list of requirements or items that you want to accomplish

---

* Note that the form "will be being checked" is rarely used. To convey a future progressive passive, use the present progressive passive.

choose

	ACTIVE	PASSIVE
Infinitive	to choose	to be chosen
Past Infinitive	to have chosen	to have been chosen
Past Participle	chosen	been chosen
Present Participle	choosing	being chosen

ACTIVE

	I	you/we/they	he/she/it

SIMPLE PRESENT	SIMPLE PAST	SIMPLE FUTURE
choose	chose	will choose
choose	chose	will choose
chooses	chose	will choose

PRESENT PROGRESSIVE	PAST PROGRESSIVE	FUTURE PROGRESSIVE
am choosing	was choosing	will be choosing
are choosing	were choosing	will be choosing
is choosing	was choosing	will be choosing

PRESENT PERFECT	PAST PERFECT	FUTURE PERFECT
have chosen	had chosen	will have chosen
have chosen	had chosen	will have chosen
has chosen	had chosen	will have chosen

PRESENT PERFECT PROGRESSIVE	PAST PERFECT PROGRESSIVE	FUTURE PERFECT PROGRESSIVE
have been choosing	had been choosing	will have been choosing
have been choosing	had been choosing	will have been choosing
has been choosing	had been choosing	will have been choosing

EXAMPLES:

We choose a different flavor of ice cream every time we come to this shop.

She chose the red dress even though I preferred the blue.

She will already have chosen the appetizer and the entrée for everyone.

PASSIVE

SIMPLE PRESENT	SIMPLE PAST	SIMPLE FUTURE
am chosen	was chosen	will be chosen
are chosen	were chosen	will be chosen
is chosen	was chosen	will be chosen

PRESENT PROGRESSIVE	PAST PROGRESSIVE	FUTURE PROGRESSIVE*
am being chosen	was being chosen	will be being chosen*
are being chosen	were being chosen	will be being chosen*
is being chosen	was being chosen	will be being chosen*

PRESENT PERFECT	PAST PERFECT	FUTURE PERFECT
have been chosen	had been chosen	will have been chosen
have been chosen	had been chosen	will have been chosen
has been chosen	had been chosen	will have been chosen

EXAMPLES:

The surprise of the night was when Helen's song was chosen for best new composition.

How many different colors will be chosen for the costumes in act one?

PRINCIPAL CONDITIONALS

PRESENT	PRESENT PROGRESSIVE	PRESENT PASSIVE
would choose	would be choosing	would be chosen
would choose	would be choosing	would be chosen
would choose	would be choosing	would be chosen

PAST	PAST PROGRESSIVE	PAST PASSIVE
would have chosen	would have been choosing	would have been chosen
would have chosen	would have been choosing	would have been chosen
would have chosen	would have been choosing	would have been chosen

EXAMPLES:

Your script certainly would have been chosen if you had submitted it.

We would choose for you, but we don't know your taste in music.

choose

PRINCIPAL PARTS: choose, chose, chosen

Important Forms in Use

IF/THEN CONDITIONALS

	IF ...	... THEN	EXAMPLE
Real Present/ Future	choose/ chooses	simple present will + base form	*If you <u>choose</u> this dish, I can try some of it.* *If my daughter <u>chooses</u> to go to an expensive private college, we'll have to take out loans.*
Unreal Present/ Future	chose	would + base form	*If she <u>chose</u> me, I would be happy.*
Unreal Past	had chosen	would have + past participle	*If I <u>had chosen</u> the other play, you wouldn't have liked it either.*

SUBJUNCTIVE

ACTIVE	choose	*It is required that the children <u>choose</u> the subjects they want to study in a Montessori school.*
PASSIVE	be chosen	*They recommend that places <u>be chosen</u> for the guests.*

PHRASAL VERBS

to choose (something or someone) over

to choose with a preference
He chose me over her; at least he has some sense!

IDIOMS

to choose wisely

to make a decision using good judgment
Choose wisely, my friend; one of these doors leads to a pit of snakes!

RELATED WORDS

choosy (adj.)	describes someone who is particular, who doesn't accept something unless he or she is very satisfied with it
pro-choice (adj.)	describes someone who believes that women have the right to decide for themselves whether or not to have an abortion (US)

* Note that the form "will be being chosen" is rarely used. To convey a future progressive passive, use the present progressive passive.

Verb Chart

close

	ACTIVE	PASSIVE
Infinitive	to close	to be closed
Past Infinitive	to have closed	to have been closed
Past Participle	closed	been closed
Present Participle	closing	being closed

ACTIVE

I
you/we/they
he/she/it

SIMPLE PRESENT	SIMPLE PAST	SIMPLE FUTURE
close	closed	will close
close	closed	will close
closes	closed	will close

PRESENT PROGRESSIVE	PAST PROGRESSIVE	FUTURE PROGRESSIVE
am closing	was closing	will be closing
are closing	were closing	will be closing
is closing	was closing	will be closing

PRESENT PERFECT	PAST PERFECT	FUTURE PERFECT
have closed	had closed	will have closed
have closed	had closed	will have closed
has closed	had closed	will have closed

PRESENT PERFECT PROGRESSIVE	PAST PERFECT PROGRESSIVE	FUTURE PERFECT PROGRESSIVE
have been closing	had been closing	will have been closing
have been closing	had been closing	will have been closing
has been closing	had been closing	will have been closing

EXAMPLES:

They were closing the doors just as we arrived. *I have been closing the cottage with you for years. I'll be happy to help again this year.* *The inspector charged the suspect with murder and closed the case.*

PASSIVE

SIMPLE PRESENT	SIMPLE PAST	SIMPLE FUTURE
am closed	was closed	will be closed
are closed	were closed	will be closed
is closed	was closed	will be closed

PRESENT PROGRESSIVE	PAST PROGRESSIVE	FUTURE PROGRESSIVE*
am being closed	was being closed	will be being closed*
are being closed	were being closed	will be being closed*
is being closed	was being closed	will be being closed*

PRESENT PERFECT	PAST PERFECT	FUTURE PERFECT
have been closed	had been closed	will have been closed
have been closed	had been closed	will have been closed
has been closed	had been closed	will have been closed

EXAMPLES:

The swimming pool is closed for cleaning on Mondays. *The top hadn't been closed properly and the water spilled into the bag.* *The case was closed after the man was convicted of murder.*

PRINCIPAL CONDITIONALS

PRESENT	PRESENT PROGRESSIVE	PRESENT PASSIVE
would close	would be closing	would be closed
would close	would be closing	would be closed
would close	would be closing	would be closed

PAST	PAST PROGRESSIVE	PAST PASSIVE
would have closed	would have been closing	would have been closed
would have closed	would have been closing	would have been closed
would have closed	would have been closing	would have been closed

EXAMPLES:

I would close the kitchen for you if you asked me to. *We would've closed up earlier if we had known you were coming.*

Important Forms in Use

IF/THEN CONDITIONALS

	IF . . .	. . . THEN	EXAMPLE
Real Present/ Future	close/closes	simple present	*If I <u>close</u> the windows upstairs, you close the ones in the living room and kitchen.*
		will + base form	*If we don't <u>close</u> up, she'll get angry.*
Unreal Present/ Future	closed	would + base form	*If we <u>closed</u> on time every day, we wouldn't get home so late.*
Unreal Past	had closed	would have + past participle	*If I <u>had closed</u> up yesterday, the store would have been in perfect order.*

SUBJUNCTIVE

ACTIVE	close	*We suggest that he <u>close</u> on the house before he goes on vacation.*
PASSIVE	be closed	*It is important that the bags <u>be closed</u> securely before they are checked in.*

PHRASAL VERBS

close down (something)	to shut down (a business) *The grocery on the corner closed down when the supermarket chain moved in next door.*
close off (something)	to designate an area inaccessible to people, cars, etc. *The street was closed off because they were making a film.*
close on (something)	to make the final arrangements for purchasing something, especially a house *We closed on our house just before the prices began to rise.*
close up (something)	to not be open to the public temporarily *What time does the store close up for the night?*

IDIOMS

to not close any doors	to not eliminate any available options *You might want to explore that job offer further; don't close any doors just yet.*
to close someone's doors	to close a business *Our local boutique closed its doors in Oak Park when business dropped off after the mall was built.*
to close up shop	to finish up work for the day *Let's complete this report and then close up shop.*
to close the books on something	to decide that you will no longer work on or investigate something *The detective closed the books on the case after their main witness died.*

RELATED WORDS

closed-minded (adj.)	not open to new ideas
closeout sale (n.)	a sale in which a store is trying to get rid of items they will no longer stock

* Note that the form "will be being closed" is rarely used. To convey a future progressive passive, use the present progressive passive.

Verb Chart

come

	ACTIVE	PASSIVE
Infinitive	to come	to be come
Past Infinitive	to have come	to have been come
Past Participle	come	been come
Present Participle	coming	being come

ACTIVE

I		
you/we/they		
he/she/it		

SIMPLE PRESENT	SIMPLE PAST	SIMPLE FUTURE
come	came	will come
come	came	will come
comes	came	will come

PRESENT PROGRESSIVE	PAST PROGRESSIVE	FUTURE PROGRESSIVE
am coming	was coming	will be coming
are coming	were coming	will be coming
is coming	was coming	will be coming

PRESENT PERFECT	PAST PERFECT	FUTURE PERFECT
have come	had come	will have come
have come	had come	will have come
has come	had come	will have come

PRESENT PERFECT PROGRESSIVE	PAST PERFECT PROGRESSIVE	FUTURE PERFECT PROGRESSIVE
have been coming	had been coming	will have been coming
have been coming	had been coming	will have been coming
has been coming	had been coming	will have been coming

EXAMPLES:

Peter and Daree are coming to the picnic on Friday.   *This sweater comes in navy blue and white.*   *They had been coming to visit us for years before they bought their own cottage in Michigan.*

PASSIVE

SIMPLE PRESENT	SIMPLE PAST	SIMPLE FUTURE
am come	was come	will be come
are come	were come	will be come
is come	was come	will be come

PRESENT PROGRESSIVE	PAST PROGRESSIVE	FUTURE PROGRESSIVE*
am being come	was being come	will be being come*
are being come	were being come	will be being come*
is being come	was being come	will be being come*

PRESENT PERFECT	PAST PERFECT	FUTURE PERFECT
have been come	had been come	will have been come
have been come	had been come	will have been come
has been come	had been come	will have been come

EXAMPLES:

When we arrived at the brainstorming meeting, all of the ideas had already been come up with.   *She was come over with a feeling of sickness.*

PRINCIPAL CONDITIONALS

PRESENT	PRESENT PROGRESSIVE	PRESENT PASSIVE
would come	would be coming	would be come
would come	would be coming	would be come
would come	would be coming	would be come

PAST	PAST PROGRESSIVE	PAST PASSIVE
would have come	would have been coming	would have been come
would have come	would have been coming	would have been come
would have come	would have been coming	would have been come

EXAMPLES:

I didn't think she would come, but she did.   *They would have come if they had been invited.*

come

Important Forms in Use

IF/THEN CONDITIONALS

	IF . . .	. . . THEN	EXAMPLE
Real Present/ Future	come/comes	simple present	*If the snow <u>comes</u> early, we are often caught without our snow tires.*
		will + base form	*If he <u>comes</u> next year, we'll do everything we didn't have time to do this time.*
Unreal Present/ Future	came	would + base form	*If they <u>came</u> right now, we could still be on time.*
Unreal Past	had come	would have + past participle	*If you <u>had come</u> for a visit, we would have shown you a good time.*

SUBJUNCTIVE

ACTIVE	come	*We advise that she <u>come</u> on the train rather than the bus.*
PASSIVE	be come	*We ask that new ideas <u>be come</u> up with for the new advertising campaign.*

PHRASAL VERBS

come in	to enter *I was a bit startled when you came in.*
come up with (something)	to think of an idea or concept *How did you come up with the idea for your new business?*
come through	to fulfill an expectation that someone has for you *As usual, Jim came through for me and found me a date for the dance next week.*
come down with (something)	to catch a cold, the flu, or some other illness *He came down with the flu and couldn't come with us.*

IDIOMS

to come and go	to be present inconsistently *The pain in my leg doesn't bother me all the time. It comes and goes.*
come on	used to tell someone to hurry up *Come on! Let's go! We're going to be late.*
to come to blows	to have an argument that escalates to physical confrontation *John and Frank almost came to blows during the meeting.*
to come face to face with something	to confront a problem *It's about time Henry came face to face with his alcohol problem.*

RELATED WORDS

newcomer (n.)	somebody who has recently arrived
comeback (n.)	a regaining of popularity

* Note that the form "will be being come" is rarely used. To convey a future progressive passive, use the present progressive passive.

Verb Chart

cross

	ACTIVE	PASSIVE
Infinitive	to cross	to be crossed
Past Infinitive	to have crossed	to have been crossed
Past Participle	crossed	been crossed
Present Participle	crossing	being crossed

ACTIVE

I		
you/we/they		
he/she/it		

SIMPLE PRESENT	SIMPLE PAST	SIMPLE FUTURE
cross	crossed	will cross
cross	crossed	will cross
crosses	crossed	will cross

PRESENT PROGRESSIVE	PAST PROGRESSIVE	FUTURE PROGRESSIVE
am crossing	was crossing	will be crossing
are crossing	were crossing	will be crossing
is crossing	was crossing	will be crossing

PRESENT PERFECT	PAST PERFECT	FUTURE PERFECT
have crossed	had crossed	will have crossed
have crossed	had crossed	will have crossed
has crossed	had crossed	will have crossed

PRESENT PERFECT PROGRESSIVE	PAST PERFECT PROGRESSIVE	FUTURE PERFECT PROGRESSIVE
have been crossing	had been crossing	will have been crossing
have been crossing	had been crossing	will have been crossing
has been crossing	had been crossing	will have been crossing

EXAMPLES:
Only cross the street at the light. *The Queen Mary II will be crossing the Atlantic several times this summer.* *She had been crossing the same street for months and had never noticed the new restaurant on the corner.*

PASSIVE

SIMPLE PRESENT	SIMPLE PAST	SIMPLE FUTURE
am crossed	was crossed	will be crossed
are crossed	were crossed	will be crossed
is crossed	was crossed	will be crossed

PRESENT PROGRESSIVE	PAST PROGRESSIVE	FUTURE PROGRESSIVE*
am being crossed	was being crossed	will be being crossed*
are being crossed	were being crossed	will be being crossed*
is being crossed	was being crossed	will be being crossed*

PRESENT PERFECT	PAST PERFECT	FUTURE PERFECT
have been crossed	had been crossed	will have been crossed
have been crossed	had been crossed	will have been crossed
has been crossed	had been crossed	will have been crossed

EXAMPLES:
Several items on the list were crossed off by the budget committee because they were too expensive. *His name is being crossed off because he has no support among the church members.*

PRINCIPAL CONDITIONALS

PRESENT	PRESENT PROGRESSIVE	PRESENT PASSIVE
would cross	would be crossing	would be crossed
would cross	would be crossing	would be crossed
would cross	would be crossing	would be crossed

PAST	PAST PROGRESSIVE	PAST PASSIVE
would have crossed	would have been crossing	would have been crossed
would have crossed	would have been crossing	would have been crossed
would have crossed	would have been crossing	would have been crossed

EXAMPLES:
They would be crossing the street at this intersection if it hadn't been blocked off. *I would have crossed out my mistakes but I was having trouble finding them.*

cross

PRINCIPAL PARTS: cross, crossed, crossed

Important Forms in Use

IF/THEN CONDITIONALS

	IF . . .	. . . THEN	EXAMPLE
Real Present/ Future	cross/crosses	simple present will + base form	*If I cross out ice cream, he buys it anyway.* *If he crosses at the light, he will be safer.*
Unreal Present/ Future	crossed	would + base form	*If we crossed the beach off our list of activities for the day, the kids would be disappointed.*
Unreal Past	had crossed	would have + past participle	*If she had crossed over into the creative department, she wouldn't have lost her job.*

SUBJUNCTIVE

ACTIVE	cross	*I ask that you cross the street only with the crossing guard.*
PASSIVE	be crossed	*We demand that Mr. Burton be crossed off the list of possible members immediately.*

PHRASAL VERBS

cross (something) off	to rule out an option *I think we'll have to cross that one off the list until we have more money.*
cross out	to draw a line through something that you have written, such as a mistake or an item on a list that you have completed *Cross out each item on the shopping list as we get it, will you?*
cross over	to move from one area to another, often over a distinct border *Did you hear that Phil crossed over into sales from acquisitions?*

IDIOMS

to cross that bridge when you come to it	to postpone dealing with something until it is necessary *Don't ask me how we're going to convince the board to give us more money for the renovation. We'll cross that bridge when we come to it.*
to cross one's fingers	to make a sign of hope for good fortune *My job interview is today! Cross your fingers for me!*

RELATED WORDS

crossing guard (n.)	a person that helps others, usually children, cross the street at busy intersections
cross-country (adj.)	a type of running in which runners go for long distances
to double-cross (v.)	to do something bad to someone with whom you had already planned to do something bad
to cross yourself (v.)	to make the sign of the cross with your hand, done in church or out of church by people of Christian faiths, especially Catholic

* Note that the form "will be being crossed" is rarely used. To convey a future progressive passive, use the present progressive passive.

cry

	ACTIVE	PASSIVE
Infinitive	to cry	to be cried
Past Infinitive	to have cried	to have been cried
Past Participle	cried	been cried
Present Participle	crying	being cried

ACTIVE

I
you/we/they
he/she/it

SIMPLE PRESENT	SIMPLE PAST	SIMPLE FUTURE
cry	cried	will cry
cry	cried	will cry
cries	cried	will cry

PRESENT PROGRESSIVE	PAST PROGRESSIVE	FUTURE PROGRESSIVE
am crying	was crying	will be crying
are crying	were crying	will be crying
is crying	was crying	will be crying

PRESENT PERFECT	PAST PERFECT	FUTURE PERFECT
have cried	had cried	will have cried
have cried	had cried	will have cried
has cried	had cried	will have cried

PRESENT PERFECT PROGRESSIVE	PAST PERFECT PROGRESSIVE	FUTURE PERFECT PROGRESSIVE
have been crying	had been crying	will have been crying
have been crying	had been crying	will have been crying
has been crying	had been crying	will have been crying

EXAMPLES:
Don't cry about it. There's nothing you can do.

What's wrong with her? She's been crying for hours.

Somebody had been crying out from the street below, which prompted us to call the police.

PASSIVE

SIMPLE PRESENT	SIMPLE PAST	SIMPLE FUTURE
am cried	was cried	will be cried
are cried	were cried	will be cried
is cried	was cried	will be cried

PRESENT PROGRESSIVE	PAST PROGRESSIVE	FUTURE PROGRESSIVE*
am being cried	was being cried	will be being cried*
are being cried	were being cried	will be being cried*
is being cried	was being cried	will be being cried*

PRESENT PERFECT	PAST PERFECT	FUTURE PERFECT
have been cried	had been cried	will have been cried
have been cried	had been cried	will have been cried
has been cried	had been cried	will have been cried

EXAMPLES:
The girls were all cried out after the death of their dog and fell asleep quickly.

No tears have been cried over the gangster who was shot down in the street.

PRINCIPAL CONDITIONALS

PRESENT	PRESENT PROGRESSIVE	PRESENT PASSIVE
would cry	would be crying	would be cried
would cry	would be crying	would be cried
would cry	would be crying	would be cried

PAST	PAST PROGRESSIVE	PAST PASSIVE
would have cried	would have been crying	would have been cried
would have cried	would have been crying	would have been cried
would have cried	would have been crying	would have been cried

EXAMPLES:
I'm glad you're not upset by the news. I thought you would be crying.

She would be crying if she weren't in shock.

cry

PRINCIPAL PARTS: cry, cried, cried

VERB CHART
24

Important Forms in Use

IF/THEN CONDITIONALS

	IF...	...THEN	EXAMPLE
Real Present/ Future	cry/cries	simple present will + base form	*If he cries, I know something is really wrong.* *If they cry, she'll be convinced to do anything.*
Unreal Present/ Future	cried	would + base form	*If we cried over spilled milk, we would be wasting our time.*
Unreal Past	had cried	would have + past participle	*If I had cried during the movie, you would have made fun of me.*

SUBJUNCTIVE

ACTIVE cry — *She advised that I not cry in front of the reporters.*
PASSIVE be cried — *It is essential that donations be cried out for by the charity.*

PHRASAL VERBS

cry out — to make a loud noise due to fear or pain, or to ask for something with urgency
The kids cried out for help when the boat began to sink.

IDIOMS

to cry over spilled milk — to waste time feeling bad about a mistake that you made
Perhaps you shouldn't have changed jobs, but there's no point in crying over spilled milk.

to cry your eyes out — to cry without stopping
I cried my eyes out when I heard that I had failed my final exam.

to cry wolf — to falsely claim that something has happened or that you need help
My brother had cried wolf so many times, we didn't believe him when he said that he was in trouble.

RELATED WORDS

crybaby (n.) — somebody who complains often
far cry (n.) — not at all like something else

* Note that the form "will be being cried" is rarely used. To convey a future progressive passive, use the present progressive passive.

Verb Chart

cut

	ACTIVE	PASSIVE
Infinitive	to cut	to be cut
Past Infinitive	to have cut	to have been cut
Past Participle	cut	been cut
Present Participle	cutting	being cut

ACTIVE

I
you/we/they
he/she/it

SIMPLE PRESENT	SIMPLE PAST	SIMPLE FUTURE
cut	cut	will cut
cut	cut	will cut
cuts	cut	will cut

PRESENT PROGRESSIVE	PAST PROGRESSIVE	FUTURE PROGRESSIVE
am cutting	was cutting	will be cutting
are cutting	were cutting	will be cutting
is cutting	was cutting	will be cutting

PRESENT PERFECT	PAST PERFECT	FUTURE PERFECT
have cut	had cut	will have cut
have cut	had cut	will have cut
has cut	had cut	will have cut

PRESENT PERFECT PROGRESSIVE	PAST PERFECT PROGRESSIVE	FUTURE PERFECT PROGRESSIVE
have been cut	had been cut	will have been cut
have been cut	had been cut	will have been cut
has been cut	had been cut	will have been cut

EXAMPLES:

The chef cuts herself every once in a while when she is preparing dinner.

My mother always cut my hair when I was a child.

I am cutting you off. You've had too much to drink.

PASSIVE

SIMPLE PRESENT	SIMPLE PAST	SIMPLE FUTURE
am cut	was cut	will be cut
are cut	were cut	will be cut
is cut	was cut	will be cut

PRESENT PROGRESSIVE	PAST PROGRESSIVE	FUTURE PROGRESSIVE*
am being cut	was being cut	will be being cut*
are being cut	were being cut	will be being cut*
is being cut	was being cut	will be being cut*

PRESENT PERFECT	PAST PERFECT	FUTURE PERFECT
have been cut	had been cut	will have been cut
have been cut	had been cut	will have been cut
has been cut	had been cut	will have been cut

EXAMPLES:

The boys were cut from the football team after several trials.

The grass had been cut recently.

The telephone had been cut off for months because they hadn't paid their bills.

PRINCIPAL CONDITIONALS

PRESENT	PRESENT PROGRESSIVE	PRESENT PASSIVE
would cut	would be cutting	would be cut
would cut	would be cutting	would be cut
would cut	would be cutting	would be cut

PAST	PAST PROGRESSIVE	PAST PASSIVE
would have cut	would have been cutting	would have been cut
would have cut	would have been cutting	would have been cut
would have cut	would have been cutting	would have been cut

EXAMPLES:

I would be cutting the cake if she hadn't offered to do it.

I would have cut in line but the owner was looking at me.

Important Forms in Use

IF/THEN CONDITIONALS

	IF . . .	. . . THEN	EXAMPLE
Real Present/ Future	cut/cuts	simple present	*If she <u>cuts</u> herself, she puts on a bandage.*
		will + base form	*If we <u>cut</u> through the park, we'll get there more quickly.*
Unreal Present/ Future	cut	would + base form	*If we <u>cut</u> a deal, would you buy the car?*
Unreal Past	had cut	would have + past participle	*If I <u>had cut</u> the meat into smaller pieces, it would've cooked faster.*

SUBJUNCTIVE

ACTIVE	cut	*We suggest that you <u>cut</u> all the material before you begin to sew.*
PASSIVE	be cut	*It is important that the fabric <u>be cut</u> on a bias.*

PHRASAL VERBS

cut (someone) down	to make someone feel less important *You are so negative. You are always cutting people down.*
cut off	to stop something completely, often related to access *She cut off our relationship when she learned that I was still friends with my ex-girlfriend.*
cut up	to divide into smaller pieces *His mother cut up the meat for him so that he would be able to eat it.*
cut in	to interrupt *Sorry to cut in, but did I just hear you say you've been to Moldavia?*

IDIOMS

to cut to the chase	to get right to the point *What do you want? Don't give me any details, just cut to the chase.*
to cut in line	to place yourself ahead of others who are waiting in line *I hate people who cut in line at movie theaters.*
to cut it	to live up to a certain level of skill or ability, to do well *He wanted to get a job as a reporter, but he just didn't cut it.*

RELATED WORDS

cut-and-dried (adj.)	describes an issue that has only one outcome
cutthroat (adj.)	extremely competitive
shortcut (n.)	a way to arrive somewhere more quickly than by the usual route

* Note that the form "will be being cut" is rarely used. To convey a future progressive passive, use the present progressive passive.

Verb Chart

die

	ACTIVE	PASSIVE
Infinitive	to die	-
Past Infinitive	to have died	-
Past Participle	died	-
Present Participle	dying	-

ACTIVE

I		
you/we/they		
he/she/it		

SIMPLE PRESENT	SIMPLE PAST	SIMPLE FUTURE
die	died	will die
die	died	will die
dies	died	will die

PRESENT PROGRESSIVE	PAST PROGRESSIVE	FUTURE PROGRESSIVE
am dying	was dying	will be dying
are dying	were dying	will be dying
is dying	was dying	will be dying

PRESENT PERFECT	PAST PERFECT	FUTURE PERFECT
have died	had died	will have died
have died	had died	will have died
has died	had died	will have died

PRESENT PERFECT PROGRESSIVE	PAST PERFECT PROGRESSIVE	FUTURE PERFECT PROGRESSIVE
have been dying	had been dying	will have been dying
have been dying	had been dying	will have been dying
has been dying	had been dying	will have been dying

EXAMPLES:

If our cat dies, we're not going to get another one.

We were dying to find out who would play the lead in the movie.

Interest in the television series has been dying off slowly.

PASSIVE

SIMPLE PRESENT	SIMPLE PAST	SIMPLE FUTURE
-	-	-
-	-	-
-	-	-

PRESENT PROGRESSIVE	PAST PROGRESSIVE	FUTURE PROGRESSIVE
-	-	-
-	-	-
-	-	-

PRESENT PERFECT	PAST PERFECT	FUTURE PERFECT
-	-	-
-	-	-
-	-	-

PRINCIPAL CONDITIONALS

PRESENT	PRESENT PROGRESSIVE	PRESENT PASSIVE
would die	would be dying	-
would die	would be dying	-
would die	would be dying	-

PAST	PAST PROGRESSIVE	PAST PASSIVE
would have died	would have been dying	-
would have died	would have been dying	-
would have died	would have been dying	-

EXAMPLES:

My mother would die if she found out what we were doing.

If the movie star had spoken to me, I would have died.

die

Important Forms in Use

IF/THEN CONDITIONALS

	IF...	...THEN	EXAMPLE
Real Present/ Future	die/dies	simple present	*If interest in a class <u>dies</u> out over the years, we cancel it.*
		will + base form	*If I <u>die</u> before you do, who will take care of you?*
Unreal Present/ Future	died	would + base form	*If the tribe <u>died</u> out today, we would have no record of their customs or language.*
Unreal Past	had died	would have + past participle	*If he <u>had died</u> in the car accident, his family would have been devastated.*

SUBJUNCTIVE

ACTIVE	die	*We suggested that the giant monster <u>die</u> in the movie by falling off a tall building.*
PASSIVE	-	

PHRASAL VERBS

die away	to slowly disappear or fade out *The sound of the concert died away as we walked across the park.*
die down	when the noise made by a crowd, the wind etc., decreases, it dies down *When the applause died down, the politician went on with his speech.*
die off	to die one by one until there are none left, as in a group of people or animals *When the last member of the tribe dies off, there will be no one left who speaks their language.*
die out	to become extinct *Recent sightings of the ivory-billed woodpecker make scientists believe that perhaps it has not died out, as previously thought.*

IDIOMS

to die of embarrassment/shame	to be very embarrassed/ashamed *When his pants fell down on stage, he died of embarrassment.*
to die a thousand deaths	to be devastated by something *If he ever left me, I'd die a thousand deaths.*
to be dying to do something	to have a strong desire to do something *Our favorite actor is in a new movie, and we're dying to see it.*
to be dying	to be completely exhausted *We were dying after the twelve-mile canoe trip, but Tim still had lots of energy.*

RELATED WORDS

do-or-die (adj.)	describes a situation in which you must do something, even if it is dangerous or risky, or you will fail
to be to die for (v.)	to be extremely good, especially relating to food

Verb Chart

dive

	ACTIVE	PASSIVE
Infinitive	to dive	to be dived
Past Infinitive	to have dived	to have been dived
Past Participle	dived	been dived
Present Participle	diving	being dived

ACTIVE

I		
you/we/they		
he/she/it		

SIMPLE PRESENT	SIMPLE PAST	SIMPLE FUTURE
dive	dived	will dive
dive	dived	will dive
dives	dived	will dive

PRESENT PROGRESSIVE	PAST PROGRESSIVE	FUTURE PROGRESSIVE
am diving	was diving	will be diving
are diving	were diving	will be diving
is diving	was diving	will be diving

PRESENT PERFECT	PAST PERFECT	FUTURE PERFECT
have dived	had dived	will have dived
have dived	had dived	will have dived
has dived	had dived	will have dived

PRESENT PERFECT PROGRESSIVE	PAST PERFECT PROGRESSIVE	FUTURE PERFECT PROGRESSIVE
have been diving	had been diving	will have been diving
have been diving	had been diving	will have been diving
has been diving	had been diving	will have been diving

EXAMPLES:
I like to dive off the diving board whenever I go to the swimming pool.

Harry dived into the paperwork and was finished before dinner.

PASSIVE

SIMPLE PRESENT	SIMPLE PAST	SIMPLE FUTURE
am dived	was dived	will be dived
are dived	were dived	will be dived
is dived	was dived	will be dived

PRESENT PROGRESSIVE	PAST PROGRESSIVE	FUTURE PROGRESSIVE*
am being dived	was being dived	will be being dived*
are being dived	were being dived	will be being dived*
is being dived	was being dived	will be being dived*

PRESENT PERFECT	PAST PERFECT	FUTURE PERFECT
have been dived	had been dived	will have been dived
have been dived	had been dived	will have been dived
has been dived	had been dived	will have been dived

EXAMPLES:
The backflip was dived nearly perfectly for a score of 99.

When we got to the party, the food was being heartily dived into by a group of hungry guests.

The pier is being dived off by some kids.

PRINCIPAL CONDITIONALS

PRESENT	PRESENT PROGRESSIVE	PRESENT PASSIVE
would dive	would be diving	would be dived
would dive	would be diving	would be dived
would dive	would be diving	would be dived

PAST	PAST PROGRESSIVE	PAST PASSIVE
would have dived	would have been diving	would have been dived
would have dived	would have been diving	would have been dived
would have dived	would have been diving	would have been dived

EXAMPLES:
I'm sure Sarah would be diving into the river with the other kids if she knew how to swim.

Sam would have dived under the bed if he had heard anyone enter the house.

Important Forms in Use

IF/THEN CONDITIONALS

	IF...	...THEN	EXAMPLE
Real Present/ Future	dive/dives	simple present	*If we <u>dive</u> into this, we can finish before the end of the day.*
		will + base form	*If she <u>dives</u> off the side of the pool, she'll win the race.*
Unreal Present/ Future	dived/dove	would + base form	*If they <u>dived</u> into the food, it would mean they were hungry.*
Unreal Past	had dived	would have + past participle	*If I <u>had dived</u> better, I would have won the competition.*

SUBJUNCTIVE

ACTIVE	dive	*It is important that the swimmers <u>dive</u> only at the deep end of the pool.*
PASSIVE	be dived	*It is essential that the first round be <u>dived</u> by our best teammate.*

PHRASAL VERBS

dive in/into something — to begin something suddenly and with a lot of energy
The kids dived into the bags of toys that had been brought to the orphanage.

RELATED WORDS

dive-bomber (n.)	a military airplane designed to drop bombs close to the ground
swan dive (n.)	a type of dive in which the hands are brought forward and above the head
diver (n.)	an athlete whose specialty is diving
dive (n.)	a seedy bar

* Note that the form "will be being dived" is rarely used. To convey a future progressive passive, use the present passive progressive.

Verb Chart

do

	ACTIVE	PASSIVE
Infinitive	to do	to be done
Past Infinitive	to have done	to have been done
Past Participle	done	been done
Present Participle	doing	being done

ACTIVE

	I	you/we/they	he/she/it

SIMPLE PRESENT
do
do
does

SIMPLE PAST
did
did
did

SIMPLE FUTURE
will do
will do
will do

PRESENT PROGRESSIVE
am doing
are doing
is doing

PAST PROGRESSIVE
was doing
were doing
was doing

FUTURE PROGRESSIVE
will be doing
will be doing
will be doing

PRESENT PERFECT
have done
have done
has done

PAST PERFECT
had done
had done
had done

FUTURE PERFECT
will have done
will have done
will have done

PRESENT PERFECT PROGRESSIVE
have been doing
have been doing
has been doing

PAST PERFECT PROGRESSIVE
had been doing
had been doing
had been doing

FUTURE PERFECT PROGRESSIVE
will have been doing
will have been doing
will have been doing

EXAMPLES:
I did a lot of stage acting when I was younger, but now I do television.

Have you done the housework yet?

The mechanic told me that he will have done most of the work by this afternoon.

PASSIVE

SIMPLE PRESENT
am done
are done
is done

SIMPLE PAST
was done
were done
was done

SIMPLE FUTURE
will be done
will be done
will be done

PRESENT PROGRESSIVE
am being done
are being done
is being done

PAST PROGRESSIVE
was being done
were being done
was being done

FUTURE PROGRESSIVE*
will be being done*
will be being done*
will be being done*

PRESENT PERFECT
have been done
have been done
has been done

PAST PERFECT
had been done
had been done
had been done

FUTURE PERFECT
will have been done
will have been done
will have been done

EXAMPLES:
The more delicate sewing is done by the owner of the shop.

If my photos will be done within the hour, I'll just wait in the lobby.

This type of experiment has never been done before.

PRINCIPAL CONDITIONALS

PRESENT
would do
would do
would do

PRESENT PROGRESSIVE
would be doing
would be doing
would be doing

PRESENT PASSIVE
would be done
would be done
would be done

PAST
would have done
would have done
would have done

PAST PROGRESSIVE
would have been doing
would have been doing
would have been doing

PAST PASSIVE
would have been done
would have been done
would have been done

EXAMPLES:
Bill would do you the favor if you did something for him.

You would have done the same thing if you had been in my position.

Andy would be doing more painting if he had his own studio.

Important Forms in Use

IF/THEN CONDITIONALS

	IF ...	...THEN	EXAMPLE
Real Present/ Future	do/does	simple present	*If she <u>does</u> the shopping for him, he makes lunch for her.*
		will + base form	*If you <u>do</u> everything on your list, you'll wear yourself out.*
Unreal Present/ Future	did	would + base form	*If Cecilia <u>did</u> a more thorough job, she would be more successful.*
Unreal Past	had done	would have + past participle	*If you <u>had done</u> it as I asked, we would have finished hours ago.*

SUBJUNCTIVE

ACTIVE	do	*I suggest that you <u>do</u> sightseeing at the port this morning and then do the museums in the afternoon.*
PASSIVE	be done	*We demand that the work <u>be done</u> immediately.*

PHRASAL VERBS

do away with (something)	to get rid of something *We had to do away with that menu because we don't serve some of the items anymore.*
do (something) over	to do something again *I realized that my essay was not on topic and that I would have to do it over.*
do (someone) in	to cause someone to become completely exhausted *All of that biking today really did me in.*
do (something) up	to fix up something to make it have a better appearance *Let's do up your apartment before the party.*
do without (someone/ something)	to manage without someone or something *We did without a car for so long, now I feel like I don't want one.*

IDIOMS

to do your best	to try very hard *He didn't win the competition but he did his best.*
to do it up	to make effort or enjoy something without limitations *Tonight's your birthday. Let's do it up!*
to do for a living	to work to earn enough money to pay for expenses *What do you do for a living?*
to have something/nothing to do with something	to have or not have any relation to another thing *Don't look at me! I had nothing to do with the accident. / I overheard a bit of news that has something to do with you.*

RELATED WORDS

to-do (n.)	a big deal, a fuss
done deal (n.)	something that is certain to happen
do-it-yourself (DIY) (adj.)	describes a job that you complete yourself instead of having it done for you
dos and don'ts (n.)	things that are good or not good to do in certain situations

* Note that the form "will be being done" is rarely used. To convey a future progressive passive, use the present progressive passive.

Verb Chart

draw

	ACTIVE	PASSIVE
Infinitive	to draw	to be drawn
Past Infinitive	to have drawn	to have been drawn
Past Participle	drawn	been drawn
Present Participle	drawing	being drawn

ACTIVE

I
you/we/they
he/she/it

SIMPLE PRESENT	SIMPLE PAST	SIMPLE FUTURE
draw	drew	will draw
draw	drew	will draw
draws	drew	will draw

PRESENT PROGRESSIVE	PAST PROGRESSIVE	FUTURE PROGRESSIVE
am drawing	was drawing	will be drawing
are drawing	were drawing	will be drawing
is drawing	was drawing	will be drawing

PRESENT PERFECT	PAST PERFECT	FUTURE PERFECT
have drawn	had drawn	will have drawn
have drawn	had drawn	will have drawn
has drawn	had drawn	will have drawn

PRESENT PERFECT PROGRESSIVE	PAST PERFECT PROGRESSIVE	FUTURE PERFECT PROGRESSIVE
have been drawing	had been drawing	will have been drawing
have been drawing	had been drawing	will have been drawing
has been drawing	had been drawing	will have been drawing

EXAMPLES:

I'll draw you a picture of the building we're hoping to buy.

The lawyer drew up the contract and the two parties were ready to sign.

The meeting was drawing to a close when the president brought up an important issue.

PASSIVE

SIMPLE PRESENT	SIMPLE PAST	SIMPLE FUTURE
am drawn	was drawn	will be drawn
are drawn	were drawn	will be drawn
is drawn	was drawn	will be drawn

PRESENT PROGRESSIVE	PAST PROGRESSIVE	FUTURE PROGRESSIVE*
am being drawn	was being drawn	will be being drawn*
are being drawn	were being drawn	will be being drawn*
is being drawn	was being drawn	will be being drawn*

PRESENT PERFECT	PAST PERFECT	FUTURE PERFECT
have been drawn	had been drawn	will have been drawn
have been drawn	had been drawn	will have been drawn
has been drawn	had been drawn	will have been drawn

EXAMPLES:

The curtains are being drawn so that they can see the film projection better.

The plans for the hospital were being drawn up by a well-known architect.

Her expertise in the field of non-profits will certainly be drawn on.

PRINCIPAL CONDITIONALS

PRESENT	PRESENT PROGRESSIVE	PRESENT PASSIVE
would draw	would be drawing	would be drawn
would draw	would be drawing	would be drawn
would draw	would be drawing	would be drawn

PAST	PAST PROGRESSIVE	PAST PASSIVE
would have drawn	would have been drawing	would have been drawn
would have drawn	would have been drawing	would have been drawn
would have drawn	would have been drawing	would have been drawn

EXAMPLES:

She's an excellent artist and would happily draw a sketch of the garden for you.

She's shy, but she would have been drawn out if my uncle Bill had started asking her questions.

draw

PRINCIPAL PARTS: draw, drew, drawn

Important Forms in Use

IF/THEN CONDITIONALS

	IF ...	... THEN	EXAMPLE
Real Present/ Future	draw/draws	simple present	If I <u>draw</u> a blank, Tim reminds me of the names of all the students in the class.
		will + base form	If you <u>draw</u> your arms back a little, you'll be safer.
Unreal Present/ Future	drew	would + base form	If I <u>drew</u> a picture of you, it would not be very flattering.
Unreal Past	had drawn	would have + past participle	If I <u>had drawn</u> the water for a bath, you would've told me you wanted to take a shower.

SUBJUNCTIVE

ACTIVE	draw	It is important that the lawyer <u>draw</u> up the papers so that we can move on with the process.
PASSIVE	be drawn	It is essential that a sketch of the alleged arsonist <u>be drawn</u> as soon as possible.

PHRASAL VERBS

draw back	to move away from someone or something *The bystanders drew back as the fire in the house began to grow.*
draw on (something)	to use knowledge, expertise, or experience in one area to help you in another area *Eileen drew on her many years' experience on the debate team to help her become a better public speaker in her new life as a politician.*
draw (someone) out	to make someone feel comfortable so that he or she is more willing to express himself or herself *Patty is usually a very shy girl, but her uncle has no problem drawing her out.*
draw (something) up	to prepare a written plan *I think that the ideas for the new business are excellent. Will someone volunteer to draw up a final plan?*

IDIOMS

to draw a blank	to not be able to remember something in the moment that you would like to *I'm sorry that I can't tell you about the last thing on my list, but I'm drawing a blank.*
to draw fire	to do something or to have an idea that causes you to be criticized by others *The director's decision to cut back on the support staff drew fire from all of the departments.*
to draw the line at something	to limit what you are willing to do *Cindi wanted to help her son do his homework, but she drew the line at sitting down and actually doing it for him.*
to draw the short straw	to be chosen to do a job that nobody wants to do *Unfortunately, our team drew the short straw and got stuck with cleanup after the barbecue.*

RELATED WORDS

drawing (n.)	a picture that is done by hand using some type of pencil or pen
drawback (n.)	a disadvantage
drawn-out (adj.)	something that is longer and more tedious than necessary

* Note that the form "will be being drawn" is rarely used. To convey a future progressive passive, use the present progressive passive.

Verb Chart

drive

	ACTIVE	PASSIVE
Infinitive	to drive	to be driven
Past Infinitive	to have driven	to have been driven
Past Participle	driven	been driven
Present Participle	driving	being driven

ACTIVE

I		
you/we/they		
he/she/it		

SIMPLE PRESENT	**SIMPLE PAST**	**SIMPLE FUTURE**
drive	drove	will drive
drive	drove	will drive
drives	drove	will drive

PRESENT PROGRESSIVE	**PAST PROGRESSIVE**	**FUTURE PROGRESSIVE**
am driving	was driving	will be driving
are driving	were driving	will be driving
is driving	was driving	will be driving

PRESENT PERFECT	**PAST PERFECT**	**FUTURE PERFECT**
have driven	had driven	will have driven
have driven	had driven	will have driven
has driven	had driven	will have driven

PRESENT PERFECT PROGRESSIVE	**PAST PERFECT PROGRESSIVE**	**FUTURE PERFECT PROGRESSIVE**
have been driving	had been driving	will have been driving
have been driving	had been driving	will have been driving
has been driving	had been driving	will have been driving

EXAMPLES:
Are you driving today or should I? *We had been driving for hours before we stopped for lunch.* *Either my mother or I will be driving to the service today if you would like a ride.*

PASSIVE

SIMPLE PRESENT	**SIMPLE PAST**	**SIMPLE FUTURE**
am driven	was driven	will be driven
are driven	were driven	will be driven
is driven	was driven	will be driven

PRESENT PROGRESSIVE	**PAST PROGRESSIVE**	**FUTURE PROGRESSIVE***
am being driven	was being driven	will be being driven*
are being driven	were being driven	will be being driven*
is being driven	was being driven	will be being driven*

PRESENT PERFECT	**PAST PERFECT**	**FUTURE PERFECT**
have been driven	had been driven	will have been driven
have been driven	had been driven	will have been driven
has been driven	had been driven	will have been driven

EXAMPLES:
The elderly couple was driven to the grocery store twice a week. *The truck is being driven by a professional.* *The kids had been driven to school by the same bus driver during all of their elementary school years.*

PRINCIPAL CONDITIONALS

PRESENT	**PRESENT PROGRESSIVE**	**PRESENT PASSIVE**
would drive	would be driving	would be driven
would drive	would be driving	would be driven
would drive	would be driving	would be driven

PAST	**PAST PROGRESSIVE**	**PAST PASSIVE**
would have driven	would have been driving	would have been driven
would have driven	would have been driving	would have been driven
would have driven	would have been driving	would have been driven

EXAMPLES:
We would have been driven mad by now if you hadn't shown up. *Ellen would be driving if her car weren't in the shop.*

drive

Important Forms in Use

IF/THEN CONDITIONALS

	IF ...	... THEN	EXAMPLE
Real Present/ Future	drive/drives	simple present	*If Jim <u>drives</u> instead of taking the train, he inevitably runs into traffic during rush hour.*
		will + base form	*If you <u>drive</u> me to the store, I'll be able to get there before it closes.*
Unreal Present/ Future	drove	would + base form	*If I <u>drove</u> to work, I would save time but spend more money.*
Unreal Past	had driven	would have + past participle	*If they <u>had driven</u>, they wouldn't have gotten any exercise.*

SUBJUNCTIVE

ACTIVE	drive	*Environmentalists suggest that we <u>drive</u> only when no other alternative transportation is available.*
PASSIVE	be driven	*My mother insists that I <u>be driven</u> to school.*

PHRASAL VERBS

drive at (something)	to communicate your main point *What are you driving at?*
drive (someone) away	to force someone into a distance, physically or emotionally *I was trying to help him but the closer I got, the more he drove me away.*
drive off	to leave in a car; to force someone or something to scatter *He drove off without giving me his name or number. /* *They drove off the enemy with scare tactics.*

IDIOMS

to drive a hard bargain	to ask for a lot *My last boss didn't ask much of us, but my new boss drives a hard bargain.*
to drive someone crazy	to frustrate or infuriate another person *His indecision is driving me crazy!*
to drive someone up the wall	to annoy someone *The children's antics were driving me up the wall.*
to drive something home	to emphasize a point *The antiwar movie really drove its message home.*

RELATED WORDS

driver (n.)	a person who drives
driver's education (n.)	courses in school that teach you how to drive
driver's license (n.)	a document that shows that you are permitted to drive
driven (adj.)	extremely motivated

* Note that the form "will be being driven" is rarely used. To convey a future progressive passive, use the present progressive passive.

Verb Chart

drop

	ACTIVE	PASSIVE
Infinitive	to drop	to be dropped
Past Infinitive	to have dropped	to have been dropped
Past Participle	dropped	been dropped
Present Participle	dropping	being dropped

ACTIVE

I		
you/we/they		
he/she/it		

SIMPLE PRESENT
drop
drop
drops

SIMPLE PAST
dropped
dropped
dropped

SIMPLE FUTURE
will drop
will drop
will drop

PRESENT PROGRESSIVE
am dropping
are dropping
is dropping

PAST PROGRESSIVE
was dropping
were dropping
was dropping

FUTURE PROGRESSIVE
will be dropping
will be dropping
will be dropping

PRESENT PERFECT
have dropped
have dropped
has dropped

PAST PERFECT
had dropped
had dropped
had dropped

FUTURE PERFECT
will have dropped
will have dropped
will have dropped

PRESENT PERFECT PROGRESSIVE
have been dropping
have been dropping
has been dropping

PAST PERFECT PROGRESSIVE
had been dropping
had been dropping
had been dropping

FUTURE PERFECT PROGRESSIVE
will have been dropping
will have been dropping
will have been dropping

EXAMPLES:
Did you drop the film off to be developed?

Twenty-five percent of the kids in inner-city high schools will have dropped out before graduation.

I didn't know that she had dropped chemistry this semester.

PASSIVE

SIMPLE PRESENT
am dropped
are dropped
is dropped

SIMPLE PAST
was dropped
were dropped
was dropped

SIMPLE FUTURE
will be dropped
will be dropped
will be dropped

PRESENT PROGRESSIVE
am being dropped
are being dropped
is being dropped

PAST PROGRESSIVE
was being dropped
were being dropped
was being dropped

FUTURE PROGRESSIVE*
will be being dropped*
will be being dropped*
will be being dropped*

PRESENT PERFECT
have been dropped
have been dropped
has been dropped

PAST PERFECT
had been dropped
had been dropped
had been dropped

FUTURE PERFECT
will have been dropped
will have been dropped
will have been dropped

EXAMPLES:
The flyers were being dropped from a small plane.

The money will be dropped off at the corner of 6th and Green.

I thought you were being dropped off by Mom and Dad.

PRINCIPAL CONDITIONALS

PRESENT
would drop
would drop
would drop

PRESENT PROGRESSIVE
would be dropping
would be dropping
would be dropping

PRESENT PASSIVE
would be dropped
would be dropped
would be dropped

PAST
would have dropped
would have dropped
would have dropped

PAST PROGRESSIVE
would have been dropping
would have been dropping
would have been dropping

PAST PASSIVE
would have been dropped
would have been dropped
would have been dropped

EXAMPLES:
Would you drop my prescription at the pharmacy on your way to the bank?

I would be dropping math this semester if my parents let me.

drop

PRINCIPAL PARTS: drop, dropped, dropped

Important Forms in Use

IF/THEN CONDITIONALS

	IF ...	...THEN	EXAMPLE
Real Present/ Future	drop/drops	simple present	If you <u>drop</u> me at the front door, don't forget to pick me up there too.
		will + base form	If she <u>drops</u> too many classes, she'll have to go to summer school.
Unreal Present/ Future	dropped	would + base form	If we <u>dropped</u> by, would they be upset?
Unreal Past	had dropped	would have + past participle	If I <u>had dropped</u> him off at 5:00, you would have had to give him dinner.

SUBJUNCTIVE

ACTIVE	drop	We suggested that they <u>drop</u> off their luggage before exploring the city.
PASSIVE	be dropped	He requests that the package <u>be dropped</u> off with the super if he isn't home.

PHRASAL VERBS

drop back	to fall behind Gabby was with me for most of the marathon, but she dropped back during the last few miles.
drop by/in	to visit someone without making a previous arrangement Henry dropped by while we were having dinner.
drop (someone) off	to deliver someone to a specific destination, usually in a car Can you drop me off at my sister's house?
drop out	to withdraw from an organized activity, such as school, before it is finished My father dropped out of school at age sixteen.

IDIOMS

to drop dead	said to someone to express anger or contempt with his or her actions or requests (informal) He asked me to come to the dance with him, but I told him to drop dead.
to drop names	to make yourself appear more important by associating yourself with famous or important people It's so annoying how Jim always tries to make himself look better by dropping names.
to drop someone a line/note	to send someone a short letter to say hi or to inform him or her of something Drop me a line when you get there so that I know how you're doing.
to drop the ball	to not complete something that others expected you to complete The lease on that great apartment would have been ours if the real estate agent hadn't dropped the ball.

RELATED WORDS

drop-dead gorgeous (adj.)	extremely good-looking or handsome
drop-in appointment (n.)	an office visit (to a doctor, dentist, etc.) for which a specific time is not needed
name-dropping (n.)	the act of making yourself seem important by associating yourself with famous or important people

Verb Chart

* Note that the form "will be being dropped" is rarely used. To convey a future progressive passive, use the present progressive passive.

95

dry

	ACTIVE	PASSIVE
Infinitive	to dry	to be dried
Past Infinitive	to have dried	to have been dried
Past Participle	dried	been dried
Present Participle	drying	being dried

I
you/we/they
he/she/it

ACTIVE

SIMPLE PRESENT	SIMPLE PAST	SIMPLE FUTURE
dry	dried	will dry
dry	dried	will dry
dries	dried	will dry

PRESENT PROGRESSIVE	PAST PROGRESSIVE	FUTURE PROGRESSIVE
am drying	was drying	will be drying
are drying	were drying	will be drying
is drying	was drying	will be drying

PRESENT PERFECT	PAST PERFECT	FUTURE PERFECT
have dried	had dried	will have dried
have dried	had dried	will have dried
has dried	had dried	will have dried

PRESENT PERFECT PROGRESSIVE	PAST PERFECT PROGRESSIVE	FUTURE PERFECT PROGRESSIVE
have been drying	had been drying	will have been drying
have been drying	had been drying	will have been drying
has been drying	had been drying	will have been drying

EXAMPLES:

Can you dry the dishes after I wash them?

The clothes will dry quickly in the sun.

Do you think the paint will have dried enough to add a second layer by the end of the day?

PASSIVE

SIMPLE PRESENT	SIMPLE PAST	SIMPLE FUTURE
am dried	was dried	will be dried
are dried	were dried	will be dried
is dried	was dried	will be dried

PRESENT PROGRESSIVE	PAST PROGRESSIVE	FUTURE PROGRESSIVE*
am being dried	was being dried	will be being dried*
are being dried	were being dried	will be being dried*
is being dried	was being dried	will be being dried*

PRESENT PERFECT	PAST PERFECT	FUTURE PERFECT
have been dried	had been dried	will have been dried
have been dried	had been dried	will have been dried
has been dried	had been dried	will have been dried

EXAMPLES:

All laundry will be dried on a cool setting.

The flowers were dried by my mother.

The dishes have already been dried.

PRINCIPAL CONDITIONALS

PRESENT	PRESENT PROGRESSIVE	PRESENT PASSIVE
would dry	would be drying	would be dried
would dry	would be drying	would be dried
would dry	would be drying	would be dried

PAST	PAST PROGRESSIVE	PAST PASSIVE
would have dried	would have been drying	would have been dried
would have dried	would have been drying	would have been dried
would have dried	would have been drying	would have been dried

EXAMPLES:

I didn't think that thick sweater would dry so quickly.

We thought the bread would have been dried out by now so we bought another loaf.

Verb Chart

Important Forms in Use

IF/THEN CONDITIONALS

	IF ...	... THEN	EXAMPLE
Real Present/ Future	dry/dries	simple present	*If she washes and <u>dries</u> the dishes, I fix the dessert.*
		will + base form	*If we <u>dry</u> off before we go inside, we won't get the house all wet.*
Unreal Present/ Future	dried	would + base form	*If the lake <u>dried</u> up, the villagers would have to travel a long distance to get water.*
Unreal Past	had dried	would have + past participle	*If the river <u>hadn't dried</u> up years ago, the town wouldn't have disappeared.*

SUBJUNCTIVE

ACTIVE	dry	*He suggested that we <u>dry</u> off before we come into the house.*
PASSIVE	be dried	*The chef asked that the fruit <u>be dried</u> according to the instructions in the cookbook.*

PHRASAL VERBS

dry off	to become dry *She dried off in the sun when she got out of the lake.*
dry (someone) off	to make dry *His mother dried him off quickly so that he didn't become cold.*
dry out	to become completely dry *The bread was left on the table and had dried out by dinner.*
dry up	to no longer have any moisture, especially a river or a lake *The creek behind our house dried up every fall.*

IDIOMS

to be dry as a bone	to no longer contain water *The lake in the village, the only water source, was dry as a bone after they built the nearby dam.*
to run dry	to no longer provide what had been previously provided *Our ideas ran dry toward the end of the year, but picked up after everyone had had a couple of weeks' vacation.*

RELATED WORDS

dry cleaning (n.)	a process used to clean delicate fabrics
drywall (n.)	a type of board used to make walls and ceilings in a house or other building
washer and drier (n.)	two machines that are used for doing laundry

* Note that the form "will be being dried" is rarely used. To convey a future progressive passive, use the present progressive passive.

eat

	ACTIVE	PASSIVE
Infinitive	to eat	to be eaten
Past Infinitive	to have eaten	to have been eaten
Past Participle	eaten	been eaten
Present Participle	eating	being eaten

ACTIVE

I
you/we/they
he/she/it

SIMPLE PRESENT	SIMPLE PAST	SIMPLE FUTURE
eat	ate	will eat
eat	ate	will eat
eats	ate	will eat

PRESENT PROGRESSIVE	PAST PROGRESSIVE	FUTURE PROGRESSIVE
am eating	was eating	will be eating
are eating	were eating	will be eating
is eating	was eating	will be eating

PRESENT PERFECT	PAST PERFECT	FUTURE PERFECT
have eaten	had eaten	will have eaten
have eaten	had eaten	will have eaten
has eaten	had eaten	will have eaten

PRESENT PERFECT PROGRESSIVE	PAST PERFECT PROGRESSIVE	FUTURE PERFECT PROGRESSIVE
have been eating	had been eating	will have been eating
have been eating	had been eating	will have been eating
has been eating	had been eating	will have been eating

EXAMPLES:
He eats eggs for breakfast. *The kids will have eaten by the time they get over to your house.* *Will you be eating with us tonight?*

PASSIVE

SIMPLE PRESENT	SIMPLE PAST	SIMPLE FUTURE
am eaten	was eaten	will be eaten
are eaten	were eaten	will be eaten
is eaten	was eaten	will be eaten

PRESENT PROGRESSIVE	PAST PROGRESSIVE	FUTURE PROGRESSIVE*
am being eaten	was being eaten	will be being eaten*
are being eaten	were being eaten	will be being eaten*
is being eaten	was being eaten	will be being eaten*

PRESENT PERFECT	PAST PERFECT	FUTURE PERFECT
have been eaten	had been eaten	will have been eaten
have been eaten	had been eaten	will have been eaten
has been eaten	had been eaten	will have been eaten

EXAMPLES:
Fish is not eaten on Fridays during Lent. *The cookies had all been eaten, and so we had ice cream for dessert.* *The pie you made is being eaten as we speak, and it's delicious.*

PRINCIPAL CONDITIONALS

PRESENT	PRESENT PROGRESSIVE	PRESENT PASSIVE
would eat	would be eating	would be eaten
would eat	would be eating	would be eaten
would eat	would be eating	would be eaten

PAST	PAST PROGRESSIVE	PAST PASSIVE
would have eaten	would have been eating	would have been eaten
would have eaten	would have been eating	would have been eaten
would have eaten	would have been eating	would have been eaten

EXAMPLES:
Would you eat fish if I made it? *I thought that all of the bread I made would have been eaten by now.*

eat

PRINCIPAL PARTS: eat, ate, eaten

Important Forms in Use

IF/THEN CONDITIONALS

	IF ...	... THEN	EXAMPLE
Real Present/ Future	eat/eats	simple present will + base form	*If I eat seafood, I break out in hives.* *If we eat at that table, we'll be too close to the door.*
Unreal Present/ Future	ate	would + base form	*If she ate more proteins, she'd have more energy during the day.*
Unreal Past	had eaten	would have + past participle	*If I had eaten what the doctor wanted me to, I would have gained a million pounds.*

SUBJUNCTIVE

ACTIVE	eat	*The nutritionist suggests that we eat four to five times a day.*
PASSIVE	be eaten	*The medical technician insists that nothing be eaten for twelve hours before the test is done.*

PHRASAL VERBS

eat away at (someone or something)	to erode something little by little *The high water level was eating away at the rocks along the coast.*
eat at (someone)	to bother *I can't remember her name; it's really eating at me.*
eat in	to eat at home *Restaurants in this neighborhood have become so expensive that we started eating in almost every night.*
eat out	to go out to a restaurant to have a meal *I don't feel like cooking tonight. Let's eat out.*
eat up	to use all of something *Our society is eating up all of the world's resources.*

IDIOMS

to eat like a horse/pig	to eat a lot *Frank always eats like a pig at the all-you-can-eat buffets.*
to have your cake and eat it too	to get the best of something, without having to pay the price *Jim wants to be rich, but he's really lazy. I have to tell him, you can't have your cake and eat it too.*
to eat someone out of house and home	to eat a lot of the food in someone's home, often used for growing teenagers *I loved having them for the weekend, but they ate me out of house and home.*
to eat your words	to recognize that you were incorrect about something you said *Linda made me eat my words when she proved to me that the tree was a redwood and not a sequoia.*
to eat your heart out	an expression that is said to someone who is envious of something you have *I know you wanted the starring role in the play, but I got it! Eat your heart out!*

RELATED WORDS

edible (adj.)	able to be eaten
eatery (n.)	a restaurant

* Note that the form "will be being eaten" is rarely used. To convey a future progressive passive, use the present progressive passive.

Verb Chart

end

	ACTIVE	PASSIVE
Infinitive	to end	to be ended
Past Infinitive	to have ended	to have been ended
Past Participle	ended	been ended
Present Participle	ending	being ended

ACTIVE

I		
you/we/they		
he/she/it		

SIMPLE PRESENT	SIMPLE PAST	SIMPLE FUTURE
end	ended	will end
end	ended	will end
ends	ended	will end

PRESENT PROGRESSIVE	PAST PROGRESSIVE	FUTURE PROGRESSIVE
am ending	was ending	will be ending
are ending	were ending	will be ending
is ending	was ending	will be ending

PRESENT PERFECT	PAST PERFECT	FUTURE PERFECT
have ended	had ended	will have ended
have ended	had ended	will have ended
has ended	had ended	will have ended

PRESENT PERFECT PROGRESSIVE	PAST PERFECT PROGRESSIVE	FUTURE PERFECT PROGRESSIVE
have been ending	had been ending	will have been ending
have been ending	had been ending	will have been ending
has been ending	had been ending	will have been ending

EXAMPLES:
I'll be surprised if their relation-ship ends on a good note.   *That relationship has been ending or years.*   *Let's plan to arrive just before the performance will have ended.*

PASSIVE

SIMPLE PRESENT	SIMPLE PAST	SIMPLE FUTURE
am ended	was ended	will be ended
are ended	were ended	will be ended
is ended	was ended	will be ended

PRESENT PROGRESSIVE	PAST PROGRESSIVE	FUTURE PROGRESSIVE*
am being ended	was being ended	will be being ended*
are being ended	were being ended	will be being ended*
is being ended	was being ended	will be being ended*

PRESENT PERFECT	PAST PERFECT	FUTURE PERFECT
have been ended	had been ended	will have been ended
have been ended	had been ended	will have been ended
has been ended	had been ended	will have been ended

EXAMPLES:
We managed to put all of the kids to bed, and another day was ended.   *They left when the ceremony was being ended.*

PRINCIPAL CONDITIONALS

PRESENT	PRESENT PROGRESSIVE	PRESENT PASSIVE
would end	would be ending	would be ended
would end	would be ending	would be ended
would end	would be ending	would be ended

PAST	PAST PROGRESSIVE	PAST PASSIVE
would have ended	would have been ending	would have been ended
would have ended	would have been ending	would have been ended
would have ended	would have been ending	would have been ended

EXAMPLES:
I didn't think the book would end that way.   *We couldn't imagine that their friendship would have ended so suddenly.*

end

Important Forms in Use

IF/THEN CONDITIONALS

	IF . . .	. . . THEN	EXAMPLE
Real Present/ Future	end/ends	simple present	*If the movie <u>ends</u> with someone's death, it doesn't have as wide an audience as if the movie has a happy ending.*
		will + base form	*If we <u>end</u> on a bad note, it will be difficult to get them to agree to another meeting.*
Unreal Present/ Future	ended	would + base form	*If we <u>ended</u> this game now, I would be the winner by default.*
Unreal Past	had ended	would have + past participle	*If he <u>had ended</u> up becoming an artist, his family would have been so proud.*

SUBJUNCTIVE

ACTIVE	end	*We asked that the band <u>end</u> before 12:00.*
PASSIVE	be ended	*The director insisted that the presentation <u>be ended</u> exactly at 9:00.*

PHRASAL VERBS

end in
to finish in a specific way, such as in disaster or triumph
The soccer game ended in disaster when all of the public ran onto the field to protest the referee's decision.

end up
to finish in a particular position, place, etc.
Terry drove his car home from the bar when he was drunk and ended up in jail.

IDIOMS

to end on a good note
to finish positively
There were some rough spots during our meeting today, but I'm happy to say that we ended on a good note.

to come to a bad end
when someone gets involved in something that destroys his or her life
Several kids from our high school joined gangs and came to a bad end.

the end justifies the means
an expression that means that it is okay to do whatever is necessary, even if it is ethically or morally questionable, in order to achieve your objective
Many civilians died in the war. We must question whether the end justified the means.

the be-all and end-all
someone or something that is better than everyone or everything else
I know you enjoy spending time with Frank, but he's not the be-all and end-all. There are other men out there.

RELATED WORDS

ending (n.)
the final part of a movie, story, etc.

endless (adj.)
without end

* Note that the form "will be being ended" is rarely used. To convey a future progressive passive, use the present progressive passive.

Verb Chart

face

	ACTIVE	PASSIVE
Infinitive	to face	to be faced
Past Infinitive	to have faced	to have been faced
Past Participle	faced	been faced
Present Participle	facing	being faced

ACTIVE

I
you/we/they
he/she/it

SIMPLE PRESENT	SIMPLE PAST	SIMPLE FUTURE
face	faced	will face
face	faced	will face
faces	faced	will face

PRESENT PROGRESSIVE	PAST PROGRESSIVE	FUTURE PROGRESSIVE
am facing	was facing	will be facing
are facing	were facing	will be facing
is facing	was facing	will be facing

PRESENT PERFECT	PAST PERFECT	FUTURE PERFECT
have faced	had faced	will have faced
have faced	had faced	will have faced
has faced	had faced	will have faced

PRESENT PERFECT PROGRESSIVE	PAST PERFECT PROGRESSIVE	FUTURE PERFECT PROGRESSIVE
have been facing	had been facing	will have been facing
have been facing	had been facing	will have been facing
has been facing	had been facing	will have been facing

EXAMPLES:

The house faced west and so we were treated to a beautiful sunset every evening.

Everybody in our yoga class was facing the same direction.

She hasn't faced up to the part she played in the collapse of the company.

PASSIVE

SIMPLE PRESENT	SIMPLE PAST	SIMPLE FUTURE
am faced	was faced	will be faced
are faced	were faced	will be faced
is faced	was faced	will be faced

PRESENT PROGRESSIVE	PAST PROGRESSIVE	FUTURE PROGRESSIVE*
am being faced	was being faced	will be being faced*
are being faced	were being faced	will be being faced*
is being faced	was being faced	will be being faced*

PRESENT PERFECT	PAST PERFECT	FUTURE PERFECT
have been faced	had been faced	will have been faced
have been faced	had been faced	will have been faced
has been faced	had been faced	will have been faced

EXAMPLES:

I am faced with difficult tasks on a daily basis.

We were faced with many problems in our childhood, such as the death of our parents.

The building was being faced with a special material to protect it from weather damage.

PRINCIPAL CONDITIONALS

PRESENT	PRESENT PROGRESSIVE	PRESENT PASSIVE
would face	would be facing	would be faced
would face	would be facing	would be faced
would face	would be facing	would be faced

PAST	PAST PROGRESSIVE	PAST PASSIVE
would have faced	would have been facing	would have been faced
would have faced	would have been facing	would have been faced
would have faced	would have been facing	would have been faced

EXAMPLES:

I reminded her of all the things he had done to her, but she wouldn't face the facts.

We didn't expect that we would be facing a budget crisis so soon in the year.

Important Forms in Use

IF/THEN CONDITIONALS

	IF ...	... THEN	EXAMPLE
Real Present/ Future	face/faces	simple present	If I _face_ her about the problem, she gets angry and refuses to speak to me.
		will + base form	If she _faces_ up to the consequences of her action, she'll make a lot of people have more confidence in her.
Unreal Present/ Future	faced	would + base form	If we _faced_ them now, we wouldn't have to deal with this later.
Unreal Past	had faced	would have + past participle	If our team _had faced_ the Rangers and not the Blue Jays, we would have won the competition.

SUBJUNCTIVE

ACTIVE	face	It is important that the patient _face_ the problem immediately.
PASSIVE	be faced	It is essential that certain key problems _be faced_ if we plan to go through with building the new hospital.

PHRASAL VERBS

face (someone) down	to deal with a person with strength _Harry always knew how to face down his opponent in a wrestling match._
face off	to fight _The boxing match was especially exciting because we had no idea what would happen when the two men faced off._
face up to (something)	to deal with something unpleasant _He needs to face up to the reality that he may not get into medical school._

IDIOMS

to face the music	to be punished after you have done something wrong, or to deal with the consequences of your actions, good or bad _I couldn't believe that he got ten years in jail. I never thought he would have to face the music._
to face (the) facts	to look at the reality of a situation _Why don't you face the facts? We don't want you here anymore!_

RELATED WORDS

face-off (n.)	a confrontation
face-lift (n.)	cosmetic surgery meant to remove wrinkles from the face
face-to-face (adv.)	directly in front of someone or something

* Note that the form "will be being faced" is rarely used. To convey a future progressive passive, use the present progressive passive.

Verb Chart

fall

	ACTIVE	PASSIVE
Infinitive	to fall	to be fallen
Past Infinitive	to have fallen	to have been fallen
Past Participle	fallen	been fallen
Present Participle	falling	being fallen

ACTIVE

I		
you/we/they		
he/she/it		

SIMPLE PRESENT	SIMPLE PAST	SIMPLE FUTURE
fall	fell	will fall
fall	fell	will fall
falls	fell	will fall

PRESENT PROGRESSIVE	PAST PROGRESSIVE	FUTURE PROGRESSIVE
am falling	was falling	will be falling
are falling	were falling	will be falling
is falling	was falling	will be falling

PRESENT PERFECT	PAST PERFECT	FUTURE PERFECT
have fallen	had fallen	will have fallen
have fallen	had fallen	will have fallen
has fallen	had fallen	will have fallen

PRESENT PERFECT PROGRESSIVE	PAST PERFECT PROGRESSIVE	FUTURE PERFECT PROGRESSIVE
have been falling	had been falling	will have been falling
have been falling	had been falling	will have been falling
has been falling	had been falling	will have been falling

EXAMPLES:
John fell off the front porch and broke his leg.
Snow was falling when we left the house.

PASSIVE

SIMPLE PRESENT	SIMPLE PAST	SIMPLE FUTURE
am fallen	was fallen	will be fallen
are fallen	were fallen	will be fallen
is fallen	was fallen	will be fallen

PRESENT PROGRESSIVE	PAST PROGRESSIVE	FUTURE PROGRESSIVE*
am being fallen	was being fallen	will be being fallen*
are being fallen	were being fallen	will be being fallen*
is being fallen	was being fallen	will be being fallen*

PRESENT PERFECT	PAST PERFECT	FUTURE PERFECT
have been fallen	had been fallen	will have been fallen
have been fallen	had been fallen	will have been fallen
has been fallen	had been fallen	will have been fallen

EXAMPLES:
My practical joke has been fallen for by all those people who thought they were so smart!
Hard times had been fallen on before; the villagers would make it through.

PRINCIPAL CONDITIONALS

PRESENT	PRESENT PROGRESSIVE	PRESENT PASSIVE
would fall	would be falling	would be fallen
would fall	would be falling	would be fallen
would fall	would be falling	would be fallen

PAST	PAST PROGRESSIVE	PAST PASSIVE
would have fallen	would have been falling	would have been fallen
would have fallen	would have been falling	would have been fallen
would have fallen	would have been falling	would have been fallen

EXAMPLES:
Who knew the temperature would fall so drastically during the night?
Prices would be falling faster if companies flooded the market with goods.

fall

PRINCIPAL PARTS: fall, fell, fallen.

Important Forms in Use

IF/THEN CONDITIONALS

	IF . . .	. . . THEN	EXAMPLE
Real Present/ Future	fall/falls	simple present	*If Bobby falls off his bicycle, he gets up, dusts himself off, and gets back on again.*
		will + base form	*If sales fall off drastically, we'll have to close the business.*
Unreal Present/ Future	fell	would + base form	*If you fell, I would catch you.*
Unreal Past	had fallen	would have + past participle	*If the proposal had fallen short of expectations, we wouldn't have accepted it.*

SUBJUNCTIVE

ACTIVE	fall	*The teacher recommends that we not fall behind in class, as it will be hard to catch up.*
PASSIVE	be fallen	*It is essential that our story be fallen for if we expect him to be surprised.*

PHRASAL VERBS

fall apart	to break into pieces, to no longer function, or to have an emotional reaction to something painful *Their marriage fell apart after their son died. / She tried not to cry at the funeral, but afterward she fell apart.*
fall for (something)	to become strongly and suddenly attracted to someone, or to get tricked *John fell for Suzanne the moment he saw her. / We fell for their scheme and lost thousands of dollars.*
fall in	when the roof of a home or other building can no longer stand *After the huge snowstorm, the roof of their garage fell in.*
fall through	to not succeed or be completed, usually used with plans *We had planned the takeover very carefully, but even well-laid plans can fall through.*

IDIOMS

to fall asleep	to begin sleeping *I can't fall asleep with the light on.*
to fall by the wayside	to lose importance and no longer be the focus of attention *We considered putting an addition on our building, but after looking at the numbers, that idea fell by the wayside.*
to fall from grace	to lose the respect of others or a position of authority *His fall from grace was complete. He lost his position, his friends, and the respect of his coworkers.*
to fall in love	to begin to have strong romantic feelings for someone *I don't think it's just a fling. I'm really falling in love with her.*
to fall short	to not meet expectations, to be insufficient *Our sales fell short of the target.*
to fall victim/prey to	to be cheated by a scheme *People often fall prey to swindlers who call and pretend to represent legitimate companies.*

RELATED WORDS

fallback (adj.)	describes something that can be used when the usual supply runs out
fall guy (n.)	the person who takes the blame when something has gone wrong
fallout (n.)	radiation that is found in the air after a nuclear reaction, or the aftermath of any significant event

* Note that the form "will be being fallen" is rarely used. To convey a future progressive passive, use the present progressive passive.

feel

	ACTIVE	PASSIVE
Infinitive	to feel	to be felt
Past Infinitive	to have felt	to have been felt
Past Participle	felt	been felt
Present Participle	feeling	being felt

ACTIVE

I	
you/we/they	
he/she/it	

SIMPLE PRESENT	SIMPLE PAST	SIMPLE FUTURE
feel	felt	will feel
feel	felt	will feel
feels	felt	will feel

PRESENT PROGRESSIVE	PAST PROGRESSIVE	FUTURE PROGRESSIVE
am feeling	was feeling	will be feeling
are feeling	were feeling	will be feeling
is feeling	was feeling	will be feeling

PRESENT PERFECT	PAST PERFECT	FUTURE PERFECT
have felt	had felt	will have felt
have felt	had felt	will have felt
has felt	had felt	will have felt

PRESENT PERFECT PROGRESSIVE	PAST PERFECT PROGRESSIVE	FUTURE PERFECT PROGRESSIVE
have been feeling	had been feeling	will have been feeling
have been feeling	had been feeling	will have been feeling
has been feeling	had been feeling	will have been feeling

EXAMPLES:

Do you feel well enough to come downstairs for dinner?

After the storm, the entire house felt damp.

How has Jim been feeling since his heart attack?

PASSIVE

SIMPLE PRESENT	SIMPLE PAST	SIMPLE FUTURE
am felt	was felt	will be felt
are felt	were felt	will be felt
is felt	was felt	will be felt

PRESENT PROGRESSIVE	PAST PROGRESSIVE	FUTURE PROGRESSIVE*
am being felt	was being felt	will be being felt*
are being felt	were being felt	will be being felt*
is being felt	was being felt	will be being felt*

PRESENT PERFECT	PAST PERFECT	FUTURE PERFECT
have been felt	had been felt	will have been felt
have been felt	had been felt	will have been felt
has been felt	had been felt	will have been felt

EXAMPLES:

The effects of the recession were felt by everyone.

Emotions are felt more strongly by some people than others.

PRINCIPAL CONDITIONALS

PRESENT	PRESENT PROGRESSIVE	PRESENT PASSIVE
would feel	would be feeling	would be felt
would feel	would be feeling	would be felt
would feel	would be feeling	would be felt

PAST	PAST PROGRESSIVE	PAST PASSIVE
would have felt	would have been feeling	would have been felt
would have felt	would have been feeling	would have been felt
would have felt	would have been feeling	would have been felt

EXAMPLES:

Sara's parents would feel better if they knew more about her boyfriend.

She would have felt fine if not for her allergies.

feel

Important Forms in Use

IF/THEN CONDITIONALS

	IF ...	... THEN	EXAMPLE
Real Present/ Future	feel/feels	simple present	*If you <u>feel</u> bad, please call us immediately.*
		will + base form	*If I <u>feel</u> like going to the movies, I'll call Jack.*
Unreal Present/ Future	felt	would + base form	*If we <u>felt</u> uncomfortable, we would leave.*
Unreal Past	had felt	would have + past participle	*If I <u>had felt</u> that she knew what she was doing, I wouldn't have asked for more help.*

SUBJUNCTIVE

ACTIVE	feel	*It is important that the customers <u>feel</u> welcome.*
PASSIVE	be felt	*He suggested that the fabric samples <u>be felt</u> before we made a decision.*

PHRASAL VERBS

feel for (someone)	to sympathize with someone *I know you have a lot of work to do, and I really feel for you, especially on such a beautiful weekend.*
feel (someone) out	to try to find out someone's feelings about something in an indirect way *I have no idea whether John is interested in investing but I'll try to feel him out when we go away this weekend.*
feel up to (something)	to have the energy to do something *I would love to help you out but I just don't feel up to it.*

IDIOMS

to feel blue	to be depressed *He's felt blue ever since the dog ran away.*
to feel like a million dollars	to have the sense that everything is great, to be fit *I feel like a million dollars now that I've started doing yoga.*
to have/get the feeling	to believe that you know something is true *I get the feeling that you aren't really interested in working with us on the project.*
to have a bad/funny feeling	to believe that there is something wrong with a certain situation *I have a bad feeling that what I said in class today is going to give people the wrong idea.*
to have a feel for something	to have a special ability to do something *He has a real feel for cooking.*

RELATED WORDS

feeling (n.)	an emotion or sense
feelers (n.)	antennae that protrude from an insect

* Note that the form "will be being felt" is rarely used. To convey a future progressive passive, use the present progressive passive.

Verb Chart

figure

	ACTIVE	PASSIVE
Infinitive	to figure	to be figured
Past Infinitive	to have figured	to have been figured
Past Participle	figured	been figured
Present Participle	figuring	being figured

ACTIVE

I
you/we/they
he/she/it

SIMPLE PRESENT	SIMPLE PAST	SIMPLE FUTURE
figure	figured	will figure
figure	figured	will figure
figures	figured	will figure

PRESENT PROGRESSIVE	PAST PROGRESSIVE	FUTURE PROGRESSIVE
am figuring	was figuring	will be figuring
are figuring	were figuring	will be figuring
is figuring	was figuring	will be figuring

PRESENT PERFECT	PAST PERFECT	FUTURE PERFECT
have figured	had figured	will have figured
have figured	had figured	will have figured
has figured	had figured	will have figured

PRESENT PERFECT PROGRESSIVE	PAST PERFECT PROGRESSIVE	FUTURE PERFECT PROGRESSIVE
have been figuring	had been figuring	will have been figuring
have been figuring	had been figuring	will have been figuring
has been figuring	had been figuring	will have been figuring

EXAMPLES:
Can you figure out how much of a tip we should leave the waitress? *The accountant is figuring out our budget for next year.* *When will you have figured this out?*

PASSIVE

SIMPLE PRESENT	SIMPLE PAST	SIMPLE FUTURE
am figured	was figured	will be figured
are figured	were figured	will be figured
is figured	was figured	will be figured

PRESENT PROGRESSIVE	PAST PROGRESSIVE	FUTURE PROGRESSIVE*
am being figured	was being figured	will be being figured*
are being figured	were being figured	will be being figured*
is being figured	was being figured	will be being figured*

PRESENT PERFECT	PAST PERFECT	FUTURE PERFECT
have been figured	had been figured	will have been figured
have been figured	had been figured	will have been figured
has been figured	had been figured	will have been figured

EXAMPLES:
The total price is being figured out at the moment. *Has an answer been figured out?* *Tax will be figured in to the final price.*

PRINCIPAL CONDITIONALS

PRESENT	PRESENT PROGRESSIVE	PRESENT PASSIVE
would figure	would be figuring	would be figured
would figure	would be figuring	would be figured
would figure	would be figuring	would be figured

PAST	PAST PROGRESSIVE	PAST PASSIVE
would have figured	would have been figuring	would have been figured
would have figured	would have been figuring	would have been figured
would have figured	would have been figuring	would have been figured

EXAMPLES:
Who would have figured that it would rain for the whole weekend? *Everything would have been figured out if we had had more time.*

figure

PRINCIPAL PARTS: figure, figured, figured

Important Forms in Use

IF/THEN CONDITIONALS

	IF...	...THEN	EXAMPLE
Real Present/ Future	figure/figures	simple present	*If I figure on having ten people for dinner, I usually buy two chickens.*
		will + base form	*If he figures out his next move soon, then it'll be my turn.*
Unreal Present/ Future	figured	would + base form	*If we figured out why he is behaving so strangely, we would talk to him about it.*
Unreal Past	had figured	would have + past participle	*If I had figured on you coming, I would have set another place at the table.*

SUBJUNCTIVE

ACTIVE	figure	*It is important that the accountant figure in all of the business expenses.*
PASSIVE	be figured	*It is essential that the menu be figured out several weeks in advance.*

PHRASAL VERBS

figure on	to plan for something *We figure on having approximately 125 guests at the wedding.*
figure out	to find the solution to a problem after thinking about it carefully *It took us hours before we were able to figure out the solution to the problem our physics teacher had assigned us.*

IDIOMS

Go figure!	said when you find a situation, action, or attitude puzzling or confusing *I can't believe that Joe and Gabrielle, two people that seem to have nothing in common, are dating. Go figure!*
that/it figures	said when something happens as you expect it to *It figures that Peggy wouldn't talk to me now, after so many years of friendship. She rejects anyone who gets too close to her.*

RELATED WORDS

facts and figures (n.)	statistics and other information relating to a specific area of knowledge

* Note that the form "will be being figured" is rarely used. To convey a future progressive passive, use the present progressive passive.

Verb Chart

fill

	ACTIVE	PASSIVE
Infinitive	to fill	to be filled
Past Infinitive	to have filled	to have been filled
Past Participle	filled	been filled
Present Participle	filling	being filled

ACTIVE

I		
you/we/they		
he/she/it		

SIMPLE PRESENT	SIMPLE PAST	SIMPLE FUTURE
fill	filled	will fill
fill	filled	will fill
fills	filled	will fill

PRESENT PROGRESSIVE	PAST PROGRESSIVE	FUTURE PROGRESSIVE
am filling	was filling	will be filling
are filling	were filling	will be filling
is filling	was filling	will be filling

PRESENT PERFECT	PAST PERFECT	FUTURE PERFECT
have filled	had filled	will have filled
have filled	had filled	will have filled
has filled	had filled	will have filled

PRESENT PERFECT PROGRESSIVE	PAST PERFECT PROGRESSIVE	FUTURE PERFECT PROGRESSIVE
have been filling	had been filling	will have been filling
have been filling	had been filling	will have been filling
has been filling	had been filling	will have been filling

EXAMPLES:

The students filled out the forms quickly.

The seats were filling up quickly five minutes before the performance.

She had been filling the gas tank with premium gasoline before the prices went up.

PASSIVE

SIMPLE PRESENT	SIMPLE PAST	SIMPLE FUTURE
am filled	was filled	will be filled
are filled	were filled	will be filled
is filled	was filled	will be filled

PRESENT PROGRESSIVE	PAST PROGRESSIVE	FUTURE PROGRESSIVE*
am being filled	was being filled	will be being filled*
are being filled	were being filled	will be being filled*
is being filled	was being filled	will be being filled*

PRESENT PERFECT	PAST PERFECT	FUTURE PERFECT
have been filled	had been filled	will have been filled
have been filled	had been filled	will have been filled
has been filled	had been filled	will have been filled

EXAMPLES:

We regret to inform you that all of the positions in our company have already been filled.

The forms had been filled out, but the personal statement had not been completed when I saw his application yesterday.

We hope the holes left by the last tenants will be filled in and painted over before we move in.

PRINCIPAL CONDITIONALS

PRESENT	PRESENT PROGRESSIVE	PRESENT PASSIVE
would fill	would be filling	would be filled
would fill	would be filling	would be filled
would fill	would be filling	would be filled

PAST	PAST PROGRESSIVE	PAST PASSIVE
would have filled	would have been filling	would have been filled
would have filled	would have been filling	would have been filled
would have filled	would have been filling	would have been filled

EXAMPLES:

Would you fill me in on what happened during the meeting?

I didn't think the vacancy would be filled so quickly.

fill

PRINCIPAL PARTS: fill, filled, filled

Important Forms in Use

IF/THEN CONDITIONALS

	IF ...	... THEN	EXAMPLE
Real Present/ Future	fill/fills	simple present	*If Benji fills up on junk food, he's not hungry at dinner time.*
		will + base form	*If Harriet fills in for me on Friday night, I'll do her shift on Saturday morning.*
Unreal Present/ Future	filled	would + base form	*If we filled the refrigerator with beer, it would be gone by tomorrow.*
Unreal Past	had filled	would have + past participle	*If they had filled my wineglass the first time, I wouldn't have asked for more.*

SUBJUNCTIVE

ACTIVE	fill	*We suggest that you fill your gas tank and your water containers at this station, because there won't be another station until you cross the desert.*
PASSIVE	be filled	*It is essential that we be filled in on all the details before we begin the negotiations.*

PHRASAL VERBS

fill in/out (something)	to write your basic personal information on a form, application, etc. *Please fill in this form before you see the doctor.*
fill (someone) in	to give all the details about something that has happened *Fill us in on what happened last night!*
fill in for (someone)	to replace someone temporarily *Laura is filling in for Cindy until she gets back from vacation.*
fill out	to begin to have a fuller figure *He's filled out a lot since he turned forty.*
fill (something) up	to add liquid or solid matter to a container until you can't add any more *I haven't been filling up the gas tank of my SUV since gas has become so expensive.*
fill up on (something)	to eat so much of one thing that you can't eat anything else *The kids filled up on ice cream and candy, and weren't hungry at dinner time.*

IDIOMS

to fill someone's shoes	to adequately replace someone in a position, such as in the workplace *We haven't been able to find anyone to fill the vice president's shoes since she retired.*
to fill the void	to do an activity that takes up time, especially to avoid missing someone or feeling sad *Hillary took up ceramics to fill the void when her husband died.*

RELATED WORDS

filler (n.)	material in a pillow, mattress, etc., that makes it fluffy; music or conversation used to take up time, often in a movie or television show

---

* Note that the form "will be being filled" is rarely used. To convey a future progressive passive, use the present progressive passive.

Verb Chart

find

	ACTIVE	PASSIVE
Infinitive	to find	to be found
Past Infinitive	to have found	to have been found
Past Participle	found	been found
Present Participle	finding	being found

ACTIVE

I		
you/we/they		
he/she/it		

SIMPLE PRESENT	SIMPLE PAST	SIMPLE FUTURE
find	found	will find
find	found	will find
finds	found	will find

PRESENT PROGRESSIVE	PAST PROGRESSIVE	FUTURE PROGRESSIVE
am finding	was finding	will be finding
are finding	were finding	will be finding
is finding	was finding	will be finding

PRESENT PERFECT	PAST PERFECT	FUTURE PERFECT
have found	had found	will have found
have found	had found	will have found
has found	had found	will have found

PRESENT PERFECT PROGRESSIVE	PAST PERFECT PROGRESSIVE	FUTURE PERFECT PROGRESSIVE
have been finding	had been finding	will have been finding
have been finding	had been finding	will have been finding
has been finding	had been finding	will have been finding

EXAMPLES:

My son and I find the chocolate ice cream to be the best at this restaurant.

We found out about the test when we got to school this morning.

He has been finding his new apartment to his liking so far.

PASSIVE

SIMPLE PRESENT	SIMPLE PAST	SIMPLE FUTURE
am found	was found	will be found
are found	were found	will be found
is found	was found	will be found

PRESENT PROGRESSIVE	PAST PROGRESSIVE	FUTURE PROGRESSIVE*
am being found	was being found	will be being found*
are being found	were being found	will be being found*
is being found	was being found	will be being found*

PRESENT PERFECT	PAST PERFECT	FUTURE PERFECT
have been found	had been found	will have been found
have been found	had been found	will have been found
has been found	had been found	will have been found

EXAMPLES:

A European cigarette was found at the scene of the crime.

They promise me that a solution will be found by the end of the day.

PRINCIPAL CONDITIONALS

PRESENT	PRESENT PROGRESSIVE	PRESENT PASSIVE
would find	would be finding	would be found
would find	would be finding	would be found
would find	would be finding	would be found

PAST	PAST PROGRESSIVE	PAST PASSIVE
would have found	would have been finding	would have been found
would have found	would have been finding	would have been found
would have found	would have been finding	would have been found

EXAMPLES:

You would have found the experience as disagreeable as I did.

We would have been found out if we hadn't hidden in the closet.

find

Important Forms in Use

IF/THEN CONDITIONALS

	IF . . .	. . . THEN	EXAMPLE
Real Present/ Future	find/finds	simple present	*If I find that the produce is not fresh in a grocery store, I never go back there.*
		will + base form	*If she finds that she's not comfortable staying with them, she'll call us.*
Unreal Present/ Future	found	would + base form	*If you found out more about the show, I would go with you.*
Unreal Past	had found	would have + past participle	*If Ben had found her more agreeable, he would've gone out with her again.*

SUBJUNCTIVE

ACTIVE	find	*They insist that we find an apartment for them.*
PASSIVE	be found	*It is imperative that a solution be found.*

PHRASAL VERBS

find out (about) (something)	to discover some information *Can you find out what time the movie begins? / How did they find out about the car accident?*

IDIOMS

finders keepers (losers weepers)	used when someone has found something that he or she intends to keep, even if the original owner asserts a claim *"What are you going to do with the money you found last night?"* *"Finders keepers!"*
to find oneself	to discover what it is that you want to do or more about who you are *Naomi went on a week-long yoga retreat hoping to find herself.*

RELATED WORDS

lost and found (n.)	the place where lost items are stored so that their owners may come to retrieve them
newfound (adj.)	newly discovered
finder's fee (n.)	money that you must pay someone who has helped you to find something, such as a home or an apartment

* Note that the form "will be being found" is rarely used. To convey a future progressive passive, use the present progressive passive.

Verb Chart

fly

	ACTIVE	PASSIVE
Infinitive	to fly	to be flown
Past Infinitive	to have flown	to have been flown
Past Participle	flown	been flown
Present Participle	flying	being flown

ACTIVE

	I	you/we/they	he/she/it

SIMPLE PRESENT	SIMPLE PAST	SIMPLE FUTURE
fly	flew	will fly
fly	flew	will fly
flies	flew	will fly

PRESENT PROGRESSIVE	PAST PROGRESSIVE	FUTURE PROGRESSIVE
am flying	was flying	will be flying
are flying	were flying	will be flying
is flying	was flying	will be flying

PRESENT PERFECT	PAST PERFECT	FUTURE PERFECT
have flown	had flown	will have flown
have flown	had flown	will have flown
has flown	had flown	will have flown

PRESENT PERFECT PROGRESSIVE	PAST PERFECT PROGRESSIVE	FUTURE PERFECT PROGRESSIVE
have been flying	had been flying	will have been flying
have been flying	had been flying	will have been flying
has been flying	had been flying	will have been flying

EXAMPLES:

As they were leaving the cave, bats were flying out into the night.

Have you ever flown overseas before?

We had been flying for years and had never experienced turbulence like we did in the last flight we took.

PASSIVE

SIMPLE PRESENT	SIMPLE PAST	SIMPLE FUTURE
am flown	was flown	will be flown
are flown	were flown	will be flown
is flown	was flown	will be flown

PRESENT PROGRESSIVE	PAST PROGRESSIVE	FUTURE PROGRESSIVE*
am being flown	was being flown	will be being flown*
are being flown	were being flown	will be being·flown*
is being flown	was being flown	will be being flown*

PRESENT PERFECT	PAST PERFECT	FUTURE PERFECT
have been flown	had been flown	will have been flown
have been flown	had been flown	will have been flown
has been flown	had been flown	will have been flown

EXAMPLES:

The packages were flown in by overnight mail.

The airplane was being flown by a new pilot.

PRINCIPAL CONDITIONALS

PRESENT	PRESENT PROGRESSIVE	PRESENT PASSIVE
would fly	would be flying	would be flown
would fly	would be flying	would be flown
would fly	would be flying	would be flown

PAST	PAST PROGRESSIVE	PAST PASSIVE
would have flown	would have been flying	would have been flown
would have flown	would have been flying	would have been flown
would have flown	would have been flying	would have been flown

EXAMPLES:

I would fly if I could get a ticket, but the flight is sold out.

We would have flown you in if we had known that you wanted to come.

fly

Important Forms in Use

IF/THEN CONDITIONALS

	IF...	...THEN	EXAMPLE
Real Present/ Future	fly/flies	simple present	*If I fly with my kids, the trip is much more difficult.*
		will + base form	*If she flies here for my birthday, I'll pay for her ticket.*
Unreal Present/ Future	flew	would + base form	*If we flew more often, the kids would get used to air travel.*
Unreal Past	had flown	would have + past participle	*If I had flown to Chicago instead of taking the train, I would have gotten there faster.*

SUBJUNCTIVE

ACTIVE	fly	*It is important that the pilot fly at an altitude that will avoid turbulence.*
PASSIVE	be flown	*It is essential that we be flown directly to Phoenix.*

PHRASAL VERBS

fly at
to attack someone, usually by speaking to him or her angrily
I don't know why I flew at Julia like that. What she said made me so angry.

IDIOMS

to fly by the seat of one's pants
to do something without making any plans
I love visiting Ben, but he flies by the seat of his pants, so it can be exhausting.

to fly in the face of danger
to do something without any regard to the danger involved
If you want to be a firefighter, you have to be willing to fly in the face of danger.

to fly off the handle
to lose your temper, to become angry
My father flew off the handle when he found out about the car accident.

to fly the coop
to leave home
After my kids had all flown the coop, the house was so peaceful that I didn't know what to do with myself.

to go fly a kite
an expression said when you're being annoyed by someone and you want him or her to leave (informal)
Why do you always have to hang around with us? Go fly a kite!

to fly right
to do the right thing
I'm upset by the things that my son is doing after school. I don't know what to do to get him to fly right.

RELATED WORDS

fly-by-night (adj.)
questionable, not trustworthy

---

* Note that the form "will be being flown" is rarely used. To convey a future progressive passive, use the present progressive passive.

Verb Chart

follow

	ACTIVE	PASSIVE
Infinitive	to follow	to be followed
Past Infinitive	to have followed	to have been followed
Past Participle	followed	been followed
Present Participle	following	being followed

ACTIVE

I		
you/we/they		
he/she/it		

SIMPLE PRESENT	SIMPLE PAST	SIMPLE FUTURE
follow	followed	will follow
follow	followed	will follow
follows	followed	will follow

PRESENT PROGRESSIVE	PAST PROGRESSIVE	FUTURE PROGRESSIVE
am following	was following	will be following
are following	were following	will be following
is following	was following	will be following

PRESENT PERFECT	PAST PERFECT	FUTURE PERFECT
have followed	had followed	will have followed
have followed	had followed	will have followed
has followed	had followed	will have followed

PRESENT PERFECT PROGRESSIVE	PAST PERFECT PROGRESSIVE	FUTURE PERFECT PROGRESSIVE
have been following	had been following	will have been following
have been following	had been following	will have been following
has been following	had been following	will have been following

EXAMPLES:

I don't follow you. Could you explain that again?

We followed all of the directions and still got lost.

I called 911 because I was certain a strange man had been following me.

PASSIVE

SIMPLE PRESENT	SIMPLE PAST	SIMPLE FUTURE
am followed	was followed	will be followed
are followed	were followed	will be followed
is followed	was followed	will be followed

PRESENT PROGRESSIVE	PAST PROGRESSIVE	FUTURE PROGRESSIVE*
am being followed	was being followed	will be being followed*
are being followed	were being followed	will be being followed*
is being followed	was being followed	will be being followed*

PRESENT PERFECT	PAST PERFECT	FUTURE PERFECT
have been followed	had been followed	will have been followed
have been followed	had been followed	will have been followed
has been followed	had been followed	will have been followed

EXAMPLES:

The appetizer was followed by a main course of prime rib or lobster.

We had this uncomfortable feeling that we were being followed.

I was glad to learn that the rules had been followed while we were away.

PRINCIPAL CONDITIONALS

PRESENT	PRESENT PROGRESSIVE	PRESENT PASSIVE
would follow	would be following	would be followed
would follow	would be following	would be followed
would follow	would be following	would be followed

PAST	PAST PROGRESSIVE	PAST PASSIVE
would have followed	would have been following	would have been followed
would have followed	would have been following	would have been followed
would have followed	would have been following	would have been followed

EXAMPLES:

Would you follow me please?

We would have followed you but we couldn't tell which car was yours.

Important Forms in Use

IF/THEN CONDITIONALS

	IF . . .	. . . THEN	EXAMPLE
Real Present/ Future	follow/follows	simple present	If the cat _follows_ me down the block, I tell her to go home.
		will + base form	If she _follows_ her dream, she won't make any money.
Unreal Present/ Future	followed	would + base form	If they _followed_ him around, he wouldn't have any freedom.
Unreal Past	had followed	would have + past participle	If we _had followed_ the news of the storm, we would have known that it was going to rain.

SUBJUNCTIVE

ACTIVE	follow	It is important that you _follow_ me.
PASSIVE	be followed	He asked that the dinner _be followed_ by drinks and dancing.

PHRASAL VERBS

follow along	to read with or play music at the same rate as someone else *I know you're not familiar with this piece, but see if you can follow along.*
follow up	to return to something that you worked on previously to get more information, to do more work on it because you think it's worthwhile *Did you follow up on the young boy who saved three kids from drowning? I think that would make a good cover story.*
follow through	to complete or pursue something you have begun working on *The problem with Rob as a salesperson is that he never follows through on possible sales.*

IDIOMS

to follow something to the letter	to do exactly what instructions or directions tell you to do *We followed the directions to the letter, and we still got lost.*
to follow someone's example	to do as someone else has done *He treated people kindly, and all of the children followed his example.*
to follow suit	to do exactly what someone else has done after you see what he or she has done *The Smiths left the housekeeper a fifteen dollar tip, and we followed suit.*
to follow in somebody's footsteps	to end up choosing the same career, lifestyle, etc., as someone older than you *Sid followed in his father's footsteps when he joined the fire department.*

RELATED WORDS

follow-up (n.)	something done to go more in depth on a subject
following (n.)	a group of people who have an appreciation for the talents of someone, such as an artist or performer

* Note that the form "will be being followed" is rarely used. To convey a future progressive passive, use the present progressive passive.

Verb Chart

117

forbid

	ACTIVE	PASSIVE
Infinitive	to forbid	to be forbidden
Past Infinitive	to have forbidden	to have been forbidden
Past Participle	forbidden	been forbidden
Present Participle	forbidding	being forbidden

ACTIVE

I		
you/we/they		
he/she/it		

SIMPLE PRESENT	SIMPLE PAST	SIMPLE FUTURE
forbid	forbade	will forbid
forbid	forbade	will forbid
forbids	forbade	will forbid

PRESENT PROGRESSIVE	PAST PROGRESSIVE	FUTURE PROGRESSIVE
am forbidding	was forbidding	will be forbidding
are forbidding	were forbidding	will be forbidding
is forbidding	was forbidding	will be forbidding

PRESENT PERFECT	PAST PERFECT	FUTURE PERFECT
have forbidden	had forbidden	will have forbidden
have forbidden	had forbidden	will have forbidden
has forbidden	had forbidden	will have forbidden

PRESENT PERFECT PROGRESSIVE	PAST PERFECT PROGRESSIVE	FUTURE PERFECT PROGRESSIVE
have been forbidding	had been forbidding	will have been forbidding
have been forbidding	had been forbidding	will have been forbidding
has been forbidding	had been forbidding	will have been forbidding

EXAMPLES:
The school had forbidden the kids from playing anywhere but in the playground behind the school. *My friend Jim has forbidden me to tell anyone his age.* *The state law forbids the sale of liquor to anyone under the age of twenty-one.*

PASSIVE

SIMPLE PRESENT	SIMPLE PAST	SIMPLE FUTURE
am forbidden	was forbidden	will be forbidden
are forbidden	were forbidden	will be forbidden
is forbidden	was forbidden	will be forbidden

PRESENT PROGRESSIVE	PAST PROGRESSIVE	FUTURE PROGRESSIVE*
am being forbidden	was being forbidden	will be being forbidden*
are being forbidden	were being forbidden	will be being forbidden*
is being forbidden	was being forbidden	will be being forbidden*

PRESENT PERFECT	PAST PERFECT	FUTURE PERFECT
have been forbidden	had been forbidden	will have been forbidden
have been forbidden	had been forbidden	will have been forbidden
has been forbidden	had been forbidden	will have been forbidden

EXAMPLES:
Smoking has been forbidden in many bars and restaurants across the country. *It is forbidden to use a cell phone in the classroom.* *Any mention of Uncle Charles in my family was strictly forbidden after his marriage to a trapeze artist caused such a scandal.*

PRINCIPAL CONDITIONALS

PRESENT	PRESENT PROGRESSIVE	PRESENT PASSIVE
would forbid	would be forbidding	would be forbidden
would forbid	would be forbidding	would be forbidden
would forbid	would be forbidding	would be forbidden

PAST	PAST PROGRESSIVE	PAST PASSIVE
would have forbidden	would have been forbidding	would have been forbidden
would have forbidden	would have been forbidding	would have been forbidden
would have forbidden	would have been forbidding	would have been forbidden

EXAMPLES:
I would forbid you from going out at night if you began to have any problems in school. *My parents would have forbidden my hanging out with Johanna if they had had any idea what we were up to.*

forbid

PRINCIPAL PARTS: forbid, forbade, forbidden

Important Forms in Use

IF/THEN CONDITIONALS

	IF...	...THEN	EXAMPLE
Real Present/ Future	forbid/forbids	simple present	*If I <u>forbid</u> him from seeing his friends, he becomes furious.*
		will + base form	*If she <u>forbids</u> me, I will do it anyway.*
Unreal Present/ Future	forbade	would + base form	*If the teacher <u>forbade</u> the use of dictionaries, the students would all fail.*
Unreal Past	had forbidden	would have + past participle	*If the doctor <u>had forbidden</u> him any indulgences, he certainly wouldn't have stayed on his diet.*

SUBJUNCTIVE

ACTIVE	forbid	*We recommend that he <u>forbid</u> his daughter from spending time with several problem students with whom she has recently fallen in.*
PASSIVE	be forbidden	*It is essential that speaking other languages <u>be forbidden</u> in our English class.*

IDIOMS

heaven forbid	an expression used when one hopes that something bad will not happen *Heaven forbid he ever find out how much I really paid for these new shoes.*

* Note that the form "will be being forbidden" is rarely used. To convey a future progressive passive, use the present progressive passive.

get

	ACTIVE	PASSIVE
Infinitive	to get	to be gotten
Past Infinitive	to have gotten	to have been gotten
Past Participle	gotten	been gotten
Present Participle	getting	being gotten

ACTIVE

I
you/we/they
he/she/it

SIMPLE PRESENT	SIMPLE PAST	SIMPLE FUTURE
get	got	will get
get	got	will get
gets	got	will get

PRESENT PROGRESSIVE	PAST PROGRESSIVE	FUTURE PROGRESSIVE
am getting	was getting	will be getting
are getting	were getting	will be getting
is getting	was getting	will be getting

PRESENT PERFECT	PAST PERFECT	FUTURE PERFECT
have gotten	had gotten	will have gotten
have gotten	had gotten	will have gotten
has gotten	had gotten	will have gotten

PRESENT PERFECT PROGRESSIVE	PAST PERFECT PROGRESSIVE	FUTURE PERFECT PROGRESSIVE
have been getting	had been getting	will have been getting
have been getting	had been getting	will have been getting
has been getting	had been getting	will have been getting

EXAMPLES:

He gets his hair cut once a month. *I finally got a new job, but I haven't gotten my first paycheck yet.* *She was getting very good grades, which makes it hard to understand why she dropped out.*

PASSIVE

SIMPLE PRESENT	SIMPLE PAST	SIMPLE FUTURE
am gotten	was gotten	will be gotten
are gotten	were gotten	will be gotten
is gotten	was gotten	will be gotten

PRESENT PROGRESSIVE	PAST PROGRESSIVE	FUTURE PROGRESSIVE*
am being gotten	was being gotten	will be being gotten*
are being gotten	were being gotten	will be being gotten*
is being gotten	was being gotten	will be being gotten*

PRESENT PERFECT	PAST PERFECT	FUTURE PERFECT
have been gotten	had been gotten	will have been gotten
have been gotten	had been gotten	will have been gotten
has been gotten	had been gotten	will have been gotten

EXAMPLES:

I am not usually gotten up by bad weather, but the storm last night woke me up. *The prize will be gotten by the best dressed couple.*

PRINCIPAL CONDITIONALS

PRESENT	PRESENT PROGRESSIVE	PRESENT PASSIVE
would get	would be getting	would be gotten
would get	would be getting	would be gotten
would get	would be getting	would be gotten

PAST	PAST PROGRESSIVE	PAST PASSIVE
would have gotten	would have been getting	would have been gotten
would have gotten	would have been getting	would have been gotten
would have gotten	would have been getting	would have been gotten

EXAMPLES:

Cynthia would get a new car if she had enough money. *Lotsa Luck would have gotten first prize if the other horse hadn't run into him.* *Sam would be getting a much better salary if he moved to New York.*

Important Forms in Use

IF/THEN CONDITIONALS

	IF ...	... THEN	EXAMPLE
Real Present/ Future	get/gets	simple present	*If I get cold, I put on a sweater.*
		will + base form	*If mom gets tired, she won't take us to the movies.*
Unreal Present/ Future	got	would + base form	*If we got a deal on the car, we would buy it.*
Unreal Past	had gotten	would have + past participle	*If you had gotten here earlier, you would have seen the play.*

SUBJUNCTIVE

ACTIVE	get	*It is suggested that the divers get their own equipment.*
PASSIVE	be gotten	*It is essential that approval be gotten before we begin the work.*

PHRASAL VERBS

get (something) across
to make something clear
He got his idea across after explaining it several times.

get around to (something)
to do something after a delay
I haven't been able to get around to cleaning the office because I've been so busy.

get back at (someone)
to do something bad to someone who has done something bad to you
Sarah wanted to get back at me when I got the position instead of her.

get by
to manage to survive with the minimum
Mark's family didn't have a lot of money, but they always got by.

get over (something)
to recover
Luckily, Sally got over her cold before the filming began.

get through (something)
to complete a task
I know we've been working on this for hours, but let's try to get through this before we leave for the day.

IDIOMS

to get it
to understand
Frank got it when I told him I didn't want him banging around anymore.

to get (someone) nowhere
to have little or no success
These negotiations are getting us nowhere.

to get on the stick
to work hard
He'll have to get on the stick if he expects to finish by Friday.

to get into trouble
to do something to cause problems for yourself
He got into trouble for throwing the baseball through the neighbor's window.

RELATED WORDS

getaway (n.)
a short trip, or the escape of a criminal

get-together (n.)
a small informal gathering of friends

---

* Note that the form "will be being gotten" is rarely used. To convey a future progressive passive, use the present progressive passive.

Verb Chart

give

	ACTIVE	PASSIVE
Infinitive	to give	to be given
Past Infinitive	have given	have been given
Past Participle	given	been given
Present Participle	giving	being given

ACTIVE

SIMPLE PRESENT	**SIMPLE PAST**	**SIMPLE FUTURE**
give	gave	will give
give	gave	will give
gives	gave	will give
PRESENT PROGRESSIVE	**PAST PROGRESSIVE**	**FUTURE PROGRESSIVE**
am giving	was giving	will be giving
are giving	were giving	will be giving
is giving	was giving	will be giving
PRESENT PERFECT	**PAST PERFECT**	**FUTURE PERFECT**
have given	had given	will have given
have given	had given	will have given
has given	had given	will have given
PRESENT PERFECT PROGRESSIVE	**PAST PERFECT PROGRESSIVE**	**FUTURE PERFECT PROGRESSIVE**
have been giving	had been giving	will have been giving
have been giving	had been giving	will have been giving
has been giving	had been giving	will have been giving

I
you/we/they
he/she/it

EXAMPLES:

We usually give money to the public radio station.

She has been given an award for her documentary about immigrants in New York.

The Women's Alliance will be giving a luncheon and everyone is welcome.

PASSIVE

SIMPLE PRESENT	**SIMPLE PAST**	**SIMPLE FUTURE**
am given	was given	will be given
are given	were given	will be given
is given	was given	will be given
PRESENT PROGRESSIVE	**PAST PROGRESSIVE**	**FUTURE PROGRESSIVE***
am being given	was being given	will be being given*
are being given	were being given	will be being given*
is being given	was being given	will be being given*
PRESENT PERFECT	**PAST PERFECT**	**FUTURE PERFECT**
have been given	had been given	will have been given
have been given	had been given	will have been given
has been given	had been given	will have been given

EXAMPLES:

The children are given too many gifts at Christmas time.

When I got home, my brother was being given a talking-to by my dad.

I think Suzanne will be given the position when the vice president steps down.

PRINCIPAL CONDITIONALS

PRESENT	**PRESENT PROGRESSIVE**	**PRESENT PASSIVE**
would give	would be giving	would be given
would give	would be giving	would be given
would give	would be giving	would be given
PAST	**PAST PROGRESSIVE**	**PAST PASSIVE**
would have given	would have been giving	would have been given
would have given	would have been giving	would have been given
would have given	would have been giving	would have been given

EXAMPLES:

We would have given her a gift if we had known it was her birthday.

The event would have been given during the daytime if the space had been available.

give

Important Forms in Use

IF/THEN CONDITIONALS

	IF...	...THEN	EXAMPLE
Real Present/ Future	give/gives	simple present	*If you give her money freely, she doesn't understand its value.*
		will + base form	*If you give me some money, I'll pick up your dry cleaning for you.*
Unreal Present/ Future	gave	would + base form	*If they gave you a raise, would you stay at your current job?*
Unreal Past	had given	would have + past participle	*If the clerk had given me some more attention, I wouldn't have been so angry.*

SUBJUNCTIVE

ACTIVE	give	*We recommend that you give a tip to your guide.*
PASSIVE	be given	*We propose that a toast be given in the name of the organizer.*

PHRASAL VERBS

give (something) away	to make a gift of something *I never watch television, so I gave mine away.*
give (something) back	to return something that was borrowed *Joe refuses to lend out CDs because people never give them back.*
give out	to stop functioning *Just as we were about to finish mowing the lawn, the lawn mower gave out.*
give in	to accept something or to do something after resisting it *Mr. and Ms. Gonzalez didn't want to move, but they finally gave in after their daughter's entreaties.*
give up	to stop trying *We spent hours trying to find the solution the math problem, but we finally gave up.*
give (something) up	to relinquish *We weren't in a position to raise a child, so we gave the baby up for adoption.*

IDIOMS

something has to give	said when one feels that a difficult situation must decrease in difficulty *It's 110 degrees out and it hasn't rained in three weeks. Something has to give.*
to give something a shot/a go	to try something to see if it works or if you can do it *I'm not very good at playing the piano, but I'll give it a shot.*

RELATED WORDS

giveaway (n.)	something that can be taken for free
(dead) giveaway (n.)	information that exposes someone or something for what he, she, or it really is
give-and-take (n.)	compromise

* Note that the form "will be being given" is rarely used. To convey a future progressive passive, use the present progressive passive.

go

	ACTIVE	PASSIVE
Infinitive	to go	to be gone
Past Infinitive	to have gone	to have been gone
Past Participle	gone	been gone
Present Participle	going	being gone

ACTIVE

I	you/we/they	he/she/it

SIMPLE PRESENT	SIMPLE PAST	SIMPLE FUTURE
go	went	will go
go	went	will go
goes	went	will go

PRESENT PROGRESSIVE	PAST PROGRESSIVE	FUTURE PROGRESSIVE
am going	was going	will be going
are going	were going	will be going
is going	was going	will be going

PRESENT PERFECT	PAST PERFECT	FUTURE PERFECT
have gone	had gone	will have gone
have gone	had gone	will have gone
has gone	had gone	will have gone

PRESENT PERFECT PROGRESSIVE	PAST PERFECT PROGRESSIVE	FUTURE PERFECT PROGRESSIVE
have been going	had been going	will have been going
have been going	had been going	will have been going
has been going	had been going	will have been going

EXAMPLES:
I'm going to work and I'll be home at 8:00. *They hadn't gone far before they realized that they hadn't locked the door.* *This car will have been going for twenty years by the time I buy a new one.*

PASSIVE

SIMPLE PRESENT	SIMPLE PAST	SIMPLE FUTURE
am gone	was gone	will be gone
are gone	were gone	will be gone
is gone	was gone	will be gone

PRESENT PROGRESSIVE	PAST PROGRESSIVE	FUTURE PROGRESSIVE*
am being gone	was being gone	will be being gone*
are being gone	were being gone	will be being gone*
is being gone	was being gone	will be being gone*

PRESENT PERFECT	PAST PERFECT	FUTURE PERFECT
have been gone	had been gone	will have been gone
have been gone	had been gone	will have been gone
has been gone	had been gone	will have been gone

EXAMPLES:
Her work was gone over many times before they found any mistakes. *The plan is being gone along with by the committee members.*

PRINCIPAL CONDITIONALS

PRESENT	PRESENT PROGRESSIVE	PRESENT PASSIVE
would go	would be going	would be gone
would go	would be going	would be gone
would go	would be going	would be gone

PAST	PAST PROGRESSIVE	PAST PASSIVE
would have gone	would have been going	would have been gone
would have gone	would have been going	would have been gone
would have gone	would have been going	would have been gone

EXAMPLES:
I would go to the party if I knew you were going to be there. *We would have gone to the concert, but we had another obligation.*

Important Forms in Use

IF/THEN CONDITIONALS

	IF ...	...THEN	EXAMPLE
Real Present/ Future	go/goes	simple present	*If he goes early, he has a better chance of catching them.*
		will + base form	*If Don goes to church, he will expect us to go with him.*
Unreal Present/ Future	went	would + base form	*If Anne went with you, she could help you carry the groceries.*
Unreal Past	had gone	would have + past participle	*If I had gone to the gym more often, I wouldn't have had the skiing accident.*

SUBJUNCTIVE

ACTIVE	go	*It is expected that all students go to the assembly.*
PASSIVE	be gone	*I urge that the papers be gone over once again before they are handed in to the judge.*

PHRASAL VERBS

go along with	to be willing to agree to something or with someone even if you may have another idea or opinion *My colleague went along with my suggestion, even though she didn't completely agree.*
go away	to disappear, to leave *I was allergic to cats when I was young, but my allergy went away as I got older.*
go for (something)	to attempt to get something *Harold is going for the job at the Boston Globe.*
go in for (something)	to be interested in or appreciate something *My girlfriend had never gone in for foreign movies before, but we watch them all the time now.*
go off	to ring, especially an alarm or a timer; to explode *Can you turn off the oven when the timer goes off? / The bomb went off in a deserted building, so no one was hurt in the explosion.*
go on	to keep talking, to continue *I'm sorry, I didn't mean to interrupt. Please, go on.*
go out (with) (someone)	to be involved romantically with someone *How long have Mary and Tom been going out?*
go over (something)	to carefully review something *Can you go over this scene with me again before I go on stage?*

IDIOMS

what goes around comes around	said when something negative happens to suggest that something positive will follow, or when you've done something positive, to suggest that something positive will also happen to you *He's been playing tricks on me forever. What goes around comes around!*
to be on the go	to be very busy *I would like to read more, but ever since I started working on Wall Street, I'm constantly on the go.*
to go for it	to not hesitate to do something *If you're interested in that job, you should go for it.*

RELATED WORDS

go-getter (n.)	someone who is constantly working to achieve more
goings-on (n.)	an interesting event or occasion
go-ahead (n.)	permission to do something

* Note that the form "will be being gone" is rarely used. To convey a future progressive passive, use the present progressive passive.

Verb Chart

grow

	ACTIVE	PASSIVE
Infinitive	to grow	to be grown
Past Infinitive	to have grown	to have been grown
Past Participle	grown	been grown
Present Participle	growing	being grown

ACTIVE

I		
you/we/they		
he/she/it		

SIMPLE PRESENT	SIMPLE PAST	SIMPLE FUTURE
grow	grew	will grow
grow	grew	will grow
grows	grew	will grow

PRESENT PROGRESSIVE	PAST PROGRESSIVE	FUTURE PROGRESSIVE
am growing	was growing	will be growing
are growing	were growing	will be growing
is growing	was growing	will be growing

PRESENT PERFECT	PAST PERFECT	FUTURE PERFECT
have grown	had grown	will have grown
have grown	had grown	will have grown
has grown	had grown	will have grown

PRESENT PERFECT PROGRESSIVE	PAST PERFECT PROGRESSIVE	FUTURE PERFECT PROGRESSIVE
have been growing	had been growing	will have been growing
have been growing	had been growing	will have been growing
has been growing	had been growing	will have been growing

EXAMPLES:
What kinds of fruits and vegetables grow in this climate? | *Your kids have grown so much since I last saw them, I hardly recognize them.* | *This year we will be growing only strawberries, blueberries, and raspberries.*

PASSIVE

SIMPLE PRESENT	SIMPLE PAST	SIMPLE FUTURE
am grown	was grown	will be grown
are grown	were grown	will be grown
is grown	was grown	will be grown

PRESENT PROGRESSIVE	PAST PROGRESSIVE	FUTURE PROGRESSIVE*
am being grown	was being grown	will be being grown*
are being grown	were being grown	will be being grown*
is being grown	was being grown	will be being grown*

PRESENT PERFECT	PAST PERFECT	FUTURE PERFECT
have been grown	had been grown	will have been grown
have been grown	had been grown	will have been grown
has been grown	had been grown	will have been grown

EXAMPLES:
Harry was grown up by the age of twelve. | *Grasses and small bushes are being grown to mark the division between our property and theirs.*

PRINCIPAL CONDITIONALS

PRESENT	PRESENT PROGRESSIVE	PRESENT PASSIVE
would grow	would be growing	would be grown
would grow	would be growing	would be grown
would grow	would be growing	would be grown

PAST	PAST PROGRESSIVE	PAST PASSIVE
would have grown	would have been growing	would have been grown
would have grown	would have been growing	would have been grown
would have grown	would have been growing	would have been grown

EXAMPLES:
I didn't know you would be growing corn this year. | *They would have grown up in Wisconsin if their mother hadn't gotten a job in Chicago.*

grow

PRINCIPAL PARTS: grow, grew, grown

Important Forms in Use

IF/THEN CONDITIONALS

	IF ...	... THEN	EXAMPLE
Real Present/ Future	grow/grows	simple present	*If the day <u>grows</u> cloudy, we usually move indoors.*
		will + base form	*If we <u>grow</u> enough of them, we will give you a bushel of peaches.*
Unreal Present/ Future	grew	would + base form	*If he <u>grew</u> another two inches, he would play on the basketball team this year.*
Unreal Past	had grown	would have + past participle	*If I <u>had grown</u> up with my grandparents, I would have spoken German.*

SUBJUNCTIVE

ACTIVE	grow	*We insist that the actor <u>grow</u> his hair long for the part.*
PASSIVE	be grown	*It is essential that plants <u>be grown</u> in fertile soil.*

PHRASAL VERBS

grow apart	to develop a distance between two people or things *We were very close as children, but over the years we've grown apart.*
grow on (someone)	to begin to become appealing or tolerable to someone *I didn't like Ely when I met him, but he's grown on me.*
grow out of (something)	to become too big for something *My kids grow out of their clothes so quickly that I am constantly buying them new sizes.*
grow up	to develop from a child to an adult *After the death of his father, Abe grew up quickly.*

IDIOMS

to grow like a weed	to grow very quickly *The boys are growing like weeds!*
to grow close(r) to someone	to develop a strong(er) relationship *We have grown closer since I moved back to Chicago.*

RELATED WORDS

growing pains (n.)	difficulties that someone or something experiences as he, she, or it develops
grown-up (n.)	an adult
growth hormone (n.)	a hormone that controls growth
growth rate (n.)	how quickly something grows

---

* Note that the form "will be being grown" is rarely used. To convey a future progressive passive, use the present progressive passive.

hand

	ACTIVE	PASSIVE
Infinitive	to hand	to be handed
Past Infinitive	to have handed	to have been handed
Past Participle	handed	been handed
Present Participle	handing	being handed

ACTIVE

I
you/we/they
he/she/it

SIMPLE PRESENT	SIMPLE PAST	SIMPLE FUTURE
hand	handed	will hand
hand	handed	will hand
hands	handed	will hand

PRESENT PROGRESSIVE	PAST PROGRESSIVE	FUTURE PROGRESSIVE
am handing	was handing	will be handing
are handing	were handing	will be handing
is handing	was handing	will be handing

PRESENT PERFECT	PAST PERFECT	FUTURE PERFECT
have handed	had handed	will have handed
have handed	had handed	will have handed
has handed	had handed	will have handed

PRESENT PERFECT PROGRESSIVE	PAST PERFECT PROGRESSIVE	FUTURE PERFECT PROGRESSIVE
have been handing	had been handing	will have been handing
have been handing	had been handing	will have been handing
has been handing	had been handing	will have been handing

EXAMPLES:
Hand me the sugar, would you? *They are handing out brochures for the new ceramics school.* *Anna will have handed all of her papers in on Friday and will be ready to celebrate.*

PASSIVE

SIMPLE PRESENT	SIMPLE PAST	SIMPLE FUTURE
am handed	was handed	will be handed
are handed	were handed	will be handed
is handed	was handed	will be handed

PRESENT PROGRESSIVE	PAST PROGRESSIVE	FUTURE PROGRESSIVE*
am being handed	was being handed	will be being handed*
are being handed	were being handed	will be being handed*
is being handed	was being handed	will be being handed*

PRESENT PERFECT	PAST PERFECT	FUTURE PERFECT
have been handed	had been handed	will have been handed
have been handed	had been handed	will have been handed
has been handed	had been handed	will have been handed

EXAMPLES:
He was handed a warrant for his arrest. *How many newspapers have been handed out so far?* *The keys for the apartment were being handed over this morning at 10:00.*

PRINCIPAL CONDITIONALS

PRESENT	PRESENT PROGRESSIVE	PRESENT PASSIVE
would hand	would be handing	would be handed
would hand	would be handing	would be handed
would hand	would be handing	would be handed

PAST	PAST PROGRESSIVE	PAST PASSIVE
would have handed	would have been handing	would have been handed
would have handed	would have been handing	would have been handed
would have handed	would have been handing	would have been handed

EXAMPLES:
I would have handed you a napkin if you had asked. *The dress would have been handed down to you if it had been in decent condition.*

Important Forms in Use

IF/THEN CONDITIONALS

	IF ...	... THEN	EXAMPLE
Real Present/ Future	hand/hands	simple present	*If she <u>hands</u> me an important document, I make sure it is filed properly.*
		will + base form	*If I <u>hand</u> you the clean sheets, will you get up on the stool and put them in the closet?*
Unreal Present/ Future	handed	would + base form	*If we <u>handed</u> out samples, we'd get some new customers.*
Unreal Past	had handed	would have + past participle	*If I <u>had handed</u> in the paper on time, I wouldn't have been marked down.*

SUBJUNCTIVE

ACTIVE	hand	*The director insists that the reporter <u>hand</u> in the article immediately.*
PASSIVE	be handed	*The police request that any important evidence <u>be handed</u> over to them at our earliest convenience.*

PHRASAL VERBS

hand (something) down	to give an official decision, such as one made by a court or another ruling body *When they handed down the guilty verdict, the defendant began to cry.*
hand (something) in	to give paperwork or an assignment to someone who asks for it *You have to hand in a police report and several other documents before they will give you a visa.*
hand (something) out	to distribute *The teacher handed out the tests when everybody had been seated.*
hand (someone or something) over	to turn someone or something over to someone else who will take responsibility for him, her, or it *Brad handed the keys over to his wife when he decided to have a beer.*

IDIOMS

to hand it to (someone)	to give someone credit for something *I've got to hand it to you. Without your help, I wouldn't have been able to finish editing the film.*

RELATED WORDS

hand-me-down (n.)	something that is given to someone else after the original owner no longer has use for it
handout (n.)	something that is given out, such as a paper given out by a teacher

* Note that the form "will be being handed" is rarely used. To convey a future progressive passive, use the present progressive passive.

Verb Chart

hang

	ACTIVE	PASSIVE
Infinitive	to hang	to be hung
Past Infinitive	to have hung	to have been hung
Past Participle	hung	been hung
Present Participle	hanging	being hung

ACTIVE

I
you/we/they
he/she/it

SIMPLE PRESENT
hang
hang
hangs

SIMPLE PAST
hung
hung
hung

SIMPLE FUTURE
will hang
will hang
will hang

PRESENT PROGRESSIVE
am hanging
are hanging
is hanging

PAST PROGRESSIVE
was hanging
were hanging
was hanging

FUTURE PROGRESSIVE
will be hanging
will be hanging
will be hanging

PRESENT PERFECT
have hung
have hung
has hung

PAST PERFECT
had hung
had hung
had hung

FUTURE PERFECT
will have hung
will have hung
will have hung

PRESENT PERFECT PROGRESSIVE
have been hanging
have been hanging
has been hanging

PAST PERFECT PROGRESSIVE
had been hanging
had been hanging
had been hanging

FUTURE PERFECT PROGRESSIVE
will have been hanging
will have been hanging
will have been hanging

EXAMPLES:

The kids hung around until Ben had finished eating dinner.

The keys are hanging on the rack by the door.

That portrait of my family will have been hanging on the same wall for twenty years when we sell our house next year.

PASSIVE

SIMPLE PRESENT
am hung
are hung
is hung

SIMPLE PAST
was hung
were hung
was hung

SIMPLE FUTURE
will be hung
will be hung
will be hung

PRESENT PROGRESSIVE
am being hung
are being hung
is being hung

PAST PROGRESSIVE
was being hung
were being hung
was being hung

FUTURE PROGRESSIVE*
will be being hung*
will be being hung*
will be being hung*

PRESENT PERFECT
have been hung
have been hung
has been hung

PAST PERFECT
had been hung
had been hung
had been hung

FUTURE PERFECT
will have been hung
will have been hung
will have been hung

EXAMPLES:

Only towels and bathing suits are hung from the racks in the shower.

The sign for the restaurant was being hung while we were having dinner.

How many posters will have been hung by the time the party begins?

PRINCIPAL CONDITIONALS

PRESENT
would hang
would hang
would hang

PRESENT PROGRESSIVE
would be hanging
would be hanging
would be hanging

PRESENT PASSIVE
would be hung
would be hung
would be hung

PAST
would have hung
would have hung
would have hung

PAST PROGRESSIVE
would have been hanging
would have been hanging
would have been hanging

PAST PASSIVE
would have been hung
would have been hung
would have been hung

EXAMPLES:

We wouldn't have been hanging around the back door of the theater, except that we thought the actors would come out.

We would have hung the tapestry up if we had known where you wanted it.

hang

Important Forms in Use

IF/THEN CONDITIONALS

	IF . . .	. . . THEN	EXAMPLE
Real Present/ Future	hang/hangs	simple present	*If I hang the clothes out in the morning, they are dry by the afternoon.*
		will + base form	*If she hangs on tightly, she won't fall off.*
Unreal Present/ Future	hung	would + base form	*If we hung the coats in the back closet, we would have a lot more room in the front closet.*
Unreal Past	had hung	would have + past participle	*If we had hung in there instead of selling those stocks, we would have made a lot of money.*

SUBJUNCTIVE

ACTIVE	hang	*The principal insisted that teachers hang students' grades on the classroom door.*
PASSIVE	be hung	*We ask that all wet clothes be hung on the drying racks outside.*

PHRASAL VERBS

hang on	to hold on tightly; to wait *Hang on! The bus is going around a corner. / Hang on! I need to tie my shoelace.*
hang out	to spend time not doing any focused activity *A lot of high school students like to hang out in the recreational center after school.*
hang together	to stay together, especially during difficult times *If we kids hadn't hung together after Dad's death, I don't think we would have made it.*
hang up (something)	to put something on a hanger (clothes) or a wall (decorations) *Hang up your dress shirt so it doesn't get wrinkled.*
hang up on (someone)	to end a phone call abruptly without saying good-bye *I know that Mena didn't like my suggestion, but that's no excuse for hanging up on me.*

IDIOMS

to get the hang of something	to begin to feel comfortable doing something *After a few lessons, I got the hang of sailing the small boat.*
to hang in there	to persevere, especially through a difficult time *It seemed the school year would never end, but I knew if we hung in there, we would all be celebrating at graduation.*
to hang on someone's every word	to listen attentively to what someone says *Sylvia was so in love with her history professor that she hung on his every word.*
to hang up one's hat	to retire *After his most difficult case, the lawyer decided to hang up his hat.*

RELATED WORDS

hangover (n.)	an ill feeling, usually a headache and nausea, that occurs the day after drinking too much alcohol
hang-up (n.)	a fear or similar discomfort that prevents someone from doing something
hanger (n.)	a triangular device with a hook on top used to hold clothes

* Note that the form "will be being hung" is rarely used. To convey a future progressive passive, use the present progressive passive.

** Please note that this conjugation refers to hanging things. When using the verb "to hang" in reference to people, it is conjugated using Verb Chart 1.

Verb Chart

have

	ACTIVE	PASSIVE
Infinitive	to have	to be had
Past Infinitive	to have had	to have been had
Past Participle	had	been had
Present Participle	having	being had

ACTIVE

I		
you/we/they		
he/she/it		

SIMPLE PRESENT	SIMPLE PAST	SIMPLE FUTURE
have	had	will have
have	had	will have
has	had	will have

PRESENT PROGRESSIVE	PAST PROGRESSIVE	FUTURE PROGRESSIVE
am having	was having	will be having
are having	were having	will be having
is having	was having	will be having

PRESENT PERFECT	PAST PERFECT	FUTURE PERFECT
have had	had had	will have had
have had	had had	will have had
has had	had had	will have had

PRESENT PERFECT PROGRESSIVE	PAST PERFECT PROGRESSIVE	FUTURE PERFECT PROGRESSIVE
have been having	had been having	will have been having
have been having	had been having	will have been having
has been having	had been having	will have been having

EXAMPLES:
She has a car, but she doesn't have insurance yet. *I've had some doubts about the new schedule.* *Will you be having dinner, or just drinks?*

PASSIVE

SIMPLE PRESENT	SIMPLE PAST	SIMPLE FUTURE
am had	was had	will be had
are had	were had	will be had
is had	was had	will be had

PRESENT PROGRESSIVE	PAST PROGRESSIVE	FUTURE PROGRESSIVE*
am being had	was being had	will be being had*
are being had	were being had	will be being had*
is being had	was being had	will be being had*

PRESENT PERFECT	PAST PERFECT	FUTURE PERFECT
have been had	had been had	will have been had
have been had	had been had	will have been had
has been had	had been had	will have been had

EXAMPLES:
The party went well, and a good time was had by all. *This must be a joke; I'm being had.*

PRINCIPAL CONDITIONALS

PRESENT	PRESENT PROGRESSIVE	PRESENT PASSIVE
would have	would be having	would be had
would have	would be having	would be had
would have	would be having	would be had

PAST	PAST PROGRESSIVE	PAST PASSIVE
would have had	would have been having	would have been had
would have had	would have been having	would have been had
would have had	would have been having	would have been had

EXAMPLES:
I would have lunch with you, but I have a meeting with my boss. *She would have had a copy of the book if her student hadn't borrowed it.* *The girls would be having a good time at camp if it weren't so hot.*

have

PRINCIPAL PARTS: have, had, had

VERB CHART
50

Important Forms in Use

IF/THEN CONDITIONALS

	IF ...	... THEN	EXAMPLE
Real Present/ Future	have/has	simple present	If I _have_ time in the afternoons, I take a walk in the park.
		will + base form	If she _has_ pneumonia, they'll keep her in the hospital.
Unreal Present/ Future	had	would + base form	If I _had_ enough money, I would lend you some.
Unreal Past	had had	would have + past participle	If you _hadn't had_ that last piece of cake, you wouldn't feel so ill right now.

SUBJUNCTIVE

ACTIVE	have	We recommend that the candidates _have_ the proper training.
PASSIVE	be had	I would suggest that this wine _be had_ with fish, not beef.

PHRASAL VERBS

have (something) out   to remove something
He had his tooth out after it had been bothering him for a few days.

IDIOMS

to have had it	to have no tolerance for something or someone anymore *I have had it with your attitude!*
to have something against someone/something	to have a negative attitude toward someone or something *What do you have against dogs? They're lovely animals!*
to have a good/bad time	to enjoy oneself/not enjoy oneself *The kids had a good time at the party last night.*
to have time	to be able to do something because your schedule permits it *We wanted to go to the concert but we didn't have time.*
to have it in you	to have the energy to do something *I would like to join you for a movie this evening, but I don't have it in me.*

RELATED WORDS

have-nots (n.)	people who often live without enough to live comfortably
haves (n.)	people who live well

---

* Note that the form "will be being had" is rarely used. To convey a future progressive passive, use the present progressive passive.

Verb Chart

133

head

	ACTIVE	PASSIVE
Infinitive	to head	to be headed
Past Infinitive	to have headed	to have been headed
Past Participle	headed	been headed
Present Participle	heading	being headed

ACTIVE

I		
you/we/they		
he/she/it		

SIMPLE PRESENT	SIMPLE PAST	SIMPLE FUTURE
head	headed	will head
head	headed	will head
heads	headed	will head

PRESENT PROGRESSIVE	PAST PROGRESSIVE	FUTURE PROGRESSIVE
am heading	was heading	will be heading
are heading	were heading	will be heading
is heading	was heading	will be heading

PRESENT PERFECT	PAST PERFECT	FUTURE PERFECT
have headed	had headed	will have headed
have headed	had headed	will have headed
has headed	had headed	will have headed

PRESENT PERFECT PROGRESSIVE	PAST PERFECT PROGRESSIVE	FUTURE PERFECT PROGRESSIVE
have been heading	had been heading	will have been heading
have been heading	had been heading	will have been heading
has been heading	had been heading	will have been heading

EXAMPLES:

The man who heads up our department is an old friend from high school.

If he continues on that track, he's heading for trouble.

We had been heading in the wrong direction for hours and had to turn around and retrace our steps.

PASSIVE

SIMPLE PRESENT	SIMPLE PAST	SIMPLE FUTURE
am headed	was headed	will be headed
are headed	were headed	will be headed
is headed	was headed	will be headed

PRESENT PROGRESSIVE	PAST PROGRESSIVE	FUTURE PROGRESSIVE*
am being headed	was being headed	will be being headed*
are being headed	were being headed	will be being headed*
is being headed	was being headed	will be being headed*

PRESENT PERFECT	PAST PERFECT	FUTURE PERFECT
have been headed	had been headed	will have been headed
have been headed	had been headed	will have been headed
has been headed	had been headed	will have been headed

EXAMPLES:

The advertising campaign was being headed by a new hire in the company.

Our department had been headed up for years by a very competent director.

PRINCIPAL CONDITIONALS

PRESENT	PRESENT PROGRESSIVE	PRESENT PASSIVE
would head	would be heading	would be headed
would head	would be heading	would be headed
would head	would be heading	would be headed

PAST	PAST PROGRESSIVE	PAST PASSIVE
would have headed	would have been heading	would have been headed
would have headed	would have been heading	would have been headed
would have headed	would have been heading	would have been headed

EXAMPLES:

Matthew would be heading in our direction if it weren't for the terrible weather.

The parade would have been headed by our float if we had finished it on time.

head

Important Forms in Use

IF/THEN CONDITIONALS

	IF . . .	. . . THEN	EXAMPLE
Real Present/ Future	head/heads	simple present will + base form	*If he <u>heads</u> the excursion, we always get lost.* *If we <u>head</u> to the north, we'll be able to see the moon.*
Unreal Present/ Future	headed	would + base form	*If we <u>headed</u> here more often, we'd get out into nature on a more regular basis.*
Unreal Past	had headed	would have + past participle	*If Bill and Hillary <u>had headed</u> for the beach this morning, they would have gotten in a good swim before it began to rain.*

SUBJUNCTIVE

ACTIVE	head	*It is important that the campers <u>head</u> in the direction of the lake.*
PASSIVE	be headed	*We ask that their outing <u>be headed</u> by someone with outdoor skills.*

PHRASAL VERBS

head back	to move in the direction that you came from, or back to where you came from *Sorry you won't be able to spend much time with Cody and Tim. They're heading back to California in the morning.*
head for	to go in the direction of something *They were heading for the cabin when the blizzard struck.*
head off	to leave and go in the direction of another place *I'm sorry to leave so soon, but I'm heading off to visit my parents tonight, and I've got to catch a plane.*
head out	to leave *We've got to head out, or we'll miss our train.*

IDIOMS

to be heading in the right direction	to be working on something and feel that your actions are taking you where you want to go *I believe that the negotiations are heading in the right direction.*
to be heading/headed for trouble	to be taking actions that will lead you to problems *The counselor could tell immediately that the boy was heading for trouble.*
to head somebody off at the pass	to try to stop somebody from doing something that you don't approve of *This idea of traveling alone in Mexico doesn't please me. I hope we can head him off at the pass.*

RELATED WORDS

head-on collision (n.)	an accident in which the fronts of two vehicles hit
head start (n.)	when someone is given an advantage over others
headway (n.)	forward movement, progress

* Note that the form "will be being headed" is rarely used. To convey a future progressive passive, use the present progressive passive.

hear

	ACTIVE	PASSIVE
Infinitive	to hear	to be heard
Past Infinitive	to have heard	to have been heard
Past Participle	heard	been heard
Present Participle	hearing	being heard

ACTIVE

I		
you/we/they		
he/she/it		

SIMPLE PRESENT	SIMPLE PAST	SIMPLE FUTURE
hear	heard	will hear
hear	heard	will hear
hears	heard	will hear

PRESENT PROGRESSIVE	PAST PROGRESSIVE	FUTURE PROGRESSIVE
am hearing	was hearing	will be hearing
are hearing	were hearing	will be hearing
is hearing	was hearing	will be hearing

PRESENT PERFECT	PAST PERFECT	FUTURE PERFECT
have heard	had heard	will have heard
have heard	had heard	will have heard
has heard	had heard	will have heard

PRESENT PERFECT PROGRESSIVE	PAST PERFECT PROGRESSIVE	FUTURE PERFECT PROGRESSIVE
have been hearing	had been hearing	will have been hearing
have been hearing	had been hearing	will have been hearing
has been hearing	had been hearing	will have been hearing

EXAMPLES:
I hear what you're saying, but I don't agree with you. *You will be hearing the emergency warning system.* *I have been hearing strange noises in my house.*

PASSIVE

SIMPLE PRESENT	SIMPLE PAST	SIMPLE FUTURE
am heard	was heard	will be heard
are heard	were heard	will be heard
is heard	was heard	will be heard

PRESENT PROGRESSIVE	PAST PROGRESSIVE	FUTURE PROGRESSIVE*
am being heard	was being heard	will be being heard*
are being heard	were being heard	will be being heard*
is being heard	was being heard	will be being heard*

PRESENT PERFECT	PAST PERFECT	FUTURE PERFECT
have been heard	had been heard	will have been heard
have been heard	had been heard	will have been heard
has been heard	had been heard	will have been heard

EXAMPLES:
The concert was being heard by thousands of people over the radio. *Do you think what I'm saying will be heard by enough staff members to make a difference?*

PRINCIPAL CONDITIONALS

PRESENT	PRESENT PROGRESSIVE	PRESENT PASSIVE
would hear	would be hearing	would be heard
would hear	would be hearing	would be heard
would hear	would be hearing	would be heard

PAST	PAST PROGRESSIVE	PAST PASSIVE
would have heard	would have been hearing	would have been heard
would have heard	would have been hearing	would have been heard
would have heard	would have been hearing	would have been heard

EXAMPLES:
We would be hearing the lecture right now if it weren't for the interference on this station. *I didn't think the new recording would be heard until next week.*

hear

PRINCIPAL PARTS: hear, heard, heard

Important Forms in Use

IF/THEN CONDITIONALS

	IF ...	...THEN	EXAMPLE
Real Present/ Future	hear/hears	simple present	If I <u>hear</u> you correctly, you want me to stop working and help you with dinner.
		will + base form	If she <u>hears</u> me yelling, she'll turn around.
Unreal Present/ Future	heard	would + base form	If I <u>heard</u> you, I would answer you.
Unreal Past	had heard	would have + past participle	If we <u>had heard</u> the timer, our dinner wouldn't have burned.

SUBJUNCTIVE

ACTIVE	hear	It is vital that the judge <u>hear</u> both sides of the story.
PASSIVE	be heard	We ask that Danny's story <u>be heard</u> first.

PHRASAL VERBS

hear from (someone)	to receive news from someone *Have you heard from Phil lately?*
hear of (something)	to be familiar with something *I have never heard of that group, but I'd love to listen to their music.*
hear (someone) out	to listen to all of what someone has to say *Please hear me out before you make any comments or criticisms.*

IDIOMS

to hear something through the grapevine	to hear news or gossip from other people rather than directly from the source *I heard through the grapevine that Sal and Maureen are splitting up.*
to not hear of something	to consider something unacceptable *Tim said he would sleep on the couch in the living room, but I won't hear of it! We have an extra bed upstairs.*
you could hear a pin drop	an expression that means that it is very quiet, often after surprising or disturbing news has been given *When she announced her marriage to Jane's ex-husband, the room became so quiet that you could hear a pin drop.*
to be hard of hearing	to have difficulty hearing *My father got a hearing aid when he started to become hard of hearing.*

RELATED WORDS

hearing (n.)	the ability to hear sound
hearing aid (n.)	a device used to improve hearing
hearsay (n.)	repeating something that you've heard but that you aren't sure is true

* Note that the form "will be being heard" is rarely used. To convey a future progressive passive, use the present progressive passive.

help

	ACTIVE	PASSIVE
Infinitive	to help	to be helped
Past Infinitive	to have helped	to have been helped
Past Participle	helped	been helped
Present Participle	helping	being helped

ACTIVE

I		
you/we/they		
he/she/it		

SIMPLE PRESENT	SIMPLE PAST	SIMPLE FUTURE
help	helped	will help
help	helped	will help
helps	helped	will help

PRESENT PROGRESSIVE	PAST PROGRESSIVE	FUTURE PROGRESSIVE
am helping	was helping	will be helping
are helping	were helping	will be helping
is helping	was helping	will be helping

PRESENT PERFECT	PAST PERFECT	FUTURE PERFECT
have helped	had helped	will have helped
have helped	had helped	will have helped
has helped	had helped	will have helped

PRESENT PERFECT PROGRESSIVE	PAST PERFECT PROGRESSIVE	FUTURE PERFECT PROGRESSIVE
have been helping	had been helping	will have been helping
have been helping	had been helping	will have been helping
has been helping	had been helping	will have been helping

EXAMPLES:
We'll help out if you need us on your moving day.

Our company will have helped thousands of people find reasonably priced homes by our anniversary next year.

They had been helping themselves to the liquor in the cabinet for weeks before we realized it.

PASSIVE

SIMPLE PRESENT	SIMPLE PAST	SIMPLE FUTURE
am helped	was helped	will be helped
are helped	were helped	will be helped
is helped	was helped	will be helped

PRESENT PROGRESSIVE	PAST PROGRESSIVE	FUTURE PROGRESSIVE*
am being helped	was being helped	will be being helped*
are being helped	were being helped	will be being helped*
is being helped	was being helped	will be being helped*

PRESENT PERFECT	PAST PERFECT	FUTURE PERFECT
have been helped	had been helped	will have been helped
have been helped	had been helped	will have been helped
has been helped	had been helped	will have been helped

EXAMPLES:
Are you being helped?

I was helped by the clerk in the red dress.

We have never been helped so much before. Thanks a lot!

PRINCIPAL CONDITIONALS

PRESENT	PRESENT PROGRESSIVE	PRESENT PASSIVE
would help	would be helping	would be helped
would help	would be helping	would be helped
would help	would be helping	would be helped

PAST	PAST PROGRESSIVE	PAST PASSIVE
would have helped	would have been helping	would have been helped
would have helped	would have been helping	would have been helped
would have helped	would have been helping	would have been helped

EXAMPLES:
I would help them if they asked me

Harry and Sue would have helped with the dinner but they got caught up in traffic.

PRINCIPAL PARTS: help, helped, helped

Important Forms in Use

IF/THEN CONDITIONALS

	IF...	...THEN	EXAMPLE
Real Present/ Future	help/helps	simple present	If I _help_ him with his assignments, then he is happy to return the favor.
		will + base form	If she _helps_ him with his homework, he'll finish up on time.
Unreal Present/ Future	helped	would + base form	If you _helped_ us move our furniture, we would be eternally grateful.
Unreal Past	had helped	would have + past participle	If I _had helped_ him do his taxes, he probably wouldn't have been audited.

SUBJUNCTIVE

ACTIVE	help	It is important that we _help_ others.
PASSIVE	be helped	They suggested that the older patients _be helped_ first.

PHRASAL VERBS

help out   to assist
            Your kids are great! They always help out when they come to visit.

IDIOMS

to help yourself to something	to take what you need by yourself without waiting for someone to give it to you _Help yourself to a drink while I get the door._
something can't be helped	said when a situation or action is unavoidable _The president of the company didn't want to fire anyone, but it couldn't be helped._

RELATED WORDS

helping (n.)   one serving of food

* Note that the form "will be being helped" is rarely used. To convey a future progressive passive, use the present progressive passive.

Verb Chart

hide

	ACTIVE	PASSIVE
Infinitive	to hide	to be hidden
Past Infinitive	to have hidden	to have been hidden
Past Participle	hidden	been hidden
Present Participle	hiding	being hidden

ACTIVE

I		
you/we/they		
he/she/it		

SIMPLE PRESENT	SIMPLE PAST	SIMPLE FUTURE
hide	hid	will hide
hide	hid	will hide
hides	hid	will hide

PRESENT PROGRESSIVE	PAST PROGRESSIVE	FUTURE PROGRESSIVE
am hiding	was hiding	will be hiding
are hiding	were hiding	will be hiding
is hiding	was hiding	will be hiding

PRESENT PERFECT	PAST PERFECT	FUTURE PERFECT
have hidden	had hidden	will have hidden
have hidden	had hidden	will have hidden
has hidden	had hidden	will have hidden

PRESENT PERFECT PROGRESSIVE	PAST PERFECT PROGRESSIVE	FUTURE PERFECT PROGRESSIVE
have been hiding	had been hiding	will have been hiding
have been hiding	had been hiding	will have been hiding
has been hiding	had been hiding	will have been hiding

EXAMPLES:
I always hide a bottle of brandy in the kitchen. *The children hid behind the door when their mother got home.* *He had been hiding the truth from me for years.*

PASSIVE

SIMPLE PRESENT	SIMPLE PAST	SIMPLE FUTURE
am hidden	was hidden	will be hidden
are hidden	were hidden	will be hidden
is hidden	was hidden	will be hidden

PRESENT PROGRESSIVE	PAST PROGRESSIVE	FUTURE PROGRESSIVE*
am being hidden	was being hidden	will be being hidden*
are being hidden	were being hidden	will be being hidden*
is being hidden	was being hidden	will be being hidden*

PRESENT PERFECT	PAST PERFECT	FUTURE PERFECT
have been hidden	had been hidden	will have been hidden
have been hidden	had been hidden	will have been hidden
has been hidden	had been hidden	will have been hidden

EXAMPLES:
The money was hidden under her mattress. *The drugs had been hidden in the lining of his suitcase, but they were detected by the equipment.*

PRINCIPAL CONDITIONALS

PRESENT	PRESENT PROGRESSIVE	PRESENT PASSIVE
would hide	would be hiding	would be hidden
would hide	would be hiding	would be hidden
would hide	would be hiding	would be hidden

PAST	PAST PROGRESSIVE	PAST PASSIVE
would have hidden	would have been hiding	would have been hidden
would have hidden	would have been hiding	would have been hidden
would have hidden	would have been hiding	would have been hidden

EXAMPLES:
We would have hidden the documents more carefully if we had known.

hide

PRINCIPAL PARTS: hide, hid, hidden

Important Forms in Use

IF/THEN CONDITIONALS

	IF . . .	. . . THEN	EXAMPLE
Real Present/ Future	hide/hides	simple present	*If the government hides the facts, the public remains uniformed.*
		will + base form	*If she hides the money in the back of the closet, nobody will find it.*
Unreal Present/ Future	hid	would + base form	*If we hid out in the woods, the other kids wouldn't be able to find us.*
Unreal Past	had hidden	would have + past participle	*If I hadn't hidden your present so well, I would have been able to find it when I wanted to give it to you.*

SUBJUNCTIVE

ACTIVE	hide	*I recommend that we hide in the kitchen so that he is surprised when he comes.*
PASSIVE	be hidden	*It is essential the his gift be hidden well or he will find it before his birthday.*

IDIOMS

to have nothing to hide	to be completely open about your actions because you feel you have done nothing wrong *Ask me anything, because I have nothing to hide.*

RELATED WORDS

hide-and-seek (n.)	a children's game in which several children hide and one must find them
hidden agenda (n.)	an additional objective that has been concealed
hideaway (n.)	a place where you can escape from the everyday cares of life
hiding place (n.)	a place where you yourself can hide or where you can hide something
hideout (n.)	someplace where you cannot be found

* Note that the form "will be being hidden" is rarely used. To convey a future progressive passive, use the present progressive passive.

hit

	ACTIVE	PASSIVE
Infinitive	to hit	to be hit
Past Infinitive	to have hit	to have been hit
Past Participle	hit	been hit
Present Participle	hitting	being hit

ACTIVE

I
you/we/they
he/she/it

SIMPLE PRESENT	SIMPLE PAST	SIMPLE FUTURE
hit	hit	will hit
hit	hit	will hit
hits	hit	will hit

PRESENT PROGRESSIVE	PAST PROGRESSIVE	FUTURE PROGRESSIVE
am hitting	was hitting	will be hitting
are hitting	were hitting	will be hitting
is hitting	was hitting	will be hitting

PRESENT PERFECT	PAST PERFECT	FUTURE PERFECT
have hit	had hit	will have hit
have hit	had hit	will have hit
has hit	had hit	will have hit

PRESENT PERFECT PROGRESSIVE	PAST PERFECT PROGRESSIVE	FUTURE PERFECT PROGRESSIVE
have been hitting	had been hitting	will have been hitting
have been hitting	had been hitting	will have been hitting
has been hitting	had been hitting	will have been hitting

EXAMPLES:

The buyout of the family company hit them hard.

We've hit on a new plan for the renovation of the recreational center.

After practicing, the team members were hitting the ball more consistently.

PASSIVE

SIMPLE PRESENT	SIMPLE PAST	SIMPLE FUTURE
am hit	was hit	will be hit
are hit	were hit	will be hit
is hit	was hit	will be hit

PRESENT PROGRESSIVE	PAST PROGRESSIVE	FUTURE PROGRESSIVE*
am being hit	was being hit	will be being hit*
are being hit	were being hit	will be being hit*
is being hit	was being hit	will be being hit*

PRESENT PERFECT	PAST PERFECT	FUTURE PERFECT
have been hit	had been hit	will have been hit
have been hit	had been hit	will have been hit
has been hit	had been hit	will have been hit

EXAMPLES:

Her car was hit by an SUV that ran a stop sign.

She looked up just as the ball was being hit by the batter.

The entire area was hit by severe thunderstorms.

PRINCIPAL CONDITIONALS

PRESENT	PRESENT PROGRESSIVE	PRESENT PASSIVE
would hit	would be hitting	would be hit
would hit	would be hitting	would be hit
would hit	would be hitting	would be hit

PAST	PAST PROGRESSIVE	PAST PASSIVE
would have hit	would have been hitting	would have been hit
would have hit	would have been hitting	would have been hit
would have hit	would have been hitting	would have been hit

EXAMPLES:

Would you hit the play button so we can watch the movie?

Nobody predicted that the rookie baseball player would be hitting so many home runs this year.

Important Forms in Use

IF/THEN CONDITIONALS

	IF ...	... THEN	EXAMPLE
Real Present/ Future	hit/hits	simple present	*If he hits well during a game, the coach gives him a lot of encouragement.*
		will + base form	*If she hits me up for money one more time, I'll give her a piece of my mind.*
Unreal Present/ Future	hit	would + base form	*If she hit her child and we suspected it was a pattern, we'd alert child welfare.*
Unreal Past	had hit	would have + past participle	*If I had hit the jackpot, I would have treated you to dinner.*

SUBJUNCTIVE

ACTIVE	hit	*The coach recommended that the boy hit the ball farther down on the bat.*
PASSIVE	be hit	*It is essential that the target for donations be hit by the close of this quarter.*

PHRASAL VERBS

hit on (someone)	to flirt with someone (usually unreciprocated) *Some guy was hitting on me in the bar, so I left.*
hit (someone) up for (something)	to ask someone for something, usually money *How much did you hit him up for this time?*

IDIOMS

to hit the spot	to satisfy, to be exactly the right thing at the right moment *That glass of lemonade really hit the spot. It was exactly what I wanted.*
to hit the road	to begin a trip, to leave a place *We've got to hit the road if we want to be home before dark. / It's late. Let's hit the road.*
to hit the nail on the head	to make a correct analysis of something *I think you hit the nail on the head when you said he did it because he was feeling guilty.*
to hit the hay	to go to sleep *Sorry to interrupt the party, but I've got to hit the hay.*
to hit it big	to become very successful or rich *The musician went to New York hoping that he would hit it big.*
to hit the deck	to quickly drop to the floor or ground *They're shooting! Hit the deck!*

RELATED WORDS

hit or miss (adv.)	very uneven, not consistent
hit-and-run (adj.)	describes an accident in which the driver hits another car or a person and then leaves the scene of the accident without providing identification
hit man (n.)	a person who commits murders as a job, an assassin

* Note that the form "will be being hit" is rarely used. To convey a future progressive passive, use the present progressive passive.

hold

	ACTIVE	PASSIVE
Infinitive	to hold	to be held
Past Infinitive	to have held	to have been held
Past Participle	held	been held
Present Participle	holding	being held

ACTIVE

I
you/we/they
he/she/it

SIMPLE PRESENT	SIMPLE PAST	SIMPLE FUTURE
hold	held	will hold
hold	held	will hold
holds	held	will hold

PRESENT PROGRESSIVE	PAST PROGRESSIVE	FUTURE PROGRESSIVE
am holding	was holding	will be holding
are holding	were holding	will be holding
is holding	was holding	will be holding

PRESENT PERFECT	PAST PERFECT	FUTURE PERFECT
have held	had held	will have held
have held	had held	will have held
has held	had held	will have held

PRESENT PERFECT PROGRESSIVE	PAST PERFECT PROGRESSIVE	FUTURE PERFECT PROGRESSIVE
have been holding	had been holding	will have been holding
have been holding	had been holding	will have been holding
has been holding	had been holding	will have been holding

EXAMPLES:
The store has been holding the dress for me while I make up my mind.
Her daughter held her hand while they crossed the street.

PASSIVE

SIMPLE PRESENT	SIMPLE PAST	SIMPLE FUTURE
am held	was held	will be held
are held	were held	will be held
is held	was held	will be held

PRESENT PROGRESSIVE	PAST PROGRESSIVE	FUTURE PROGRESSIVE*
am being held	was being held	will be being held*
are being held	were being held	will be being held*
is being held	was being held	will be being held*

PRESENT PERFECT	PAST PERFECT	FUTURE PERFECT
have been held	had been held	will have been held
have been held	had been held	will have been held
has been held	had been held	will have been held

EXAMPLES:
They were held up by the rush hour traffic.
The baby was being held by his grandmother.

PRINCIPAL CONDITIONALS

PRESENT	PRESENT PROGRESSIVE	PRESENT PASSIVE
would hold	would be holding	would be held
would hold	would be holding	would be held
would hold	would be holding	would be held

PAST	PAST PROGRESSIVE	PAST PASSIVE
would have held	would have been holding	would have been held
would have held	would have been holding	would have been held
would have held	would have been holding	would have been held

EXAMPLES:
A larger container would hold more water.
I would have held out if I had known that you had made dinner.

hold

Important Forms in Use

IF/THEN CONDITIONALS

	IF...	...THEN	EXAMPLE
Real Present/ Future	hold/holds	simple present	*If I hold the mirror in a certain way, I can see into the next room.*
		will + base form	*If she holds him back any longer, he will resent her for it.*
Unreal Present/ Future	held	would + base form	*If we held the party next week, Jim wouldn't be able to come.*
Unreal Past	had held	would have + past participle	*If the traffic hadn't held me up, I would have been here hours ago.*

SUBJUNCTIVE

ACTIVE	hold	*The owner insists that we hold on to the furniture in the lounge.*
PASSIVE	be held	*The manager recommended that a meeting be held once a week.*

PHRASAL VERBS

hold (something) against (somebody)	to consider something that someone did a reason to treat him or her differently (usually with dislike) *Henrietta didn't invite me to her wedding and I still hold it against her.*
hold (someone or something) back	to keep someone or something from moving forward . *My son was held back in first grade even though he was supposed to move to the second grade. / He had really hurt me but I held back the tears.*
hold on to (something or someone)	to not let something or someone go *You should hold on to your mother's paintings. They could be valuable someday.*
hold out for	to wait until you have exactly what you want *She could've married any man but she was holding out for Mr. Perfect.*
hold (someone or something) up	to delay someone who is in the process of doing something or something that is in the process of being done; to raise *I'm sorry I'm late. I got held up by traffic. / Hold up your hand if you've ever been to China.*

IDIOMS

to hold a grudge	to remain angry at someone about something that he or she did *She's still holding a grudge about my not showing up for dinner a few weeks ago.*
to hold down the fort	to be in charge of a place, especially when those usually in charge have left temporarily *I've got to run out for milk. Can you hold down the fort?*
hold your horses	an expression said when you want someone to stop *Tom wanted to start on the painting job before we had cleaned the walls. "Hold your horses," I said.*
to hold one's own	to successfully do something with others who are more experienced *We weren't sure if she would be able to run with the advanced team, but she's holding her own.*

RELATED WORDS

holder (n.)	something that holds something else
holding pattern (n.)	a configuration of planes waiting to land at an airport, usually after some delay

---

* Note that the form "will be being held" is rarely used. To convey a future progressive passive, use the present progressive passive.

Verb Chart

jump

	ACTIVE	PASSIVE
Infinitive	to jump	to be jumped
Past Infinitive	to have jumped	to have been jumped
Past Participle	jumped	been jumped
Present Participle	jumping	being jumped

ACTIVE

I		
you/we/they		
he/she/it		

SIMPLE PRESENT	SIMPLE PAST	SIMPLE FUTURE
jump	jumped	will jump
jump	jumped	will jump
jumps	jumped	will jump

PRESENT PROGRESSIVE	PAST PROGRESSIVE	FUTURE PROGRESSIVE
am jumping	was jumping	will be jumping
are jumping	were jumping	will be jumping
is jumping	was jumping	will be jumping

PRESENT PERFECT	PAST PERFECT	FUTURE PERFECT
have jumped	had jumped	will have jumped
have jumped	had jumped	will have jumped
has jumped	had jumped	will have jumped

PRESENT PERFECT PROGRESSIVE	PAST PERFECT PROGRESSIVE	FUTURE PERFECT PROGRESSIVE
have been jumping	had been jumping	will have been jumping
have been jumping	had been jumping	will have been jumping
has been jumping	had been jumping	will have been jumping

EXAMPLES:

The horse easily jumped over the fence.

Whenever the boss asks her to do something, she jumps.

The birds have been jumping from tree to tree, which makes it harder to identify them.

PASSIVE

SIMPLE PRESENT	SIMPLE PAST	SIMPLE FUTURE
am jumped	was jumped	will be jumped
are jumped	were jumped	will be jumped
is jumped	was jumped	will be jumped

PRESENT PROGRESSIVE	PAST PROGRESSIVE	FUTURE PROGRESSIVE*
am being jumped	was being jumped	will be being jumped*
are being jumped	were being jumped	will be being jumped*
is being jumped	was being jumped	will be being jumped*

PRESENT PERFECT	PAST PERFECT	FUTURE PERFECT
have been jumped	had been jumped	will have been jumped
have been jumped	had been jumped	will have been jumped
has been jumped	had been jumped	will have been jumped

EXAMPLES:

How many hedges will be jumped before the horse completes the steeplechase?

They were jumped as they rounded the corner.

PRINCIPAL CONDITIONALS

PRESENT	PRESENT PROGRESSIVE	PRESENT PASSIVE
would jump	would be jumping	would be jumped
would jump	would be jumping	would be jumped
would jump	would be jumping	would be jumped

PAST	PAST PROGRESSIVE	PAST PASSIVE
would have jumped	would have been jumping	would have been jumped
would have jumped	would have been jumping	would have been jumped
would have jumped	would have been jumping	would have been jumped

EXAMPLES:

She would jump through hoops to make him happy.

The kids would have jumped off the diving board, but their mother didn't let them.

jump

PRINCIPAL PARTS: jump, jumped, jumped

VERB CHART
57

Important Forms in Use

IF/THEN CONDITIONALS

	IF . . .	. . . THEN	EXAMPLE
Real Present/ Future	jump/jumps	simple present	*If I __jump__ into the pool, I always get water in my nose.*
		will + base form	*If she __jumps__ far enough, she'll make the final rounds.*
Unreal Present/ Future	jumped	would + base form	*If the horse __jumped__ better during the practice rounds, it would make it to the finals.*
Unreal Past	had jumped	would have + past participle	*If you __had jumped__ on that idea, we would have been rich!*

SUBJUNCTIVE

ACTIVE	jump	*It is essential that we __jump__ on this deal soon if we don't want to lose an excellent opportunity.*
PASSIVE	be jumped	*We recommend that the offer __be jumped__ on before the close of today's trading.*

PHRASAL VERBS

jump in	to interrupt, or to get involved in a conversation
	If I can jump in for a moment, I have a few ideas on this topic also.
jump on (something)	to quickly act on something
	We need to jump on this opportunity while we still have the chance.
jump out at	to attract attention
	I didn't like the Picasso I saw, but Jackson Pollock's work at the Met jumped out at me.

IDIOMS

to jump to attention	to eagerly follow someone's orders
	When I asked those kids to clean up the campsite, they really jumped to attention.
to jump the gun	to do something too soon
	He jumped the gun when he asked her out on a date so soon after they had met.
to jump through hoops	to do whatever is necessary to get something that you want
	I felt sorry for Sam, seeing the way his company made him jump through hoops for that promotion.
to jump all over someone	to chastise
	Why do you always jump all over me for every little thing I do?

RELATED WORDS

jumping jacks (n.)	a type of exercise in which you move your feet out and in while moving your hands up and down
jumpy (adj.)	uneasy, nervous

---

* Note that the form "will be being jumped" is rarely used. To convey a future progressive passive, use the present progressive passive.

keep

	ACTIVE	PASSIVE
Infinitive	to keep	to be kept
Past Infinitive	to have kept	to have been kept
Past Participle	kept	been kept
Present Participle	keeping	being kept

ACTIVE

SIMPLE PRESENT	**SIMPLE PAST**	**SIMPLE FUTURE**
keep	kept	will keep
keep	kept	will keep
keeps	kept	will keep
PRESENT PROGRESSIVE	**PAST PROGRESSIVE**	**FUTURE PROGRESSIVE**
am keeping	was keeping	will be keeping
are keeping	were keeping	will be keeping
is keeping	was keeping	will be keeping
PRESENT PERFECT	**PAST PERFECT**	**FUTURE PERFECT**
have kept	had kept	will have kept
have kept	had kept	will have kept
has kept	had kept	will have kept
PRESENT PERFECT PROGRESSIVE	**PAST PERFECT PROGRESSIVE**	**FUTURE PERFECT PROGRESSIVE**
have been keeping	had been keeping	will have been keeping
have been keeping	had been keeping	will have been keeping
has been keeping	had been keeping	will have been keeping

I

you/we/they

he/she/it

EXAMPLES:

Can you keep a secret?

Are you keeping track of all the money we spend?

He had kept the ribbons all of his life by which to remember his mother.

PASSIVE

SIMPLE PRESENT	**SIMPLE PAST**	**SIMPLE FUTURE**
am kept	was kept	will be kept
are kept	were kept	will be kept
is kept	was kept	will be kept
PRESENT PROGRESSIVE	**PAST PROGRESSIVE**	**FUTURE PROGRESSIVE***
am being kept	was being kept	will be being kept*
are being kept	were being kept	will be being kept*
is being kept	was being kept	will be being kept*
PRESENT PERFECT	**PAST PERFECT**	**FUTURE PERFECT**
have been kept	had been kept	will have been kept
have been kept	had been kept	will have been kept
has been kept	had been kept	will have been kept

EXAMPLES:

She has been kept from finding a solution to the problem due to a lack of funding.

The gold bricks are being kept in the Federal Reserve.

Your money will kept in a safe-deposit box until you wish to pick it up.

PRINCIPAL CONDITIONALS

PRESENT	**PRESENT PROGRESSIVE**	**PRESENT PASSIVE**
would keep	would be keeping	would be kept
would keep	would be keeping	would be kept
would keep	would be keeping	would be kept
PAST	**PAST PROGRESSIVE**	**PAST PASSIVE**
would have kept	would have been keeping	would have been kept
would have kept	would have been keeping	would have been kept
would have kept	would have been keeping	would have been kept

EXAMPLES:

I'm sure she would keep your cat for you for just a week.

You wouldn't have kept up with me if the race had been last week.

keep

Important Forms in Use

IF/THEN CONDITIONALS

	IF ...	...THEN	EXAMPLE
Real Present/ Future	keep/keeps	simple present	*If he keeps up the good work, he gets a gold star.*
		will + base form	*If you keep her in sight, we won't lose her.*
Unreal Present/ Future	kept	would + base form	*If they kept in touch with us, we'd keep in touch with them.*
Unreal Past	had kept	would have + past participle	*If I had kept her as a friend, I would have been happier.*

SUBJUNCTIVE

ACTIVE	keep	*He suggests that you keep to your regular exercise schedule.*
PASSIVE	be kept	*It is essential that the cat and the dog be kept away from each other.*

PHRASAL VERBS

keep at (something)	to work hard on something without stopping *I thought he would give up dancing, but he kept at it for many years.*
keep (someone) away	to not allow people to come close to someone or something *You need to keep the children away from the fire!*
keep off (something)	to stay away from or avoid (usually indicates prohibition from standing on something) *Keep off the grass.*
keep on (doing something)	to continue *We know that learning a language can be difficult, but we want to encourage you to keep on studying.*
keep (someone or something) out	to prevent (someone or something) from entering *When I was a child, my parents kept me out of the attic.*
keep up	to maintain the same pace as others *It was hard, but I kept up with John during the marathon last year.*

IDIOMS

to keep a secret	to not tell anyone about something *Can you keep a secret?*
to keep in touch	to stay in contact *Let's keep in touch when you move to New Jersey.*
to keep someone posted	to inform someone if there are any changes in your life, a situation, etc. *I know you just started in your new job. You'll have to keep me posted as to how things are going.*

RELATED WORDS

keepsake (n.)	something that you keep to remind you of something or someone
keeper (n.)	something or someone worth keeping

Verb Chart

* Note that the form "will be being kept" is rarely used. To convey a future progressive passive, use the present progressive passive.

kick

	ACTIVE	PASSIVE
Infinitive	to kick	to be kicked
Past Infinitive	to have kicked	to have been kicked
Past Participle	kicked	been kicked
Present Participle	kicking	being kicked

ACTIVE

I		
you/we/they		
he/she/it		

SIMPLE PRESENT	SIMPLE PAST	SIMPLE FUTURE
kick	kicked	will kick
kick	kicked	will kick
kicks	kicked	will kick

PRESENT PROGRESSIVE	PAST PROGRESSIVE	FUTURE PROGRESSIVE
am kicking	was kicking	will be kicking
are kicking	were kicking	will be kicking
is kicking	was kicking	will be kicking

PRESENT PERFECT	PAST PERFECT	FUTURE PERFECT
have kicked	had kicked	will have kicked
have kicked	had kicked	will have kicked
has kicked	had kicked	will have kicked

PRESENT PERFECT PROGRESSIVE	PAST PERFECT PROGRESSIVE	FUTURE PERFECT PROGRESSIVE
have been kicking	had been kicking	will have been kicking
have been kicking	had been kicking	will have been kicking
has been kicking	had been kicking	will have been kicking

EXAMPLES:
The chancellor kicked the students out of the program because they had plagiarized. *The kids were kicking the ball around in the playground.* *Hal has been trying to quit smoking for years, but he still hasn't kicked the habit.*

PASSIVE

SIMPLE PRESENT	SIMPLE PAST	SIMPLE FUTURE
am kicked	was kicked	will be kicked
are kicked	were kicked	will be kicked
is kicked	was kicked	will be kicked

PRESENT PROGRESSIVE	PAST PROGRESSIVE	FUTURE PROGRESSIVE*
am being kicked	was being kicked	will be being kicked*
are being kicked	were being kicked	will be being kicked*
is being kicked	was being kicked	will be being kicked*

PRESENT PERFECT	PAST PERFECT	FUTURE PERFECT
have been kicked	had been kicked	will have been kicked
have been kicked	had been kicked	will have been kicked
has been kicked	had been kicked	will have been kicked

EXAMPLES:
The boys were kicked out of school because of inappropriate behavior. *Sam will be kicked off the team if he doesn't get into shape.* *How many ideas had been kicked around before the final decision was made?*

PRINCIPAL CONDITIONALS

PRESENT	PRESENT PROGRESSIVE	PRESENT PASSIVE
would kick	would be kicking	would be kicked
would kick	would be kicking	would be kicked
would kick	would be kicking	would be kicked

PAST	PAST PROGRESSIVE	PAST PASSIVE
would have kicked	would have been kicking	would have been kicked
would have kicked	would have been kicking	would have been kicked
would have kicked	would have been kicking	would have been kicked

EXAMPLES:
If this sleeping pill would kick in, I could get some sleep. *They would have been kicked out if they hadn't apologized to the director.*

kick

Important Forms in Use

IF/THEN CONDITIONALS

	IF ...	... THEN	EXAMPLE
Real Present/ Future	kick/kicks	simple present	If I <u>kick</u> them off the team, I have no good players left.
		will + base form	If the kids <u>kick</u> the ball right in front of the house, they will break a window.
Unreal Present/ Future	kicked	would + base form	If we <u>kicked</u> the idea around for a little bit longer, we would make a better decision.
Unreal Past	had kicked	would have + past participle	If I <u>had kicked</u> my son out of the house after he disobeyed me, he wouldn't have had anywhere to go.

SUBJUNCTIVE

ACTIVE	kick	We ask that you <u>kick</u> around a few ideas before making a final choice.
PASSIVE	be kicked	It is essential that anyone not following the rules and regulations <u>be kicked</u> out of the club.

PHRASAL VERBS

kick (someone or something) around	to abuse someone The teachers didn't do anything when I got kicked around by the other kids in class.
kick back	to relax You can just kick back while I get our dinner.
kick in	to begin to take effect The sleeping pills finally began to kick in and I was able to get some rest.
kick out	to force someone to leave If you don't follow the school rules, you will be kicked out.

IDIOMS

to kick someone when he or she is down	to do something bad to someone when he or she is already suffering Firing him now, after he just lost his mother and got divorced, would be kicking him when he was down.
to get a kick out of something	to really enjoy something I don't know why, but your mother really gets a kick out of taking cruises.
to kick the habit	to get rid of a bad habit I have been smoking for years, and although I've tried, I just can't seem to kick the habit.
to kick the bucket	to die (informal) Has that old lady next door kicked the bucket yet?
to kick yourself	to be angry or frustrated due to something that you did or didn't do I kicked myself for not buying the house before the market made it unaffordable.
to kick around the idea	to consider an idea I've been kicking around the idea of traveling to South Africa this summer.

RELATED WORDS

kickback (n.)	a sum of money that is given in return for a favor
for kicks (adv.)	for fun

* Note that the form "will be being kicked" is rarely used. To convey a future progressive passive, use the present progressive passive.

Verb Chart

knock

	ACTIVE	PASSIVE
Infinitive	to knock	to be knocked
Past Infinitive	to have knocked	to have been knocked
Past Participle	knocked	been knocked
Present Participle	knocking	being knocked

I
you/we/they
he/she/it

ACTIVE

SIMPLE PRESENT	SIMPLE PAST	SIMPLE FUTURE
knock	knocked	will knock
knock	knocked	will knock
knocks	knocked	will knock

PRESENT PROGRESSIVE	PAST PROGRESSIVE	FUTURE PROGRESSIVE
am knocking	was knocking	will be knocking
are knocking	were knocking	will be knocking
is knocking	was knocking	will be knocking

PRESENT PERFECT	PAST PERFECT	FUTURE PERFECT
have knocked	had knocked	will have knocked
have knocked	had knocked	will have knocked
has knocked	had knocked	will have knocked

PRESENT PERFECT PROGRESSIVE	PAST PERFECT PROGRESSIVE	FUTURE PERFECT PROGRESSIVE
have been knocking	had been knocking	will have been knocking
have been knocking	had been knocking	will have been knocking
has been knocking	had been knocking	will have been knocking

EXAMPLES:

The boxer knocked out his opponent in three rounds.

The engine was knocking, which prompted us to drop the car off at the mechanic's.

Our neighbor had been knocking on the door for several minutes before I heard anything.

PASSIVE

SIMPLE PRESENT	SIMPLE PAST	SIMPLE FUTURE
am knocked	was knocked	will be knocked
are knocked	were knocked	will be knocked
is knocked	was knocked	will be knocked

PRESENT PROGRESSIVE	PAST PROGRESSIVE	FUTURE PROGRESSIVE*
am being knocked	was being knocked	will be being knocked*
are being knocked	were being knocked	will be being knocked*
is being knocked	was being knocked	will be being knocked*

PRESENT PERFECT	PAST PERFECT	FUTURE PERFECT
have been knocked	had been knocked	will have been knocked
have been knocked	had been knocked	will have been knocked
has been knocked	had been knocked	will have been knocked

EXAMPLES:

The chairs were knocked over by the strong wind.

When I got home, I found that all of my work had been knocked to the floor.

Tim had been knocked down by some older kids in the fight.

PRINCIPAL CONDITIONALS

PRESENT	PRESENT PROGRESSIVE	PRESENT PASSIVE
would knock	would be knocking	would be knocked
would knock	would be knocking	would be knocked
would knock	would be knocking	would be knocked

PAST	PAST PROGRESSIVE	PAST PASSIVE
would have knocked	would have been knocking	would have been knocked
would have knocked	would have been knocking	would have been knocked
would have knocked	would have been knocking	would have been knocked

EXAMPLES:

We would have knocked, but we didn't think you were home.

I didn't expect that I would be knocked over by the blast.

Important Forms in Use

IF/THEN CONDITIONALS

	IF . . .	. . . THEN	EXAMPLE
Real Present/ Future	knock/knocks	simple present	*If she <u>knocks</u> on the door, you need to answer it.*
		will + base form	*If we <u>knock</u> anything over, my mom will kill me!*
Unreal Present/ Future	knocked	would + base form	*If the committee <u>knocked</u> the idea around, I'm sure they'd see that it has a lot of merit.*
Unreal Past	had knocked	would have + past participle	*If he <u>had knocked</u> out his opponent in the first round, the fight wouldn't have been very exciting.*

SUBJUNCTIVE

ACTIVE	knock	*It is vital that we <u>knock</u> this report out quickly.*
PASSIVE	be knocked	*We recommend that several ideas <u>be knocked</u> around before a decision is made.*

PHRASAL VERBS

knock (someone) around	to bully or physically abuse someone *The kids always knocked me around after school.*
knock (something) around	to discuss an idea for a time before making a decision *We knocked around the idea of dividing the department in two, but decided against it.*
knock (someone) out	to make someone unconscious *The firefighters found her after she had been knocked out by smoke inhalation.*
knock (something) out	to do something quickly *There's not much work left on the first draft. Let's knock it out before we go home.*
knock (someone or something) over	to hit so that someone or something falls over *The wind knocked over the container of plants on the terrace.*
knock (someone) up	to make someone pregnant (informal) *Did you hear that Elizabeth got knocked up?*

IDIOMS

to knock something	to criticize something *I know you don't like our suggestion, but don't knock it until you have an idea of your own.*
to knock it off	to quit doing something that is annoying someone else *Would you knock it off? I need to study.*
to knock on wood	to wish for good luck to continue (based on a superstition that when something is said, one must knock on wood to keep the opposite from happening) *We've never had an accident—knock on wood.*
to knock the wind out of somebody	to cause difficulty breathing for a moment, usually with a blow to the torso *The punch to the stomach knocked the wind out of him.*
to knock someone off his or her feet	to give someone a big surprise *His marriage proposal knocked me off my feet.*

RELATED WORDS

knockoff (n.)	something that is made to resemble the original but is not of the same quality
knockout (n.)	someone who is very attractive (informal)
hard knocks (n.)	difficult experiences

* Note that the form "will be being knocked" is rarely used. To convey a future progressive passive, use the present progressive passive.

Verb Chart

know

	ACTIVE	PASSIVE
Infinitive	to know	to be known
Past Infinitive	to have known	to have been known
Past Participle	known	been known
Present Participle	knowing*	being known

ACTIVE

	I	you/we/they	he/she/it

SIMPLE PRESENT	SIMPLE PAST	SIMPLE FUTURE
know	knew	will know
know	knew	will know
knows	knew	will know

PRESENT PROGRESSIVE	PAST PROGRESSIVE	FUTURE PROGRESSIVE
am knowing*	was knowing*	will be knowing*
are knowing*	were knowing*	will be knowing*
is knowing*	was knowing*	will be knowing*

PRESENT PERFECT	PAST PERFECT	FUTURE PERFECT
have known	had known	will have known
have known	had known	will have known
has known	had known	will have known

PRESENT PERFECT PROGRESSIVE	PAST PERFECT PROGRESSIVE	FUTURE PERFECT PROGRESSIVE
have been knowing*	had been knowing*	will have been knowing*
have been knowing*	had been knowing*	will have been knowing*
has been knowing*	had been knowing*	will have been knowing*

EXAMPLES:
Sarah and Jessica have known each other since childhood.

Had we known he wasn't coming, we might have postponed the meeting.

I will know the answer to your question by next week.

PASSIVE

SIMPLE PRESENT	SIMPLE PAST	SIMPLE FUTURE
am known	was known	will be known
are known	were known	will be known
is known	was known	will be known

PRESENT PROGRESSIVE	PAST PROGRESSIVE	FUTURE PROGRESSIVE**
am being known*	was being known*	will be being known**
are being known*	were being known*	will be being known**
is being known*	was being known*	will be being known**

PRESENT PERFECT	PAST PERFECT	FUTURE PERFECT
have been known	had been known	will have been known
have been known	had been known	will have been known
has been known	had been known	will have been known

EXAMPLES:
He was known for his discovery of dark stars.

You will always be known as the boy who saved us from the fire.

PRINCIPAL CONDITIONALS

PRESENT	PRESENT PROGRESSIVE	PRESENT PASSIVE
would know	would be knowing*	would be known
would know	would be knowing*	would be known
would know	would be knowing*	would be known

PAST	PAST PROGRESSIVE	PAST PASSIVE
would have known	would have been knowing*	would have been known
would have known	would have been knowing*	would have been known
would have known	would have been knowing*	would have been known

EXAMPLES:
You would know if you were in love with him.

Would he have known about the affair if you hadn't told him?

know

Important Forms in Use

IF/THEN CONDITIONALS

	IF ...	... THEN	EXAMPLE
Real Present/ Future	know/knows	simple present	*If I <u>know</u> it's going to snow, I put on my galoshes.*
		will + base form	*If he <u>knows</u> where we we keep the spare towels, he'll get you one.*
Unreal Present/ Future	knew	would + base form	*If she <u>knew</u> who you were, she wouldn't talk to you.*
Unreal Past	had known	would have + past participle	*If the kids <u>had known</u> the food was for the party, they wouldn't have eaten it.*

SUBJUNCTIVE

ACTIVE	know	*It is important that the teacher <u>know</u> about this immediately.*
PASSIVE	be known	*We recommend that all conjugations of all verbs in the present tense <u>be known</u> before taking the exam.*

PHRASAL VERBS

know about
    to be aware of certain information
    Does your mom know about our plan to go camping this summer?

know of
    to have heard about someone or something but not know him, her, or it directly
    I don't know Harry personally, but I know of him.

IDIOMS

to know the ropes/one's way around
    to be familiar with procedures in an office or similar institution
    If you have any questions, ask me. I've been here for years, so I know the ropes.

to not know someone from Adam
    to have no idea who someone is
    I was worried about hiring him to paint my house considering that I didn't know him from Adam, but I was desperate.

to be in the know
    to have information about something
    If you want to work for the National Enquirer, you have to be in the know.

RELATED WORDS

know-how (n.)
    the knowledge or skill required to do a job

know-it-all (n.)
    a person who believes that he or she knows a lot about everything

well-known (adj.)
    familiar to many people

---

* Note that "know" is a stative verb and is rarely used in the progressive form.

** Note that the form "will be being known" is rarely used. To convey a future progressive passive, use the present progressive passive.

Verb Chart

lay

	ACTIVE	PASSIVE
Infinitive	to lay	to be laid
Past Infinitive	to have laid	to have been laid
Past Participle	laid	been laid
Present Participle	laying	being laid

ACTIVE

	I
	you/we/they
	he/she/it

SIMPLE PRESENT	SIMPLE PAST	SIMPLE FUTURE
lay	laid	will lay
lay	laid	will lay
lays	laid	will lay

PRESENT PROGRESSIVE	PAST PROGRESSIVE	FUTURE PROGRESSIVE
am laying	was laying	will be laying
are laying	were laying	will be laying
is laying	was laying	will be laying

PRESENT PERFECT	PAST PERFECT	FUTURE PERFECT
have laid	had laid	will have laid
have laid	had laid	will have laid
has laid	had laid	will have laid

PRESENT PERFECT PROGRESSIVE	PAST PERFECT PROGRESSIVE	FUTURE PERFECT PROGRESSIVE
have been laying	had been laying	will have been laying
have been laying	had been laying	will have been laying
has been laying	had been laying	will have been laying

EXAMPLES:

She laid the baby down for a nap. *The hens have been laying more eggs than usual.* *Tom will have laid the keys on the counter. Can you get them for me?*

PASSIVE

SIMPLE PRESENT	SIMPLE PAST	SIMPLE FUTURE
am laid	was laid	will be laid
are laid	were laid	will be laid
is laid	was laid	will be laid

PRESENT PROGRESSIVE	PAST PROGRESSIVE	FUTURE PROGRESSIVE*
am being laid	was being laid	will be being laid*
are being laid	were being laid	will be being laid*
is being laid	was being laid	will be being laid*

PRESENT PERFECT	PAST PERFECT	FUTURE PERFECT
have been laid	had been laid	will have been laid
have been laid	had been laid	will have been laid
has been laid	had been laid	will have been laid

EXAMPLES:

Thousands of workers were laid off in the recent factory closings. *His body will be laid to rest in Graceland Cemetery.* *The trap had been laid and the hunters expected to catch a small animal for dinner.*

PRINCIPAL CONDITIONALS

PRESENT	PRESENT PROGRESSIVE	PRESENT PASSIVE
would lay	would be laying	would be laid
would lay	would be laying	would be laid
would lay	would be laying	would be laid

PAST	PAST PROGRESSIVE	PAST PASSIVE
would have laid	would have been laying	would have been laid
would have laid	would have been laying	would have been laid
would have laid	would have been laying	would have been laid

EXAMPLES:

I would lay the carpet in the upstairs only after you have finished painting. *He would have laid to rest any rumors if they weren't true.*

PRINCIPAL PARTS: lay, laid, laid

Important Forms in Use

IF/THEN CONDITIONALS

	IF ...	... THEN	EXAMPLE
Real Present/ Future	lay/lays	simple present	*If I lay the keys on the table, I know exactly where they are.*
		will + base form	*If she lays it on thick, he'll give her whatever she wants.*
Unreal Present/ Future	laid	would + base form	*If we laid the carpet ourselves, we wouldn't have to pay the professionals.*
Unreal Past	had laid	would have + past participle	*If I had laid off the coffee, I wouldn't have been so anxious during the interview.*

SUBJUNCTIVE

ACTIVE	lay	*It is important that the counselor not lay into the kids, even if she is angry.*
PASSIVE	be laid	*We ask that the carpet be laid and the walls be painted before we move in.*

PHRASAL VERBS

lay into	to attack someone because you are angry *If Mom lays into me again about not having a job, I'm moving out.*
lay (someone) off	to take someone's job away *Our entire team was laid off after we lost the contract with the multinational.*
lay off (something)	to stop doing something that is not healthy for you *I'm going to lay off playing basketball until my shoulder has healed.*
lay (something) out	to arrange *All of the plans were laid out long before we left on vacation.*

IDIOMS

to lay something on the line	to state something clearly even though it might be upsetting *I'm going to lay it on the line. The work you're doing for us is just not adequate.*
to lay something to rest	to stop discussing, working on, or worrying about something *We were all happy when Tom laid his career as a drummer to rest.*
to lay it on thick	to overdo something, especially flattery *When Harry started to compliment Helen excessively, I could only wonder why he was laying it on so thick.*
I hate to lay this on you	an expression used when giving someone a job that he or she does not want to do or telling someone something that he or she doesn't want to know *I hate to lay this on you now, right before vacation, but I really need these reports before you go.*

RELATED WORDS

layaway (n.)	when money is put down little by little in order to purchase something
layoff (n.)	when a workplace takes jobs away from workers
layout (n.)	the way a room or building is organized
laid-back (adj.)	relaxed, easygoing

Verb Chart

* Note that the form "will be being laid" is rarely used. To convey a future progressive passive, use the present progressive passive.

lead

	ACTIVE	PASSIVE
Infinitive	to lead	to be led
Past Infinitive	to have led	to have been led
Past Participle	led	been led
Present Participle	leading	being led

ACTIVE

I		
you/we/they		
he/she/it		

SIMPLE PRESENT	SIMPLE PAST	SIMPLE FUTURE
lead	led	will lead
lead	led	will lead
leads	led	will lead

PRESENT PROGRESSIVE	PAST PROGRESSIVE	FUTURE PROGRESSIVE
am leading	was leading	will be leading
are leading	were leading	will be leading
is leading	was leading	will be leading

PRESENT PERFECT	PAST PERFECT	FUTURE PERFECT
have led	had led	will have led
have led	had led	will have led
has led	had led	will have led

PRESENT PERFECT PROGRESSIVE	PAST PERFECT PROGRESSIVE	FUTURE PERFECT PROGRESSIVE
have been leading	had been leading	will have been leading
have been leading	had been leading	will have been leading
has been leading	had been leading	will have been leading

EXAMPLES:

Lead the horse over in this direction, and I'll take him into the stable.

The White Sox first baseman led the league in home runs.

The yoga instructor was leading the class through a series of breathing exercises.

PASSIVE

SIMPLE PRESENT	SIMPLE PAST	SIMPLE FUTURE
am led	was led	will be led
are led	were led	will be led
is led	was led	will be led

PRESENT PROGRESSIVE	PAST PROGRESSIVE	FUTURE PROGRESSIVE*
am being led	was being led	will be being led*
are being led	were being led	will be being led*
is being led	was being led	will be being led*

PRESENT PERFECT	PAST PERFECT	FUTURE PERFECT
have been led	had been led	will have been led
have been led	had been led	will have been led
has been led	had been led	will have been led

EXAMPLES:

The choir was led by a graduate student from Oberlin College.

Tommy was a good boy until he was led astray by some of the older kids.

PRINCIPAL CONDITIONALS

PRESENT	PRESENT PROGRESSIVE	PRESENT PASSIVE
would lead	would be leading	would be led
would lead	would be leading	would be led
would lead	would be leading	would be led

PAST	PAST PROGRESSIVE	PAST PASSIVE
would have led	would have been leading	would have been led
would have led	would have been leading	would have been led
would have led	would have been leading	would have been led

EXAMPLES:

Mr. Smith promised that he would lead the group of spelunkers through the cave.

Mr. Pekela would have been leading the choir if he hadn't come down with the flu.

lead

Important Forms in Use

IF/THEN CONDITIONALS

	IF ...	...THEN	EXAMPLE
Real Present/ Future	lead/leads	simple present	*If I lead the debate team in wins, it's because I spend so much time preparing.*
		will + base form	*If you lead me to the canned fruit aisle, I'll be able to find what I'm looking for.*
Unreal Present/ Future	led	would + base form	*If she led a healthier lifestyle, she wouldn't be seeing so many doctors.*
Unreal Past	had led	would have + past participle	*If I had led the team to victory, I would have been selected to coach next year.*

SUBJUNCTIVE

ACTIVE	lead	*It is important that he lead the way if he wants things done properly.*
PASSIVE	be led	*It is essential that we be led by a competent director.*

PHRASAL VERBS

lead into (something)	to provoke or introduce *Our conversation about religion led into our discussion on ethics.*
lead (someone) on	to deceive someone into thinking that you are interested in him or her or in something he or she has to offer *Sarah led him on until months later, when she finally told him that she was in love with someone else.*
lead to (something)	to cause something else to happen *One thing led to another, and before I knew it, I was the owner of a new dog. / My friendship with John led to my interest in English literature.*

IDIOMS

to lead someone astray	to cause someone to make a mistake or do something bad *She has been led astray by the kids at school that she hangs out with.*
to lead a charmed life	to have a life filled with good fortune *With all the money and opportunities you've had, you certainly have led a charmed life!*
you can lead a horse to water (but you can't make it drink)	you can show a person what's right, but you can't make him or her do it *He knew he should follow the doctor's advice if he wanted to become healthy, but he didn't. It just goes to show that you can lead a horse to water but you can't make it drink.*

RELATED WORDS

leader (n.)	a person who takes charge
leadoff (adj.)	the one that goes first
leading (adj.)	the first, the best, or the most important

---

* Note that the form "will be being led" is rarely used. To convey a future progressive passive, use the present progressive passive.

Verb Chart

159

leave

	ACTIVE	PASSIVE
Infinitive	to leave	to be left
Past Infinitive	to have left	to have been left
Past Participle	left	been left
Present Participle	leaving	being left

ACTIVE

	I	you/we/they	he/she/it

SIMPLE PRESENT	**SIMPLE PAST**	**SIMPLE FUTURE**
leave	left	will leave
leave	left	will leave
leaves	left	will leave

PRESENT PROGRESSIVE	**PAST PROGRESSIVE**	**FUTURE PROGRESSIVE**
am leaving	was leaving	will be leaving
are leaving	were leaving	will be leaving
is leaving	was leaving	will be leaving

PRESENT PERFECT	**PAST PERFECT**	**FUTURE PERFECT**
have left	had left	will have left
have left	had left	will have left
has left	had left	will have left

PRESENT PERFECT PROGRESSIVE	**PAST PERFECT PROGRESSIVE**	**FUTURE PERFECT PROGRESSIVE**
have been leaving	had been leaving	will have been leaving
have been leaving	had been leaving	will have been leaving
has been leaving	had been leaving	will have been leaving

EXAMPLES:
The train is leaving at night, and we will arrive in Pittsburgh in the morning.   *The hurricane left many families homeless.*   *By the time we arrive in Zurich, they will have left.*

PASSIVE

SIMPLE PRESENT	**SIMPLE PAST**	**SIMPLE FUTURE**
am left	was left	will be left
are left	were left	will be left
is left	was left	will be left

PRESENT PROGRESSIVE	**PAST PROGRESSIVE**	**FUTURE PROGRESSIVE***
am being left	was being left	will be being left*
are being left	were being left	will be being left*
is being left	was being left	will be being left*

PRESENT PERFECT	**PAST PERFECT**	**FUTURE PERFECT**
have been left	had been left	will have been left
have been left	had been left	will have been left
has been left	had been left	will have been left

EXAMPLES:
The congregation was left without a church after the fire.   *Only a few dishes will be left to choose from when we get to the restaurant.*   *The children had been left at home unsupervised.*

PRINCIPAL CONDITIONALS

PRESENT	**PRESENT PROGRESSIVE**	**PRESENT PASSIVE**
would leave	would be leaving	would be left
would leave	would be leaving	would be left
would leave	would be leaving	would be left

PAST	**PAST PROGRESSIVE**	**PAST PASSIVE**
would have left	would have been left	would have been left
would have left	would have been left	would have been left
would have left	would have been left	would have been left

EXAMPLES:
We would have left earlier if we had known about the storm.   *Nothing would have been left if the police hadn't gotten here so quickly.*

leave

PRINCIPAL PARTS: leave, left, left

Important Forms in Use

IF/THEN CONDITIONALS

	IF...	...THEN	EXAMPLE
Real Present/ Future	leave/leaves	simple present	*If I <u>leave</u> at 7:00, I can be home by 7:45.*
		will + base form	*If she <u>leaves</u> him, she won't have anywhere to go.*
Unreal Present/ Future	left	would + base form	*If we <u>left</u> him behind, we would be able to go more quickly.*
Unreal Past	had left	would have + past participle	*If her parents <u>had left</u> her alone in the house, she would have thrown a huge party.*

SUBJUNCTIVE

ACTIVE	leave	*We recommend that you <u>leave</u> immediately after you have packed your bags.*
PASSIVE	be left	*The hotel suggests that all valuables <u>be left</u> in the safe.*

PHRASAL VERBS

leave (something) behind	to not bring something along *I wanted to bring the wine, but my bag was already heavy, so I left it behind.*
leave off	to stop doing something in the middle that you will return to later *Where did we leave off reading last week?*
leave (something) out	to omit *It took forever to get my tax returns this year because I left out my signature on the original documents.*

IDIOMS

to leave (someone) hanging	to make someone wait for a decision *He's left me hanging for weeks about whether or not he's going to rent the room in the back of my house.*
to leave well enough alone	to stop meddling with a situation that would be better off without anyone's help *Bob doesn't want your help. Why don't you leave well enough alone?*
to leave someone	to end a romantic relationship *Did you hear that Hillary left Stan?*
I could take it or leave it	an expression used when you have ambivalent feelings about something *As for the new color that you chose for the dining room, I could take it or leave it.*

RELATED WORDS

leftover (adj.)	anything that remains after the rest has been used
leftovers (n.)	food that remains after a meal has been eaten
left-wing (adj.)	political thought that is to the opposite extreme of conservatism
left-handed (adj.)	describes someone who uses his or her left hand

* Note that the form "will be being left" is rarely used. To convey a future progressive passive, use the present progressive passive.

Verb Chart

let

	ACTIVE	PASSIVE
Infinitive	to let	to be let
Past Infinitive	to have let	to have been let
Past Participle	let	been let
Present Participle	letting	being let

ACTIVE

SIMPLE PRESENT	**SIMPLE PAST**	**SIMPLE FUTURE**
let	let	will let
let	let	will let
lets	let	will let

PRESENT PROGRESSIVE	**PAST PROGRESSIVE**	**FUTURE PROGRESSIVE**
am letting	was letting	will be letting
are letting	were letting	will be letting
is letting	was letting	will be letting

PRESENT PERFECT	**PAST PERFECT**	**FUTURE PERFECT**
have let	had let	will have let
have let	had let	will have let
has let	had let	will have let

PRESENT PERFECT PROGRESSIVE	**PAST PERFECT PROGRESSIVE**	**FUTURE PERFECT PROGRESSIVE**
have been letting	had been letting	will have been letting
have been letting	had been letting	will have been letting
has been letting	had been letting	will have been letting

EXAMPLES:
She let out the seam on her new pants to make them a little longer. *I was letting my dog out this morning when he got out of his collar and ran away.* *We have let too many good opportunities go by.*

PASSIVE

SIMPLE PRESENT	**SIMPLE PAST**	**SIMPLE FUTURE**
am let	was let	will be let
are let	were let	will be let
is let	was let	will be let

PRESENT PROGRESSIVE	**PAST PROGRESSIVE**	**FUTURE PROGRESSIVE***
am being let	was being let	will be being let*
are being let	were being let	will be being let*
is being let	was being let	will be being let*

PRESENT PERFECT	**PAST PERFECT**	**FUTURE PERFECT**
have been let	had been let	will have been let
have been let	had been let	will have been let
has been let	had been let	will have been let

EXAMPLES:
I had been let down so many times by my mother, I finally decided to only rely on myself. *My new pants are being let out by the seamstress.*

PRINCIPAL CONDITIONALS

PRESENT	**PRESENT PROGRESSIVE**	**PRESENT PASSIVE**
would let	would be letting	would be let
would let	would be letting	would be let
would let	would be letting	would be let

PAST	**PAST PROGRESSIVE**	**PAST PASSIVE**
would have let	would have been letting	would have been let
would have let	would have been letting	would have been let
would have let	would have been letting	would have been let

EXAMPLES:
I would let you take the car tonight, but I have to use it for work. *Angelica would have let me in, but she didn't have a key.*

I
you/we/they
he/she/it

let

PRINCIPAL PARTS: let, let, let

Important Forms in Use

IF/THEN CONDITIONALS

	IF ...	... THEN	EXAMPLE
Real Present/ Future	let/lets	simple present	*If she <u>lets</u> me stay up late, I know she's in a good mood.*
		will + base form	*If I <u>let</u> on that I'm upset, she'll never let me hear the end of it.*
Unreal Present/ Future	let	would + base form	*If we <u>let</u> them, they'd take over the entire house.*
Unreal Past	had let	would have + past participle	*If I <u>had let</u> Harry know sooner, he would've been able to come.*

SUBJUNCTIVE

ACTIVE	let	*The counselor recommends that each student <u>let</u> someone from the faculty review his or her course choices.*
PASSIVE	be let	*It is important that latecomers <u>be let</u> in only after the first movement is finished.*

PHRASAL VERBS

let (someone) down	to disappoint someone who was expecting something from you or thought highly of you *Jim really let me down when he didn't show up for my party.*
let (someone) off	to absolve from punishment, or to drop someone at a certain place *I'll let you off this time, but the next time you come home late, you'll be grounded. / The bus driver let me off at the wrong stop, so I had to walk a few blocks to get here.*
let on	to expose one's emotions without stating them directly *Maurice let on that he was unhappy about how the evening turned out, but he wouldn't tell us why.*
let (someone) out	to open the doors so that someone can leave a building, or to drop someone at a certain place in your car *The janitor let me out after the doors had all been locked. / Can you let me out at the corner of Smith and Bergen?*

IDIOMS

to let something go	to not take notice of someone else's improper actions or behavior *His behavior was inappropriate but the teacher let it go, considering he was usually the best-behaved student in the class.*
to let someone have it	to openly express your anger toward someone *My roommate really let me have it when I didn't clean up after the party.*
to let someone off the hook	to not punish someone *If you go and visit Aunt Elizabeth in the hospital tonight, I'll let you off the hook for not going last night.*
to let off steam	to do something in order to get rid of anger or stress *I find that running really helps me let off steam.*

RELATED WORDS

letdown (n.)	a disappointment
let's (mod.)	the contraction of "let us," used by someone to make a suggestion to a group of people
sublet (n.)	a situation in which someone rents a room, apartment, etc., for a period of time while the owner or renter is away

* Note that the form "will be being let" is rarely used. To convey a future progressive passive, use the present progressive passive.

lie

	ACTIVE	PASSIVE
Infinitive	to lie	-
Past Infinitive	to have lain	-
Past Participle	lain	-
Present Participle	lying	-

ACTIVE

	SIMPLE PRESENT	SIMPLE PAST	SIMPLE FUTURE
I	lie	lay	will lie
you/we/they	lie	lay	will lie
he/she/it	lies	lay	will lie

PRESENT PROGRESSIVE	PAST PROGRESSIVE	FUTURE PROGRESSIVE
am lying	was lying	will be lying
are lying	were lying	will be lying
is lying	was lying	will be lying

PRESENT PERFECT	PAST PERFECT	FUTURE PERFECT
have lain	had lain	will have lain
have lain	had lain	will have lain
has lain	had lain	will have lain

PRESENT PERFECT PROGRESSIVE	PAST PERFECT PROGRESSIVE	FUTURE PERFECT PROGRESSIVE
have been lying	had been lying	will have been lying
have been lying	had been lying	will have been lying
has been lying	had been lying	will have been lying

EXAMPLES:

I told him to lie down for a while if he wasn't feeling well.

During the entire semester, his books lay on the table untouched.

His future has always lain in his ability to succeed in school.

PASSIVE

SIMPLE PRESENT	SIMPLE PAST	SIMPLE FUTURE
-	-	-
-	-	-
-	-	-

PRESENT PROGRESSIVE	PAST PROGRESSIVE	FUTURE PROGRESSIVE*
-	-	-
-	-	-
-	-	-

PRESENT PERFECT	PAST PERFECT	FUTURE PERFECT
-	-	-
-	-	-
-	-	-

PRINCIPAL CONDITIONALS

PRESENT	PRESENT PROGRESSIVE	PRESENT PASSIVE
would lie	would be lying	-
would lie	would be lying	-
would lie	would be lying	-

PAST	PAST PROGRESSIVE	PAST PASSIVE
would have lain	would have been lying	-
would have lain	would have been lying	-
would have lain	would have been lying	-

EXAMPLES:

If they accepted the proposal, the new high-rise would lie in the center of town next to the river.

I would have lain in bed all day if I hadn't had to go to work.

lie

Important Forms in Use

IF/THEN CONDITIONALS

	IF ...	... THEN	EXAMPLE
Real Present/ Future	lie/lies	simple present	*If I <u>lie</u> down and take an aspirin, my headache usually goes away quickly.*
		will + base form	*If we <u>lie</u> low for a few days, maybe the police won't catch us.*
Unreal Present/ Future	lay	would + base form	*If your success <u>lay</u> only in the quality of your writing, your book would be a best-seller.*
Unreal Past	had lain	would have + past participle	*If the city <u>hadn't lain</u> in a valley, perhaps it wouldn't have been hit by the tornado.*

SUBJUNCTIVE

ACTIVE	lie	*It is important that he <u>lie</u> down immediately.*
PASSIVE	-	

PHRASAL VERBS

lie around	to spend time doing very little *Every time I come home you're just lying around.*
lie behind	to be the real reason for something *I have no idea what lay behind their plan to split our department in two.*
lie down	to put your body in a flat position, usually on the floor, a bed, etc. *Can I lie down for a few minutes before dinner?*
lie with someone or something	when blame or responsibility rests with someone or something *The responsibility for the failure of the schools lies with the mayor.*

IDIOMS

to lie low	to hide in order to avoid being caught *When the police came looking for Bobby, I called him and warned him to lie low.*
lie ahead/lie in store	to be coming in the future *We don't know what lies ahead for our company.*
let sleeping dogs lie	to not discuss something that has caused problems in the past *The manager wanted to bring up her attendance from the previous year, but I suggested that we let sleeping dogs lie.*
lie heavy on someone	to take something seriously, especially when it makes you feel bad *The decision to fire several loyal employees lay heavy on him.*

RELATED WORDS

lie-down (n.)	a short rest

Verb Chart

light

	ACTIVE	PASSIVE
Infinitive	to light	to be lit/lighted
Past Infinitive	to have lit/lighted	to have been lit/lighted
Past Participle	lit/lighted	been lit/lighted
Present Participle	lighting	being lit/lighted

ACTIVE

I		
you/we/they		
he/she/it		

SIMPLE PRESENT	SIMPLE PAST	SIMPLE FUTURE
light	lit/lighted	will light
light	lit/lighted	will light
lights	lit/lighted	will light

PRESENT PROGRESSIVE	PAST PROGRESSIVE	FUTURE PROGRESSIVE
am lighting	was lighting	will be lighting
are lighting	were lighting	will be lighting
is lighting	was lighting	will be lighting

PRESENT PERFECT	PAST PERFECT	FUTURE PERFECT
have lit/lighted	had lit/lighted	will have lit/lighted
have lit/lighted	had lit/lighted	will have lit/lighted
has lit/lighted	had lit/lighted	will have lit/lighted

PRESENT PERFECT PROGRESSIVE	PAST PERFECT PROGRESSIVE	FUTURE PERFECT PROGRESSIVE
have been lighting	had been lighting	will have been lighting
have been lighting	had been lighting	will have been lighting
has been lighting	had been lighting	will have been lighting

EXAMPLES:

Light a fire in the fireplace. It's freezing in here!

The sky lights up with fireworks every Fourth of July.

The room started to look beautiful as we were lighting the candles.

PASSIVE

SIMPLE PRESENT	SIMPLE PAST	SIMPLE FUTURE
am lit/lighted	was lit/lighted	will be lit/lighted
are lit/lighted	were lit/lighted	will be lit/lighted
is lit/lighted	was lit/lighted	will be lit/lighted

PRESENT PROGRESSIVE	PAST PROGRESSIVE	FUTURE PROGRESSIVE*
am being lit/lighted	was being lit/lighted	will be being lit/lighted*
are being lit/lighted	were being lit/lighted	will be being lit/lighted*
is being lit/lighted	was being lit/lighted	will be being lit/lighted*

PRESENT PERFECT	PAST PERFECT	FUTURE PERFECT
have been lit/lighted	had been lit/lighted	will have been lit/lighted
have been lit/lighted	had been lit/lighted	will have been lit/lighted
has been lit/lighted	had been lit/lighted	will have been lit/lighted

EXAMPLES:

Tell the birthday girl to come in. The candles are being lit as we speak.

Her cigarette was lit by a tall, dark stranger who appeared out of nowhere.

His face had been lit up by the news of the arrival of his best friend.

PRINCIPAL CONDITIONALS

PRESENT	PRESENT PROGRESSIVE	PRESENT PASSIVE
would light	would be lighting	would be lit/lighted
would light	would be lighting	would be lit/lighted
would light	would be lighting	would be lit/lighted

PAST	PAST PROGRESSIVE	PAST PASSIVE
would have lit/lighted	would have been lighting	would have been lit/lighted
would have lit/lighted	would have been lighting	would have been lit/lighted
would have lit/lighted	would have been lighting	would have been lit/lighted

EXAMPLES:

Would you light the candles on the dining room table?

They told us that the room would be lit with indirect lighting.

light

PRINCIPAL PARTS: light, lit/lighted, lit/lighted

Important Forms in Use

IF/THEN CONDITIONALS

	IF ...	... THEN	EXAMPLE
Real Present/ Future	light/lights	simple present	*If I <u>light</u> the fire too early, it goes out before we're in bed.*
		will + base form	*If Nathan <u>lights</u> another cigarette in the house, Ryan will ask him to step outside.*
Unreal Present/ Future	lit/lighted	would + base form	*If we <u>lit</u> up the stairway, it would be safer at night.*
Unreal Past	had lit/ had lighted	would have + past participle	*If dad <u>had lit</u> a fire, we wouldn't have been so cold.*

SUBJUNCTIVE

ACTIVE	light	*It is important that someone experienced <u>light</u> the fire.*
PASSIVE	be lit/lighted	*We recommended that the candles <u>be lit</u> in case of a power outage.*

PHRASAL VERBS

light on/upon (something)	to have an idea suddenly *After thinking about it for hours, we lit upon an idea that we all could agree on.*
light out	to leave quickly *We lit out for the meeting place as soon as our parents were in bed.*
light up	to make a room or other space fill with light; to start smoking a cigarette *The room lit up when we turned on the lamps in each corner. / He lit up as soon as his mother left the room.*

IDIOMS

to light a fire under someone	to motivate someone *What he needs to get him going is someone to light a fire under him.*
to see the light	to understand or be enlightened *I've explained my side of the situation, and I think she's beginning to see the light.*

RELATED WORDS

well/poorly-lit (adj.)	(of a space) either adequately or inadequately filled with light
lighter (n.)	a small gadget used to light a cigarette

* Note that the form "will be being lit/lighted" is rarely used. To convey a future progressive passive, use the present progressive passive.

live

	ACTIVE	PASSIVE
Infinitive	to live	to be lived
Past Infinitive	to have lived	to have been lived
Past Participle	lived	been lived
Present Participle	living	being lived

ACTIVE

I		
you/we/they		
he/she/it		

SIMPLE PRESENT	SIMPLE PAST	SIMPLE FUTURE
live	lived	will live
live	lived	will live
lives	lived	will live

PRESENT PROGRESSIVE	PAST PROGRESSIVE	FUTURE PROGRESSIVE
am living	was living	will be living
are living	were living	will be living
is living	was living	will be living

PRESENT PERFECT	PAST PERFECT	FUTURE PERFECT
have lived	had lived	will have lived
have lived	had lived	will have lived
has lived	had lived	will have lived

PRESENT PERFECT PROGRESSIVE	PAST PERFECT PROGRESSIVE	FUTURE PERFECT PROGRESSIVE
have been living	had been living	will have been living
have been living	had been living	will have been living
has been living	had been living	will have been living

EXAMPLES:

I was living in a studio apartment before I bought my own one-bedroom apartment.

She had always lived in fear of being rejected.

By next year, the hawks will have been living in the park for ten years.

PASSIVE

SIMPLE PRESENT	SIMPLE PAST	SIMPLE FUTURE
am lived	was lived	will be lived
are lived	were lived	will be lived
is lived	was lived	will be lived

PRESENT PROGRESSIVE	PAST PROGRESSIVE	FUTURE PROGRESSIVE*
am being lived	was being lived	will be being lived*
are being lived	were being lived	will be being lived*
is being lived	was being lived	will be being lived*

PRESENT PERFECT	PAST PERFECT	FUTURE PERFECT
have been lived	had been lived	will have been lived
have been lived	had been lived	will have been lived
has been lived	had been lived	will have been lived

EXAMPLES:

After the long journey, they felt as if several years had been lived instead of several months.

The February House was lived in by W. H. Auden, Carson McCullers, and Gypsy Rose Lee.

PRINCIPAL CONDITIONALS

PRESENT	PRESENT PROGRESSIVE	PRESENT PASSIVE
would live	would be living	would be lived
would live	would be living	would be lived
would live	would be living	would be lived

PAST	PAST PROGRESSIVE	PAST PASSIVE
would have lived	would have been living	would have been lived
would have lived	would have been living	would have been lived
would have lived	would have been living	would have been lived

EXAMPLES:

My husband, who grew up in a small town, said that he would never live in New York City.

We would be living closer to my work if we could find a reasonably-priced apartment.

Important Forms in Use

Verb Chart

IF/THEN CONDITIONALS

	IF ...	... THEN	EXAMPLE
Real Present/ Future	live/lives	simple present	*If you <u>live</u> in that building, then it means we're neighbors!*
		will + base form	*If she <u>lives</u> down the road, she'll certainly come to the party.*
Unreal Present/ Future	lived	would + base form	*If I <u>lived</u> in a big city, I wouldn't own a car.*
Unreal Past	had lived	would have + past participle	*If my grandmother <u>had lived</u> longer, I would've gotten to know her better.*

SUBJUNCTIVE

ACTIVE	live	*We suggest that you <u>live</u> in on-campus housing.*
PASSIVE	be lived	*It is asked that the high standards of the university <u>be lived</u> up to.*

PHRASAL VERBS

live (something) down	to be able to make others forget a mistake or blunder *That was some party. You'll never live this one down.*
live off (something)	to rely on something as your main source of income *She's been living off the meager salary they pay her at the restaurant.*
live through (something)	to survive a negative or difficult experience *Pravir lived through the divorce, but not without difficulty.*
live up to (something)	to fulfill an expectation *She never lived up to what her parents expected of her.*

IDIOMS

to live and let live	to allow people to do what they want, just as you do what you want *I don't particularly agree with the neighbors' lifestyle, but I figure that I should live and let live.*
to live beyond your means	to spend more money than you really can afford *My parents taught me not to live beyond my means.*
to live on borrowed time	to continue living even after one should have or might have died *After the car accident, he felt that he was living on borrowed time. He was lucky to be alive.*
to live from hand to mouth	to earn barely enough money to survive *Our salary is so low that we are forced to live from hand to mouth.*
to live it up	to enjoy yourself fully, especially by going out and eating and drinking without limit *We've been working so hard. Let's go out tonight and live it up.*

RELATED WORDS

livelihood (n.)	a means of earning one's money or living
lived-in (adj.)	comfortable

* Note that the form "will be being lived" is rarely used. To convey a future progressive passive, use the present progressive passive.

lock

	ACTIVE	PASSIVE
Infinitive	to lock	to be locked
Past Infinitive	to have locked	to have been locked
Past Participle	locked	been locked
Present Participle	locking	being locked

ACTIVE

I
you/we/they
he/she/it

SIMPLE PRESENT	SIMPLE PAST	SIMPLE FUTURE
lock	locked	will lock
lock	locked	will lock
locks	locked	will lock

PRESENT PROGRESSIVE	PAST PROGRESSIVE	FUTURE PROGRESSIVE
am locking	was locking	will be locking
are locking	were locking	will be locking
is locking	was locking	will be locking

PRESENT PERFECT	PAST PERFECT	FUTURE PERFECT
have locked	had locked	will have locked
have locked	had locked	will have locked
has locked	had locked	will have locked

PRESENT PERFECT PROGRESSIVE	PAST PERFECT PROGRESSIVE	FUTURE PERFECT PROGRESSIVE
have been locking	had been locking	will have been locking
have been locking	had been locking	will have been locking
has been locking	had been locking	will have been locking

EXAMPLES:
Don't forget to lock the door before you go to bed.
Had he locked the doors or did the burglars just walk in?
We haven't been locking the windows at night because it feels so safe here.

PASSIVE

SIMPLE PRESENT	SIMPLE PAST	SIMPLE FUTURE
am locked	was locked	will be locked
are locked	were locked	will be locked
is locked	was locked	will be locked

PRESENT PROGRESSIVE	PAST PROGRESSIVE	FUTURE PROGRESSIVE*
am being locked	was being locked	will be being locked*
are being locked	were being locked	will be being locked*
is being locked	was being locked	will be being locked*

PRESENT PERFECT	PAST PERFECT	FUTURE PERFECT
have been locked	had been locked	will have been locked
have been locked	had been locked	will have been locked
has been locked	had been locked	will have been locked

EXAMPLES:
The gate will be locked, so make sure that you have the code.
Luckily, the doors hadn't been locked yet when we ran back into the store to find my purse.
The dog had been locked up for hours and was ready to get out.

PRINCIPAL CONDITIONALS

PRESENT	PRESENT PROGRESSIVE	PRESENT PASSIVE
would lock	would be locking	would be locked
would lock	would be locking	would be locked
would lock	would be locking	would be locked

PAST	PAST PROGRESSIVE	PAST PASSIVE
would have locked	would have been locking	would have been locked
would have locked	would have been locking	would have been locked
would have locked	would have been locking	would have been locked

EXAMPLES:
Would you lock my locker for me please?
This door would have been locked if Jim had come home.

lock

Important Forms in Use

IF/THEN CONDITIONALS

	IF...	...THEN	EXAMPLE
Real Present/ Future	lock/locks	simple present	*If I don't <u>lock</u> up the bikes, I run the risk of getting one stolen.*
		will + base form	*If we <u>lock</u> you out by mistake, you'll find a key under the mat.*
Unreal Present/ Future	locked	would + base form	*If we <u>locked</u> the door every night, we would sleep more soundly.*
Unreal Past	had locked	would have + past participle	*If I <u>hadn't locked</u> the door, the cat would have gotten out.*

SUBJUNCTIVE

ACTIVE	lock	*It is important that the custodian <u>lock</u> up the office when he's finished cleaning.*
PASSIVE	be locked	*It is essential that doors <u>be locked</u> before nine p.m.*

PHRASAL VERBS

lock (someone) out	to close the door so that the person on the other side cannot enter *After she found out that her husband had been cheating on her she locked him out of the house.*
lock (someone or something) in	to close the door from the outside so that the person or thing inside cannot get out or be gotten out *I managed to lock my keys in the car for the third time this week.*
lock up	to arrest someone and put him or her in jail *The drunk driver was arrested and locked up at the local jail for the night.*

IDIOMS

to lock horns with someone	to get into an argument with someone *The two managing directors locked horns during the meeting.*
to lock lips	to kiss (informal) *My little brother turned away whenever the main characters in the film locked lips.*
lock, stock, and barrel	everything *The yard sale was great! We got rid of everything, lock, stock, and barrel.*
to be under lock and key	to be in a safe, locked place, or guarded carefully *After all the robberies recently, I made sure my valuables were under lock and key.*

RELATED WORDS

locker (n.)	a small place where you can store things temporarily such as at a gym
locket (n.)	a piece of jewelry that can be opened and can hold something inside
locksmith (n.)	a person who installs locks, unlocks doors, etc.
lockup (n.)	prison

* Note that the form "will be being locked" is rarely used. To convey a future progressive passive, use the present progressive passive.

Verb Chart

look

	ACTIVE	PASSIVE
Infinitive	to look	to be looked
Past Infinitive	to have looked	to have been looked
Past Participle	looked	been looked
Present Participle	looking	being looked

ACTIVE

I		
you/we/they		
he/she/it		

SIMPLE PRESENT	SIMPLE PAST	SIMPLE FUTURE
look	looked	will look
look	looked	will look
looks	looked	will look

PRESENT PROGRESSIVE	PAST PROGRESSIVE	FUTURE PROGRESSIVE
am looking	was looking	will be looking
are looking	were looking	will be looking
is looking	was looking	will be looking

PRESENT PERFECT	PAST PERFECT	FUTURE PERFECT
have looked	had looked	will have looked
have looked	had looked	will have looked
has looked	had looked	will have looked

PRESENT PERFECT PROGRESSIVE	PAST PERFECT PROGRESSIVE	FUTURE PERFECT PROGRESSIVE
have been looking	had been looking	will have been looking
have been looking	had been looking	will have been looking
has been looking	had been looking	will have been looking

EXAMPLES:

The sky was looking gray and we decided to leave the beach early.

We will be looking forward to hearing from you.

The manager had been looking for the keys for days when he found them in the laundry basket.

PASSIVE

SIMPLE PRESENT	SIMPLE PAST	SIMPLE FUTURE
am looked	was looked	will be looked
are looked	were looked	will be looked
is looked	was looked	will be looked

PRESENT PROGRESSIVE	PAST PROGRESSIVE	FUTURE PROGRESSIVE*
am being looked	was being looked	will be being looked*
are being looked	were being looked	will be being looked*
is being looked	was being looked	will be being looked*

PRESENT PERFECT	PAST PERFECT	FUTURE PERFECT
have been looked	had been looked	will have been looked
have been looked	had been looked	will have been looked
has been looked	had been looked	will have been looked

EXAMPLES:

Her artwork was always looked on fondly by her father.

Our house will be looked after by the management company.

PRINCIPAL CONDITIONALS

PRESENT	PRESENT PROGRESSIVE	PRESENT PASSIVE
would look	would be looking	would be looked
would look	would be looking	would be looked
would look	would be looking	would be looked

PAST	PAST PROGRESSIVE	PAST PASSIVE
would have looked	would have been looking	would have been looked
would have looked	would have been looking	would have been looked
would have looked	would have been looking	would have been looked

EXAMPLES:

I'm sure the tomatoes would be looking better if they got more sun.

I would have looked through the books if you had given me a little bit more time.

Important Forms in Use

IF/THEN CONDITIONALS

	IF...	...THEN	EXAMPLE
Real Present/ Future	look/looks	simple present	*If we <u>look</u> in on her once a day, she's fine.*
		will + base form	*If she <u>looks</u> over here, we'll say hello to her.*
Unreal Present/ Future	looked	would + base form	*If we <u>looked</u> around a little bit more, we'd find something that we liked.*
Unreal Past	had looked	would have + past participle	*If I <u>had looked</u> more closely, I would never have signed the contract.*

SUBJUNCTIVE

ACTIVE	look	*I recommend that the potential buyers <u>look</u> at the apartment again before you discuss prices.*
PASSIVE	be looked	*We ask that the lease <u>be looked</u> at by a lawyer before we sign.*

PHRASAL VERBS

look after (someone or something)	to take care of, watch, or guard someone or something *Our neighbor is looking after the house while we are away.*
look forward to (something)	to be excited about something that is going to happen in the future *After not taking a vacation for so many years, we were looking forward to our trip to Italy.*
look into (something)	to investigate *The police were looking into the robbery. / I know that you haven't received your refund yet and I'll be happy to look into it for you.*
look over	to examine something *Can you look over this document quickly before I sign it? / The mechanic looked over the engine carefully before we even thought about buying the car.*

IDIOMS

to look down your nose at someone	to not think highly of someone *My father always looked down his nose at the next-door neighbors.*
to look for the silver lining/ to look on the bright side	to be optimistic *I told him to look on the bright side when he got into the accident. After all, nobody was hurt.*
to look out for number one	to protect yourself at the expense of helping others *He was the most selfish person I ever knew. The only advice he ever gave me was to look out for number one.*
to not look a gift horse in the mouth	to be appreciative, instead of critical, of something that someone has given you or offered you *My brother didn't want to stay in Susan's apartment because it was too dark. I reminded him not to look a gift horse in the mouth.*

RELATED WORDS

good-looking (adj.)	attractive
looking glass (n.)	an old-fashioned term for a mirror
look-see (n.)	a brief look at something

* Note that the form "will be being looked" is rarely used. To convey a future progressive passive, use the present progressive passive.

Verb Chart

lose

	ACTIVE	PASSIVE
Infinitive	to lose	to be lost
Past Infinitive	to have lost	to have been lost
Past Participle	lost	been lost
Present Participle	losing	being lost

ACTIVE

I	
you/we/they	
he/she/it	

SIMPLE PRESENT	SIMPLE PAST	SIMPLE FUTURE
lose	lost	will lose
lose	lost	will lose
loses	lost	will lose

PRESENT PROGRESSIVE	PAST PROGRESSIVE	FUTURE PROGRESSIVE
am losing	was losing	will be losing
are losing	were losing	will be losing
is losing	was losing	will be losing

PRESENT PERFECT	PAST PERFECT	FUTURE PERFECT
have lost	had lost	will have lost
have lost	had lost	will have lost
has lost	had lost	will have lost

PRESENT PERFECT PROGRESSIVE	PAST PERFECT PROGRESSIVE	FUTURE PERFECT PROGRESSIVE
have been losing	had been losing	will have been losing
have been losing	had been losing	will have been losing
has been losing	had been losing	will have been losing

EXAMPLES:
Have you lost your keys again? | *I had already lost most of my money when I finally decided to leave the casino.* | *How many soldiers will have lost their lives by the end of this conflict?*

PASSIVE

SIMPLE PRESENT	SIMPLE PAST	SIMPLE FUTURE
am lost	was lost	will be lost
are lost	were lost	will be lost
is lost	was lost	will be lost

PRESENT PROGRESSIVE	PAST PROGRESSIVE	FUTURE PROGRESSIVE*
am being lost	was being lost	will be being lost*
are being lost	were being lost	will be being lost*
is being lost	was being lost	will be being lost*

PRESENT PERFECT	PAST PERFECT	FUTURE PERFECT
have been lost	had been lost	will have been lost
have been lost	had been lost	will have been lost
has been lost	had been lost	will have been lost

EXAMPLES:
The kids were lost in the woods for hours. | *The letter had been lost in the mail.* | *Whatever you do, don't give Terry the cash. It will be lost by the time we get there.*

PRINCIPAL CONDITIONALS

PRESENT	PRESENT PROGRESSIVE	PRESENT PASSIVE
would lose	would be losing	would be lost
would lose	would be losing	would be lost
would lose	would be losing	would be lost

PAST	PAST PROGRESSIVE	PAST PASSIVE
would have lost	would have been losing	would have been lost
would have lost	would have been losing	would have been lost
would have lost	would have been losing	would have been lost

EXAMPLES:
I would be lost if I didn't have such great assistants. | *The game would have been lost if it weren't for Sosa's home run in the last inning.*

lose

Important Forms in Use

IF/THEN CONDITIONALS

	IF...	...THEN	EXAMPLE
Real Present/ Future	lose/loses	simple present	*If we <u>lose</u> each other, let's meet on the steps near the lions in an hour.*
		will + base form	*If the tenors <u>lose</u> their place again, we'll have to call another rehearsal.*
Unreal Present/ Future	lost	would + base form	*If Sam <u>lost</u> his job, he would have trouble finding another one.*
Unreal Past	had lost	would have + past participle	*If he <u>had lost</u> his nerve, he never would have asked me out.*

SUBJUNCTIVE

ACTIVE	lose	*We advise that you not <u>lose</u> track of your spending.*
PASSIVE	be lost	*The mayor asked that a few key documents inadvertently <u>be lost</u> before the inspector showed up.*

PHRASAL VERBS

lose out on	to not benefit from
	If you don't go for the internship, you will be losing out on a great opportunity!

IDIOMS

to lose track	to not be able to keep up with the details of a certain situation
	If I don't write down all of the money that I spend, I tend to lose track of it.
to lose ground	to stop making progress and instead begin to move backward
	Due to delays in getting a shuttle to the space station, the space program is losing ground.
Get lost!	said when you want someone to leave (informal)
	You are really bothering me. Get lost!
to lose touch	to not remain in contact with someone
	Sylvia and I lost touch after she got a job in another city.
to lose face	to feel embarrassment or that your honor has been offended
	The negotiations had to be very delicate so that the prime minister wouldn't lose face.

RELATED WORDS

loser (n.)	a person who has failed to win a competition, game, bet, etc.
loss (n.)	the state of not having something that you once had
lost (adj.)	misplaced

* Note that the form "will be being lost" is rarely used. To convey a future progressive passive, use the present progressive passive.

Verb Chart

make

	ACTIVE	PASSIVE
Infinitive	to make	to be made
Past Infinitive	have made	have been made
Past Participle	made	been made
Present Participle	making	being made

ACTIVE

I
you/we/they
he/she/it

SIMPLE PRESENT	SIMPLE PAST	SIMPLE FUTURE
make	made	will make
make	made	will make
makes	made	will make

PRESENT PROGRESSIVE	PAST PROGRESSIVE	FUTURE PROGRESSIVE
am making	was making	will be making
are making	were making	will be making
is making	was making	will be making

PRESENT PERFECT	PAST PERFECT	FUTURE PERFECT
have made	had made	will have made
have made	had made	will have made
has made	had made	will have made

PRESENT PERFECT PROGRESSIVE	PAST PERFECT PROGRESSIVE	FUTURE PERFECT PROGRESSIVE
have been making	had been making	will have been making
have been making	had been making	will have been making
has been making	had been making	will have been making

EXAMPLES:

John is making all of the furniture for our new house.

Drink a cup of hot tea. That will make you feel better.

When we arrived at the restaurant, we realized that we hadn't made a reservation.

PASSIVE

SIMPLE PRESENT	SIMPLE PAST	SIMPLE FUTURE
am made	was made	will be made
are made	were made	will be made
is made	was made	will be made

PRESENT PROGRESSIVE	PAST PROGRESSIVE	FUTURE PROGRESSIVE*
am being made	was being made	will be being made*
are being made	were being made	will be being made*
is being made	was being made	will be being made*

PRESENT PERFECT	PAST PERFECT	FUTURE PERFECT
have been made	had been made	will have been made
have been made	had been made	will have been made
has been made	had been made	will have been made

EXAMPLES:

Most of the clothing I am wearing was made in China.

After months of deliberations, a decision has finally been made.

It was disappointing to find out that the telephone call still hadn't been made.

PRINCIPAL CONDITIONALS

PRESENT	PRESENT PROGRESSIVE	PRESENT PASSIVE
would make	would be making	would be made
would make	would be making	would be made
would make	would be making	would be made

PAST	PAST PROGRESSIVE	PAST PASSIVE
would have made	would have been making	would have been made
would have made	would have been making	would have been made
would have made	would have been making	would have been made

EXAMPLES:

I would happily make you a cup of tea if you asked.

Sally wouldn't have made so many mistakes if she had been more careful.

Important Forms in Use

IF/THEN CONDITIONALS

	IF...	...THEN	EXAMPLE
Real Present/ Future	make/makes	simple present	*If we <u>make</u> too much food, we have leftovers for the following day.*
		will + base form	*If you <u>make</u> the cake from scratch, it will be delicious.*
Unreal Present/ Future	made	would + base form	*If they <u>made</u> it here for the surprise party, my mother would be so happy.*
Unreal Past	had made	would have + past participle	*If Ben and Terry <u>hadn't made</u> it to the finish line, they would have shocked everyone.*

SUBJUNCTIVE

ACTIVE	make	*It is important that we <u>make</u> this experience a valuable one.*
PASSIVE	be made	*We recommend that an effort <u>be made</u> to finish the work before the deadline.*

PHRASAL VERBS

make away with (something)	to steal *The robbers made away with all of my mother's china.*
make (something) into	to change something so that it has a different use or form *We're going to make this into the baby's room.*
make out (something)	to be able to understand something at a minimal level *We tried to read her great-grandfather's letters from the Civil War, but we couldn't make out the handwriting.*
make (something) over	to redo, often used with decoration, makeup, or fashion *We made over the downstairs bathroom and kitchen.*
make (something) up	to invent a story to deceive or entertain *I didn't know how to explain my lateness so I made something up.*

IDIOMS

to make a go of something	to attempt to be successful in a venture *We didn't think he could make a go of it, but the new restaurant is doing very well.*
to make do	to manage with less then the perfect amount *The hostess didn't have enough chairs for the party, but she made do.*
to make time	to find space in your schedule for something or someone *Can you make time for me this afternoon?*
to make a mountain out of a molehill	to exaggerate a small issue into a big one *My boss was really making a mountain out of a molehill when he threatened to fire me over the article I wrote.*
to make the most (out) of something	to take full advantage of something *We really made the most of this weekend. I can't believe how many things we did.*

RELATED WORDS

make-believe (adj.)	not real, imaginary
maker (n.)	the entity that produces something
makeover (n.)	a process in which the appearance of something is changed to make it look better
makeup (n.)	what something is composed of, or cosmetics that are applied to the face

Verb Chart

* Note that the form "will be being made" is rarely used. To convey a future progressive passive, use the present progressive passive.

open

	ACTIVE	PASSIVE
Infinitive	to open	to be opened
Past Infinitive	to have opened	to have been opened
Past Participle	opened	been opened
Present Participle	opening	being opened

ACTIVE

I
you/we/they
he/she/it

SIMPLE PRESENT	SIMPLE PAST	SIMPLE FUTURE
open	opened	will open
open	opened	will open
opens	opened	will open

PRESENT PROGRESSIVE	PAST PROGRESSIVE	FUTURE PROGRESSIVE
am opening	was opening	will be opening
are opening	were opening	will be opening
is opening	was opening	will be opening

PRESENT PERFECT	PAST PERFECT	FUTURE PERFECT
have opened	had opened	will have opened
have opened	had opened	will have opened
has opened	had opened	will have opened

PRESENT PERFECT PROGRESSIVE	PAST PERFECT PROGRESSIVE	FUTURE PERFECT PROGRESSIVE
have been opening	had been opening	will have been opening
have been opening	had been opening	will have been opening
has been opening	had been opening	will have been opening

EXAMPLES:
She opened her wallet and discovered that all of her money and credit cards had been taken.

The kids will be opening their presents first thing in the morning.

If I leave the house at 8:00, the bank will have opened by the time I get there.

PASSIVE

SIMPLE PRESENT	SIMPLE PAST	SIMPLE FUTURE
am opened	was opened	will be opened
are opened	were opened	will be opened
is opened	was opened	will be opened

PRESENT PROGRESSIVE	PAST PROGRESSIVE	FUTURE PROGRESSIVE*
am being opened	was being opened	will be being opened*
are being opened	were being opened	will be being opened*
is being opened	was being opened	will be being opened*

PRESENT PERFECT	PAST PERFECT	FUTURE PERFECT
have been opened	had been opened	will have been opened
have been opened	had been opened	will have been opened
has been opened	had been opened	will have been opened

EXAMPLES:
The milk was opened yesterday; it should be fine to drink.

The doors of the theater were being opened when we got there.

I was upset to find out that my package had been opened by someone before it arrived at my house.

PRINCIPAL CONDITIONALS

PRESENT	PRESENT PROGRESSIVE	PRESENT PASSIVE
would open	would be opening	would be opened
would open	would be opening	would be opened
would open	would be opening	would be opened

PAST	PAST PROGRESSIVE	PAST PASSIVE
would have opened	would have been opening	would have been opened
would have opened	would have been opening	would have been opened
would have opened	would have been opening	would have been opened

EXAMPLES:
She was excited to hear that her favorite band would open for Bruce Springsteen on his tour this year.

I would have opened an account at another bank if I had known how much my bank was going to charge me.

PRINCIPAL PARTS: open, opened, opened

Important Forms in Use

IF/THEN CONDITIONALS

	IF ...	... THEN	EXAMPLE
Real Present/ Future	open/opens	simple present	*If I <u>open</u> the doors for you, you need to promise that you will lock them before you leave.*
		will + base form	*If he <u>opens</u> the present now, he'll be able to use it on his vacation.*
Unreal Present/ Future	opened	would + base form	*If you <u>opened</u> your eyes, you would see that he's making a fool out of you.*
Unreal Past	had opened	would have + past participle	*If I <u>had opened</u> with a more popular song, the audience would have liked my concert more.*

SUBJUNCTIVE

ACTIVE	open	*We suggest that you <u>open</u> the package before you leave the store to make sure that everything has been included.*
PASSIVE	be opened	*We ask that the doors <u>be opened</u> before five p.m.*

PHRASAL VERBS

open out	to lead to something else *A door in my living room opens out onto the back terrace.*
open up	to become vacant or available *Call my boss sometime this week; several positions in the graphics department are opening up.*
open up to someone	to become more candid about your feelings *My colleague only opened up to me after we had worked together for several years.*

IDIOMS

to open doors	to create possibilities for someone *Having my uncle on the board certainly opened doors for me at the foundation.*
to open your mind to something	to be willing to have new experiences or be accepting of new ideas or things *You can't just dismiss the neighbors as being strange; you need to open your mind to new cultures and learn more about their customs.*
to open your heart to someone	to share personal thoughts and feelings with someone *Sam and I were just friends, but after he separated from his wife, he began to open his heart to me.*
to open someone's eyes	to make something clear to someone who hadn't been able to see it before *The lecture that we heard last night about the media really opened my eyes to a lot of truths that I didn't know about before.*

RELATED WORDS

open-and-shut (adj.)	describes a situation that is black-and-white, where there is no doubt about the answer or outcome
opener (n.)	a device used to open cans, bottles, etc.; the first game of the season, act of the show, etc.

* Note that the form "will be being opened" is rarely used. To convey a future progressive passive, use the present progressive passive.

panic

	ACTIVE	PASSIVE
Infinitive	to panic	to be panicked
Past Infinitive	to have panicked	to have been panicked
Past Participle	panicked	been panicked
Present Participle	panicking	being panicked

ACTIVE

I		
you/we/they		
he/she/it		

SIMPLE PRESENT	SIMPLE PAST	SIMPLE FUTURE
panic	panicked	will panic
panic	panicked	will panic
panics	panicked	will panic

PRESENT PROGRESSIVE	PAST PROGRESSIVE	FUTURE PROGRESSIVE
am panicking	was panicking	will be panicking
are panicking	were panicking	will be panicking
is panicking	was panicking	will be panicking

PRESENT PERFECT	PAST PERFECT	FUTURE PERFECT
have panicked	had panicked	will have panicked
have panicked	had panicked	will have panicked
has panicked	had panicked	will have panicked

PRESENT PERFECT PROGRESSIVE	PAST PERFECT PROGRESSIVE	FUTURE PERFECT PROGRESSIVE
have been panicking	had been panicking	will have been panicking
have been panicking	had been panicking	will have been panicking
has been panicking	had been panicking	will have been panicking

EXAMPLES:
If we don't get these drafts in by the end of the day, the director will panic.
Call Mom and tell her where you are. She's been panicking all day.
The audience had panicked, which had caused delays in getting out of the theater.

PASSIVE

SIMPLE PRESENT	SIMPLE PAST	SIMPLE FUTURE
am panicked	was panicked	will be panicked
are panicked	were panicked	will be panicked
is panicked	was panicked	will be panicked

PRESENT PROGRESSIVE	PAST PROGRESSIVE	FUTURE PROGRESSIVE*
am being panicked	was being panicked	will be being panicked*
are being panicked	were being panicked	will be being panicked*
is being panicked	was being panicked	will be being panicked*

PRESENT PERFECT	PAST PERFECT	FUTURE PERFECT
have been panicked	had been panicked	will have been panicked
have been panicked	had been panicked	will have been panicked
has been panicked	had been panicked	will have been panicked

EXAMPLES:
I am always panicked by strange noises I hear in the night.
Americans were panicked by sudden drops in the value of stocks.
I was panicked by the fact that my parents would be home in an hour.

PRINCIPAL CONDITIONALS

PRESENT	PRESENT PROGRESSIVE	PRESENT PASSIVE
would panic	would be panicking	would be panicked
would panic	would be panicking	would be panicked
would panic	would be panicking	would be panicked

PAST	PAST PROGRESSIVE	PAST PASSIVE
would have panicked	would have been panicking	would have been panicked
would have panicked	would have been panicking	would have been panicked
would have panicked	would have been panicking	would have been panicked

EXAMPLES:
You would panic too if you were in my situation.
We would have panicked if we had arrived at the airport even a minute later.

Important Forms in Use

IF/THEN CONDITIONALS

	IF ...	... THEN	EXAMPLE
Real Present/ Future	panic/panics	simple present	*If I we panic now, we lose the race.*
		will + base form	*If she panics while holding on to the cliff edge with only one hand, it will mean death.*
Unreal Present/ Future	panicked	would + base form	*If he panicked instead of responding calmly, the firefighter would never make it out of the building alive.*
Unreal Past	had panicked	would have + past participle	*If I had panicked when the car began to slide, I wouldn't have been able to avoid an accident.*

SUBJUNCTIVE

ACTIVE	panic	*It is important that an airline pilot not panic in emergency situations.*
PASSIVE	be panicked	*It is essential that citizens not be panicked in the face of a natural disaster.*

IDIOMS

to press/push/hit the panic button	to make a quick, not well-thought-out response when confronted by a difficult situation *Only someone with nerves of steel, someone who won't hit the panic button, can be considered to lead the expedition to the top of Mt. Everest.*

RELATED WORDS

panic attack (n.)	the escalation of anxiety to the point at which it causes the heart to beat faster and shortness of breath
panic-stricken (adj.)	overwhelmed by a high level of anxiety or nervousness

* Note that the form "will be being panicked" is rarely used. To convey a future progressive passive, use the present progressive passive.

Verb Chart

pass

	ACTIVE	PASSIVE
Infinitive	to pass	to be passed
Past Infinitive	to have passed	to have been passed
Past Participle	passed	been passed
Present Participle	passing	being passed

ACTIVE

I	
you/we/they	
he/she/it	

SIMPLE PRESENT	SIMPLE PAST	SIMPLE FUTURE
pass	passed	will pass
pass	passed	will pass
passes	passed	will pass

PRESENT PROGRESSIVE	PAST PROGRESSIVE	FUTURE PROGRESSIVE
am passing	was passing	will be passing
are passing	were passing	will be passing
is passing	was passing	will be passing

PRESENT PERFECT	PAST PERFECT	FUTURE PERFECT
have passed	had passed	will have passed
have passed	had passed	will have passed
has passed	had passed	will have passed

PRESENT PERFECT PROGRESSIVE	PAST PERFECT PROGRESSIVE	FUTURE PERFECT PROGRESSIVE
have been passing	had been passing	will have been passing
have been passing	had been passing	will have been passing
has been passing	had been passing	will have been passing

EXAMPLES:

He passes by here a couple of times a year on his way to Florida.

How many students have passed the college entrance examination so far this year?

Hopefully, I will have passed all of my courses by the end of the year.

PASSIVE

SIMPLE PRESENT	SIMPLE PAST	SIMPLE FUTURE
am passed	was passed	will be passed
are passed	were passed	will be passed
is passed	was passed	will be passed

PRESENT PROGRESSIVE	PAST PROGRESSIVE	FUTURE PROGRESSIVE*
am being passed	was being passed	will be being passed*
are being passed	were being passed	will be being passed*
is being passed	was being passed	will be being passed*

PRESENT PERFECT	PAST PERFECT	FUTURE PERFECT
have been passed	had been passed	will have been passed
have been passed	had been passed	will have been passed
has been passed	had been passed	will have been passed

EXAMPLES:

She was passed over for a promotion.

The torch will be passed from athlete to athlete until it arrives in the Olympic city.

What is the dish that is being passed around?

PRINCIPAL CONDITIONALS

PRESENT	PRESENT PROGRESSIVE	PRESENT PASSIVE
would pass	would be passing	would be passed
would pass	would be passing	would be passed
would pass	would be passing	would be passed

PAST	PAST PROGRESSIVE	PAST PASSIVE
would have passed	would have been passing	would have been passed
would have passed	would have been passing	would have been passed
would have passed	would have been passing	would have been passed

EXAMPLES:

I didn't know that the honor would be passed on to me.

I thought she would pass me by without saying anything.

pass

Important Forms in Use

IF/THEN CONDITIONALS

	IF . . .	. . . THEN	EXAMPLE
Real Present/ Future	pass/passes	simple present	If he <u>passes</u> his exams, we take him to Pederson's for ice cream.
		will + base form	If we <u>pass</u> a gas station on the way, I'll stop and fill up.
Unreal Present/ Future	passed	would + base form	If she <u>passed</u> by here, we would see her.
Unreal Past	had passed	would have + past participle	If I <u>had passed</u> the grocery store, I would have bought some milk.

SUBJUNCTIVE

ACTIVE	pass	They asked that he <u>pass</u> by on the way to school in the morning.
PASSIVE	be passed	It is important that the tests <u>be passed</u> out only after all students are seated and all books are put away.

PHRASAL VERBS

pass by	to proceed past somewhere on your way to another place *She passed by the restaurant on her way home.*
pass (something) down	to give something that belongs to you to someone in the next generation of your family; to send something, such as orders, through a chain of communication from top to bottom *The rings were passed down from her mother.*
pass (something) on	to give something (usually information) to someone else *These are the figures. Can you pass them on to accounting?*
pass (something) out	to hand out, to distribute *We need volunteers to pass out the flyers.*
pass out	to lose consciousness *The room was very stuffy and Hillary passed out.*
pass (someone) over	to not consider someone for something *I thought that Randy would be good for the position, but they passed him over.*

IDIOMS

to pass the buck	to make someone else responsible for something that you should be responsible for *Their department always passes the buck, which means a lot more work for us.*
to pass muster	to be acceptable *Do you think our cleaning job will pass muster, or should we have done a more careful job?*
to (have to) pass (on something)	to reject or refuse in a polite manner *I'm going to pass on the apple pie. I'm way too full.*
this too shall pass	an expression meaning that life goes on even after something difficult or unpleasant happens *I know your divorce has been difficult, but this too shall pass.*

RELATED WORDS

passing interest/fancy (n.)	a short-term interest in something
passable (adj.)	acceptable

* Note that the form "will be being passed" is rarely used. To convey a future progressive passive, use the present progressive passive.

pay

	ACTIVE	PASSIVE
Infinitive	to pay	to be paid
Past Infinitive	to have paid	to have been paid
Past Participle	paid	been paid
Present Participle	paying	being paid

ACTIVE

I		
you/we/they		
he/she/it		

SIMPLE PRESENT	SIMPLE PAST	SIMPLE FUTURE
pay	paid	will pay
pay	paid	will pay
pays	paid	will pay

PRESENT PROGRESSIVE	PAST PROGRESSIVE	FUTURE PROGRESSIVE
am paying	was paying	will be paying
are paying	were paying	will be paying
is paying	was paying	will be paying

PRESENT PERFECT	PAST PERFECT	FUTURE PERFECT
have paid	had paid	will have paid
have paid	had paid	will have paid
has paid	had paid	will have paid

PRESENT PERFECT PROGRESSIVE	PAST PERFECT PROGRESSIVE	FUTURE PERFECT PROGRESSIVE
have been paying	had been paying	will have been paying
have been paying	had been paying	will have been paying
has been paying	had been paying	will have been paying

EXAMPLES:

If you pay attention, you can pick up a lot from Howard's TV show.

We haven't paid our taxes yet this year and it's already April 1st.

While Johanna was paying, Danny went outside to get a taxi.

PASSIVE

SIMPLE PRESENT	SIMPLE PAST	SIMPLE FUTURE
am paid	was paid	will be paid
are paid	were paid	will be paid
is paid	was paid	will be paid

PRESENT PROGRESSIVE	PAST PROGRESSIVE	FUTURE PROGRESSIVE*
am being paid	was being paid	will be being paid*
are being paid	were being paid	will be being paid*
is being paid	was being paid	will be being paid*

PRESENT PERFECT	PAST PERFECT	FUTURE PERFECT
have been paid	had been paid	will have been paid
have been paid	had been paid	will have been paid
has been paid	had been paid	will have been paid

EXAMPLES:

Mary was paid very well for the job.

The workers were being paid too little for the amount of labor the job involved.

PRINCIPAL CONDITIONALS

PRESENT	PRESENT PROGRESSIVE	PRESENT PASSIVE
would pay	would be paying	would be paid
would pay	would be paying	would be paid
would pay	would be paying	would be paid

PAST	PAST PROGRESSIVE	PAST PASSIVE
would have paid	would have been paid	would have been paid
would have paid	would have been paid	would have been paid
would have paid	would have been paid	would have been paid

EXAMPLES:

He would pay you more if he felt that the job had been well done.

We didn't know how much we would be paid for painting her house.

Sally would have been paid more if she had asked for more.

PRINCIPAL PARTS: pay, paid, paid

Important Forms in Use

IF/THEN CONDITIONALS

	IF . . .	. . . THEN	EXAMPLE
Real Present/ Future	pay/pays	simple present	*If I _pay_ attention, I understand everything when she speaks in Spanish.*
		will + base form	*If she _pays_ that much money for this piece of junk, I'll die.*
Unreal Present/ Future	paid	would + base form	*If we _paid_ off our debts, we'd be able to take a vacation.*
Unreal Past	had paid	would have + past participle	*If I _had paid_ for you at the movies, I wouldn't have had any money for dinner.*

SUBJUNCTIVE

ACTIVE	pay	*It is required that your son _pay_ the bill in full.*
PASSIVE	be paid	*It is essential that we _be paid_ before we begin to work.*

PHRASAL VERBS

pay (someone) back	to repay *Simon still hasn't paid me back the money I lent him when we went sailing.*
pay off	to give the entire sum of money that you owe for something; to bribe *I'll never pay off the money I owe for college.*
pay up	to give the money that you owe, especially when you are reluctant to do so *They sent a collector to his house to make sure he paid up.*

IDIOMS

to pay someone a compliment	to say something nice to someone about his or her abilities, appearance, or performance *She paid me the nicest compliment I had ever received when she compared my performance to Bette Davis.*
to pay the price	to suffer the consequences of a bad decision *He paid the price for quitting his job without thinking, because he is still out of work.*
to pay for something	to suffer or receive retribution for something done; often used as a threat *He'll pay for the way he treated my family.*
to pay through the nose	to pay too much for something *The hotel was beautiful but we paid through the nose.*
to pay your respects	to send your regards to someone, often at a funeral *We wanted to talk to the widow and pay our respects.*
to pay attention	to listen or watch closely *You need to pay attention to her lecture; we'll be tested on it later.*

RELATED WORDS

down payment (n.)	the money that you put down before you make a large purchase, such as a house or a car
paycheck (n.)	the money that you receive each time your workplace pays you
payday (n.)	the day each week, month, etc., that you receive your paycheck
pay raise (n.)	an increase in salary
payroll (n.)	a list kept by employers of people in their employ to be paid and the amount owed to each

* Note that the form "will be being paid" is rarely used. To convey a future progressive passive, use the present progressive passive.

plan

	ACTIVE	PASSIVE
Infinitive	to plan	to be planned
Past Infinitive	to have planned	to have been planned
Past Participle	planned	been planned
Present Participle	planning	being planned

ACTIVE

I
you/we/they
he/she/it

SIMPLE PRESENT	SIMPLE PAST	SIMPLE FUTURE
plan	planned	will plan
plan	planned	will plan
plans	planned	will plan

PRESENT PROGRESSIVE	PAST PROGRESSIVE	FUTURE PROGRESSIVE
am planning	was planning	will be planning
are planning	were planning	will be planning
is planning	was planning	will be planning

PRESENT PERFECT	PAST PERFECT	FUTURE PERFECT
have planned	had planned	will have planned
have planned	had planned	will have planned
has planned	had planned	will have planned

PRESENT PERFECT PROGRESSIVE	PAST PERFECT PROGRESSIVE	FUTURE PERFECT PROGRESSIVE
have been planning	had been planning	will have been planning
have been planning	had been planning	will have been planning
has been planning	had been planning	will have been planning

EXAMPLES:

He is planning to move to an apartment that is closer to his work.

How long have you been planning your vacation?

They had planned to go to Colorado at Christmas time but there was a huge blizzard the day before their flight left.

PASSIVE

SIMPLE PRESENT	SIMPLE PAST	SIMPLE FUTURE
am planned	was planned	will be planned
are planned	were planned	will be planned
is planned	was planned	will be planned

PRESENT PROGRESSIVE	PAST PROGRESSIVE	FUTURE PROGRESSIVE*
am being planned	was being planned	will be being planned*
are being planned	were being planned	will be being planned*
is being planned	was being planned	will be being planned*

PRESENT PERFECT	PAST PERFECT	FUTURE PERFECT
have been planned	had been planned	will have been planned
have been planned	had been planned	will have been planned
has been planned	had been planned	will have been planned

EXAMPLES:

Our day is being planned by the tour guide.

I didn't know what had been planned and, unfortunately, showed up along with the guest of honor at the surprise party.

By the time you get here, all the camp activities will have been planned.

PRINCIPAL CONDITIONALS

PRESENT	PRESENT PROGRESSIVE	PRESENT PASSIVE
would plan	would be planning	would be planned
would plan	would be planning	would be planned
would plan	would be planning	would be planned

PAST	PAST PROGRESSIVE	PAST PASSIVE
would have planned	would have been planning	would have been planned
would have planned	would have been planning	would have been planned
would have planned	would have been planning	would have been planned

EXAMPLES:

I would plan on cold weather. Bring a sweater and a jacket.

We would have planned better if we had known how many people were coming.

Important Forms in Use

IF/THEN CONDITIONALS

	IF ...	...THEN	EXAMPLE
Real Present/ Future	plan/plans	simple present	If I _plan_ on rain, the sun always shines, and if I plan on sun, it always rains.
		will + base form	If she _plans_ the event with me, then I won't have as much work.
Unreal Present/ Future	planned	would + base form	If they _planned_ on coming, they would tell us.
Unreal Past	had planned	would have + past participle	If I _had planned_ the dinner, I would have had fish instead of red meat.

SUBJUNCTIVE

ACTIVE	plan	It is important that we _plan_ the reception right away if we want to find any available space.
PASSIVE	be planned	It is essential that our weekend _be planned_ down to the last minute so we don't lose any time.

PHRASAL VERBS

plan ahead	to make plans well in advance for something that is going to happen in the future If you don't plan ahead, especially by booking hotels, there will certainly be problems once you get to Paris.
plan for	to prepare for something that may happen in the future We didn't plan for rain, but all of the guests gathered under the tent and had a great time anyway.
plan on	to count on or expect that something will happen We plan on having his help for the move.
plan out	to prepare for something that is going to happen in the future by looking carefully at every detail and potential problems The architect has planned out every step in the building of our house.

IDIOMS

to go as planned	when something happens exactly as you prepared The wedding was perfect. Everything went as planned.
to have plans	when you have an agreement to do something, you say that you have plans I'm sorry I can't come with you tonight but I already have plans.
to make plans	to make an arrangement to do something I haven't seen Harry for weeks but we're making plans to get together soon.
You can plan on it!	an expression that is said to let someone know that something is going to happen "Are you going to come to my party tonight?" "You can plan on it!"

RELATED WORDS

plan (n.)	an arrangement
plan of attack (n.)	a plan to accomplish something
well-laid plans (n.)	arrangements that have been thought out carefully

Verb Chart

* Note that the form "will be being planned" is rarely used. To convey a future progressive passive, use the present progressive passive.

play

	ACTIVE	PASSIVE
Infinitive	to play	to be played
Past Infinitive	to have played	to have been played
Past Participle	played	been played
Present Participle	playing	being played

ACTIVE

I		
you/we/they		
he/she/it		

SIMPLE PRESENT	SIMPLE PAST	SIMPLE FUTURE
play	played	will play
play	played	will play
plays	played	will play

PRESENT PROGRESSIVE	PAST PROGRESSIVE	FUTURE PROGRESSIVE
am playing	was playing	will be playing
are playing	were playing	will be playing
is playing	was playing	will be playing

PRESENT PERFECT	PAST PERFECT	FUTURE PERFECT
have played	had played	will have played
have played	had played	will have played
has played	had played	will have played

PRESENT PERFECT PROGRESSIVE	PAST PERFECT PROGRESSIVE	FUTURE PERFECT PROGRESSIVE
have been playing	had been playing	will have been playing
have been playing	had been playing	will have been playing
has been playing	had been playing	will have been playing

EXAMPLES:

The kids play in the supervised playground area after school.

We were playing duets for hours.

The new act will be playing at the Apollo Theater.

PASSIVE

SIMPLE PRESENT	SIMPLE PAST	SIMPLE FUTURE
am played	was played	will be played
are played	were played	will be played
is played	was played	will be played

PRESENT PROGRESSIVE	PAST PROGRESSIVE	FUTURE PROGRESSIVE*
am being played	was being played	will be being played*
are being played	were being played	will be being played*
is being played	was being played	will be being played*

PRESENT PERFECT	PAST PERFECT	FUTURE PERFECT
have been played	had been played	will have been played
have been played	had been played	will have been played
has been played	had been played	will have been played

EXAMPLES:

A symphony by Mozart was being played in the waiting room.

The cricket match was played for days.

I hope they won't have played my favorite song before we get there.

PRINCIPAL CONDITIONALS

PRESENT	PRESENT PROGRESSIVE	PRESENT PASSIVE
would play	would be playing	would be played
would play	would be playing	would be played
would play	would be playing	would be played

PAST	PAST PROGRESSIVE	PAST PASSIVE
would have played	would have been playing	would have been played
would have played	would have been playing	would have been played
would have played	would have been playing	would have been played

EXAMPLES:

The team manager didn't know who would be playing first base in that night's game.

Alice would have played if she hadn't sprained her ankle.

play

PRINCIPAL PARTS: play, played, played

VERB CHART
78

Important Forms in Use

IF/THEN CONDITIONALS

	IF...	...THEN	EXAMPLE
Real Present/ Future	play/plays	simple present	If I _play_ with him in the morning, he still wants me to play with him again at night.
		will + base form	If she _plays_ the music too loud, the neighbors will complain.
Unreal Present/ Future	played	would + base form	If we _played_ bridge more often, we'd be able to compete with the Wheats.
Unreal Past	had played	would have + past participle	If she _had played_ that song earlier, the audience would have stayed longer.

SUBJUNCTIVE

ACTIVE	play	It is important that the actors _play_ the parts as the director stipulated.
PASSIVE	be played	It is essential that the wedding march _be played_ as the bride enters the church.

PHRASAL VERBS

play down (something)	to make something appear less important than it is _Ira is an excellent pianist but he always plays down his talents._
play out	to come to a conclusion or an end _We were all tense as we waited to find out how the negotiations would play out._
play up (something or someone)	to make something appear more important than it is _He always plays up his relationship with the president of the company._
play with (something or someone)	to use something or someone for amusement _The kids were playing with the old clothes that I had thrown into a trunk in the attic._

IDIOMS

to play with fire	to involve yourself in something dangerous _I don't think Tom should invest in that new company. In my opinion, he's playing with fire._
to play something for all it's worth	to take full advantage of something _We'll only get the grant once, so let's play it for all it's worth._
to play it by ear	to not make specific plans, to make plans as things happen _Audrey doesn't know when she'll get off work, so let's just play it by ear tonight._
to play someone for a fool	to treat someone like he or she is stupid _Don't play me for a fool! I know that you didn't give me the money for the rent last month._
to play second fiddle to someone	to be less important than someone else _Joe didn't want to play second fiddle to Leslie and so he quit._

RELATED WORDS

player (n.)	a person who participates in a game or plays a musical instrument
play (n.)	a written piece in which actors take different parts and perform on stage
play-by-play (n.)	a description of a sports game as it is happening that can be heard on TV or on the radio

Verb Chart

* Note that the form "will be being played" is rarely used. To convey a future progressive passive, use the present progressive passive.

pull

	ACTIVE	PASSIVE
Infinitive	to pull	to be pulled
Past Infinitive	to have pulled	to have been pulled
Past Participle	pulled	been pulled
Present Participle	pulling	being pulled

ACTIVE

I
you/we/they
he/she/it

SIMPLE PRESENT	SIMPLE PAST	SIMPLE FUTURE
pull	pulled	will pull
pull	pulled	will pull
pulls	pulled	will pull

PRESENT PROGRESSIVE	PAST PROGRESSIVE	FUTURE PROGRESSIVE
am pulling	was pulling	will be pulling
are pulling	were pulling	will be pulling
is pulling	was pulling	will be pulling

PRESENT PERFECT	PAST PERFECT	FUTURE PERFECT
have pulled	had pulled	will have pulled
have pulled	had pulled	will have pulled
has pulled	had pulled	will have pulled

PRESENT PERFECT PROGRESSIVE	PAST PERFECT PROGRESSIVE	FUTURE PERFECT PROGRESSIVE
have been pulling	had been pulling	will have been pulling
have been pulling	had been pulling	will have been pulling
has been pulling	had been pulling	will have been pulling

EXAMPLES:
The horse pulls too much weight when it carries the buggy.

I had pulled a muscle and therefore couldn't compete.

They pulled up in a beautiful new BMW convertible.

PASSIVE

SIMPLE PRESENT	SIMPLE PAST	SIMPLE FUTURE
am pulled	was pulled	will be pulled
are pulled	were pulled	will be pulled
is pulled	was pulled	will be pulled

PRESENT PROGRESSIVE	PAST PROGRESSIVE	FUTURE PROGRESSIVE*
am being pulled	was being pulled	will be being pulled*
are being pulled	were being pulled	will be being pulled*
is being pulled	was being pulled	will be being pulled*

PRESENT PERFECT	PAST PERFECT	FUTURE PERFECT
have been pulled	had been pulled	will have been pulled
have been pulled	had been pulled	will have been pulled
has been pulled	had been pulled	will have been pulled

EXAMPLES:
The students feel that they are pulled in too many different directions.

The trailer was being pulled by a pickup truck.

PRINCIPAL CONDITIONALS

PRESENT	PRESENT PROGRESSIVE	PRESENT PASSIVE
would pull	would be pulling	would be pulled
would pull	would be pulling	would be pulled
would pull	would be pulling	would be pulled

PAST	PAST PROGRESSIVE	PAST PASSIVE
would have pulled	would have been pulling	would have been pulled
would have pulled	would have been pulling	would have been pulled
would have pulled	would have been pulling	would have been pulled

EXAMPLES:
Would you pull the cart toward you please?

He would have pulled a muscle if he hadn't warmed up before the game.

Important Forms in Use

IF/THEN CONDITIONALS

	IF ...	... THEN	EXAMPLE
Real Present/ Future	pull/pulls	simple present	*If I <u>pull</u> my weight, my boss is happy.*
		will + base form	*If she <u>pulls</u> this rope, it'll raise the curtains.*
Unreal Present/ Future	pulled	would + base form	*If we <u>pulled</u> together, we would have a better chance of surviving.*
Unreal Past	had pulled past participle	would have +	*If I <u>had pulled</u> her hair any harder, it would have come out.*

SUBJUNCTIVE

ACTIVE	pull	*We suggest that someone <u>pull</u> the boat and someone get behind and push.*
PASSIVE	be pulled	*She asked that the drapes <u>be pulled</u> closed before we left.*

PHRASAL VERBS

pull apart	to separate *You need to pull the pieces apart before you begin the puzzle again.*
pull (something) off	to only barely manage to do something, usually because you have not properly prepared for it *I can't believe we pulled off the concert last night. We hadn't practiced in ages.*
pull through	to make it through a difficult situation *She's very ill and we're not sure if she's going to pull through.*
pull together	when a group of people band together in order to confront a problem or some difficult situation *During the Great Depression, Americans had to pull together in order to make it through.*

IDIOMS

to pull a fast one	to trick someone *She pulled a fast one when she told me she was broke and got me to lend her money.*
to pull oneself together	to get one's life back together after a spate of problems, or to stop behaving in a nervous or frightened way. *I know you're upset, but you've got to talk to the judge. Pull yourself together.*
to pull oneself up by one's bootstraps	to make a success of one's life without anybody else's help *Both of his parents died when he was a child and he had to pull himself up by his bootstraps.*
to pull someone's leg	to tease someone *Come on! You aren't almost sixty, are you? You're pulling my leg.*
to have (no) pull	to have some (or no) influence on a situation *I'm sorry I can't help you get a job here but I have no pull.*

RELATED WORDS

pullover (n.)	a sweater that you put on by pulling it over your head
pull-up (n.)	an exercise in which you grab onto a bar and pull yourself up

Verb Chart

---

* Note that the form "will be being pulled" is rarely used. To convey a future progressive passive, use the present progressive passive.

put

	ACTIVE	PASSIVE
Infinitive	to put	to be put
Past Infinitive	to have put	to have been put
Past Participle	put	been put
Present Participle	putting	being put

ACTIVE

I		
you/we/they		
he/she/it		

SIMPLE PRESENT	SIMPLE PAST	SIMPLE FUTURE
put	put	will put
put	put	will put
puts	put	will put

PRESENT PROGRESSIVE	PAST PROGRESSIVE	FUTURE PROGRESSIVE
am putting	was putting	will be putting
are putting	were putting	will be putting
is putting	was putting	will be putting

PRESENT PERFECT	PAST PERFECT	FUTURE PERFECT
have put	had put	will have put
have put	had put	will have put
has put	had put	will have put

PRESENT PERFECT PROGRESSIVE	PAST PERFECT PROGRESSIVE	FUTURE PERFECT PROGRESSIVE
have been putting	had been putting	will have been putting
have been putting	had been putting	will have been putting
has been putting	had been putting	will have been putting

EXAMPLES:

The bellhop put our suitcases in our room.	They are putting new gutters on the first and second floors of our house.	She had put the children to sleep before we began to watch the movie.

PASSIVE

SIMPLE PRESENT	SIMPLE PAST	SIMPLE FUTURE
am put	was put	will be put
are put	were put	will be put
is put	was put	will be put

PRESENT PROGRESSIVE	PAST PROGRESSIVE	FUTURE PROGRESSIVE*
am being put	was being put	will be being put*
are being put	were being put	will be being put*
is being put	was being put	will be being put*

PRESENT PERFECT	PAST PERFECT	FUTURE PERFECT
have been put	had been put	will have been put
have been put	had been put	will have been put
has been put	had been put	will have been put

EXAMPLES:

The final touches are being put on the cake.	Any book on hold will be put back on the shelf if it is not picked up in three days.	Your tickets have been put in "will call" under your husband's name.

PRINCIPAL CONDITIONALS

PRESENT	PRESENT PROGRESSIVE	PRESENT PASSIVE
would put	would be putting	would be put
would put	would be putting	would be put
would put	would be putting	would be put

PAST	PAST PROGRESSIVE	PAST PASSIVE
would have put	would have been putting	would have been put
would have put	would have been putting	would have been put
would have put	would have been putting	would have been put

EXAMPLES:

We would be putting them up if they hadn't come with their children.	Normally, the receipt would have been put in this folder.	

Important Forms in Use

IF/THEN CONDITIONALS

	IF...	...THEN	EXAMPLE
Real Present/ Future	put/puts	simple present	*If you put too much salt in the sauce, we can't do anything to change the flavor.*
		will + base form	*If she puts me in the room next to her, I'll see her more often.*
Unreal Present/ Future	put	would + base form	*If we put the dogs out, we wouldn't have to worry about their barking.*
Unreal Past	had put	would have + past participle	*If I had put that question to him, I don't think he would've answered it.*

SUBJUNCTIVE

ACTIVE	put	*We suggest that the officer put her gun on the table.*
PASSIVE	be put	*It is important that all valuables be put in a safe place.*

PHRASAL VERBS

put (something) away	to return something to its original position *When you finish working on your pottery, you need to put away all of the equipment and clean up your station.*
put (something) off	to postpone *I'm supposed to work on my history assignment but I keep putting it off.*
put (something) out	to extinguish *The firefighters put out the fire quickly.*
put (something) together	to assemble *The only problem with this furniture is that you have to put it together by yourself.*
put up with	to stand for behavior that is difficult or less than acceptable *I don't know how you put up with your next-door neighbors. They're having parties every weekend.*

IDIOMS

to put a stop to something	to end something that you believe shouldn't have been happening in the first place *We finally put a stop to his bad behavior by instituting a system of rewards.*
to put someone on the spot	to put someone in the uncomfortable position of having to give an answer immediately *I'm sorry to put you on the spot, but could we stay with you while we're in the city?*
to put up a fight	to not surrender or give in to what someone else wants *The two young boys tried to steal his wallet, but he put up a fight.*
to put your nose to the grindstone	to work very hard *If I'm going to finish this report before tomorrow, I'll have to put my nose to the grindstone.*

RELATED WORDS

put-down (n.)	something said to criticize someone else or to make him or her feel bad or stupid
put out (adj.)	when you feel upset, angry, or as if you have done too much for another person

Verb Chart

* Note that the form "will be being put" is rarely used. To convey a future progressive passive, use the present progressive passive.

quiz

	ACTIVE	PASSIVE
Infinitive	to quiz	to be quizzed
Past Infinitive	to have quizzed	to have been quizzed
Past Participle	quizzed	been quizzed
Present Participle	quizzing	being quizzed

ACTIVE

	I	you/we/they	he/she/it

SIMPLE PRESENT
quiz
quiz
quizzes

SIMPLE PAST
quizzed
quizzed
quizzed

SIMPLE FUTURE
will quiz
will quiz
will quiz

PRESENT PROGRESSIVE
am quizzing
are quizzing
is quizzing

PAST PROGRESSIVE
was quizzing
were quizzing
was quizzing

FUTURE PROGRESSIVE
will be quizzing
will be quizzing
will be quizzing

PRESENT PERFECT
have quizzed
have quizzed
has quizzed

PAST PERFECT
had quizzed
had quizzed
had quizzed

FUTURE PERFECT
will have quizzed
will have quizzed
will have quizzed

PRESENT PERFECT PROGRESSIVE
have been quizzing
have been quizzing
has been quizzing

PAST PERFECT PROGRESSIVE
had been quizzing
had been quizzing
had been quizzing

FUTURE PERFECT PROGRESSIVE
will have been quizzing
will have been quizzing
will have been quizzing

EXAMPLES:
The teacher is quizzing the class on the material they learned yesterday.

I'll quiz you on state capitals if you quiz me on the presidents.

PASSIVE

SIMPLE PRESENT
am quizzed
are quizzed
is quizzed

SIMPLE PAST
was quizzed
were quizzed
was quizzed

SIMPLE FUTURE
will be quizzed
will be quizzed
will be quizzed

PRESENT PROGRESSIVE
am being quizzed
are being quizzed
is being quizzed

PAST PROGRESSIVE
was being quizzed
were being quizzed
was being quizzed

FUTURE PROGRESSIVE*
will be being quizzed*
will be being quizzed*
will be being quizzed*

PRESENT PERFECT
have been quizzed
have been quizzed
has been quizzed

PAST PERFECT
had been quizzed
had been quizzed
had been quizzed

FUTURE PERFECT
will have been quizzed
will have been quizzed
will have been quizzed

EXAMPLES:
The students will be quizzed on lessons five and six.

Richard is being quizzed by my father on his knowledge of antique cars.

PRINCIPAL CONDITIONALS

PRESENT
would quiz
would quiz
would quiz

PRESENT PROGRESSIVE
would be quizzing
would be quizzing
would be quizzing

PRESENT PASSIVE
would be quizzed
would be quizzed
would be quizzed

PAST
would have quizzed
would have quizzed
would have quizzed

PAST PROGRESSIVE
would have been quizzing
would have been quizzing
would have been quizzing

PAST PASSIVE
would have been quizzed
would have been quizzed
would have been quizzed

EXAMPLES:
Professor Hogan would have been quizzing us on the material if she hadn't broken her leg.

I would have quizzed you on your whereabouts if I didn't trust you.

Important Forms in Use

IF/THEN CONDITIONALS

	IF ...	... THEN	EXAMPLE
Real Present/ Future	quiz/quizzes	simple present	*If you <u>quiz</u> the students by surprise, they don't like it very much.*
		will + base form	*If she <u>quizzes</u> them on the material, she'll find out how much they've learned.*
Unreal Present/ Future	quizzed	would + base form	*If we <u>quizzed</u> each other on the names of the flowers, we would learn a lot faster.*
Unreal Past	had quizzed	would have + past participle	*If you <u>had quizzed</u> me on politics, you would have found out how little I know.*

SUBJUNCTIVE

ACTIVE	quiz	*They suggest that we <u>quiz</u> our children on their whereabouts every night.*
PASSIVE	be quizzed	*It is important that the students <u>be quizzed</u> on the material.*

PHRASAL VERBS

quiz (someone) on	to ask about or interrogate, sometimes aggressively or invasively *As soon as I got home, he was quizzing me on my date and how it went.*
quiz (someone) over	to ask questions on a specific subject *The teacher quizzed us over the Spanish civil war.*

RELATED WORDS

quiz (n.)	a short test
quizmaster (n.)	the person who asks questions on a game show or in a board game
quizzical (adj.)	strange, comical, weird, or inquiring (said of expressions)

* Note that the form "will be being quizzed" is rarely used. To convey a future progressive passive, use the present progressive passive.

Verb Chart

reach

	ACTIVE	PASSIVE
Infinitive	to reach	to be reached
Past Infinitive	to have reached	to have been reached
Past Participle	reached	been reached
Present Participle	reaching	being reached

I
you/we/they
he/she/it

ACTIVE

SIMPLE PRESENT	SIMPLE PAST	SIMPLE FUTURE
reach	reached	will reach
reach	reached	will reach
reaches	reached	will reach

PRESENT PROGRESSIVE	PAST PROGRESSIVE	FUTURE PROGRESSIVE
am reaching	was reaching	will be reaching
are reaching	were reaching	will be reaching
is reaching	was reaching	will be reaching

PRESENT PERFECT	PAST PERFECT	FUTURE PERFECT
have reached	had reached	will have reached
have reached	had reached	will have reached
has reached	had reached	will have reached

PRESENT PERFECT PROGRESSIVE	PAST PERFECT PROGRESSIVE	FUTURE PERFECT PROGRESSIVE
have been reaching	had been reaching	will have been reaching
have been reaching	had been reaching	will have been reaching
has been reaching	had been reaching	will have been reaching

EXAMPLES:
Call us when you reach the hotel. *We will have reached California by next Tuesday.* *They had been reaching for great things but they had a lot of bad luck.*

PASSIVE

SIMPLE PRESENT	SIMPLE PAST	SIMPLE FUTURE
am reached	was reached	will be reached
are reached	were reached	will be reached
is reached	was reached	will be reached

PRESENT PROGRESSIVE	PAST PROGRESSIVE	FUTURE PROGRESSIVE*
am being reached	was being reached	will be being reached*
are being reached	were being reached	will be being reached*
is being reached	was being reached	will be being reached*

PRESENT PERFECT	PAST PERFECT	FUTURE PERFECT
have been reached	had been reached	will have been reached
have been reached	had been reached	will have been reached
has been reached	had been reached	will have been reached

EXAMPLES:
They were reached at the house in the woods only after hours of trying. *An agreement had not been reached as of last Tuesday.*

PRINCIPAL CONDITIONALS

PRESENT	PRESENT PROGRESSIVE	PRESENT PASSIVE
would reach	would be reaching	would be reached
would reach	would be reaching	would be reached
would reach	would be reaching	would be reached

PAST	PAST PROGRESSIVE	PAST PASSIVE
would have reached	would have been reaching	would have been reached
would have reached	would have been reaching	would have been reached
would have reached	would have been reaching	would have been reached

EXAMPLES:
We would be reaching out to them more but we feel they want to be left alone. *They would have reached their final destination earlier if they hadn't run out of gas.*

reach

PRINCIPAL PARTS: reach, reached, reached

Important Forms in Use

IF/THEN CONDITIONALS

	IF ...	... THEN	EXAMPLE
Real Present/ Future	reach/reaches	simple present	If I _reach_ him at John's, that means he's staying there tonight.
		will + base form	If they _reach_ their goal by next weekend, they'll cancel the rest of the pledge drive.
Unreal Present/ Future	reached	would + base form	If we _reached_ out to them more, they would probably be better friends.
Unreal Past	had reached	would have + past participle	If I _had reached_ their offices, I would have left a message.

SUBJUNCTIVE

ACTIVE	reach	The accountant suggested that they not _reach_ their credit limit and pay off the balance each month.
PASSIVE	be reached	It is essential that we _be reached_ quickly in case of any emergency.

PHRASAL VERBS

reach out to (someone)	to try to help someone who has made efforts to distance himself or herself
	My mom tried to reach out to me when I was a teenager, but I needed more serious help.

IDIOMS

to reach for the stars	to dream wildly, or to have goals that are very hard to attain
	I'm not saying that you shouldn't do it, but I just want to remind you that applying for the grant at Harvard is reaching for the stars.
to be out of someone's reach	to be impossible for someone to achieve
	I hate to tell you this, but the leading role in the movie is out of your reach for many reasons.
to be reaching	to try to make something out to be what it isn't
	You think I look like Julia Roberts? That's definitely reaching!

RELATED WORDS

reachable (adj.)	able to be obtained

* Note that the form "will be being reached" is rarely used. To convey a future progressive passive, use the present progressive passive.

read

	ACTIVE	PASSIVE
Infinitive	to read	to be read
Past Infinitive	to have read	to have been read
Past Participle	read	been read
Present Participle	reading	being read

ACTIVE

	I	you/we/they	he/she/it

SIMPLE PRESENT
read
read
reads

SIMPLE PAST
read
read
read

SIMPLE FUTURE
will read
will read
will read

PRESENT PROGRESSIVE
am reading
are reading
is reading

PAST PROGRESSIVE
was reading
were reading
was reading

FUTURE PROGRESSIVE
will be reading
will be reading
will be reading

PRESENT PERFECT
have read
have read
has read

PAST PERFECT
had read
had read
had read

FUTURE PERFECT
will have read
will have read
will have read

PRESENT PERFECT PROGRESSIVE
have been reading
have been reading
has been reading

PAST PERFECT PROGRESSIVE
had been reading
had been reading
had been reading

FUTURE PERFECT PROGRESSIVE
will have been reading
will have been reading
will have been reading

EXAMPLES:
The teacher reads to her students every morning.

The book club is reading a book by Graham Greene.

By the time I finish my graduate degree, I will have read every book there is to read on James Joyce's Ulysses.

PASSIVE

SIMPLE PRESENT
am read
are read
is read

SIMPLE PAST
was read
were read
was read

SIMPLE FUTURE
will be read
will be read
will be read

PRESENT PROGRESSIVE
am being read
are being read
is being read

PAST PROGRESSIVE
was being read
were being read
was being read

FUTURE PROGRESSIVE*
will be being read*
will be being read*
will be being read*

PRESENT PERFECT
have been read
have been read
has been read

PAST PERFECT
had been read
had been read
had been read

FUTURE PERFECT
will have been read
will have been read
will have been read

EXAMPLES:
The Catcher in the Rye *is commonly read by high school students.*

Did you hear that my book is being read by a publisher?

Our electrical meter has already been read.

PRINCIPAL CONDITIONALS

PRESENT
would read
would read
would read

PRESENT PROGRESSIVE
would be reading
would be reading
would be reading

PRESENT PASSIVE
would be read
would be read
would be read

PAST
would have read
would have read
would have read

PAST PROGRESSIVE
would have been reading
would have been reading
would have been reading

PAST PASSIVE
would have been read
would have been read
would have been read

EXAMPLES:
I would read Swann's Way *if I were you.*

I would read your mind if I could, but I can't.

Important Forms in Use

IF/THEN CONDITIONALS

	IF ...	...THEN	EXAMPLE
Real Present/ Future	read/reads	simple present	*If you <u>read</u> out loud, I can understand better.*
		will + base form	*If they <u>read</u> about my success in the newspaper, they'll be very happy.*
Unreal Present/ Future	read	would + base form	*If Aunt Sally <u>read</u> this book, she would really like it.*
Unreal Past past participle	had read	would have +	*If I <u>hadn't read</u> his journal, I wouldn't have found out about the affair.*

SUBJUNCTIVE

ACTIVE	read	*I recommend that you <u>read</u> the newspaper daily if you want to improve your English.*
PASSIVE	be read	*It has been proposed that the essays <u>be read</u> by the committee.*

PHRASAL VERBS

read (something) over/through	to read carefully *Will you read over the contract again? I think there are several mistakes.*
read up on (something)	to learn or study more about a specific topic *I'm going to have to read up on animal behavior before I get my dog.*

IDIOMS

to read between the lines	to try to get the real meaning of what was said or written *He didn't say that he wanted to go out with her, but she could read between the lines.*
to read too much into (something)	to have an understanding of an action, behavior, etc., that may not be true *You are reading too much into this. I simply did not want to go out tonight.*

RELATED WORDS

reading (n.)	when an author chooses selections from his or her poetry or prose to read to an audience
readable (adj.)	easy to read
reader (n.)	a person who reads a written work
well-read (adj.)	a term used to describe people who have read a lot

* Note that the form "will be being read" is rarely used. To convey a future progressive passive, use the present progressive passive.

Verb Chart

roll

	ACTIVE	PASSIVE
Infinitive	to roll	to be rolled
Past Infinitive	to have rolled	to have been rolled
Past Participle	rolled	been rolled
Present Participle	rolling	being rolled

ACTIVE

I		
you/we/they		
he/she/it		

SIMPLE PRESENT	SIMPLE PAST	SIMPLE FUTURE
roll	rolled	will roll
roll	rolled	will roll
rolls	rolled	will roll

PRESENT PROGRESSIVE	PAST PROGRESSIVE	FUTURE PROGRESSIVE
am rolling	was rolling	will be rolling
are rolling	were rolling	will be rolling
is rolling	was rolling	will be rolling

PRESENT PERFECT	PAST PERFECT	FUTURE PERFECT
have rolled	had rolled	will have rolled
have rolled	had rolled	will have rolled
has rolled	had rolled	will have rolled

PRESENT PERFECT PROGRESSIVE	PAST PERFECT PROGRESSIVE	FUTURE PERFECT PROGRESSIVE
have been rolling	had been rolling	will have been rolling
have been rolling	had been rolling	will have been rolling
has been rolling	had been rolling	will have been rolling

EXAMPLES:

The mechanics rolled the car with the flat tire into the garage. | *John had just rolled up in front of our house in his brand new Mercedes when I got home.* | *The dog had been rolling over and doing other tricks since it was a puppy.*

PASSIVE

SIMPLE PRESENT	SIMPLE PAST	SIMPLE FUTURE
am rolled	was rolled	will be rolled
are rolled	were rolled	will be rolled
is rolled	was rolled	will be rolled

PRESENT PROGRESSIVE	PAST PROGRESSIVE	FUTURE PROGRESSIVE*
am being rolled	was being rolled	will be being rolled*
are being rolled	were being rolled	will be being rolled*
is being rolled	was being rolled	will be being rolled*

PRESENT PERFECT	PAST PERFECT	FUTURE PERFECT
have been rolled	had been rolled	will have been rolled
have been rolled	had been rolled	will have been rolled
has been rolled	had been rolled	will have been rolled

EXAMPLES:

The cookie dough is rolled out and then cut into shapes with cookie cutters. | *The rock in the riverbed was rolled over by the curious child.*

PRINCIPAL CONDITIONALS

PRESENT	PRESENT PROGRESSIVE	PRESENT PASSIVE
would roll	would be rolling	would be rolled
would roll	would be rolling	would be rolled
would roll	would be rolling	would be rolled

PAST	PAST PROGRESSIVE	PAST PASSIVE
would have rolled	would have been rolling	would have been rolled
would have rolled	would have been rolling	would have been rolled
would have rolled	would have been rolling	would have been rolled

EXAMPLES:

We would have rolled out the red carpet if we had known you were coming. | *I would roll down the window if I could figure out how to do it.*

roll

PRINCIPAL PARTS: roll, rolled, rolled

Important Forms in Use

IF/THEN CONDITIONALS

	IF ...	... THEN	EXAMPLE
Real Present/ Future	roll/rolls	simple present	*If the orders roll in quickly, we need to get started right away.*
		will + base form	*If we roll out of here around 7:00, we'll get there just on time.*
Unreal Present/ Future	rolled	would + base form	*If she rolled up her sleeves, she wouldn't ruin her new blouse.*
Unreal Past	had rolled	would have + past participle	*If I had rolled over that account into an IRA, I would have had more money when I retired.*

SUBJUNCTIVE

ACTIVE	roll	*We ask that the painters roll up all the rugs before laying down the drop cloths.*
PASSIVE	be rolled	*It is essential that the blueprints be rolled up carefully so that they are not damaged.*

PHRASAL VERBS

roll in	to come in in large numbers or quantity *Shortly after we launched our Web site, orders for the handmade blankets began to roll in faster than we could make them.*
roll out (something)	to lay out straight something that had been rolled up, or to distribute *After we polish the floors and let them dry, we have to roll out the Oriental rugs that are in the closet.*
roll over (something)	to convert one type of account into another *My accountant suggested that I roll over my money market account into an IRA.*
roll up (something)	to curl something into a cylinder *We roll up the carpet every Saturday night before our dancing lesson.*

IDIOMS

to roll with the punches	to go along with whatever is happening without making a fuss *Jim is usually stressed out whenever there's a change in the schedule but today he's rolling with the punches.*
to roll out the red carpet	to do everything to make someone feel welcome or important *They really rolled out the red carpet for us; they even put mints on our pillows!*
to be ready to roll	to be prepared to leave (informal) *Come and pick us up. We're ready to roll!*

RELATED WORDS

roller skates (n.)	shoes with wheels on them
rolling pin (n.)	a kitchen tool used to roll out dough

*Note that the form "will be being rolled" is rarely used. To convey a future progressive passive, use the present progressive passive.

Verb Chart

run

	ACTIVE	PASSIVE
Infinitive	to run	to be run
Past Infinitive	to have run	to have been run
Past Participle	run	been run
Present Participle	running	being run

ACTIVE

	I
	you/we/they
	he/she/it

SIMPLE PRESENT	SIMPLE PAST	SIMPLE FUTURE
run	ran	will run
run	ran	will run
runs	ran	will run

PRESENT PROGRESSIVE	PAST PROGRESSIVE	FUTURE PROGRESSIVE
am running	was running	will be running
are running	were running	will be running
is running	was running	will be running

PRESENT PERFECT	PAST PERFECT	FUTURE PERFECT
have run	had run	will have run
have run	had run	will have run
has run	had run	will have run

PRESENT PERFECT PROGRESSIVE	PAST PERFECT PROGRESSIVE	FUTURE PERFECT PROGRESSIVE
have been running	had been running	will have been running
have been running	had been running	will have been running
has been running	had been running	will have been running

EXAMPLES:
We run in the park three days a week and then go to the gym.   *We're running late. Let's get going.*   *By the time she finishes the marathon, she will have run twenty-six miles.*

PASSIVE

SIMPLE PRESENT	SIMPLE PAST	SIMPLE FUTURE
am run	was run	will be run
are run	were run	will be run
is run	was run	will be run

PRESENT PROGRESSIVE	PAST PROGRESSIVE	FUTURE PROGRESSIVE*
am being run	was being run	will be being run*
are being run	were being run	will be being run*
is being run	was being run	will be being run*

PRESENT PERFECT	PAST PERFECT	FUTURE PERFECT
have been run	had been run	will have been run
have been run	had been run	will have been run
has been run	had been run	will have been run

EXAMPLES:
The gunslinger was run out of town.   *The program will be run by Sarah Miles.*   *The retirement home had never been run as well as when Mr. Bendrix took over.*

PRINCIPAL CONDITIONALS

PRESENT	PRESENT PROGRESSIVE	PRESENT PASSIVE
would run	would be running	would be run
would run	would be running	would be run
would run	would be running	would be run

PAST	PAST PROGRESSIVE	PAST PASSIVE
would have run	would have been running	would have been run
would have run	would have been running	would have been run
would have run	would have been running	would have been run

EXAMPLES:
I didn't know that you would be running in the marathon.   *Henry would have run in the race if he hadn't twisted his ankle.*   *The contest would be run by last year's winner.*

Important Forms in Use

IF/THEN CONDITIONALS

	IF ...	... THEN	EXAMPLE
Real Present/ Future	run/runs	simple present	*If the kids <u>run</u> a lot during the day, they are tired in the evenings.*
		will + base form	*If we <u>run</u> into my cousin, we will ask him if we can stay at his house next weekend.*
Unreal Present/ Future	ran	would + base form	*If we <u>ran</u> a tighter ship, we wouldn't be losing so much money.*
Unreal Past	had run	would have + past participle	*If John Greene <u>had run</u> for office, he would have won.*

SUBJUNCTIVE

ACTIVE	run	*It is important that the film <u>run</u> on schedule.*
PASSIVE	be run	*I suggest that all plans <u>be run</u> by me first.*

PHRASAL VERBS

run away	to escape, or leave at a fast pace *I was talking to the little girl about her dog, but she suddenly ran away.*
run for	to try to get into public office through an election process *Yuri decided to run for mayor, even though his wife didn't want him to get into politics.*
run into	to meet somebody by chance *We ran into Heather last night at the movie theater.*
run out of	to reach the end of a supply of something *Last week on the way to visit my cousin in Champaign, my car ran out of gas.*
run up against	to meet with resistance *While trying to get approval for the new park, the committee ran up against the disapproval of the mayor.*

IDIOMS

to run for cover	to try to hide when something dangerous is approaching *The soldiers heard the incoming shells and ran for cover.*
to (make a) run for it	to try to escape something by running quickly *It's raining, but if we make a run for it, we might not get too wet.*
to run something by someone	to present an idea, opinion, etc., to someone *I have some thoughts about the advertising campaign and I'd like to run them by you.*
to run something into the ground	to destroy something through incompetence *John's inability to see the bigger picture was fatal for the company. He eventually ran the business into the ground.*

RELATED WORDS

runaway (n.)	a child who has escaped from home
run-down (adj.)	old and dilapidated, in bad condition, especially a building or area
runaround (n.)	evasive behavior (to give someone the runaround)

* Note that the form "will be being run" is rarely used. To convey a future progressive passive, use the present progressive passive.

Verb Chart

say

	ACTIVE	PASSIVE
Infinitive	to say	to be said
Past Infinitive	to have said	to have been said
Past Participle	said	been said
Present Participle	saying	being said

ACTIVE

	I	you/we/they	he/she/it

SIMPLE PRESENT	SIMPLE PAST	SIMPLE FUTURE
say	said	will say
say	said	will say
says	said	will say

PRESENT PROGRESSIVE	PAST PROGRESSIVE	FUTURE PROGRESSIVE
am saying	was saying	will be saying
are saying	were saying	will be saying
is saying	was saying	will be saying

PRESENT PERFECT	PAST PERFECT	FUTURE PERFECT
have said	had said	will have said
have said	had said	will have said
has said	had said	will have said

PRESENT PERFECT PROGRESSIVE	PAST PERFECT PROGRESSIVE	FUTURE PERFECT PROGRESSIVE
have been saying	had been saying	will have been saying
have been saying	had been saying	will have been saying
has been saying	had been saying	will have been saying

EXAMPLES:

She said that we should go in through the back door.

What were you saying?

Have you said everything you need to say?

PASSIVE

SIMPLE PRESENT	SIMPLE PAST	SIMPLE FUTURE
am said	was said	will be said
are said	were said	will be said
is said	was said	will be said

PRESENT PROGRESSIVE	PAST PROGRESSIVE	FUTURE PROGRESSIVE*
am being said	was being said	will be being said*
are being said	were being said	will be being said*
is being said	was being said	will be being said*

PRESENT PERFECT	PAST PERFECT	FUTURE PERFECT
have been said	had been said	will have been said
hàve been said	had been said	will have been said
has been said	had been said	will have been said

EXAMPLES:

I don't know what you're talking about. Nothing was said in the last meeting concerning this issue.

Things had been said by both parties that later caused regret.

PRINCIPAL CONDITIONALS

PRESENT	PRESENT PROGRESSIVE	PRESENT PASSIVE
would say	would be saying	would be said
would say	would be saying	would be said
would say	would be saying	would be said

PAST	PAST PROGRESSIVE	PAST PASSIVE
would have said	would have been saying	would have been said
would have said	would have been saying	would have been said
would have said	would have been saying	would have been said

EXAMPLES:

We would have said something sooner, but we thought you really liked him.

Who knew what would be said?

Important Forms in Use

IF/THEN CONDITIONALS

	IF . . .	. . . THEN	EXAMPLE
Real Present/ Future	say/says	simple present	If she _says_ that she's fine, then I believe her.
		will + base form	If we _say_ we'll be there, then we'll be there.
Unreal Present/ Future	said	would + base form	If they _said_ anything that made any sense, then we would listen to them.
Unreal Past	had said	would have + past participle	If I _had said_ that she has bad taste in music, she wouldn't have been my friend anymore.

SUBJUNCTIVE

ACTIVE	say	It is important that you _say_ exactly what you think.
PASSIVE	be said	It is essential that all of this _be said_ at the meeting.

PHRASAL VERBS

say for	to speak in favor of something There's a lot to be said for speaking your mind when everyone else disagrees with you.
say against	to speak in opposition of something There's a lot to be said against his environmental policy.

IDIOMS

to say the right thing	to say something that induces a favorable reaction Linda always says the right thing and somehow we get bumped up to first class.
to say when	to indicate that you've had enough How much coffee do you want? Just say when.
to say what's on your mind	to tell someone about something that has been bothering you I know something's up. Why don't you say what's on your mind?

RELATED WORDS

saying (n.)	an expression that has a special meaning
well-said (adj.)	stated in an articulate way

* Note that the form "will be being said" is rarely used. To convey a future progressive passive, use the present progressive passive.

Verb Chart

see

	ACTIVE	PASSIVE
Infinitive	to see	to be seen
Past Infinitive	to have seen	to have been seen
Past Participle	seen	been seen
Present Participle	seeing	being seen

I
you/we/they
he/she/it

ACTIVE

SIMPLE PRESENT	SIMPLE PAST	SIMPLE FUTURE
see	saw	will see
see	saw	will see
sees	saw	will see

PRESENT PROGRESSIVE	PAST PROGRESSIVE	FUTURE PROGRESSIVE
am seeing	was seeing	will be seeing
are seeing	were seeing	will be seeing
is seeing	was seeing	will be seeing

PRESENT PERFECT	PAST PERFECT	FUTURE PERFECT
have seen	had seen	will have seen
have seen	had seen	will have seen
has seen	had seen	will have seen

PRESENT PERFECT PROGRESSIVE	PAST PERFECT PROGRESSIVE	FUTURE PERFECT PROGRESSIVE
have been seeing	had been seeing	will have been seeing
have been seeing	had been seeing	will have been seeing
has been seeing	had been seeing	will have been seeing

EXAMPLES:

We see each other every day because we leave for work at the same time every morning.

I saw a great film last weekend, but I haven't seen the one you're talking about.

By this time next month, Sally and Rick will have been seeing each other for two years.

PASSIVE

SIMPLE PRESENT	SIMPLE PAST	SIMPLE FUTURE
am seen	was seen	will be seen
are seen	were seen	will be seen
is seen	was seen	will be seen

PRESENT PROGRESSIVE	PAST PROGRESSIVE	FUTURE PROGRESSIVE*
am being seen	was being seen	will be being seen*
are being seen	were being seen	will be being seen*
is being seen	was being seen	will be being seen*

PRESENT PERFECT	PAST PERFECT	FUTURE PERFECT
have been seen	had been seen	will have been seen
have been seen	had been seen	will have been seen
has been seen	had been seen	will have been seen

EXAMPLES:

Such violent storms are not usually seen at this time of the year!

The debate was seen by everyone, and it made a big difference in the election.

Has this report been seen by the manager yet?

PRINCIPAL CONDITIONALS

PRESENT	PRESENT PROGRESSIVE	PRESENT PASSIVE
would see	would be seeing	would be seen
would see	would be seeing	would be seen
would see	would be seeing	would be seen

PAST	PAST PROGRESSIVE	PAST PASSIVE
would have seen	would have been seeing	would have been seen
would have seen	would have been seeing	would have been seen
would have seen	would have been seeing	would have been seen

EXAMPLES:

We would have been seeing a film right now if you hadn't missed that train!

Sam would be seen as a real jerk if he doesn't apologize to everyone.

see

Important Forms in Use

IF/THEN CONDITIONALS

	IF...	...THEN	EXAMPLE
Real Present/ Future	see/sees	simple present	*If I see clouds in the morning, then I take an umbrella with me.*
		will + base form	*If she sees her neighbor on the elevator, then she'll say hello to him.*
Unreal Present/ Future	saw	would + base form	*If we saw them more often, we'd know more about their lives.*
Unreal Past	had seen	would have + past participle	*If I had seen the play, I would have told you whether it was good or not.*

SUBJUNCTIVE

ACTIVE	see	*It is important that the director see the report right away.*
PASSIVE	be seen	*It is essential that we be seen before five p.m.*

PHRASAL VERBS

see to (someone or something)	to manage, to handle, or to take responsibility for something. *Please see to the reports. / Could you see to the children and make sure they're okay?*
see (someone) in/into	to lead someone into a room *Ms. Richard's assistant saw the new clients into the conference room.*
see (something) through	to finish or complete *Gary always starts projects, but he never sees anything through.*
see (someone) off	to help someone leave, to be with a person when he or she leaves *Mr. and Ms. Park just saw their oldest son off to college.*
see after (someone)	to take care of someone *See after your grandmother while she's staying with us.*
see about (something)	to ask about something, to inquire *I went to the store to see about a new laptop, but they were all too expensive.*

IDIOMS

to see red	to be very angry *Karen saw red when she heard what Joe had done.*
to see someone	to date, to be in a relationship *How long have John and Susan been seeing each other?*
to not be able to see the forest for the trees	to become overly involved in details *Oliver can't see the forest for the trees; he spends too much time on the wording and not enough time on the theme of his essay.*
to see the big picture	to understand the most important issues of a problem *Henry is good at the details of his job, but he doesn't see the big picture.*
to see double	to be confused, especially from having too much alcohol *Kevin was seeing double after the party, so we took his keys and called him a cab.*

RELATED WORDS

Seeing Eye dog (n.)	a dog that is specially trained to help blind people; trademark of Seeing Eye, Inc.
seer (n.)	a person with mystical powers who can see the future; a clairvoyant
seesaw (n.)	a plank that children sit on across from one another and balance, going up and down

Verb Chart

* Note that the form "will be being seen" is rarely used. To convey a future progressive passive, use the present progressive passive.

sell

	ACTIVE	PASSIVE
Infinitive	to sell	to be sold
Past Infinitive	to have sold	to have been sold
Past Participle	sold	been sold
Present Participle	selling	being sold

ACTIVE

	I	you/we/they	he/she/it

SIMPLE PRESENT
sell
sell
sells

SIMPLE PAST
sold
sold
sold

SIMPLE FUTURE
will sell
will sell
will sell

PRESENT PROGRESSIVE
am selling
are selling
is selling

PAST PROGRESSIVE
was selling
were selling
was selling

FUTURE PROGRESSIVE
will be selling
will be selling
will be selling

PRESENT PERFECT
have sold
have sold
has sold

PAST PERFECT
had sold
had sold
had sold

FUTURE PERFECT
will have sold
will have sold
will have sold

PRESENT PERFECT PROGRESSIVE
have been selling
have been selling
has been selling

PAST PERFECT PROGRESSIVE
had been selling
had been selling
had been selling

FUTURE PERFECT PROGRESSIVE
will have been selling
will have been selling
will have been selling

EXAMPLES:
Her first book was selling surprisingly well.

The company's products had sold poorly before their redesign.

She sold me on the idea of buying a new car.

PASSIVE

SIMPLE PRESENT
am sold
are sold
is sold

SIMPLE PAST
was sold
were sold
was sold

SIMPLE FUTURE
will be sold
will be sold
will be sold

PRESENT PROGRESSIVE
am being sold
are being sold
is being sold

PAST PROGRESSIVE
was being sold
were being sold
was being sold

FUTURE PROGRESSIVE*
will be being sold*
will be being sold*
will be being sold*

PRESENT PERFECT
have been sold
have been sold
has been sold

PAST PERFECT
had been sold
had been sold
had been sold

FUTURE PERFECT
will have been sold
will have been sold
will have been sold

EXAMPLES:
The family was sold on the idea of living on the third floor of our new building.

You can buy our product wherever magazines and newspapers are sold.

Unfortunately, the desk has already been sold.

PRINCIPAL CONDITIONALS

PRESENT
would sell
would sell
would sell

PRESENT PROGRESSIVE
would be selling
would be selling
would be selling

PRESENT PASSIVE
would be sold
would be sold
would be sold

PAST
would have sold
would have sold
would have sold

PAST PROGRESSIVE
would have been selling
would have been selling
would have been selling

PAST PASSIVE
would have been sold
would have been sold
would have been sold

EXAMPLES:
The books would be selling better if you did a book tour.

Our house would have sold already if we had lowered the price.

sell

PRINCIPAL PARTS: sell, sold, sold

Important Forms in Use

IF/THEN CONDITIONALS

	IF ...	... THEN	EXAMPLE
Real Present/ Future	sell/sells	simple present	*If my boss <u>sells</u> a lot in any certain month, he gives us a bonus.*
		will + base form	*If she <u>sells</u> her house, we'll have new neighbors.*
Unreal Present/ Future	sold	would + base form	*If we <u>sold</u> them on the idea, we'd have enough money to start our company.*
Unreal Past	had sold	would have + past participle	*If Sheila <u>had sold</u> out, she might have been more successful in the short term, but her work wouldn't have been as well received.*

SUBJUNCTIVE

ACTIVE	sell	*We suggest you <u>sell</u> your car and buy a smaller one.*
PASSIVE	be sold	*It is essential that the house <u>be sold</u> before winter.*

PHRASAL VERBS

sell off	to try to get rid of something, usually by selling it cheaply *We lowered the prices in hopes of selling off the rest of our inventory quickly.*
sell out (of) (something)	to exhaust a supply of a saleable item *The store sold out of the popular book almost as soon as it arrived.*
sell out	to let your values or beliefs take second place to making money *I couldn't believe the kind of music my favorite musician is making. She's really sold out.*

IDIOMS

to sell (someone) on (something)	to convince someone of something *After I talked to the car salesperson for an hour, I was sold on buying the convertible.*
to sell like hotcakes	to sell very quickly *I was afraid that my idea wouldn't be successful, but my T-shirts began to sell like hotcakes.*
to undersell	to offer a service or product at a lower price than someone else is offering *Our prices our so low, we won't be undersold.*

RELATED WORDS

sold out (adj.)	when a performance or any show that requires the purchase of tickets no longer has tickets available
best-seller (n.)	an item that sells extremely well
salesperson (n.)	a person whose profession is selling things to others

* Note that the form "will be being sold" is rarely used. To convey a future progressive passive, use the present progressive passive.

Verb Chart

send

	ACTIVE	PASSIVE
Infinitive	to send	to be sent
Past Infinitive	to have sent	to have been sent
Past Participle	sent	been sent
Present Participle	sending	being sent

I
you/we/they
he/she/it

ACTIVE

SIMPLE PRESENT	SIMPLE PAST	SIMPLE FUTURE
send	sent	will send
send	sent	will send
sends	sent	will send

PRESENT PROGRESSIVE	PAST PROGRESSIVE	FUTURE PROGRESSIVE
am sending	was sending	will be sending
are sending	were sending	will be sending
is sending	was sending	will be sending

PRESENT PERFECT	PAST PERFECT	FUTURE PERFECT
have sent	had sent	will have sent
have sent	had sent	will have sent
has sent	had sent	will have sent

PRESENT PERFECT PROGRESSIVE	PAST PERFECT PROGRESSIVE	FUTURE PERFECT PROGRESSIVE
have been sending	had been sending	will have been sending
have been sending	had been sending	will have been sending
has been sending	had been sending	will have been sending

EXAMPLES:
I will send you out of the room if you can't behave. *My grandparents are sending me some money for my birthday.* *Have you sent the packages yet?*

PASSIVE

SIMPLE PRESENT	SIMPLE PAST	SIMPLE FUTURE
am sent	was sent	will be sent
are sent	were sent	will be sent
is sent	was sent	will be sent

PRESENT PROGRESSIVE	PAST PROGRESSIVE	FUTURE PROGRESSIVE*
am being sent	was being sent	will be being sent*
are being sent	were being sent	will be being sent*
is being sent	was being sent	will be being sent*

PRESENT PERFECT	PAST PERFECT	FUTURE PERFECT
have been sent	had been sent	will have been sent
have been sent	had been sent	will have been sent
has been sent	had been sent	will have been sent

EXAMPLES:
A specialist was sent for when the doctor couldn't diagnose the patient's illness. *Your package will be sent by first-class mail and should arrive on Tuesday.* *Letters had been sent home with all of the students informing the parents about the open house.*

PRINCIPAL CONDITIONALS

PRESENT	PRESENT PROGRESSIVE	PRESENT PASSIVE
would send	would be sending	would be sent
would send	would be sending	would be sent
would send	would be sending	would be sent

PAST	PAST PROGRESSIVE	PAST PASSIVE
would have sent	would have been sending	would have been sent
would have sent	would have been sending	would have been sent
would have sent	would have been sending	would have been sent

EXAMPLES:
The teacher would have sent him home earlier if she had known he wasn't feeling well. *I would be sending you more clients if you agreed to take on more cases.*

send

Important Forms in Use

IF/THEN CONDITIONALS

	IF...	...THEN	EXAMPLE
Real Present/ Future	send/sends	simple present	*If you <u>send</u> a letter on Monday, it arrives here on Wednesday.*
		will + base form	*If she <u>sends</u> me an e-mail, I'll forward it to you.*
Unreal Present/ Future	sent	would + base form	*If we <u>sent</u> for the doctor immediately, she would have a better chance of survival.*
Unreal Past	had sent	would have + past participle	*If Mike <u>had sent</u> word sooner, we would have advised you of the changes.*

SUBJUNCTIVE

ACTIVE	send	*They asked that we <u>send</u> the drafts out before the close of business today.*
PASSIVE	be sent	*I suggest that any correspondence <u>be sent</u> by overnight mail.*

PHRASAL VERBS

send back	to return *I sent him several letters but they were all sent back.*
send in	to have something delivered to a place where it can be taken care of *I sent in an entry for the raffle. Hopefully, I'll win something.*
send out	to distribute, often to many different destinations *We sent out invitations to our going-away party.*
send up	to make the value of something increase *The new park sent up the housing prices in the area.*

IDIOMS

to send someone packing	to make someone leave because he or she is no longer wanted *She sent her husband packing when she found out he had been unfaithful.*
to send chills/shivers up and down someone's spine	to cause an emotional reaction, such as fear or excitement *The idea that several people were killed in this room sent shivers up and down my spine.*
to send word	to let someone know something by sending him or her a written or oral message *When you want me to come and help you, just send word.*

RELATED WORDS

sender (n.)	the person who has mailed a package or letter
send-off (n.)	the time in which you say good-bye to a person who is leaving
send-up (n.)	a parody or spoof

* Note that the form "will be being sent" is rarely used. To convey a future progressive passive, use the present progressive passive.

Verb Chart

set

	ACTIVE	PASSIVE
Infinitive	to set	to be set
Past Infinitive	to have set	to have been set
Past Participle	set	been set
Present Participle	setting	being set

ACTIVE

I		
you/we/they		
he/she/it		

SIMPLE PRESENT	SIMPLE PAST	SIMPLE FUTURE
set	set	will set
set	set	will set
sets	set	will set

PRESENT PROGRESSIVE	PAST PROGRESSIVE	FUTURE PROGRESSIVE
am setting	was setting	will be setting
are setting	were setting	will be setting
is setting	was setting	will be setting

PRESENT PERFECT	PAST PERFECT	FUTURE PERFECT
have set	had set	will have set
have set	had set	will have set
has set	had set	will have set

PRESENT PERFECT PROGRESSIVE	PAST PERFECT PROGRESSIVE	FUTURE PERFECT PROGRESSIVE
have been setting	had been setting	will have been setting
have been setting	had been setting	will have been setting
has been setting	had been setting	will have been setting

EXAMPLES:
I don't know what set him off, but he's very angry.

We were still setting up the buffet table when the guests began to arrive.

She didn't like how I had set up the furniture.

PASSIVE

SIMPLE PRESENT	SIMPLE PAST	SIMPLE FUTURE
am set	was set	will be set
are set	were set	will be set
is set	was set	will be set

PRESENT PROGRESSIVE	PAST PROGRESSIVE	FUTURE PROGRESSIVE*
am being set	was being set	will be being set*
are being set	were being set	will be being set*
is being set	was being set	will be being set*

PRESENT PERFECT	PAST PERFECT	FUTURE PERFECT
have been set	had been set	will have been set
have been set	had been set	will have been set
has been set	had been set	will have been set

EXAMPLES:
The alarm clock is set for 5:30.

The chairs were being set up for the reception.

The table will have been set by the time dinner is ready.

PRINCIPAL CONDITIONALS

PRESENT	PRESENT PROGRESSIVE	PRESENT PASSIVE
would set	would be setting	would be set
would set	would be setting	would be set
would set	would be setting	would be set

PAST	PAST PROGRESSIVE	PAST PASSIVE
would have set	would have been setting	would have been set
would have set	would have been setting	would have been set
would have set	would have been setting	would have been set

EXAMPLES:
We would have set the table for more people if we had known they were going to come.

I didn't think the plans would be set so soon.

set

Important Forms in Use

IF/THEN CONDITIONALS

	IF ...	... THEN	EXAMPLE
Real Present/ Future	set/sets	simple present	*If he <u>sets</u> up before lunch, he usually joins us at the Mexican restaurant.*
		will + base form	*If we <u>set</u> out the sheets, they'll make their own beds.*
Unreal Present/ Future	set	would + base form	*If Harry <u>set</u> out to accomplish more, we'd be able to get a better house.*
Unreal Past	had set	would have + past participle	*If I <u>had set</u> you up with Mike, you wouldn't have liked him.*

SUBJUNCTIVE

ACTIVE	set	*We ask that you <u>set</u> the tables before the caterers arrive.*
PASSIVE	be set	*I suggest that the new book display <u>be set</u> up in that corner.*

PHRASAL VERBS

set back	to keep something from moving forward *We were set back time and time again by the lack of funding.*
set (something) down	to place an object on a surface *Set the food down and help me get the grill ready.*
set (someone) off	to make angry or agitated *The unkind way he spoke to me really set me off!*
set out	to begin a trip *The girls set out on their camping trip early yesterday morning.*
set up	to begin a new business, group, etc., or to prepare the equipment before a show, performance, party, etc. *Many immigrants have set up businesses in this neighborhood. / Can you help me set up the stage for act one?*

IDIOMS

to set out to do something	to have a very focused plan of what you want to accomplish *He set out to become a partner in the law firm and he accomplished his goal by age forty.*
to set your heart on something	to have a strong desire to get or do something, so much so that you will be disappointed if your wishes don't come true *The kids have set their hearts on going to Natalie's party today. Can't you take the day off and bring them?*
to set up shop	to begin operating *Why don't you set up shop right here?*
to set someone straight	to correct someone or tell him or her how to act in a more acceptable manner *He doesn't know how to treat his mother. Someone needs to set him straight.*
to set someone on edge	to make someone nervous or agitated *How long are the kids going to practice? Their music is really setting me on edge.*

RELATED WORDS

setback (n.)	a delay in progress

* Note that the form "will be being set" is rarely used. To convey a future progressive passive, use the present progressive passive.

Verb Chart

shake

	ACTIVE	PASSIVE
Infinitive	to shake	to be shaken
Past Infinitive	to have shaken	to have been shaken
Past Participle	shaken	been shaken
Present Participle	shaking	being shaken

ACTIVE

I
you/we/they
he/she/it

SIMPLE PRESENT	SIMPLE PAST	SIMPLE FUTURE
shake	shook	will shake
shake	shook	will shake
shakes	shook	will shake

PRESENT PROGRESSIVE	PAST PROGRESSIVE	FUTURE PROGRESSIVE
am shaking	was shaking	will be shaking
are shaking	were shaking	will be shaking
is shaking	was shaking	will be shaking

PRESENT PERFECT	PAST PERFECT	FUTURE PERFECT
have shaken	had shaken	will have shaken
have shaken	had shaken	will have shaken
has shaken	had shaken	will have shaken

PRESENT PERFECT PROGRESSIVE	PAST PERFECT PROGRESSIVE	FUTURE PERFECT PROGRESSIVE
have been shaking	had been shaking	will have been shaking
have been shaking	had been shaking	will have been shaking
has been shaking	had been shaking	will have been shaking

EXAMPLES:
In America, people usually shake hands upon meeting for the first time.   *The house shook with each crash of thunder.*   *We had shaken on it, but we hadn't signed anything.*

PASSIVE

SIMPLE PRESENT	SIMPLE PAST	SIMPLE FUTURE
am shaken	was shaken	will be shaken
are shaken	were shaken	will be shaken
is shaken	was shaken	will be shaken

PRESENT PROGRESSIVE	PAST PROGRESSIVE	FUTURE PROGRESSIVE*
am being shaken	was being shaken	will be being shaken*
are being shaken	were being shaken	will be being shaken*
is being shaken	was being shaken	will be being shaken*

PRESENT PERFECT	PAST PERFECT	FUTURE PERFECT
have been shaken	had been shaken	will have been shaken
have been shaken	had been shaken	will have been shaken
has been shaken	had been shaken	will have been shaken

EXAMPLES:
The paint was shaken by a machine after we bought it.   *No one was hurt in the accident, but everyone was a bit shaken by the ordeal.*

PRINCIPAL CONDITIONALS

PRESENT	PRESENT PROGRESSIVE	PRESENT PASSIVE
would shake	would be shaking	would be shaken
would shake	would be shaking	would be shaken
would shake	would be shaking	would be shaken

PAST	PAST PROGRESSIVE	PAST PASSIVE
would have shaken	would have been shaking	would have been shaken
would have shaken	would have been shaking	would have been shaken
would have shaken	would have been shaking	would have been shaken

EXAMPLES:
I would shake your hand but I've been cooking and I'm covered with grease.   *Sally would have been shaken up more if her mother hadn't called her right away to talk to her.*

shake

Important Forms in Use

IF/THEN CONDITIONALS

	IF . . .	. . . THEN	EXAMPLE
Real Present/ Future	shake/shakes	simple present	If I _shake_ your hand, it doesn't guarantee anything.
		will + base form	If he _shakes_ the juice before we open it, it will taste better.
Unreal Present/ Future	shook	would + base form	If we _shook_ them up a little bit, they would come around.
Unreal Past	had shaken	would have + past participle	If I _had shaken_ out the carpet last week, it wouldn't have been so dirty for our visitors.

SUBJUNCTIVE

ACTIVE	shake	I suggest that you _shake_ on the deal to make it more formal.
PASSIVE	be shaken	It is essential that the paint _be shaken_ thoroughly before the can is opened.

PHRASAL VERBS

shake someone down	to get money from someone in a corrupt way _The gang began shaking down all the businesses in the neighborhood._
shake on (something)	to make an informal agreement _My client promised to pay me the money, but unfortunately we only shook on it. There was no written proof._
shake out (something)	to move something up and down through the air to remove something from it _We need to shake out these rugs. They're getting really dirty._
shake (someone) up	to disturb or upset someone _The car accident really shook her up._

IDIOMS

to shake a leg	to hurry _Come on! Shake a leg! We need to be there in ten minutes._
to shake like a leaf	to tremble because you are afraid of something _The girl was shaking like a leaf when the police found her after she had been separated from her parents._
to shake something to its foundations	to make major changes in something that alter it completely _The structure of the corporation was shaken to its foundations when the CEO and all of his advisors stepped down amid scandal._

RELATED WORDS

shaken (adj.)	agitated
shake-up (n.)	a reorganization
shaky (adj.)	unsure or unsteady

* Note that the form "will be being shaken" is rarely used. To convey a future progressive passive, use the present progressive passive.

shoot

	ACTIVE	PASSIVE
Infinitive	to shoot	to be shot
Past Infinitive	to have shot	to have been shot
Past Participle	shot	been shot
Present Participle	shooting	being shot

I
you/we/they
he/she/it

ACTIVE

SIMPLE PRESENT	SIMPLE PAST	SIMPLE FUTURE
shoot	shot	will shoot
shoot	shot	will shoot
shoots	shot	will shoot

PRESENT PROGRESSIVE	PAST PROGRESSIVE	FUTURE PROGRESSIVE
am shooting	was shooting	will be shooting
are shooting	were shooting	will be shooting
is shooting	was shooting	will be shooting

PRESENT PERFECT	PAST PERFECT	FUTURE PERFECT
have shot	had shot	will have shot
have shot	had shot	will have shot
has shot	had shot	will have shot

PRESENT PERFECT PROGRESSIVE	PAST PERFECT PROGRESSIVE	FUTURE PERFECT PROGRESSIVE
have been shooting	had been shooting	will have been shooting
have been shooting	had been shooting	will have been shooting
has been shooting	had been shooting	will have been shooting

EXAMPLES:

If he shoots, hit the deck!

Billy has shot up at least three inches in the past two months.

The kids were shooting at the targets in the amusement park.

PASSIVE

SIMPLE PRESENT	SIMPLE PAST	SIMPLE FUTURE
am shot	was shot	will be shot
are shot	were shot	will be shot
is shot	was shot	will be shot

PRESENT PROGRESSIVE	PAST PROGRESSIVE	FUTURE PROGRESSIVE*
am being shot	was being shot	will be being shot*
are being shot	were being shot	will be being shot*
is being shot	was being shot	will be being shot*

PRESENT PERFECT	PAST PERFECT	FUTURE PERFECT
have been shot	had been shot	will have been shot
have been shot	had been shot	will have been shot
has been shot	had been shot	will have been shot

EXAMPLES:

The man was shot in the shoulder and the abdomen.

They looked at the gun and tried to figure out how many bullets had been shot.

PRINCIPAL CONDITIONALS

PRESENT	PRESENT PROGRESSIVE	PRESENT PASSIVE
would shoot	would be shooting	would be shot
would shoot	would be shooting	would be shot
would shoot	would be shooting	would be shot

PAST	PAST PROGRESSIVE	PAST PASSIVE
would have shot	would have been shooting	would have been shot
would have shot	would have been shooting	would have been shot
would have shot	would have been shooting	would have been shot

EXAMPLES:

We would shoot the scene later at night if we had the right lighting.

The soldier would have been shot if the general hadn't made him fall to the ground.

shoot

PRINCIPAL PARTS: shoot, shot, shot

Important Forms in Use

IF/THEN CONDITIONALS

	IF . . .	. . . THEN	EXAMPLE
Real Present/ Future	shoot/shoots	simple present	*If I <u>shoot</u> down his ideas, he gets angry.*
		will + base form	*If she <u>shoots</u> off her mouth again, I won't talk to her.*
Unreal Present/ Future	shot	would + base form	*If we <u>shot</u> the breeze with them every once in a while, they would be more friendly.*
Unreal Past	had shot	would have + past participle	*If she <u>had shot</u> the man, he would have died.*

SUBJUNCTIVE

ACTIVE	shoot	*We ask that the director <u>shoot</u> from this angle.*
PASSIVE	be shot	*He recommended that the scene <u>be shot</u> outside instead of in the studio.*

PHRASAL VERBS

shoot (something) down — to dismiss an idea as not valid
I gave them several suggestions about places to eat but they were all shot down.

shoot for (something) — to try to reach something that may be hard to obtain
He's shooting for Harvard or Yale, but I don't think either is realistic.

shoot up — to grow quickly
Hal shot up to six feet in a matter of months.

IDIOMS

to shoot your mouth off — to talk, usually to a lot of people, without thinking
I didn't tell Al I had been fired because I knew he would shoot his mouth off, and I didn't want the whole neighborhood to know.

to shoot from the hip — to say something without thinking
I might be shooting from the hip here, but I think that dress is horrid.

to shoot something full of holes — to show that an idea or theory has no validity
We thought the animal getting into our attic was a neighbor's cat. That theory was shot full of holes when I opened the attic door and a squirrel jumped out at me. *

to shoot the breeze — to talk about nothing specific
On summer nights, you can find the neighbors gathered on one porch shooting the breeze.

to take a shot at something/ to give something a shot — to try something
I've never tried playing bridge before, but I'll take a shot at it.

RELATED WORDS

big shot (n.) — a person who thinks of himself as very important, or someone who is very important

shoot-out (n.) — a gunfight

shooting gallery (n.) — a place in an amusement park where people shoot at targets in order to win prizes

* Note that the form "will be being shot" is rarely used. To convey a future progressive passive, use the present progressive passive.

show

	ACTIVE	PASSIVE
Infinitive	to show	to be shown
Past Infinitive	to have showed	to have been shown
Past Participle	showed	been shown
Present Participle	showing	being shown

ACTIVE

I
you/we/they
he/she/it

SIMPLE PRESENT	SIMPLE PAST	SIMPLE FUTURE
show	showed	will show
show	showed	will show
shows	showed	will show

PRESENT PROGRESSIVE	PAST PROGRESSIVE	FUTURE PROGRESSIVE
am showing	was showing	will be showing
are showing	were showing	will be showing
is showing	was showing	will be showing

PRESENT PERFECT	PAST PERFECT	FUTURE PERFECT
have shown	had shown	will have shown
have shown	had shown	will have shown
has shown	had shown	will have shown

PRESENT PERFECT PROGRESSIVE	PAST PERFECT PROGRESSIVE	FUTURE PERFECT PROGRESSIVE
have been showing	had been showing	will have been showing
have been showing	had been showing	will have been showing
has been showing	had been showing	will have been showing

EXAMPLES:

She's showing her paintings at the gallery on Broadway and Prince.

The chef showed me how to prepare the soufflé.

Come back at 8:00. We will have shown the first movie and you can stay for the second.

PASSIVE

SIMPLE PRESENT	SIMPLE PAST	SIMPLE FUTURE
am shown	was shown	will be shown
are shown	were shown	will be shown
is shown	was shown	will be shown

PRESENT PROGRESSIVE	PAST PROGRESSIVE	FUTURE PROGRESSIVE*
am being shown	was being shown	will be being shown*
are being shown	were being shown	will be being shown*
is being shown	was being shown	will be being shown*

PRESENT PERFECT	PAST PERFECT	FUTURE PERFECT
have been shown	had been shown	will have been shown
have been shown	had been shown	will have been shown
has been shown	had been shown	will have been shown

EXAMPLES:

The painting had been shown for several weeks before it was purchased.

The movie was being shown at several theaters.

The guests will be shown a short film that explains the goal of our fund-raiser.

PRINCIPAL CONDITIONALS

PRESENT	PRESENT PROGRESSIVE	PRESENT PASSIVE
would show	would be showing	would be shown
would show	would be showing	would be shown
would show	would be showing	would be shown

PAST	PAST PROGRESSIVE	PAST PASSIVE
would have shown	would have been showing	would have been shown
would have shown	would have been showing	would have been shown
would have shown	would have been showing	would have been shown

EXAMPLES:

I'm sure she would show you the apartment if you wanted to see it.

She would be showing if she were five months pregnant.

show

Important Forms in Use

IF/THEN CONDITIONALS

	IF ...	...THEN	EXAMPLE
Real Present/ Future	show/shows	simple present	If the artwork <u>shows</u> in our gallery, the artist gets good coverage.
		will + base form	If we <u>show</u> them the house, they will want to stay.
Unreal Present/ Future	showed	would + base form	If he <u>showed</u> more of his writing to us, we would be more willing to back him.
Unreal Past	had shown	would have + past participle	If the guests <u>had shown</u> up on time, we wouldn't have been ready for them.

SUBJUNCTIVE

ACTIVE	show	They are insisting that we <u>show</u> them the contents of our luggage.
PASSIVE	be shown	It is required that ID <u>be shown</u> upon entering the building.

PHRASAL VERBS

show off	to flaunt something or brag about it *Frank bought a new Ferrari and he showed it off to all his neighbors.*
show up	to appear, especially when others are expecting you *We had just started to eat when the last guest showed up.*

IDIOMS

to show (someone) a good time	to take someone out and make sure he or she has fun *My cousin is coming to visit and we're going to show him a good time.*
to show (someone) the door	to make clear that it is time for someone to leave *When the business deal didn't work out, my partner showed him the door.*
to show (someone) who's boss	to assert your authority *He thinks he can take over this project, but I'll show him who's boss.*
to show your true colors	to do something, usually negative, that allows others to see who you really are *When he refused to take me to the hospital he showed his true colors.*

RELATED WORDS

show-and-tell (n.)	an opportunity for children to bring an item to class and explain its significance
showdown (n.)	a confrontation that results from a long-running dispute
show-off (n.)	a person who hopes to impress others by emphasizing his or her skills, talents, or possessions
show of hands (n.)	a decision made by asking a group of people to vote by raising their hands
showstopper (n.)	a very impressive performance

* Note that the form "will be being shown" is rarely used. To convey a future progressive passive, use the present progressive passive.

Verb Chart

shut

	ACTIVE	PASSIVE
Infinitive	to shut	to be shut
Past Infinitive	to have shut	to have been shut
Past Participle	shut	been shut
Present Participle	shutting	being shut

ACTIVE

I		
you/we/they		
he/she/it		

SIMPLE PRESENT	SIMPLE PAST	SIMPLE FUTURE
shut	shut	will shut
shut	shut	will shut
shuts	shut	will shut

PRESENT PROGRESSIVE	PAST PROGRESSIVE	FUTURE PROGRESSIVE
am shutting	was shutting	will be shutting
are shutting	were shutting	will be shutting
is shutting	was shutting	will be shutting

PRESENT PERFECT	PAST PERFECT	FUTURE PERFECT
have shut	had shut	will have shut
have shut	had shut	will have shut
has shut	had shut	will have shut

PRESENT PERFECT PROGRESSIVE	PAST PERFECT PROGRESSIVE	FUTURE PERFECT PROGRESSIVE
have been shutting	had been shutting	will have been shutting
have been shutting	had been shutting	will have been shutting
has been shutting	had been shutting	will have been shutting

EXAMPLES:

Please shut the door on your way out.

The diner next door is shutting its doors for the last time tomorrow.

Have you shut the trunk? I need to get out the rest of the groceries.

PASSIVE

SIMPLE PRESENT	SIMPLE PAST	SIMPLE FUTURE
am shut	was shut	will be shut
are shut	were shut	will be shut
is shut	was shut	will be shut

PRESENT PROGRESSIVE	PAST PROGRESSIVE	FUTURE PROGRESSIVE*
am being shut	was being shut	will be being shut*
are being shut	were being shut	will be being shut*
is being shut	was being shut	will be being shut*

PRESENT PERFECT	PAST PERFECT	FUTURE PERFECT
have been shut	had been shut	will have been shut
have been shut	had been shut	will have been shut
has been shut	had been shut	will have been shut

EXAMPLES:

The doors are shut every night promptly at 11:00.

The restaurant that we liked so much was shut down due to health code violations.

I went back in the house to make sure that all of the doors and windows had been shut properly.

PRINCIPAL CONDITIONALS

PRESENT	PRESENT PROGRESSIVE	PRESENT PASSIVE
would shut	would be shutting	would be shut
would shut	would be shutting	would be shut
would shut	would be shutting	would be shut

PAST	PAST PROGRESSIVE	PAST PASSIVE
would have shut	would have been shutting	would have been shut
would have shut	would have been shutting	would have been shut
would have shut	would have been shutting	would have been shut

EXAMPLES:

We thought the water would be shut off and so we bought several bottles at the store.

Would you shut the window please? It's freezing in here.

Important Forms in Use

IF/THEN CONDITIONALS

	IF ...	... THEN	EXAMPLE
Real Present/ Future	shut/shuts	simple present	*If I shut off the music too early, he insists that I turn it on again.*
		will + base form	*If she shuts him out of her life, he won't be there for her when she needs him.*
Unreal Present/ Future	shut	would + base form	*If the health department shut us down, we wouldn't be able to open up again until we had made all of the changes they required.*
Unreal Past	had shut	would have + past participle	*If you had shut the door, we would've been locked out.*

SUBJUNCTIVE

ACTIVE	shut	*It is recommended that the mechanic shut off the equipment before making any repairs.*
PASSIVE	be shut	*It is asked that the front and back doors be shut before 12:00 a.m.*

PHRASAL VERBS

to shut (someone or something) out	to not allow someone or something to enter, to exclude *Unfortunately, our team was shut out of the meeting with the board.*
to shut (something) off	to stop something mechanical, such as a television, radio, fan, car, etc., from functioning *Can you shut off the TV when you come upstairs?*
to shut up	to stop talking, or to stop someone from talking *If you don't shut up, I'm going to scream!*
to shut (something) down	to close a business, factory, etc. *The bakery near my house was shut down by the health department.*

IDIOMS

to shut your mouth/trap	to stop talking, usually given as an order in anger or annoyance *How can you say those things to me? Shut your mouth!*

RELATED WORDS

open-and-shut (adj.)	describes a situation in which the answer is clear, there is no doubt
shut-in (n.)	a person who is not able to leave the house due to illness or some other form of incapacitation
shut-eye (n.)	sleep
shutter (n.)	a piece of wood that can be opened and closed to cover a window or let light in
shutout (n.)	a game in which one team wins without allowing the other team to score any points

* Note that the form "will be being shut" is rarely used. To convey a future progressive passive, use the present

Verb Chart

sit

	ACTIVE	PASSIVE
Infinitive	to sit	to be sat
Past Infinitive	to have sat	to have been sat
Past Participle	sat	been sat
Present Participle	sitting	being sat

ACTIVE

I
you/we/they
he/she/it

SIMPLE PRESENT	SIMPLE PAST	SIMPLE FUTURE
sit	sat	will sit
sit	sat	will sit
sits	sat	will sit

PRESENT PROGRESSIVE	PAST PROGRESSIVE	FUTURE PROGRESSIVE
am sitting	was sitting	will be sitting
are sitting	were sitting	will be sitting
is sitting	was sitting	will be sitting

PRESENT PERFECT	PAST PERFECT	FUTURE PERFECT
have sat	had sat	will have sat
have sat	had sat	will have sat
has sat	had sat	will have sat

PRESENT PERFECT PROGRESSIVE	PAST PERFECT PROGRESSIVE	FUTURE PERFECT PROGRESSIVE
have been sitting	had been sitting	will have been sitting
have been sitting	had been sitting	will have been sitting
has been sitting	had been sitting	will have been sitting

EXAMPLES:

Annie sits in the same chair every night at dinner.

My mom has been sitting at the table for hours reading the newspaper.

The guest had sat in the place where my father usually sat.

PASSIVE

SIMPLE PRESENT	SIMPLE PAST	SIMPLE FUTURE
am sat	was sat	will be sat
are sat	were sat	will be sat
is sat	was sat	will be sat

PRESENT PROGRESSIVE	PAST PROGRESSIVE	FUTURE PROGRESSIVE*
am being sat	was being sat	will be being sat*
are being sat	were being sat	will be being sat*
is being sat	was being sat	will be being sat*

PRESENT PERFECT	PAST PERFECT	FUTURE PERFECT
have been sat	had been sat	will have been sat
have been sat	had been sat	will have been sat
has been sat	had been sat	will have been sat

EXAMPLES:

I can't believe Ms. Henderson and her ex-husband were sat at the same table.

The children were being sat at their desks in alphabetical order.

PRINCIPAL CONDITIONALS

PRESENT	PRESENT PROGRESSIVE	PRESENT PASSIVE
would sit	would be sitting	would be sat
would sit	would be sitting	would be sat
would sit	would be sitting	would be sat

PAST	PAST PROGRESSIVE	PAST PASSIVE
would have sat	would have been sitting	would have been sat
would have sat	would have been sitting	would have been sat
would have sat	would have been sitting	would have been sat

EXAMPLES:

We would sit down but the guest of honor hasn't arrived.

Harry would have sat next to Sally but be couldn't find her.

Important Forms in Use

IF/THEN CONDITIONALS

	IF...	...THEN	EXAMPLE
Real Present/ Future	sit/sits	simple present	*If I <u>sit</u> in this position for too long, my foot falls asleep.*
		will + base form	*If he <u>sits</u> with us at dinner, we'll have time to discuss his company's proposal.*
Unreal Present/ Future	sat	would + base form	*If you <u>sat</u> around doing nothing, you wouldn't feel relaxed; you would feel bored.*
Unreal Past	had sat	would have + past participle	*If I <u>had sat</u> through the whole movie, I would have gone crazy.*

SUBJUNCTIVE

ACTIVE	sit	*We prefer that the playwright <u>sit</u> in the front row so that we can introduce him after the show.*
PASSIVE	be sat	*It is requested that the host <u>be sat</u> at the head of the table.*

PHRASAL VERBS

sit back	to relax and get comfortable *Sit back and relax. We don't have to go anywhere for at least half an hour.*
sit down	to move from a standing position to a sitting position *Please sit down and I'll get you something to drink.*
sit (something) out	to not participate *I'm going to sit this one out. Jim, why don't you take my place?*
sit through	to stay for the entirety of something, even if it is tedious or boring *I can't believe how bad that movie was! Unfortunately, I felt like I had to sit through it or I would be insulting my friends who brought me.*
sit up	to not slouch, to not relax too much in a sitting position *Can you sit up please? I don't like it when students slouch in class.*

IDIOMS

to sit tight	to be patient *You can't expect us to get there on a magic carpet. Just sit tight. We'll be there in half an hour.*
to sit idly by	to do nothing *I can't believe that he would just sit idly by while that man was speaking to his wife so rudely!*
to be sitting pretty	to be in a good position *Don is sitting pretty. He gets all of the good jobs because the boss likes him.*
to not sit well with someone	to make someone uncomfortable *This decision to let him take the car out on his own doesn't sit well with me.*

RELATED WORDS

sit-in (n.)	a protest in which people refuse to move from somewhere until their demands have been recognized
sitting duck (n.)	a person who is in a place or a position from which he or she can be attacked
sit-up (n.)	a type of exercise in which you move your upper body from a lying position to a sitting position and back down again

Verb Chart

* Note that the form "will be being sat" is rarely used. To convey a future progressive passive, use the present progressive passive.

sleep

	ACTIVE	PASSIVE
Infinitive	to sleep	to be slept
Past Infinitive	to have slept	to have been slept
Past Participle	slept	been slept
Present Participle	sleeping	being slept

ACTIVE

I	
you/we/they	
he/she/it	

SIMPLE PRESENT	SIMPLE PAST	SIMPLE FUTURE
sleep	slept	will sleep
sleep	slept	will sleep
sleeps	slept	will sleep

PRESENT PROGRESSIVE	PAST PROGRESSIVE	FUTURE PROGRESSIVE
am sleeping	was sleeping	will be sleeping
are sleeping	were sleeping	will be sleeping
is sleeping	was sleeping	will be sleeping

PRESENT PERFECT	PAST PERFECT	FUTURE PERFECT
have slept	had slept	will have slept
have slept	had slept	will have slept
has slept	had slept	will have slept

PRESENT PERFECT PROGRESSIVE	PAST PERFECT PROGRESSIVE	FUTURE PERFECT PROGRESSIVE
have been sleeping	had been sleeping	will have been sleeping
have been sleeping	had been sleeping	will have been sleeping
has been sleeping	had been sleeping	will have been sleeping

EXAMPLES:

You have been sleeping for hours! — *If we wake her up at 10:00, she will have slept for eight hours.* — *The cat sleeps on the windowsill.*

PASSIVE

SIMPLE PRESENT	SIMPLE PAST	SIMPLE FUTURE
am slept	was slept	will be slept
are slept	were slept	will be slept
is slept	was slept	will be slept

PRESENT PROGRESSIVE	PAST PROGRESSIVE	FUTURE PROGRESSIVE*
am being slept	was being slept	will be being slept*
are being slept	were being slept	will be being slept*
is being slept	was being slept	will be being slept*

PRESENT PERFECT	PAST PERFECT	FUTURE PERFECT
have been slept	had been slept	will have been slept
have been slept	had been slept	will have been slept
has been slept	had been slept	will have been slept

EXAMPLES:

The three bears found that their beds had been slept in while they were away. — *By the morning, the drunken evening had been slept off.*

PRINCIPAL CONDITIONALS

PRESENT	PRESENT PROGRESSIVE	PRESENT PASSIVE
would sleep	would be sleeping	would be slept
would sleep	would be sleeping	would be slept
would sleep	would be sleeping	would be slept

PAST	PAST PROGRESSIVE	PAST PASSIVE
would have slept	would have been sleeping	would have been slept
would have slept	would have been sleeping	would have been slept
would have slept	would have been sleeping	would have been slept

EXAMPLES:

They would've slept more soundly if they had gotten some exercise during the day. — *A peaceful night would have been slept if it weren't for the periodic noises from outside.*

VERB CHART 96

sleep

PRINCIPAL PARTS: sleep, slept, slept

Important Forms in Use

IF/THEN CONDITIONALS

	IF ...	... THEN	EXAMPLE
Real Present/ Future	sleep/sleeps	simple present	*If the baby <u>sleeps</u> too long in the afternoon, he wakes up several times during the night.*
		will + base form	*If you don't <u>sleep</u> well tonight, you won't be ready for your big day tomorrow.*
Unreal Present/ Future	slept	would + base form	*If I <u>slept</u> better, I wouldn't be so grumpy all the time.*
Unreal Past	had slept	would have + past participle	*If the guests <u>had slept</u> on the pull-out bed in the living room, we would've woken them up in the morning.*

SUBJUNCTIVE

ACTIVE	sleep	*It is important the baby <u>sleep</u> on its back.*
PASSIVE	be slept	*The coach recommended that a good eight hours <u>be slept</u> the night before the game.*

PHRASAL VERBS

sleep in	to sleep longer than you usually do in the morning *My boyfriend has to get up at 5:30 every workday, so he likes to sleep in on the weekends.*
sleep (something) off	to sleep extra time in order to wake up fresh, such as after drinking too much *Tom won't wake up for hours. He's sleeping off the wild night we had.*
sleep over	to sleep at someone else's house *It was so late when we finished the work that I decided to sleep over instead of trying to go home.*
sleep through (something)	to fall asleep during something, such as a film, and not wake up until it's over *The lecture was a little slow and Leo slept through the whole thing.*

IDIOMS

to sleep like a log/like a baby	to sleep very well so that nothing can disturb you *Don't worry about making noise. My roommate sleeps like a baby.*
to not sleep a wink	to not sleep at all *I didn't sleep a wink last night because of those barking dogs.*
to sleep on it	to wait to make a decision until you've thought about it overnight *Why don't you sleep on it and call me tomorrow?*
to sleep with (someone)	to have sex with *We all know that they are sleeping with each other.*

RELATED WORDS

sleepover (n.)	a party, usually for children, where friends stay the night at another friend's house
to oversleep (v.)	to sleep too much when you need to get up at a certain time
sleep-deprived (adj.)	to be short on sleep
sleepwalker (n.)	a person who walks while asleep

* Note that the form "will be being slept" is rarely used. To convey a future progressive passive, use the present progressive.

Verb Chart

slip

	ACTIVE	PASSIVE
Infinitive	to slip	to be slipped
Past Infinitive	to have slipped	to have been slipped
Past Participle	slipped	been slipped
Present Participle	slipping	being slipped

ACTIVE

I
you/we/they
he/she/it

SIMPLE PRESENT	SIMPLE PAST	SIMPLE FUTURE
slip	slipped	will slip
slip	slipped	will slip
slips	slipped	will slip

PRESENT PROGRESSIVE	PAST PROGRESSIVE	FUTURE PROGRESSIVE
am slipping	was slipping	will be slipping
are slipping	were slipping	will be slipping
is slipping	was slipping	will be slipping

PRESENT PERFECT	PAST PERFECT	FUTURE PERFECT
have slipped	had slipped	will have slipped
have slipped	had slipped	will have slipped
has slipped	had slipped	will have slipped

PRESENT PERFECT PROGRESSIVE	PAST PERFECT PROGRESSIVE	FUTURE PERFECT PROGRESSIVE
have been slipping	had been slipping	will have been slipping
have been slipping	had been slipping	will have been slipping
has been slipping	had been slipping	will have been slipping

EXAMPLES:
Don't slip! There is ice on the steps. *I can't believe you slipped up and gave away the answer to the trivia question!* *His ranking among the other tennis players at the club had slipped since he had stopped practicing.*

PASSIVE

SIMPLE PRESENT	SIMPLE PAST	SIMPLE FUTURE
am slipped	was slipped	will be slipped
are slipped	were slipped	will be slipped
is slipped	was slipped	will be slipped

PRESENT PROGRESSIVE	PAST PROGRESSIVE	FUTURE PROGRESSIVE*
am being slipped	was being slipped	will be being slipped*
are being slipped	were being slipped	will be being slipped*
is being slipped	was being slipped	will be being slipped*

PRESENT PERFECT	PAST PERFECT	FUTURE PERFECT
have been slipped	had been slipped	will have been slipped
have been slipped	had been slipped	will have been slipped
has been slipped	had been slipped	will have been slipped

EXAMPLES:
Something had been slipped into his drink and he began to feel dizzy. *The bills were slipped into an envelope so that no one would notice.* *The hundred dollar bill was slipped to the maître d' and we were seated immediately.*

PRINCIPAL CONDITIONALS

PRESENT	PRESENT PROGRESSIVE	PRESENT PASSIVE
would slip	would be slipping	would be slipped
would slip	would be slipping	would be slipped
would slip	would be slipping	would be slipped

PAST	PAST PROGRESSIVE	PAST PASSIVE
would have slipped	would have been slipping	would have been slipped
would have slipped	would have been slipping	would have been slipped
would have slipped	would have been slipping	would have been slipped

EXAMPLES:
I would slip him a few dollars if he asked for it. *You would have slipped coming up the stairs if I hadn't put salt on the ice.*

slip

PRINCIPAL PARTS: slip, slipped, slipped

VERB CHART

97

Important Forms in Use

IF/THEN CONDITIONALS

	IF ...	... THEN	EXAMPLE
Real Present/ Future	slip/slips	simple present	*If I slip you fifty dollars, make sure I get a good table.*
		will + base form	*If she slips up again, her boss will fire her.*
Unreal Present/ Future	slipped	would + base form	*If we slipped out for a few minutes, nobody would notice.*
Unreal Past	had slipped	would have + past participle	*If I had slipped during the performance, it would have been embarrassing.*

SUBJUNCTIVE

ACTIVE	slip	*We ask that you slip out of the meeting for just a few moments to talk with our representative.*
PASSIVE	be slipped	*The landlord requested that rent checks be slipped under the door.*

PHRASAL VERBS

slip into	to quickly put on different clothes *She slipped into her pajamas and got into bed.*
slip out	to leave quietly and quickly in hopes that no one will notice *I guess he slipped out while we were taking a break.*
slip up	to make a mistake *The mail carrier must have slipped up when he delivered your package to our house.*

IDIOMS

to slip through your fingers	to lose a valuable opportunity when you are very close to getting it *She's a lovely girl. Don't let this one slip through your fingers.*
to slip through the cracks	to be ignored or forgotten, usually related to bureaucracy *Millions of low-income families slip through the cracks. They don't receive benefits because their salary is a few dollars above the poverty line.*
to slip one over on someone	to fool someone *The story about the new investment company was completely unbelievable. I can't believe you slipped that one over on the old lady.*
to slip one's mind	to forget *I was supposed to call Liz last night but it completely slipped my mind.*
to slip someone something	to give someone something, often money or drugs, in a way that doesn't attract attention *I slipped the bellbop a few dollars when he brought our suitcases to the room.*

RELATED WORDS

slip of the tongue (n.)	a mistake in speech
slipper (n.)	a small, lightweight shoe that is worn in the house
Freudian slip (n.)	a verbal mistake that reveals the truth of what someone was actually thinking

* Note that the form "will be being slipped" is rarely used. To convey a future progressive passive, use the present progressive passive.

Verb Chart

speak

	ACTIVE	PASSIVE
Infinitive	to speak	to be spoken
Past Infinitive	to have spoken	to have been spoken
Past Participle	spoken	been spoken
Present Participle	speaking	being spoken

ACTIVE

I
you/we/they
he/she/it

SIMPLE PRESENT	SIMPLE PAST	SIMPLE FUTURE
speak	spoke	will speak
speak	spoke	will speak
speaks	spoke	will speak

PRESENT PROGRESSIVE	PAST PROGRESSIVE	FUTURE PROGRESSIVE
am speaking	was speaking	will be speaking
are speaking	were speaking	will be speaking
is speaking	was speaking	will be speaking

PRESENT PERFECT	PAST PERFECT	FUTURE PERFECT
have spoken	had spoken	will have spoken
have spoken	had spoken	will have spoken
has spoken	had spoken	will have spoken

PRESENT PERFECT PROGRESSIVE	PAST PERFECT PROGRESSIVE	FUTURE PERFECT PROGRESSIVE
have been speaking	had been speaking	will have been speaking
have been speaking	had been speaking	will have been speaking
has been speaking	had been speaking	will have been speaking

EXAMPLES:
I can't stand when my friends speak badly about each other.

This lecture is very interesting. Do you know who is speaking?

PASSIVE

SIMPLE PRESENT	SIMPLE PAST	SIMPLE FUTURE
am spoken	was spoken	will be spoken
are spoken	were spoken	will be spoken
is spoken	was spoken	will be spoken

PRESENT PROGRESSIVE	PAST PROGRESSIVE	FUTURE PROGRESSIVE*
am being spoken	was being spoken	will be being spoken*
are being spoken	were being spoken	will be being spoken*
is being spoken	was being spoken	will be being spoken*

PRESENT PERFECT	PAST PERFECT	FUTURE PERFECT
have been spoken	had been spoken	will have been spoken
have been spoken	had been spoken	will have been spoken
has been spoken	had been spoken	will have been spoken

EXAMPLES:
The girls were spoken to sternly by the principal when he found out they had left school early.

I didn't appreciate the way I was spoken to by the clerk. I'll never go back to that store.

PRINCIPAL CONDITIONALS

PRESENT	PRESENT PROGRESSIVE	PRESENT PASSIVE
would speak	would be speaking	would be spoken
would speak	would be speaking	would be spoken
would speak	would be speaking	would be spoken

PAST	PAST PROGRESSIVE	PAST PASSIVE
would have spoken	would have been speaking	would have been spoken
would have spoken	would have been speaking	would have been spoken
would have spoken	would have been speaking	would have been spoken

EXAMPLES:
Jean would have spoken more if he hadn't felt limited by his inability to express himself in English.

Who knew that Ingrid would speak for two hours without a break?

speak

PRINCIPAL PARTS: speak, spoke, spoken

Important Forms in Use

IF/THEN CONDITIONALS

	IF ...	... THEN	EXAMPLE
Real Present/ Future	speak/speaks	simple present	*If you <u>speak</u> softly, I can't understand you.*
		will + base form	*If she <u>speaks</u> to him, certainly he'll come around.*
Unreal Present/ Future	spoke	would + base form	*If he <u>spoke</u> more convincingly, he would be the director and not just an assistant.*
Unreal Past	had spoken	would have + past participle	*If they <u>had spoken</u> to me before the event began, we would've avoided a lot of confusion.*

SUBJUNCTIVE

ACTIVE	speak	*We suggest that he <u>speak</u> to the detective in private.*
PASSIVE	be spoken	*It is important that the girls <u>be spoken</u> to so that this incident is not repeated.*

PHRASAL VERBS

speak of (someone or something)	to refer to someone or something while you are talking *Speaking of Tom, didn't he start law school last year?*
speak out	to voice your opinion about something *She never hesitated to speak out about the atrocities that were committed during the war in El Salvador.*
speak to	to talk to someone, often when he or she has done something wrong *You'll speak to him about parking in my place, won't you?*
speak up	to talk louder *You'll have to speak up because I can't hear a thing.*
speak up for (someone)	to support someone *My boss always spoke up for us whenever there was a problem.*

IDIOMS

actions speak louder than words	an expression that means that it is better to teach someone through example than through explanation *My mother always said that actions speak louder than words.*
to speak highly of someone	to express respect or admiration for someone *Her teachers spoke highly of her and so we decided to hire her.*
to speak of the devil	to be talking about someone, and he or she appears *Speak of the devil! We were just talking about you.*
to speak your mind	to state your opinions or feelings clearly *If you're upset, I'd prefer that you speak your mind.*

RELATED WORDS

speakeasy (n.)	an illegal club that served alcohol during Prohibition in the United States
speaker (n.)	a person who is addressing an audience
speech (n.)	a spoken presentation, usually formal, given to group of people
speechless (adj.)	overcome by emotion and unable to speak

* Note that the form "will be being spoken" is rarely used. To convey a future progressive passive, use the present progressive passive.

spell

	ACTIVE	PASSIVE
Infinitive	to spell	to be spelled
Past Infinitive	to have spelled	to have been spelled
Past Participle	spelled	been spelled
Present Participle	spelling	being spelled

I		
you/we/they		
he/she/it		

ACTIVE

SIMPLE PRESENT	SIMPLE PAST	SIMPLE FUTURE
spell	spelled	will spell
spell	spelled	will spell
spells	spelled	will spell

PRESENT PROGRESSIVE	PAST PROGRESSIVE	FUTURE PROGRESSIVE
am spelling	was spelling	will be spelling
are spelling	were spelling	will be spelling
is spelling	was spelling	will be spelling

PRESENT PERFECT	PAST PERFECT	FUTURE PERFECT
have spelled	had spelled	will have spelled
have spelled	had spelled	will have spelled
has spelled	had spelled	will have spelled

PRESENT PERFECT PROGRESSIVE	PAST PERFECT PROGRESSIVE	FUTURE PERFECT PROGRESSIVE
have been spelling	had been spelling	will have been spelling
have been spelling	had been spelling	will have been spelling
has been spelling	had been spelling	will have been spelling

EXAMPLES:
He spells his name with an a, not an o.

The students were spelling words on the blackboard.

She had spelled her name clearly, but the receptionist still didn't understand her.

PASSIVE

SIMPLE PRESENT	SIMPLE PAST	SIMPLE FUTURE
am spelled	was spelled	will be spelled
are spelled	were spelled	will be spelled
is spelled	was spelled	will be spelled

PRESENT PROGRESSIVE	PAST PROGRESSIVE	FUTURE PROGRESSIVE*
am being spelled	was being spelled	will be being spelled*
are being spelled	were being spelled	will be being spelled*
is being spelled	was being spelled	will be being spelled*

PRESENT PERFECT	PAST PERFECT	FUTURE PERFECT
have been spelled	had been spelled	will have been spelled
have been spelled	had been spelled	will have been spelled
has been spelled	had been spelled	will have been spelled

EXAMPLES:
My name is long and complicated and is always spelled wrong.

The owner realized the name of his restaurant had been spelled wrong on all the menus.

How will your daughter's name be spelled?

PRINCIPAL CONDITIONALS

PRESENT	PRESENT PROGRESSIVE	PRESENT PASSIVE
would spell	would be spelling	would be spelled
would spell	would be spelling	would be spelled
would spell	would be spelling	would be spelled

PAST	PAST PROGRESSIVE	PAST PASSIVE
would have spelled	would have been spelling	would have been spelled
would have spelled	would have been spelling	would have been spelled
would have spelled	would have been spelling	would have been spelled

EXAMPLES:
Would you spell that for me?

I thought huevo would be spelled without an h because it's pronounced that way.

spell

Important Forms in Use

IF/THEN CONDITIONALS

	IF ...	...THEN	EXAMPLE
Real Present/ Future	spell/spells	simple present	*If the students spell a few words wrong, don't worry about it.*
		will + base form	*If the boy spells this word correctly, he'll win the spelling bee.*
Unreal Present/ Future	spelled	would + base form	*If you spelled out exactly what you expect, they would probably do a better job.*
Unreal Past	had spelled	would have + past participle	*If I had spelled the lead actors' names wrong on the marquee, I would have been in trouble.*

SUBJUNCTIVE

ACTIVE	spell	*My mother recommended that we spell the name like her father did.*
PASSIVE	be spelled	*We ask that the duties be spelled out to us clearly before we begin working.*

PHRASAL VERBS

spell (something) out

to explain a problem or concern clearly and simply
I can't believe you don't understand what I'm saying. Do I have to spell it out for you?

IDIOMS

to spell trouble

to be likely to cause future problems
Those rusty pipes spell trouble. We should call a plumber before they burst.

to put someone under a spell

to capture the interest of someone
Andre seems to have put her under a spell.

RELATED WORDS

spellbound (adj.)	caught up in something
spell check (n.)	a device on a computer that finds mistakes in spelling
spell (n.)	a short period of time
spelling bee (n.)	a competition in which individuals win or lose according to whether they are able to spell words correctly

* Note that the form "will be being spelled" is rarely used. To convey a future progressive passive, use the present progressive passive.

Verb Chart

spend

	ACTIVE	PASSIVE
Infinitive	to spend	to be spent
Past Infinitive	to have spent	to have been spent
Past Participle	spent	been spent
Present Participle	spending	being spent

ACTIVE

	I
you/we/they	
he/she/it	

SIMPLE PRESENT	SIMPLE PAST	SIMPLE FUTURE
spend	spent	will spend
spend	spent	will spend
spends	spent	will spend

PRESENT PROGRESSIVE	PAST PROGRESSIVE	FUTURE PROGRESSIVE
am spending	was spending	will be spending
are spending	were spending	will be spending
is spending	was spending	will be spending

PRESENT PERFECT	PAST PERFECT	FUTURE PERFECT
have spent	had spent	will have spent
have spent	had spent	will have spent
has spent	had spent	will have spent

PRESENT PERFECT PROGRESSIVE	PAST PERFECT PROGRESSIVE	FUTURE PERFECT PROGRESSIVE
have been spending	had been spending	will have been spending
have been spending	had been spending	will have been spending
has been spending	had been spending	will have been spending

EXAMPLES:
We are spending too much money and we need to cut down. *How many days will you be spending in Hawaii?* *I have been spending a lot of time with Jean lately.*

PASSIVE

SIMPLE PRESENT	SIMPLE PAST	SIMPLE FUTURE
am spent	was spent	will be spent
are spent	were spent	will be spent
is spent	was spent	will be spent

PRESENT PROGRESSIVE	PAST PROGRESSIVE	FUTURE PROGRESSIVE*
am being spent	was being spent	will be being spent*
are being spent	were being spent	will be being spent*
is being spent	was being spent	will be being spent*

PRESENT PERFECT	PAST PERFECT	FUTURE PERFECT
have been spent	had been spent	will have been spent
have been spent	had been spent	will have been spent
has been spent	had been spent	will have been spent

EXAMPLES:
The money was all spent before we even considered redoing the upstairs rooms of the house. *I'm sure that a lot of time will be spent at the beach if the weather is good.*

PRINCIPAL CONDITIONALS

PRESENT	PRESENT PROGRESSIVE	PRESENT PASSIVE
would spend	would be spending	would be spent
would spend	would be spending	would be spent
would spend	would be spending	would be spent

PAST	PAST PROGRESSIVE	PAST PASSIVE
would have spent	would have been spending	would have been spent
would have spent	would have been spending	would have been spent
would have spent	would have been spending	would have been spent

EXAMPLES:
We would spend more time with them if they weren't so busy.

spend

PRINCIPAL PARTS: spend, spent, spent

VERB CHART
100

Important Forms in Use

IF/THEN CONDITIONALS

	IF ...	... THEN	EXAMPLE
Real Present/ Future	spend/spends	simple present	*If I <u>spend</u> money on going out, I don't have any left for taking a vacation.*
		will + base form	*If she <u>spends</u> too much energy on him, he won't respond.*
Unreal Present/ Future	spent	would + base form	*If we <u>spent</u> the night here, we would be ready to drive tomorrow.*
Unreal Past	had spent	would have + past participle	*If Harry <u>had spent</u> as much time studying as he did playing his guitar, he wouldn't have done so poorly on his exams.*

SUBJUNCTIVE

ACTIVE	spend	*We suggest that you <u>spend</u> some time at the Art Institute before you go to the Historical Society.*
PASSIVE	be spent	*It is essential that money <u>be spent</u> on children's programs.*

IDIOMS

to be spent

to be exhausted
I would go out with you, but I'm spent.

RELATED WORDS

spendthrift (n.)	a person who spends money without thinking, even if he or she does not have a lot of it
big spender (n.)	a person who likes to spend a lot of money
spending (n.)	the amount of money that a government, institution, etc., spends
spending money (n.)	money that you allow yourself for expenses strictly for enjoyment

* Note that the form "will be being spent" is rarely used. To convey a future progressive passive, use the present progressive passive.

Verb Chart

spin

	ACTIVE	PASSIVE
Infinitive	to spin	to be spun
Past Infinitive	to have spun	to have been spun
Past Participle	spun	been spun
Present Participle	spinning	being spun

I
you/we/they
he/she/it

ACTIVE

SIMPLE PRESENT	SIMPLE PAST	SIMPLE FUTURE
spin	spun	will spin
spin	spun	will spin
spins	spun	will spin

PRESENT PROGRESSIVE	PAST PROGRESSIVE	FUTURE PROGRESSIVE
am spinning	was spinning	will be spinning
are spinning	were spinning	will be spinning
is spinning	was spinning	will be spinning

PRESENT PERFECT	PAST PERFECT	FUTURE PERFECT
have spun	had spun	will have spun
have spun	had spun	will have spun
has spun	had spun	will have spun

PRESENT PERFECT PROGRESSIVE	PAST PERFECT PROGRESSIVE	FUTURE PERFECT PROGRESSIVE
have been spinning	had been spinning	will have been spinning
have been spinning	had been spinning	will have been spinning
has been spinning	had been spinning	will have been spinning

EXAMPLES:

The machine spins the clothes to dry them.

The car in front of us spun out of control and slid into the embankment.

The café owner's daughter was spinning a top in the doorway.

PASSIVE

SIMPLE PRESENT	SIMPLE PAST	SIMPLE FUTURE
am spun	was spun	will be spun
are spun	were spun	will be spun
is spun	was spun	will be spun

PRESENT PROGRESSIVE	PAST PROGRESSIVE	FUTURE PROGRESSIVE*
am being spun	was being spun	will be being spun*
are being spun	were being spun	will be being spun*
is being spun	was being spun	will be being spun*

PRESENT PERFECT	PAST PERFECT	FUTURE PERFECT
have been spun	had been spun	will have been spun
have been spun	had been spun	will have been spun
has been spun	had been spun	will have been spun

EXAMPLES:

The silk thread was spun in a small village in India.

A spider's web was being spun during the night.

PRINCIPAL CONDITIONALS

PRESENT	PRESENT PROGRESSIVE	PRESENT PASSIVE
would spin	would be spinning	would be spun
would spin	would be spinning	would be spun
would spin	would be spinning	would be spun

PAST	PAST PROGRESSIVE	PAST PASSIVE
would have spun	would have been spinning	would have been spun
would have spun	would have been spinning	would have been spun
would have spun	would have been spinning	would have been spun

EXAMPLES:

The room would be spinning if I had had any more to drink.

spin

Important Forms in Use

IF/THEN CONDITIONALS

	IF ...	... THEN	EXAMPLE
Real Present/ Future	spin/spins	simple present	*If I <u>spin</u> the record at the wrong speed, it sounds funny.*
		will + base form	*If she <u>spins</u> out again on the highway, I won't lend her my car anymore.*
Unreal Present/ Future	spun	would + base form	*If we <u>spun</u> around right now, we would see a famous actor.*
Unreal Past	had spun	would have + past participle	*If I <u>had spun</u> my wheels anymore, I would have gone crazy!*

SUBJUNCTIVE

ACTIVE	spin	*It is important that the clothes <u>spin</u> for a full cycle.*
PASSIVE	be spun	*It is necessary that a spider's web <u>be spun</u> in a uniform pattern in order to catch the most flies.*

PHRASAL VERBS

spin out	to move out of control in a circular fashion *The wheels of the car spun out and we just got stuck deeper in the mud.*
spin around	to turn continuously, or to make one turn quickly *Spin around! Let me see your new dress!*

IDIOMS

to spin records	to play music on vinyl for a group of people *The DJ spun records until everybody had left the club.*
to spin your wheels	to do something without any result or without a goal *This job isn't giving me any valuable experience. I feel like I'm just spinning my wheels.*
to go for a spin	to drive around without any particular destination *If you're not doing anything, we could go for a spin in my new car.*

RELATED WORDS

spinning (n.)	a type of exercise in a gym in which a group of people ride stationary bicycles while following a leader
spinning wheel (n.)	a machine that is used to make thread out of some material, such as cotton, wool, or silk
spin-off (n.)	something that develops from something else, especially a television program that develops out of another

* Note that the form "will be being spun" is rarely used. To convey a future progressive passive, use the present progressive passive.

Verb Chart

stand

	ACTIVE	PASSIVE
Infinitive	to stand	to be stood
Past Infinitive	to have stood	to have been stood
Past Participle	stood	been stood
Present Participle	standing	being stood

ACTIVE

	I	you/we/they	he/she/it

SIMPLE PRESENT	SIMPLE PAST	SIMPLE FUTURE
stand	stood	will stand
stand	stood	will stand
stands	stood	will stand

PRESENT PROGRESSIVE	PAST PROGRESSIVE	FUTURE PROGRESSIVE
am standing	was standing	will be standing
are standing	were standing	will be standing
is standing	was standing	will be standing

PRESENT PERFECT	PAST PERFECT	FUTURE PERFECT
have stood	had stood	will have stood
have stood	had stood	will have stood
has stood	had stood	will have stood

PRESENT PERFECT PROGRESSIVE	PAST PERFECT PROGRESSIVE	FUTURE PERFECT PROGRESSIVE
have been standing	had been standing	will have been standing
have been standing	had been standing	will have been standing
has been standing	had been standing	will have been standing

EXAMPLES:

The house stands on property that once belonged to my grandparents.

That building has been standing for 120 years.

We had stood the loud music long enough and left before the concert finished.

PASSIVE

SIMPLE PRESENT	SIMPLE PAST	SIMPLE FUTURE
am stood	was stood	will be stood
are stood	were stood	will be stood
is stood	was stood	will be stood

PRESENT PROGRESSIVE	PAST PROGRESSIVE	FUTURE PROGRESSIVE*
am being stood	was being stood	will be being stood*
are being stood	were being stood	will be being stood*
is being stood	was being stood	will be being stood*

PRESENT PERFECT	PAST PERFECT	FUTURE PERFECT
have been stood	had been stood	will have been stood
have been stood	had been stood	will have been stood
has been stood	had been stood	will have been stood

EXAMPLES:

It's unclear how the strong winds were stood by the villagers.

Sara had been stood up by her boyfriend for the last time.

PRINCIPAL CONDITIONALS

PRESENT	PRESENT PROGRESSIVE	PRESENT PASSIVE
would stand	would be standing	would be stood
would stand	would be standing	would be stood
would stand	would be standing	would be stood

PAST	PAST PROGRESSIVE	PAST PASSIVE
would have stood	would have been standing	would have been stood
would have stood	would have been standing	would have been stood
would have stood	would have been standing	would have been stood

EXAMPLES:

We would have stood near the front of the venue if it had been less crowded.

The two vases would have been stood next to each other on the table if they matched more perfectly.

stand

Important Forms in Use

IF/THEN CONDITIONALS

	IF . . .	. . . THEN	EXAMPLE
Real Present/ Future	stand/stands	simple present	*If I <u>stand</u> up for too long, my feet get very tired.*
		will + base form	*If she <u>stands</u> for it any longer, he'll think his behavior is acceptable.*
Unreal Present/ Future	stood	would + base form	*If you <u>stood</u> and saw the view, you would be inspired to begin a new painting.*
Unreal Past	had stood	would have + past participle	*If the rookie baseball player <u>hadn't stood</u> in for me when I broke my leg, the season would have been over.*

SUBJUNCTIVE

ACTIVE	stand	*We propose that the female lead <u>stand</u> on this side of the stage and her costar <u>stand</u> next to her.*
PASSIVE	be stood	*It is essential that the vase <u>be stood</u> on the pedestal in the corner.*

PHRASAL VERBS

stand around	to remain in one place not doing anything *We stood around for an hour waiting for Jim and Susan to arrive.*
stand for (something)	to accept behavior or a situation that is not perfect or that is undesirable *I won't stand for his behavior any longer!*
stand up	to rise *Stand up slowly so that you don't turn over the boat.*
stand down	to withdraw aggressive advances, or to step aside *Tell your troops to stand down; we don't want to fight you!*
stand out	to be obvious or different *He's dyed his hair purple since high school to stand out from the other kids.*

IDIOMS

to know where you stand with someone	to be able to assess your relationship with someone else *I like Harry because you always know where you stand with him.*
can't stand it/something	to have a strong dislike for someone or something *I can't stand this hot and humid weather!*
to stand on one's own two feet	to be an independent person *Now that he's at college he's going to have to stand on his own two feet.*
to stand a chance	to have some hope or possibility of happening or succeeding *The young boxer doesn't stand a chance against the older, more experienced one.*

RELATED WORDS

standby (adj.)	describes something that is kept on hand for a situation in which it may be needed
stand-in (n.)	someone or something who replaces someone or something else, usually temporarily
standing ovation (n.)	when an audience stands up to applaud an especially good performer or performance
stand-up comedy (n.)	a performance in which an individual entertains an audience by telling jokes

* Note that the form "will be being stood" is rarely used. To convey a future progressive passive, use the present progressive passive.

Verb Chart

stay

	ACTIVE	PASSIVE
Infinitive	to stay	to be stayed
Past Infinitive	to have stayed	to have been stayed
Past Participle	stayed	been stayed
Present Participle	staying	being stayed

I
you/we/they
he/she/it

ACTIVE

SIMPLE PRESENT	SIMPLE PAST	SIMPLE FUTURE
stay	stayed	will stay
stay	stayed	will stay
stays	stayed	will stay

PRESENT PROGRESSIVE	PAST PROGRESSIVE	FUTURE PROGRESSIVE
am staying	was staying	will be staying
are staying	were staying	will be staying
is staying	was staying	will be staying

PRESENT PERFECT	PAST PERFECT	FUTURE PERFECT
have stayed	had stayed	will have stayed
have stayed	had stayed	will have stayed
has stayed	had stayed	will have stayed

PRESENT PERFECT PROGRESSIVE	PAST PERFECT PROGRESSIVE	FUTURE PERFECT PROGRESSIVE
have been staying	had been staying	will have been staying
have been staying	had been staying	will have been staying
has been staying	had been staying	will have been staying

EXAMPLES:
We were staying in a beautiful hotel that was located on the beach.

The two of you will stay upstairs, and my husband and I will stay downstairs.

The cats have stayed away from us even though we tried to gain their trust.

PASSIVE

SIMPLE PRESENT	SIMPLE PAST	SIMPLE FUTURE
am stayed	was stayed	will be stayed
are stayed	were stayed	will be stayed
is stayed	was stayed	will be stayed

PRESENT PROGRESSIVE	PAST PROGRESSIVE	FUTURE PROGRESSIVE*
am being stayed	was being stayed	will be being stayed*
are being stayed	were being stayed	will be being stayed*
is being stayed	was being stayed	will be being stayed*

PRESENT PERFECT	PAST PERFECT	FUTURE PERFECT
have been stayed	had been stayed	will have been stayed
have been stayed	had been stayed	will have been stayed
has been stayed	had been stayed	will have been stayed

EXAMPLES:
This hotel was stayed in by Charles Dickens when he visited the United States.

PRINCIPAL CONDITIONALS

PRESENT	PRESENT PROGRESSIVE	PRESENT PASSIVE
would stay	would be staying	would be stayed
would stay	would be staying	would be stayed
would stay	would be staying	would be stayed

PAST	PAST PROGRESSIVE	PAST PASSIVE
would have stayed	would have been staying	would have been stayed
would have stayed	would have been staying	would have been stayed
would have stayed	would have been staying	would have been stayed

EXAMPLES:
Would you stay the night if there was room in the hotel?

We would have been staying in the basement if it weren't for the water damage.

stay

Important Forms in Use

IF/THEN CONDITIONALS

	IF ...	... THEN	EXAMPLE
Real Present/ Future	stay/stays	simple present	*If I <u>stay</u> with Susan, you stay with Albert.*
		will + base form	*If she <u>stays</u> late, I'll have to pick her up.*
Unreal Present/ Future	stayed	would + base form	*If we <u>stayed</u> here more often, we'd know our way around.*
Unreal Past	had stayed	would have + past participle	*If I <u>had stayed</u> a few more minutes, I would have seen the surprise ending.*

SUBJUNCTIVE

ACTIVE	stay	*It is important that the creative department <u>stay</u> until the cover design has been chosen.*
PASSIVE	be stayed	*We suggest that the Lincoln Room <u>be stayed</u> in if you have a choice.*

PHRASAL VERBS

stay in	to remain inside *Billy has to stay in today because he's got a cold.*
stay on	to remain in place, usually a job *A few employees stayed on after the strike.*
stay out	to remain outside *Harry stayed out until 3:00 in the morning.*
stay up	to remain awake *We stayed up until 12:00 watching a great movie on TV.*

IDIOMS

to stay put	to not move from a certain place *I'm going into the pharmacy for two seconds. Stay put until I get back.*
to stay the course	to not give up on something even when it is difficult *We managed to stay the course and finish the documentary even when circumstances made us want to throw in the towel.*

RELATED WORDS

staying power (n.)	the ability to last through time

* Note that the form "will be being stayed" is rarely used. To convey a future progressive passive, use the present progressive.

Verb Chart

step

	ACTIVE	PASSIVE
Infinitive	to step	to be stepped
Past Infinitive	to have stepped	to have been stepped
Past Participle	stepped	been stepped
Present Participle	stepping	being stepped

ACTIVE

I
you/we/they
he/she/it

SIMPLE PRESENT	SIMPLE PAST	SIMPLE FUTURE
step	stepped	will step
step	stepped	will step
steps	stepped	will step

PRESENT PROGRESSIVE	PAST PROGRESSIVE	FUTURE PROGRESSIVE
am stepping	was stepping	will be stepping
are stepping	were stepping	will be stepping
is stepping	was stepping	will be stepping

PRESENT PERFECT	PAST PERFECT	FUTURE PERFECT
have stepped	had stepped	will have stepped
have stepped	had stepped	will have stepped
has stepped	had stepped	will have stepped

PRESENT PERFECT PROGRESSIVE	PAST PERFECT PROGRESSIVE	FUTURE PERFECT PROGRESSIVE
have been stepping	had been stepping	will have been stepping
have been stepping	had been stepping	will have been stepping
has been stepping	had been stepping	will have been stepping

EXAMPLES:
We couldn't believe it when the mayor stepped down after he was accused of misappropriating funds. *Don't step on my toes with those boots!* *John had just stepped out when we got to the office and so we decided to wait for him in the lounge.*

PASSIVE

SIMPLE PRESENT	SIMPLE PAST	SIMPLE FUTURE
am stepped	was stepped	will be stepped
are stepped	were stepped	will be stepped
is stepped	was stepped	will be stepped

PRESENT PROGRESSIVE	PAST PROGRESSIVE	FUTURE PROGRESSIVE*
am being stepped	was being stepped	will be being stepped*
are being stepped	were being stepped	will be being stepped*
is being stepped	was being stepped	will be being stepped*

PRESENT PERFECT	PAST PERFECT	FUTURE PERFECT
have been stepped	had been stepped	will have been stepped
have been stepped	had been stepped	will have been stepped
has been stepped	had been stepped	will have been stepped

EXAMPLES:
The tempo was stepped up and the piece sounded much more like the original. *He had been stepped on one too many times when he exploded at his boss.*

PRINCIPAL CONDITIONALS

PRESENT	PRESENT PROGRESSIVE	PRESENT PASSIVE
would step	would be stepping	would be stepped
would step	would be stepping	would be stepped
would step	would be stepping	would be stepped

PAST	PAST PROGRESSIVE	PAST PASSIVE
would have stepped	would have been stepping	would have been stepped
would have stepped	would have been stepping	would have been stepped
would have stepped	would have been stepping	would have been stepped

EXAMPLES:
Would you step down if you were in his position? *The project manager would have stepped up the pace of the work if she thought the workers could handle more.*

step

PRINCIPAL PARTS: step, stepped, stepped

Important Forms in Use

IF/THEN CONDITIONALS

	IF ...	... THEN	EXAMPLE
Real Present/ Future	step/steps	simple present	*If you step on this spot, the floor creaks.*
		will + base form	*If she steps down, the position of vice president will be open.*
Unreal Present/ Future	stepped	would + base form	*If you stepped out of line, he would tell you immediately.*
Unreal Past	had stepped	would have + past participle	*If I had stepped up the pace of the campaign, we would have finished before the holidays, but we wouldn't have done such a thorough job.*

SUBJUNCTIVE

ACTIVE	step	*We suggest that you step down pending a further investigation of misdeeds.*
PASSIVE	be stepped	*They recommended that the pace be stepped up slightly in order to finish our work by the deadline.*

PHRASAL VERBS

step down	to resign *The foreign minister stepped down after the scandal.*
step out	to leave your home or office for a short time *Janice stepped out of her office to get some lunch.*
step up	to approach *If you have a question for the author, please step up to the microphone.*

IDIOMS

to step up to the plate	to not hesitate to get involved in or work on something *If you want to get that grant, you have to step up to the plate.*
to step on it	to go faster, especially when you're driving in a car (informal) *C'mon! Step on it! I need to get to the airport in fifteen minutes.*
to take a step/(some) steps	to move toward something *We haven't gotten all of the departments to agree to the changes, but we've taken some steps in that direction.*
to step on someone's toes	to upset someone by doing something that interferes with his or her responsibilities *I didn't realize when I offered to take the photos of the air and water show that I would be stepping on Melinda's toes.*
to step out of line	to do something that is inappropriate in a certain situation, to break rules or regulations *If any of the boys steps out of line, I will not hesitate to call his parents and have him taken out of the camp.*
to step it up	to increase the speed and effort with which something is done *We need to step it up if we're going to finish this report on time.*

RELATED WORDS

step-by-step (adv.)	little by little, slowly, with deliberate pace
step stool (n.)	a piece of furniture that can be stood on to reach things that are out of reach
baby steps (n.)	tiny steps toward a goal
stepladder (n.)	a small ladder that is used inside a house or building
stepmother/stepfather (n.)	someone who has married your father/mother and is not your biological parent

Verb Chart

* Note that the form "will be being stepped" is rarely used. To convey a future progressive passive, use the present progressive passive.

stick

	ACTIVE	PASSIVE
Infinitive	to stick	to be stuck
Past Infinitive	to have stuck	to have been stuck
Past Participle	stuck	been stuck
Present Participle	sticking	being stuck

ACTIVE

I
you/we/they
he/she/it

SIMPLE PRESENT	SIMPLE PAST	SIMPLE FUTURE
stick	stuck	will stick
stick	stuck	will stick
sticks	stuck	will stick

PRESENT PROGRESSIVE	PAST PROGRESSIVE	FUTURE PROGRESSIVE
am sticking	was sticking	will be sticking
are sticking	were sticking	will be sticking
is sticking	was sticking	will be sticking

PRESENT PERFECT	PAST PERFECT	FUTURE PERFECT
have stuck	had stuck	will have stuck
have stuck	had stuck	will have stuck
has stuck	had stuck	will have stuck

PRESENT PERFECT PROGRESSIVE	PAST PERFECT PROGRESSIVE	FUTURE PERFECT PROGRESSIVE
have been sticking	had been sticking	will have been sticking
have been sticking	had been sticking	will have been sticking
has been sticking	had been sticking	will have been sticking

EXAMPLES:
You have to push hard because the door sticks. *She stuck the note to the refrigerator before she left for work.* *If you don't put butter in the pan, the pancakes will stick.*

PASSIVE

SIMPLE PRESENT	SIMPLE PAST	SIMPLE FUTURE
am stuck	was stuck	will be stuck
are stuck	were stuck	will be stuck
is stuck	was stuck	will be stuck

PRESENT PROGRESSIVE	PAST PROGRESSIVE	FUTURE PROGRESSIVE*
am being stuck	was being stuck	will be being stuck*
are being stuck	were being stuck	will be being stuck*
is being stuck	was being stuck	will be being stuck*

PRESENT PERFECT	PAST PERFECT	FUTURE PERFECT
have been stuck	had been stuck	will have been stuck
have been stuck	had been stuck	will have been stuck
has been stuck	had been stuck	will have been stuck

EXAMPLES:
We were stuck in traffic for hours. *Why am I always stuck with the worst job?* *That beautiful cupboard has been stuck in that corner for years.*

PRINCIPAL CONDITIONALS

PRESENT	PRESENT PROGRESSIVE	PRESENT PASSIVE
would stick	would be sticking	would be stuck
would stick	would be sticking	would be stuck
would stick	would be sticking	would be stuck

PAST	PAST PROGRESSIVE	PAST PASSIVE
would have stuck	would have been sticking	would have been stuck
would have stuck	would have been sticking	would have been stuck
would have stuck	would have been sticking	would have been stuck

EXAMPLES:
I would stick the beers in the freezer until they were cold. *The neighbors would have been stuck if we hadn't lent them our car.*

stick

Important Forms in Use

IF/THEN CONDITIONALS

	IF ...	... THEN	EXAMPLE
Real Present/ Future	stick/sticks	simple present	*If I <u>stick</u> to my regular schedule, I get to work around 8:00.*
		will + base form	*If your guest <u>sticks</u> around a little longer, I'll give him a ride home.*
Unreal Present/ Future	stuck	would + base form	*If we <u>stuck</u> to my plan, we'd have a lot of options.*
Unreal Past	had stuck	would have + past participle	*If I <u>hadn't stuck</u> the directions in your purse, you wouldn't have known how to get here.*

SUBJUNCTIVE

ACTIVE	stick	*It is important that we <u>stick</u> to the plan if we want to succeed.*
PASSIVE	be stuck	*We suggest that posters <u>be stuck</u> to the wall with a removable adhesive.*

PHRASAL VERBS

stick around	to stay where you are for a while longer *I was glad that some of my closer friends stuck around to help me clean up after dinner.*
stick to	to persist, to keep going *She has stuck to her exercise regime and has lost ten pounds.*
stick out	to be obvious *These shoes really stick out, don't they?*
stick someone with something	to leave someone with the responsibility for something *Mom stuck me with walking the dog every morning this week.*

IDIOMS

to stick it to someone	to make someone suffer, to punish *The boss really stuck it to us when she gave our group the hardest task.*
to stick to your guns	to persist in doing something even though it is difficult or others don't support it *I was proud when my son stuck to his guns even though he didn't get the support he wanted.*
to stick out like a sore thumb	to be obviously unlike the rest of the group *It turned out to be a formal party! I stuck out like a sore thumb in my jeans and T-shirt.*
to stick your neck out for someone	to chance personal risk in order to help someone else *Andre really stuck his neck out for me when he took the blame for the broken lamp.*

RELATED WORDS

stick-to-itiveness (n.)	the ability to keep at something even though it may not be easy
stickup (n.)	a situation in which a criminal points a gun at someone and demands money

* Note that the form "will be being stuck" is rarely used. To convey a future progressive passive, use the present progressive passive.

Verb Chart

stop

	ACTIVE	PASSIVE
Infinitive	to stop	to be stopped
Past Infinitive	to have stopped	to have been stopped
Past Participle	stopped	been stopped
Present Participle	stopping	being stopped

I
you/we/they
he/she/it

ACTIVE

SIMPLE PRESENT	SIMPLE PAST	SIMPLE FUTURE
stop	stopped	will stop
stop	stopped	will stop
stops	stopped	will stop

PRESENT PROGRESSIVE	PAST PROGRESSIVE	FUTURE PROGRESSIVE
am stopping	was stopping	will be stopping
are stopping	were stopping	will be stopping
is stopping	was stopping	will be stopping

PRESENT PERFECT	PAST PERFECT	FUTURE PERFECT
have stopped	had stopped	will have stopped
have stopped	had stopped	will have stopped
has stopped	had stopped	will have stopped

PRESENT PERFECT PROGRESSIVE	PAST PERFECT PROGRESSIVE	FUTURE PERFECT PROGRESSIVE
have been stopping	had been stopping	will have been stopping
have been stopping	had been stopping	will have been stopping
has been stopping	had been stopping	will have been stopping

EXAMPLES:
We always stop off at my grandparents' house on the way to the lake.

I certainly hope this noise will have stopped by the time we go to bed.

Harold and Maude have been stopping by more often recently.

PASSIVE

SIMPLE PRESENT	SIMPLE PAST	SIMPLE FUTURE
am stopped	was stopped	will be stopped
are stopped	were stopped	will be stopped
is stopped	was stopped	will be stopped

PRESENT PROGRESSIVE	PAST PROGRESSIVE	FUTURE PROGRESSIVE*
am being stopped	was being stopped	will be being stopped*
are being stopped	were being stopped	will be being stopped*
is being stopped	was being stopped	will be being stopped*

PRESENT PERFECT	PAST PERFECT	FUTURE PERFECT
have been stopped	had been stopped	will have been stopped
have been stopped	had been stopped	will have been stopped
has been stopped	had been stopped	will have been stopped

EXAMPLES:
Thank goodness that thief was stopped before he got away with that woman's purse.

Do you know when our mail will be stopped?

The reckless driver had been stopped by the undercover police officer.

PRINCIPAL CONDITIONALS

PRESENT	PRESENT PROGRESSIVE	PRESENT PASSIVE
would stop	would be stopping	would be stopped
would stop	would be stopping	would be stopped
would stop	would be stopping	would be stopped

PAST	PAST PROGRESSIVE	PAST PASSIVE
would have stopped	would have been stopping	would have been stopped
would have stopped	would have been stopping	would have been stopped
would have stopped	would have been stopping	would have been stopped

EXAMPLES:
We would stop playing our music so late at night if anybody asked us to.

The criminals wouldn't have been stopped if their car hadn't malfunctioned.

stop

Important Forms in Use

IF/THEN CONDITIONALS

	IF ...	... THEN	EXAMPLE
Real Present/ Future	stop/stops	simple present	*If I <u>stop</u> off at the baker's on Tuesdays, I get whole wheat bread.*
		will + base form	*If she <u>stops</u> studying, she won't get into medical school.*
Unreal Present/ Future	stopped	would + base form	*If we <u>stopped</u> for a few minutes, we'd be able to catch our breath.*
Unreal Past	had stopped	would have + past participle	*If I <u>had stopped</u> him from becoming a musician, he would have been miserable.*

SUBJUNCTIVE

ACTIVE	stop	*We propose that the party <u>stop</u> at 10:30.*
PASSIVE	be stopped	*It is essential that the perpetrators <u>be stopped</u> before they commit any more crimes.*

PHRASAL VERBS

stop by/in/off	to make a short visit to someone's home or place of work *If you can stop by for a moment, I'll give you the keys to my apartment.*
stop over	to stay somewhere for a short time, especially during a longer trip *We stopped over at my aunt's house on the way to the mountains.*
stop up	to plug, to clog *The sink is all stopped up; there must be a blockage in the pipes.*

IDIOMS

to stop at nothing	to be willing to do anything to get what you want *She wanted to become a partner in her firm, and she would stop at nothing to get it.*
to stop dead in your tracks	to suddenly not move, especially when you are frightened *We heard a loud noise that stopped us dead in our tracks.*

RELATED WORDS

stopgap (n.)	a temporary solution
stoplight (n.)	a signal at an intersection that indicates when you need to stop and when you can go
stopover (n.)	an interruption in a longer journey
stopwatch (n.)	a timer used to see how long something takes, such as a race

* Note that the form "will be being stopped" is rarely used. To convey a future progressive passive, use the present progressive passive.

Verb Chart

swear

	ACTIVE	PASSIVE
Infinitive	to swear	to be sworn
Past Infinitive	to have sworn	to have been sworn
Past Participle	sworn	been sworn
Present Participle	swearing	being sworn

ACTIVE

I
you/we/they
he/she/it

SIMPLE PRESENT	SIMPLE PAST	SIMPLE FUTURE
swear	swore	will swear
swear	swore	will swear
swears	swore	will swear

PRESENT PROGRESSIVE	PAST PROGRESSIVE	FUTURE PROGRESSIVE
am swearing	was swearing	will be swearing
are swearing	were swearing	will be swearing
is swearing	was swearing	will be swearing

PRESENT PERFECT	PAST PERFECT	FUTURE PERFECT
have sworn	had sworn	will have sworn
have sworn	had sworn	will have sworn
has sworn	had sworn	will have sworn

PRESENT PERFECT PROGRESSIVE	PAST PERFECT PROGRESSIVE	FUTURE PERFECT PROGRESSIVE
have been swearing	had been swearing	will have been swearing
have been swearing	had been swearing	will have been swearing
has been swearing	had been swearing	will have been swearing

EXAMPLES:
I swear I won't do it again!   *The cashier swore that she hadn't taken the money.*   *The defendant had sworn to tell the truth.*

PASSIVE

SIMPLE PRESENT	SIMPLE PAST	SIMPLE FUTURE
am sworn	was sworn	will be sworn
are sworn	were sworn	will be sworn
is sworn	was sworn	will be sworn

PRESENT PROGRESSIVE	PAST PROGRESSIVE	FUTURE PROGRESSIVE*
am being sworn	was being sworn	will be being sworn*
are being sworn	were being sworn	will be being sworn*
is being sworn	was being sworn	will be being sworn*

PRESENT PERFECT	PAST PERFECT	FUTURE PERFECT
have been sworn	had been sworn	will have been sworn
have been sworn	had been sworn	will have been sworn
has been sworn	had been sworn	will have been sworn

EXAMPLES:
The president of the United States is sworn in by the chief justice of the Supreme Court.   *The defendant was sworn in by the bailiff.*   *Certain foods had been sworn off by the athletes.*

PRINCIPAL CONDITIONALS

PRESENT	PRESENT PROGRESSIVE	PRESENT PASSIVE
would swear	would be swearing	would be sworn
would swear	would be swearing	would be sworn
would swear	would be swearing	would be sworn

PAST	PAST PROGRESSIVE	PAST PASSIVE
would have sworn	would have been swearing	would have been sworn
would have sworn	would have been swearing	would have been sworn
would have sworn	would have been swearing	would have been sworn

EXAMPLES:
I would swear that he told me he lived in this neighborhood.   *The kids would have sworn if their mother hadn't been there.*

swear

PRINCIPAL PARTS: swear, swore, sworn

Important Forms in Use

IF/THEN CONDITIONALS

	IF . . .	. . . THEN	EXAMPLE
Real Present/ Future	swear/swears	simple present	*If I <u>swear</u> in front of my mother, she gets angry.*
		will + base form	*If she <u>swears</u> at me again, I'll call the police.*
Unreal Present/ Future	swore	would + base form	*If he <u>swore</u> his product worked, I would be convinced to buy it.*
Unreal Past	had sworn	would have + past participle	*If I <u>had sworn</u> off sweets, I wouldn't have been able to have any of your delicious cake.*

SUBJUNCTIVE

ACTIVE	swear	*We recommend that you <u>swear</u> off coffee, cigarettes, and alcohol.*
PASSIVE	be sworn	*It is required by law that each witness <u>be sworn</u> in.*

PHRASAL VERBS

swear by (something or someone)	to insist that something works or is valuable *I don't like Tony's dentist, but Tony swears by her.*
swear (someone) in	to make someone promise to perform a duty, such as in an official job *As soon as the new mayor was sworn in, he decided to start making changes to policy.*
swear off	to give up something, usually a bad habit *Jim swore off drinking for the rest of the semester after going out every night for a week.*

IDIOMS

to swear up and down	to insist that something is true *He swore up and down that he had never seen the document that was missing.*
to swear someone to secrecy	to make someone promise not to tell anyone about something *I thought it was a little exaggerated, but Anita swore me to secrecy before she would tell me who she was dating.*

RELATED WORDS

swearword (n.)	an offensive word, an expletive
swearing-in (n.)	a ceremony in which someone takes an oath to serve in office

* Note that the form "will be being sworn" is rarely used. To convey a future progressive passive, use the present progressive passive.

Verb Chart

take

	ACTIVE	PASSIVE
Infinitive	to take	to be taken
Past Infinitive	to have taken	to have been taken
Past Participle	taken	been taken
Present Participle	taking	being taken

ACTIVE

I
you/we/they
he/she/it

SIMPLE PRESENT	SIMPLE PAST	SIMPLE FUTURE
take	took	will take
take	took	will take
takes	took	will take

PRESENT PROGRESSIVE	PAST PROGRESSIVE	FUTURE PROGRESSIVE
am taking	was taking	will be taking
are taking	were taking	will be taking
is taking	was taking	will be taking

PRESENT PERFECT	PAST PERFECT	FUTURE PERFECT
have taken	had taken	will have taken
have taken	had taken	will have taken
has taken	had taken	will have taken

PRESENT PERFECT PROGRESSIVE	PAST PERFECT PROGRESSIVE	FUTURE PERFECT PROGRESSIVE
have been taking	had been taking	will have been taking
have been taking	had been taking	will have been taking
has been taking	had been taking	will have been taking

EXAMPLES:

They are taking a class in art history at Columbia University.

I will be taking the children to the park around 3:00 if you want to join us.

Have you taken any of the books in the basement? You're welcome to them.

PASSIVE

SIMPLE PRESENT	SIMPLE PAST	SIMPLE FUTURE
am taken	was taken	will be taken
are taken	were taken	will be taken
is taken	was taken	will be taken

PRESENT PROGRESSIVE	PAST PROGRESSIVE	FUTURE PROGRESSIVE*
am being taken	was being taken	will be being taken*
are being taken	were being taken	will be being taken*
is being taken	was being taken	will be being taken*

PRESENT PERFECT	PAST PERFECT	FUTURE PERFECT
have been taken	had been taken	will have been taken
have been taken	had been taken	will have been taken
has been taken	had been taken	will have been taken

EXAMPLES:

I'm afraid that I was taken advantage of when I bought this car.

When I started there, the school was being taken over by new owners.

By the end of the match, the young player had been taken down a peg or two.

PRINCIPAL CONDITIONALS

PRESENT	PRESENT PROGRESSIVE	PRESENT PASSIVE
would take	would be taking	would be taken
would take	would be taking	would be taken
would take	would be taking	would be taken

PAST	PAST PROGRESSIVE	PAST PASSIVE
would have taken	would have been taking	would have been taken
would have taken	would have been taking	would have been taken
would have taken	would have been taking	would have been taken

EXAMPLES:

They would have taken the bus if the route were more direct.

The medicine would have been taken if the nurses had left it where it could be found.

take

Important Forms in Use

IF/THEN CONDITIONALS

	IF...	...THEN	EXAMPLE
Real Present/ Future	take/takes	simple present	If we _take_ a vacation in the summer, we usually go to the Caribbean.
		will + base form	If it _takes_ them three hours, they won't be here until midnight.
Unreal Present/ Future	took	would + base form	If he _took_ more time, he would do a better job.
Unreal Past	had taken	would have + past participle	If the hurricane _had taken_ our house, we wouldn't have had anywhere to go.

SUBJUNCTIVE

ACTIVE	take	I advise that she _take_ only the classes necessary to graduate.
PASSIVE	be taken	We recommend that the medicine _be taken_ with meals.

PHRASAL VERBS

take advantage of (someone or something)	to use someone or something for your own benefit _The hotel manager took advantage of the tourists by charging them more than the room was worth._
take after (someone)	to resemble someone in appearance and/or behavior _My son takes after his father in his dislike for social events._
take (someone) in	to house or take care of someone in need of help _My aunt took us in when our house was flooded during the hurricane season last year._
take (something) out	to dispose of something, to remove something _Tommy always takes out the trash after dinner, and I do the dishes._
take over	to assume control of something _When the dictatorship ended, the interim president took over._
take on (something)	to accept a challenging responsibility _He took on the new job even though he was already quite busy._

IDIOMS

to take a break	to rest for a short period of time _We always take a break from 10:00 to 10:30._
to take it or leave it	to accept something as is or not at all _My customer didn't want to pay so much for the item, but I told him to take it or leave it._
to take (someone or something) for granted	to not appreciate the real value of someone or something _We took our boss for granted until she was promoted and we couldn't find a decent replacement._
to take into consideration	to consider _Your letters of recommendation will be taken into consideration, as will your grade point average._
to take your time	to do something at your own pace _We felt like we needed to finish the presentation, but our advisor told us to take our time._

RELATED WORDS

takeout (n./adj.)	food that will be eaten outside of the restaurant where it was purchased
takeover (n.)	the act of assuming control of a country or company
takeoff (n.)	the moment when an airplane leaves the ground
taker (n.)	a person who accepts an offer

* Note that the form "will be being taken" is rarely used. To convey a future progressive passive, use the present progressive passive.

talk

	ACTIVE	PASSIVE
Infinitive	to talk	to be talked
Past Infinitive	to have talked	to have been talked
Past Participle	talked	been talked
Present Participle	talking	being talked

ACTIVE

	I	you/we/they	he/she/it

SIMPLE PRESENT	SIMPLE PAST	SIMPLE FUTURE
talk	talked	will talk
talk	talked	will talk
talks	talked	will talk

PRESENT PROGRESSIVE	PAST PROGRESSIVE	FUTURE PROGRESSIVE
am talking	was talking	will be talking
are talking	were talking	will be talking
is talking	was talking	will be talking

PRESENT PERFECT	PAST PERFECT	FUTURE PERFECT
have talked	had talked	will have talked
have talked	had talked	will have talked
has talked	had talked	will have talked

PRESENT PERFECT PROGRESSIVE	PAST PERFECT PROGRESSIVE	FUTURE PERFECT PROGRESSIVE
have been talking	had been talking	will have been talking
have been talking	had been talking	will have been talking
has been talking	had been talking	will have been talking

EXAMPLES:

We talk about all of the people we know in common whenever we see each other.

What do you think Mom and Dad are talking about? They've been in there for hours.

Patrick talked to me about his experiences in the war.

PASSIVE

SIMPLE PRESENT	SIMPLE PAST	SIMPLE FUTURE
am talked	was talked	will be talked
are talked	were talked	will be talked
is talked	was talked	will be talked

PRESENT PROGRESSIVE	PAST PROGRESSIVE	FUTURE PROGRESSIVE*
am being talked	was being talked	will be being talked*
are being talked	were being talked	will be being talked*
is being talked	was being talked	will be being talked*

PRESENT PERFECT	PAST PERFECT	FUTURE PERFECT
have been talked	had been talked	will have been talked
have been talked	had been talked	will have been talked
has been talked	had been talked	will have been talked

EXAMPLES:

The kids are being talked to by the principal.

The recent marriage was all that was being talked about at the social last night.

This issue has already been talked about at length. Let's move on.

PRINCIPAL CONDITIONALS

PRESENT	PRESENT PROGRESSIVE	PRESENT PASSIVE
would talk	would be talking	would be talked
would talk	would be talking	would be talked
would talk	would be talking	would be talked

PAST	PAST PROGRESSIVE	PAST PASSIVE
would have talked	would have been talking	would have been talked
would have talked	would have been talking	would have been talked
would have talked	would have been talking	would have been talked

EXAMPLES:

Would you talk to the kids about making so much noise in the basement?

Henry would have talked to you sooner if he had had your number.

talk

PRINCIPAL PARTS: talk, talked, talked

Important Forms in Use

IF/THEN CONDITIONALS

	IF ...	...THEN	EXAMPLE
Real Present/ Future	talk/talks	simple present	*If I <u>talk</u> to the neighbors, I get stuck for half an hour at least.*
		will + base form	*If she <u>talks</u> some sense into him, he'll be the better for it.*
Unreal Present/ Future	talked	would + base form	*If we <u>talked</u> to your mom more often, she wouldn't be so angry with us.*
Unreal Past	had talked	would have + past participle	*If you <u>had talked</u> to the security guard before trying to get in, she wouldn't have called the police.*

SUBJUNCTIVE

ACTIVE	talk	*It is important that the teacher <u>talk</u> to each student individually.*
PASSIVE	be talked	*We request that each child <u>be talked</u> to about what is expected of him or her.*

PHRASAL VERBS

talk (someone) into (something)	to convince someone of something *Natasha didn't want to take the assistant director position, but her boss talked her into it.*
talk (something) over	to discuss something carefully *Shouldn't we talk this over carefully before we make any decisions?*
talk over (something or someone)	to speak louder than something or someone else *I'm sorry this place is so loud; we'll just have to talk over the music.*
talk (something) up	to say positive things about something *We really want to see that movie, especially since Carolyn has been talking it up for weeks.*
talk down to (someone)	to speak to someone in a way that shows you believe he or she is less intelligent than you *I can't stand the way he talks down to his wife. I don't know how she puts up with it.*
talk (someone) out of (something)	to convince someone that something is not a good idea *We were going to go to Egypt but the travel agent talked us out of it. He convinced us to wait until winter, when the temperatures aren't as high.*

IDIOMS

to talk a mile a minute	to speak very quickly *All of the characters in the movie talked a mile a minute. I couldn't understand anything.*
to talk up a storm	to speak a lot *The rest of us were tired, but we sat and listened as Ben talked up a storm last night.*
to talk shop	to speak about things related to the workplace especially when not at work *Are you guys going to talk shop all night? How boring!*
to talk the talk	to speak as if you know how to do something well *I don't know if Charles is any good at politics, but he certainly talks the talk.*
to talk some/any sense into someone	to try to make someone see the mistake he or she is making *He wants to drop out of college with only one semester left, and I can't seem to talk any sense into him.*

RELATED WORDS

walkie-talkie (n.)	a device that is used to communicate with others over short distances
talking book (n.)	a book that has been recorded on tape or CD
talking-to (n.)	a scolding

* Note that the form "will be being talked" is rarely used. To convey a future progressive passive, use the present progressive passive.

teach

	ACTIVE	PASSIVE
Infinitive	to teach	to be taught
Past Infinitive	to have taught	to have been taught
Past Participle	taught	been taught
Present Participle	teaching	being taught

ACTIVE

I		
you/we/they		
he/she/it		

SIMPLE PRESENT	SIMPLE PAST	SIMPLE FUTURE
teach	taught	will teach
teach	taught	will teach
teaches	taught	will teach

PRESENT PROGRESSIVE	PAST PROGRESSIVE	FUTURE PROGRESSIVE
am teaching	was teaching	will be teaching
are teaching	were teaching	will be teaching
is teaching	was teaching	will be teaching

PRESENT PERFECT	PAST PERFECT	FUTURE PERFECT
have taught	had taught	will have taught
have taught	had taught	will have taught
has taught	had taught	will have taught

PRESENT PERFECT PROGRESSIVE	PAST PERFECT PROGRESSIVE	FUTURE PERFECT PROGRESSIVE
have been teaching	had been teaching	will have been teaching
have been teaching	had been teaching	will have been teaching
has been teaching	had been teaching	will have been teaching

EXAMPLES:

She teaches the second grade at our old elementary school.

By the end of the semester, our professor will have taught us all about transnational migration in the twentieth century.

I'm teaching her how to tie her shoelaces.

PASSIVE

SIMPLE PRESENT	SIMPLE PAST	SIMPLE FUTURE
am taught	was taught	will be taught
are taught	were taught	will be taught
is taught	was taught	will be taught

PRESENT PROGRESSIVE	PAST PROGRESSIVE	FUTURE PROGRESSIVE*
am being taught	was being taught	will be being taught*
are being taught	were being taught	will be being taught*
is being taught	was being taught	will be being taught*

PRESENT PERFECT	PAST PERFECT	FUTURE PERFECT
have been taught	had been taught	will have been taught
have been taught	had been taught	will have been taught
has been taught	had been taught	will have been taught

EXAMPLES:

The students are being taught their ABC's.

German wasn't taught in our school; French and Spanish were taught instead.

They asked Jim to cook Thanksgiving dinner because he had been taught how to cook by a four-star chef.

PRINCIPAL CONDITIONALS

PRESENT	PRESENT PROGRESSIVE	PRESENT PASSIVE
would teach	would be teaching	would be taught
would teach	would be teaching	would be taught
would teach	would be teaching	would be taught

PAST	PAST PROGRESSIVE	PAST PASSIVE
would have taught	would have been teaching	would have been taught
would have taught	would have been teaching	would have been taught
would have taught	would have been teaching	would have been taught

EXAMPLES:

I would be teaching economics this semester if I weren't on sabbatical.

If we had the resources to buy more equipment, computer science would be taught in all of our schools.

teach

PRINCIPAL PARTS: teach, taught, taught

Important Forms in Use

IF/THEN CONDITIONALS

	IF...	...THEN	EXAMPLE
Real Present/ Future	teach/teaches	simple present	*If she <u>teaches</u> history, she knows a lot about the Second World War.*
		will + base form	*If I <u>teach</u> you how to play guitar, you'll never want to stop.*
Unreal Present/	taught	would + base form	*If they <u>taught</u> at that college, they would have better salaries.*
Unreal Past	had taught	would have + past participle	*If you <u>had taught</u> me how to cook, I would have eaten better when I lived on my own.*

SUBJUNCTIVE

ACTIVE	teach	*It is important that we <u>teach</u> life skills along with other subjects in schools.*
PASSIVE	be taught	*It is crucial that every child <u>be taught</u> how to read.*

IDIOMS

You can't teach an old dog new tricks.	an expression meaning you can't change someone's habits or behavior *I try to tell him not to chew with his mouth open, but I guess you can't teach an old dog new tricks.*

RELATED WORDS

teacher (n.)	someone who educates

* Note that the form "will be being taught" is rarely used. To convey a future progressive passive, use the present progressive passive.

tear

	ACTIVE	PASSIVE
Infinitive	to tear	to be torn
Past Infinitive	to have torn	to have been torn
Past Participle	torn	been torn
Present Participle	tearing	being torn

ACTIVE

	I	you/we/they	he/she/it

SIMPLE PRESENT	SIMPLE PAST	SIMPLE FUTURE
tear	tore	will tear
tear	tore	will tear
tears	tore	will tear

PRESENT PROGRESSIVE	PAST PROGRESSIVE	FUTURE PROGRESSIVE
am tearing	was tearing	will be tearing
are tearing	were tearing	will be tearing
is tearing	was tearing	will be tearing

PRESENT PERFECT	PAST PERFECT	FUTURE PERFECT
have torn	had torn	will have torn
have torn	had torn	will have torn
has torn	had torn	will have torn

PRESENT PERFECT PROGRESSIVE	PAST PERFECT PROGRESSIVE	FUTURE PERFECT PROGRESSIVE
have been tearing	had been tearing	will have been tearing
have been tearing	had been tearing	will have been tearing
has been tearing	had been tearing	will have been tearing

EXAMPLES:

Tear a piece of the bread off and tell me if you like it.

A nail on the chair tore a hole in my favorite jeans.

The decision had been tearing her apart.

PASSIVE

SIMPLE PRESENT	SIMPLE PAST	SIMPLE FUTURE
am torn	was torn	will be torn
are torn	were torn	will be torn
is torn	was torn	will be torn

PRESENT PROGRESSIVE	PAST PROGRESSIVE	FUTURE PROGRESSIVE*
am being torn	was being torn	will be being torn*
are being torn	were being torn	will be being torn*
is being torn	was being torn	will be being torn*

PRESENT PERFECT	PAST PERFECT	FUTURE PERFECT
have been torn	had been torn	will have been torn
have been torn	had been torn	will have been torn
has been torn	had been torn	will have been torn

EXAMPLES:

Ronald was torn between going to two different concerts on Friday.

When I walked into the room, my lottery ticket was being torn up by the dog.

The pants were brand new but had been torn in both knees.

PRINCIPAL CONDITIONALS

PRESENT	PRESENT PROGRESSIVE	PRESENT PASSIVE
would tear	would be tearing	would be torn
would tear	would be tearing	would be torn
would tear	would be tearing	would be torn

PAST	PAST PROGRESSIVE	PAST PASSIVE
would have torn	would have been tearing	would have been torn
would have torn	would have been tearing	would have been torn
would have torn	would have been tearing	would have been torn

EXAMPLES:

I would tear up that document if I were you.

If I had to make the decision today, I would be torn.

Important Forms in Use

IF/THEN CONDITIONALS

	IF ...	...THEN	EXAMPLE
Real Present/ Future	tear/tears	simple present	*If I tear him away from the TV, he forgets about the program quickly.*
		will + base form	*If Doug tears through all of the books like he did with the last one, he'll have no problem passing this class.*
Unreal Present/ Future	tore	would + base form	*If we tore into this fresh loaf of bread, Mom would get angry.*
Unreal Past	had torn	would have + past participle	*If the player had torn a ligament, he would have been out for the season.*

SUBJUNCTIVE

ACTIVE	tear	*We ask that the workers tear out the carpeting in all of the bedrooms.*
PASSIVE	be torn	*We require that the ticket stub be torn off before the moviegoer enters the theater.*

PHRASAL VERBS

tear (someone) away	to convince someone to stop doing an activity that he or she is involved in *We could barely tear the kids away from the television so that we could go to the beach.*
tear (something or someone) down	to destroy, to bring down *They tore the house down after years of neglect.*
tear (something) out	to remove something from where it is fixed *They began cleaning up the garden by tearing out all of the weeds that had grown over the summer.*
tear (someone) up	to be extremely upsetting to someone *The breakup is tearing her up.*
tear into	to eviscerate, to abuse *He tore into us for taking the car without asking permission.*

IDIOMS

to tear your hair out	to be extremely upset or anxious about something *Can you help her with her move? She's tearing her hair out.*
to tear somebody limb from limb	to physically harm someone in a violent way *If my brother ever saw my ex-boyfriend he would tear him limb from limb.*
to be torn	to not be able to decide between two options *The student was torn between taking a class with a well-respected professor and taking a class that he was especially interested in.*

RELATED WORDS

torn up (adj.)	upset

* Note that the form "will be being torn" is rarely used. To convey a future progressive passive, use the present progressive passive.

Verb Chart

tell

	ACTIVE	PASSIVE
Infinitive	to tell	to be told
Past Infinitive	to have told	to have been told
Past Participle	told	been told
Present Participle	telling	being told

ACTIVE

I
you/we/they
he/she/it

SIMPLE PRESENT	SIMPLE PAST	SIMPLE FUTURE
tell	told	will tell
tell	told	will tell
tells	told	will tell

PRESENT PROGRESSIVE	PAST PROGRESSIVE	FUTURE PROGRESSIVE
am telling	was telling	will be telling
are telling	were telling	will be telling
is telling	was telling	will be telling

PRESENT PERFECT	PAST PERFECT	FUTURE PERFECT
have told	had told	will have told
have told	had told	will have told
has told	had told	will have told

PRESENT PERFECT PROGRESSIVE	PAST PERFECT PROGRESSIVE	FUTURE PERFECT PROGRESSIVE
have been telling	had been telling	will have been telling
have been telling	had been telling	will have been telling
has been telling	had been telling	will have been telling

EXAMPLES:
The author will be telling stories at 10:00 this morning at a coffee shop in the neighborhood.

Did you tell me the truth?

We had been telling her to go to the doctor for months.

PASSIVE

SIMPLE PRESENT	SIMPLE PAST	SIMPLE FUTURE
am told	was told	will be told
are told	were told	will be told
is told	was told	will be told

PRESENT PROGRESSIVE	PAST PROGRESSIVE	FUTURE PROGRESSIVE*
am being told	was being told	will be being told*
are being told	were being told	will be being told*
is being told	was being told	will be being told*

PRESENT PERFECT	PAST PERFECT	FUTURE PERFECT
have been told	had been told	will have been told
have been told	had been told	will have been told
has been told	had been told	will have been told

EXAMPLES:
I was told to bring my social security card and birth certificate to the receptionist.

The same story had been told to me by my grandmother and now I was telling it to my daughter.

PRINCIPAL CONDITIONALS

PRESENT	PRESENT PROGRESSIVE	PRESENT PASSIVE
would tell	would be telling	would be told
would tell	would be telling	would be told
would tell	would be telling	would be told

PAST	PAST PROGRESSIVE	PAST PASSIVE
would have told	would have been telling	would have been told
would have told	would have been telling	would have been told
would have told	would have been telling	would have been told

EXAMPLES:
Would you tell the waiter that we need another bottle of wine?

I would have told you about the meeting if I had thought you would be interested.

tell

PRINCIPAL PARTS: tell, told, told

VERB CHART
112

Important Forms in Use

IF/THEN CONDITIONALS

	IF ...	...THEN	EXAMPLE
Real Present/ Future	tell/tells	simple present	*If I <u>tell</u> him to leave ten minutes before we need to, we usually leave on time.*
		will + base form	*If he <u>tells</u> his coworkers his idea, they'll be very pleased.*
Unreal Present/ Future	told	would + base form	*If we <u>told</u> them what we thought, they'd feel more comfortable.*
Unreal Past	had told	would have + past participle	*If I <u>had told</u> you to clean the kitchen, you would have cleaned the entire house.*

SUBJUNCTIVE

ACTIVE	tell	*We ask that the pilot <u>tell</u> the passengers what they should expect during the flight.*
PASSIVE	be told	*It is important that he <u>be told</u> the truth so we don't get into any trouble.*

PHRASAL VERBS

tell (someone) off	to explain to someone in an angry way what you think he or she has done wrong *My boss told me off for leaving work without letting him know.*
tell on (someone)	to alert a person of authority, such as parents or teachers, when someone has done something that he or she shouldn't have *I can't believe my sister told on me for smoking in the house. Now my parents won't let me go out this weekend.*

IDIOMS

to tell a lie	to deceive, to be dishonest *I can always tell when you're telling a lie because you begin to stutter.*
to tell the truth	to be honest *I don't want to hang out with Frances anymore because I never know when she's telling the truth.*
to tell it like it is	to explain something honestly *We need to have a meeting with the boss and tell it like it is.*

RELATED WORDS

teller (n.)	a person who works in a bank and does basic transactions for customers
fortune-teller (n.)	a person who predicts someone's future

* Note that the form "will be being told" is rarely used. To convey a future progressive passive, use the present progressive passive.

Verb Chart

257

think

	ACTIVE	PASSIVE
Infinitive	to think	to be thought
Past Infinitive	to have thought	to have been thought
Past Participle	thought	been thought
Present Participle	thinking	being thought

ACTIVE

I		
you/we/they		
he/she/it		

SIMPLE PRESENT	SIMPLE PAST	SIMPLE FUTURE
think	thought	will think
think	thought	will think
thinks	thought	will think

PRESENT PROGRESSIVE	PAST PROGRESSIVE	FUTURE PROGRESSIVE
am thinking	was thinking	will be thinking
are thinking	were thinking	will be thinking
is thinking	was thinking	will be thinking

PRESENT PERFECT	PAST PERFECT	FUTURE PERFECT
have thought	had thought	will have thought
have thought	had thought	will have thought
has thought	had thought	will have thought

PRESENT PERFECT PROGRESSIVE	PAST PERFECT PROGRESSIVE	FUTURE PERFECT PROGRESSIVE
have been thinking	had been thinking	will have been thinking
have been thinking	had been thinking	will have been thinking
has been thinking	had been thinking	will have been thinking

EXAMPLES:
I thought you said that you were coming with us.

I have been thinking, isn't it time to take a vacation?

Will you be thinking about Sarah when she leaves?

PASSIVE

SIMPLE PRESENT	SIMPLE PAST	SIMPLE FUTURE
am thought	was thought	will be thought
are thought	were thought	will be thought
is thought	was thought	will be thought

PRESENT PROGRESSIVE	PAST PROGRESSIVE	FUTURE PROGRESSIVE*
am being thought	was being thought	will be being thought*
are being thought	were being thought	will be being thought*
is being thought	was being thought	will be being thought*

PRESENT PERFECT	PAST PERFECT	FUTURE PERFECT
have been thought	had been thought	will have been thought
have been thought	had been thought	will have been thought
has been thought	had been thought	will have been thought

EXAMPLES:
He is thought to be one of the top physicians in his field.

Several options had been thought about until a final decision was made.

PRINCIPAL CONDITIONALS

PRESENT	PRESENT PROGRESSIVE	PRESENT PASSIVE
would think	would be thinking	would be thought
would think	would be thinking	would be thought
would think	would be thinking	would be thought

PAST	PAST PROGRESSIVE	PAST PASSIVE
would have thought	would have been thinking	would have been thought
would have thought	would have been thinking	would have been thought
would have thought	would have been thinking	would have been thought

EXAMPLES:
What would you think if I told you I was going to change majors in college?

I never would have thought that he was interested in gardening.

think

Important Forms in Use

IF/THEN CONDITIONALS

	IF...	...THEN	EXAMPLE
Real Present/ Future	think/thinks	simple present	*If I <u>think</u> about it too much, I get a headache.*
		will + base form	*If she <u>thinks</u> he is going to agree, she'll definitely be surprised by his answer.*
Unreal Present/ Future	thought	would + base form	*If we <u>thought</u> that it was a good idea, we would do it.*
Unreal Past	had thought	would have + past participle	*If I <u>had thought</u> more about how expensive it is to live here, I wouldn't have made the move.*

SUBJUNCTIVE

ACTIVE	think	*It is important that you <u>think</u> carefully about this.*
PASSIVE	be thought	*It is requested that a new solution <u>be thought</u> of.*

PHRASAL VERBS

think about	to consider
	I'm not sure if I'll take guitar lessons, but I'm thinking about it.
think through	to think carefully about what my happen based on a decision you make
	You can drop out of school, but you need to think it through.
think up	to come up with a new idea
	The theme for our dance is really stupid. We'll have to think up a new idea.

IDIOMS

to think before you act	to take your time and consider all options before taking action or a making a decision
	Think before you act; that way you might be able to avoid a bad decision.
to think on your feet	to respond quickly in a situation without taking time to prepare your response
	If you want to be a trader in the stock exchange, you have to be able to think on your feet.
to be lost in thought	to be thinking deeply about something
	I'm sorry. I didn't hear what you said; I was lost in thought.
to think it over	to consider something carefully
	It's a big decision. I'll have to think it over and let you know.

RELATED WORDS

unthinkable (adj.)	impossible to imagine
thinker (n.)	a person who spends a lot of time in thought
well-thought-of (adj.)	respected
think tank (n.)	a group of people with knowledge in a specific field that are hired by a government or political organization to give advice

* Note that the form "will be being thought" is rarely used. To convey a future progressive passive, use the present progressive passive.

Verb Chart

throw

	ACTIVE	PASSIVE
Infinitive	to throw	to be thrown
Past Infinitive	to have thrown	to have been thrown
Past Participle	thrown	been thrown
Present Participle	throwing	being thrown

ACTIVE

	I	you/we/they	he/she/it

SIMPLE PRESENT	SIMPLE PAST	SIMPLE FUTURE
throw	threw	will throw
throw	threw	will throw
throws	threw	will throw

PRESENT PROGRESSIVE	PAST PROGRESSIVE	FUTURE PROGRESSIVE
am throwing	was throwing	will be throwing
are throwing	were throwing	will be throwing
is throwing	was throwing	will be throwing

PRESENT PERFECT	PAST PERFECT	FUTURE PERFECT
have thrown	had thrown	will have thrown
have thrown	had thrown	will have thrown
has thrown	had thrown	will have thrown

PRESENT PERFECT PROGRESSIVE	PAST PERFECT PROGRESSIVE	FUTURE PERFECT PROGRESSIVE
have been throwing	had been throwing	will have been throwing
have been throwing	had been throwing	will have been throwing
has been throwing	had been throwing	will have been throwing

EXAMPLES:
She throws with her left hand. / *Peter threw out his back when he was trying to move the couch.* / *The Pedersens will be throwing a big party for Eva's sixtieth birthday.*

PASSIVE

SIMPLE PRESENT	SIMPLE PAST	SIMPLE FUTURE
am thrown	was thrown	will be thrown
are thrown	were thrown	will be thrown
is thrown	was thrown	will be thrown

PRESENT PROGRESSIVE	PAST PROGRESSIVE	FUTURE PROGRESSIVE*
am being thrown	was being thrown	will be being thrown*
are being thrown	were being thrown	will be being thrown*
is being thrown	was being thrown	will be being thrown*

PRESENT PERFECT	PAST PERFECT	FUTURE PERFECT
have been thrown	had been thrown	will have been thrown
have been thrown	had been thrown	will have been thrown
has been thrown	had been thrown	will have been thrown

EXAMPLES:
The leaflets were thrown from a small airplane flying over the city. / *That blender will be thrown away with the rest of the junk in the house unless you want it.*

PRINCIPAL CONDITIONALS

PRESENT	PRESENT PROGRESSIVE	PRESENT PASSIVE
would throw	would be throwing	would be thrown
would throw	would be throwing	would be thrown
would throw	would be throwing	would be thrown

PAST	PAST PROGRESSIVE	PAST PASSIVE
would have thrown	would have been throwing	would have been thrown
would have thrown	would have been throwing	would have been thrown
would have thrown	would have been throwing	would have been thrown

EXAMPLES:
Would you throw the leftover food in the garbage can please? / *He would have thrown the ball to you but he thought you weren't playing.*

throw

Important Forms in Use

IF/THEN CONDITIONALS

	IF...	...THEN	EXAMPLE
Real Present/ Future	throw/throws	simple present	*If my mom throws away my stuff, I get really angry.*
		will + base form	*If I throw you the keys, will you open the car?*
Unreal Present/ Future	threw	would + base form	*If we threw a party, the guy you're interested in would surely come.*
Unreal Past	had thrown	would have + past participle	*If you had thrown in the towel months ago when you wanted to, you wouldn't have come in first place in the competition.*

SUBJUNCTIVE

ACTIVE	throw	*He asked that we throw a party in his memory.*
PASSIVE	be thrown	*We recommend that all expired products be thrown away.*

PHRASAL VERBS

throw away	to dispose of *Don't throw away the opportunity to see* The Producers *if you can get tickets.*
throw off	to confuse or misdirect *The smell of an unusual perfume threw off the detectives, but they soon found out who the murderer was.*
throw out	to dispose of, or to dismiss someone from an organization, such as a school *Do you mind throwing out the trash?*
throw together	to prepare something at the last minute *I know we weren't planning on having dinner here, but I'd be happy to throw something together.*
throw up	to vomit *Several of us threw up after eating at the restaurant across the street.*

IDIOMS

to throw the baby out with the bathwater	to give up completely on something instead of trying to salvage the parts that might still work *The idea of a new hospital is good even if these plans are not the best. Don't throw the baby out with the bathwater by giving up on it altogether.*
to throw someone a curveball	to surprise someone *He really threw me a curveball when he said he was married.*
to throw a wrench into something	to hinder the progress of something *The car breaking down threw a wrench into our plans, as we had wanted to leave first thing the next morning.*
to throw in the towel	to give up *Studying medicine is so difficult for me. Some days I just want to throw in the towel.*

RELATED WORDS

throw rug (n.)	a small area rug
to overthrow (v.)	to take power from
a stone's throw away (n.)	a very close distance

---

* Note that the form "will be being thrown" is rarely used. To convey a future progressive passive, use the present progressive passive.

tie

	ACTIVE	PASSIVE
Infinitive	to tie	to be tied
Past Infinitive	to have tied	to have been tied
Past Participle	tied	been tied
Present Participle	tying	being tied

ACTIVE

I
you/we/they
he/she/it

SIMPLE PRESENT	SIMPLE PAST	SIMPLE FUTURE
tie	tied	will tie
tie	tied	will tie
ties	tied	will tie

PRESENT PROGRESSIVE	PAST PROGRESSIVE	FUTURE PROGRESSIVE
am tying	was tying	will be tying
are tying	were tying	will be tying
is tying	was tying	will be tying

PRESENT PERFECT	PAST PERFECT	FUTURE PERFECT
have tied	had tied	will have tied
have tied	had tied	will have tied
has tied	had tied	will have tied

PRESENT PERFECT PROGRESSIVE	PAST PERFECT PROGRESSIVE	FUTURE PERFECT PROGRESSIVE
have been tying	had been tying	will have been tying
have been tying	had been tying	will have been tying
has been tying	had been tying	will have been tying

EXAMPLES:

Anton was tying his tie but needed somebody to help him.

The sailor tied the rope around the pylon on the pier.

Jim and Sam had tied one on the night before, and were recovering from a hangover.

PASSIVE

SIMPLE PRESENT	SIMPLE PAST	SIMPLE FUTURE
am tied	was tied	will be tied
are tied	were tied	will be tied
is tied	was tied	will be tied

PRESENT PROGRESSIVE	PAST PROGRESSIVE	FUTURE PROGRESSIVE*
am being tied	was being tied	will be being tied*
are being tied	were being tied	will be being tied*
is being tied	was being tied	will be being tied*

PRESENT PERFECT	PAST PERFECT	FUTURE PERFECT
have been tied	had been tied	will have been tied
have been tied	had been tied	will have been tied
has been tied	had been tied	will have been tied

EXAMPLES:

Mr. Hyde will be tied up for hours. Can you call back tomorrow?

She was tied up in knots trying to make a decision about what to do with her children.

The boat had been tied to the tow boat that brought it to shore.

PRINCIPAL CONDITIONALS

PRESENT	PRESENT PROGRESSIVE	PRESENT PASSIVE
would tie	would be tying	would be tied
would tie	would be tying	would be tied
would tie	would be tying	would be tied

PAST	PAST PROGRESSIVE	PAST PASSIVE
would have tied	would have been tying	would have been tied
would have tied	would have been tying	would have been tied
would have tied	would have been tying	would have been tied

EXAMPLES:

They would tie the knot now if they were ever going to get married.

If I took that job, I would be tied to a nine-to-five schedule, which is not what I want.

tie

PRINCIPAL PARTS: tie, tied, tied

VERB CHART
115

Important Forms in Use

IF/THEN CONDITIONALS

	IF . . .	. . . THEN	EXAMPLE
Real Present/ Future	tie/ties	simple present	*If I <u>tie</u> my son's shoes with a double knot, they don't come untied as often.*
		will + base form	*If you <u>tie</u> her down, she'll pull out of the deal completely.*
Unreal Present/ Future	tied	would + base form	*If you <u>tied</u> your shoes tighter to begin with, they wouldn't come undone every five minutes.*
Unreal Past	had tied	would have + past participle	*If the action in the first act <u>had tied</u> in more clearly to the second act, the play would have gotten better reviews.*

SUBJUNCTIVE

ACTIVE	tie	*It is important that we <u>tie</u> up all loose ends.*
PASSIVE	be tied	*It is required that the newspapers <u>be tied</u> in a bundle before they are placed outside for recycling.*

PHRASAL VERBS

tie (someone) down	to stop someone from doing things that he or she wants to do *I would love to have a dog, but having one would tie me down and I wouldn't be able to travel.*
tie in	to connect to something else *I think that the story about the new religious group will tie in to our story about spirituality in America.*
tie (someone or something) up	to use rope or some other sort of cord to attach things together, or force someone to stay where he or she is *The bank robbers tied up the security guard so that he couldn't move while they got into the safe.*

IDIOMS

to tie yourself up in knots	to become confused or worried about something *I don't know why she always ties herself up in knots when her family comes to visit.*
to tie the knot	to get married *So you two, when are you going to tie the knot?*
to tie one on	to drink excessive amounts of alcohol *Jimmy went out with his old law school buddies and tied one on.*
to be tied up	to be busy *I'm sorry that I couldn't get back to you earlier; I was tied up.*
my hands are tied	an expression used when you are unable to do anything about a situation that someone else wants you to change *Mr. Carlson would love to give you a better price on the car but his hands are tied.*

RELATED WORDS

tie (n.)	a piece of clothing usually worn by a man that goes around the neck with a knot below the chin

* Note that the form "will be being tied" is rarely used. To convey a future progressive passive, use the present progressive passive.

Verb Chart

263

tread

	ACTIVE	PASSIVE
Infinitive	to tread	to be trodden
Past Infinitive	to have trodden	to have been trodden
Past Participle	trodden	been trodden
Present Participle	treading	being trodden

ACTIVE

I		
you/we/they		
he/she/it		

SIMPLE PRESENT	SIMPLE PAST	SIMPLE FUTURE
tread	trod	will tread
tread	trod	will tread
treads	trod	will tread

PRESENT PROGRESSIVE	PAST PROGRESSIVE	FUTURE PROGRESSIVE
am treading	was treading	will be treading
are treading	were treading	will be treading
is treading	was treading	will be treading

PRESENT PERFECT	PAST PERFECT	FUTURE PERFECT
have trodden	had trodden	will have trodden
have trodden	had trodden	will have trodden
has trodden	had trodden	will have trodden

PRESENT PERFECT PROGRESSIVE	PAST PERFECT PROGRESSIVE	FUTURE PERFECT PROGRESSIVE
have been treading	had been treading	will have been treading
have been treading	had been treading	will have been treading
has been treading	had been treading	will have been treading

EXAMPLES:
She treads water to stay afloat in the pool.

The dictator will have been treading on the rights of his people for nearly two decades.

Marie was treading the boards for the first time in her role as Juliet.

PASSIVE

SIMPLE PRESENT	SIMPLE PAST	SIMPLE FUTURE
am trodden	was trodden	will be trodden
are trodden	were trodden	will be trodden
is trodden	was trodden	will be trodden

PRESENT PROGRESSIVE	PAST PROGRESSIVE	FUTURE PROGRESSIVE*
am being trodden	was being trodden	will be being trodden*
are being trodden	were being trodden	will be being trodden*
is being trodden	was being trodden	will be being trodden*

PRESENT PERFECT	PAST PERFECT	FUTURE PERFECT
have been trodden	had been trodden	will have been trodden
have been trodden	had been trodden	will have been trodden
has been trodden	had been trodden	will have been trodden

EXAMPLES:
A path will have been trodden by those who walked before us.

Our freedoms will not be trodden upon by the leaders we elect.

PRINCIPAL CONDITIONALS

PRESENT	PRESENT PROGRESSIVE	PRESENT PASSIVE
would tread	would be treading	would be trodden
would tread	would be treading	would be trodden
would tread	would be treading	would be trodden

PAST	PAST PROGRESSIVE	PAST PASSIVE
would have trodden	would have been treading	would have been trodden
would have trodden	would have been treading	would have been trodden
would have trodden	would have been treading	would have been trodden

EXAMPLES:
If I were you I would tread lightly around the issue of his divorce.

If someone didn't speak up, his opinions would have been trodden upon.

tread

PRINCIPAL PARTS: tread, trod/treaded, trodden/trod

Important Forms in Use

IF/THEN CONDITIONALS

	IF ...	... THEN	EXAMPLE
Real Present/ Future	tread/treads	simple present	*If I <u>tread</u> water for thirty minutes, my arms are really tired.*
		will + base form	*If she <u>treads</u> lightly, she won't offend him.*
Unreal Present/ Future	trod	would + base form	*If we <u>trod</u> on his toes, he'd say something to us.*
Unreal Past	had trodden	would have + past participle	*If I <u>had trodden</u> on anyone's feelings, I would have apologized immediately.*

SUBJUNCTIVE

ACTIVE	tread	It is important that we <u>tread</u> lightly on this issue so that we don't offend anyone.
PASSIVE	be trod	It is essential that the rights of the people not <u>be trodden</u> upon through acts of violence or intimidation.

PHRASAL VERBS

tread on/upon	to oppress *Their rights were trodden upon for years before they found the courage to stand up to their ruler.*

IDIOMS

to tread water	to keep afloat, physically or metaphorically *Let's just tread water until the boss gets back into town. She can handle the situation better than we can.*
to tread lightly	to go or speak carefully without upsetting someone or something *Tread lightly around the issue of religion at dinner tonight. My family doesn't always see eye to eye on that issue.*
to tread the boards	to act on stage *I've been treading the boards in local productions ever since I was five years old.*
to tread on someone's toes	to offend someone or overstep your boundaries *I think I trod on Stewart's toes a bit when I volunteered to do the music for the party.*

RELATED WORDS

tread (n.)	the part of a tire or wheel that touches the road
treadmill (n.)	a machine with a continuous belt on which one can walk or run in place

* Note that the form "will be being trodden" is rarely used. To convey a future progressive passive, use the present progressive passive.

try

	ACTIVE	PASSIVE
Infinitive	to try	to be tried
Past Infinitive	to have tried	to have been tried
Past Participle	tried	been tried
Present Participle	trying	being tried

ACTIVE

I
you/we/they
he/she/it

SIMPLE PRESENT	SIMPLE PAST	SIMPLE FUTURE
try	tried	will try
try	tried	will try
tries	tried	will try

PRESENT PROGRESSIVE	PAST PROGRESSIVE	FUTURE PROGRESSIVE
am trying	was trying	will be trying
are trying	were trying	will be trying
is trying	was trying	will be trying

PRESENT PERFECT	PAST PERFECT	FUTURE PERFECT
have tried	had tried	will have tried
have tried	had tried	will have tried
has tried	had tried	will have tried

PRESENT PERFECT PROGRESSIVE	PAST PERFECT PROGRESSIVE	FUTURE PERFECT PROGRESSIVE
have been trying	had been trying	will have been trying
have been trying	had been trying	will have been trying
has been trying	had been trying	will have been trying

EXAMPLES:
If at first you don't succeed, try, try again. | *We were trying your number for hours. Why didn't you answer?* | *The director is trying to make some changes in the company. That's why you were hired.*

PASSIVE

SIMPLE PRESENT	SIMPLE PAST	SIMPLE FUTURE
am tried	was tried	will be tried
are tried	were tried	will be tried
is tried	was tried	will be tried

PRESENT PROGRESSIVE	PAST PROGRESSIVE	FUTURE PROGRESSIVE*
am being tried	was being tried	will be being tried*
are being tried	were being tried	will be being tried*
is being tried	was being tried	will be being tried*

PRESENT PERFECT	PAST PERFECT	FUTURE PERFECT
have been tried	had been tried	will have been tried
have been tried	had been tried	will have been tried
has been tried	had been tried	will have been tried

EXAMPLES:
Have all of the options been tried? | *The criminal was being tried at the federal court.* | *Every possible medication was tried before Cynthia agreed to look into alternative treatments.*

PRINCIPAL CONDITIONALS

PRESENT	PRESENT PROGRESSIVE	PRESENT PASSIVE
would try	would be trying	would be tried
would try	would be trying	would be tried
would try	would be trying	would be tried

PAST	PAST PROGRESSIVE	PAST PASSIVE
would have tried	would have been trying	would have been tried
would have tried	would have been trying	would have been tried
would have tried	would have been trying	would have been tried

EXAMPLES:
The team would be trying harder if they thought there were any possibility of winning the competition. | *I would have tried the salad if I had known that you had made it.*

try

Important Forms in Use

IF/THEN CONDITIONALS

	IF...	...THEN	EXAMPLE
Real Present/ Future	try/tries	simple present	*If you <u>try</u> him after 10:00 at night, he never answers his phone.*
		will + base form	*If Jon <u>tries</u> to talk to her, surely she will listen.*
Unreal Present/ Future	tried	would + base form	*If they <u>tried</u> another route to the south, they would avoid the heavy snow up north.*
Unreal Past	had tried	would have + past participle	*If you <u>had tried</u> the salsa dancing class, I think you would have loved it.*

SUBJUNCTIVE

ACTIVE	try	*I recommend that you <u>try</u> the filet mignon. It's excellent.*
PASSIVE	be tried	*It is essential that all possible solutions <u>be tried</u> before we give up.*

PHRASAL VERBS

try for (something)
: to attempt to get something
She knew it was a long shot, but she tried for the position as manager anyway.

try (something) on
: to put an item of clothing on to see if it fits
I tried on my mother's wedding dress and it fit perfectly.

try (someone or something) out
: to test someone or something to see if he, she, or it works
Try out the new CD I burned for you to see if it works. / They weren't convinced that she was the right person for the job but they agreed to try her out.

IDIOMS

to try someone's patience
: to annoy someone
The naughty children tried my patience.

try that on for size
: an expression used after you've told someone something surprising
His record collection contains over five thousand albums. Five thousand! Try that on for size.

to try your hand at something
: to attempt to do something you have never done before
When I retire I'm going to try my hand at painting.

RELATED WORDS

trying (adj.)
: difficult or annoying

tryout (n.)
: an audition or test that you must take before being accepted in a group as a musician, actor, athlete, etc.

* Note that the form "will be being tried" is rarely used. To convey a future progressive passive, use the present progressive passive.

Verb Chart

turn

	ACTIVE	PASSIVE
Infinitive	to turn	to be turned
Past Infinitive	to have turned	to have been turned
Past Participle	turned	been turned
Present Participle	turning	being turned

ACTIVE

I		
you/we/they		
he/she/it		

SIMPLE PRESENT	SIMPLE PAST	SIMPLE FUTURE
turn	turned	will turn
turn	turned	will turn
turns	turned	will turn

PRESENT PROGRESSIVE	PAST PROGRESSIVE	FUTURE PROGRESSIVE
am turning	was turning	will be turning
are turning	were turning	will be turning
is turning	was turning	will be turning

PRESENT PERFECT	PAST PERFECT	FUTURE PERFECT
have turned	had turned	will have turned
have turned	had turned	will have turned
has turned	had turned	will have turned

PRESENT PERFECT PROGRESSIVE	PAST PERFECT PROGRESSIVE	FUTURE PERFECT PROGRESSIVE
have been turning	had been turning	will have been turning
have been turning	had been turning	will have been turning
has been turning	had been turning	will have been turning

EXAMPLES:

Turn around so I can take your picture.

I was turning the key in the door when I realized that someone was inside.

My daughter will be turning eleven next year.

PASSIVE

SIMPLE PRESENT	SIMPLE PAST	SIMPLE FUTURE
am turned	was turned	will be turned
are turned	were turned	will be turned
is turned	was turned	will be turned

PRESENT PROGRESSIVE	PAST PROGRESSIVE	FUTURE PROGRESSIVE*
am being turned	was being turned	will be being turned*
are being turned	were being turned	will be being turned*
is being turned	was being turned	will be being turned*

PRESENT PERFECT	PAST PERFECT	FUTURE PERFECT
have been turned	had been turned	will have been turned
have been turned	had been turned	will have been turned
has been turned	had been turned	will have been turned

EXAMPLES:

The burgers are turned only when their bottoms are browned.

The clocks will be turned back this weekend.

The concert was sold out and hundreds of people had been turned away.

PRINCIPAL CONDITIONALS

PRESENT	PRESENT PROGRESSIVE	PRESENT PASSIVE
would turn	would be turning	would be turned
would turn	would be turning	would be turned
would turn	would be turning	would be turned

PAST	PAST PROGRESSIVE	PAST PASSIVE
would have turned	would have been turning	would have been turned
would have turned	would have been turning	would have been turned
would have turned	would have been turning	would have been turned

EXAMPLES:

I would turn the keys over to you but I know that you can't drive stick shift.

The tomatoes would have turned red by now if they had had enough water.

I didn't know that the stage would be turned in the opposite direction.

Important Forms in Use

IF/THEN CONDITIONALS

	IF . . .	. . . THEN	EXAMPLE
Real Present/ Future	turn/turns	simple present	*If I <u>turn</u> the chicken over too soon, it cooks unevenly.*
		will + base form	*If she <u>turns</u> me in to the police, I'll have to find a lawyer.*
Unreal Present/ Future	turned	would + base form	*If we <u>turned</u> to the right, we would pass by the old town square.*
Unreal Past	had turned	would have + past participle	*If you <u>had turned</u> out to be right, I would have had to give you the five dollars we bet.*

SUBJUNCTIVE

ACTIVE	turn	*I recommend that all passengers <u>turn</u> their documents over to the captain.*
PASSIVE	be turned	*It is essential that the streetlights <u>be turned</u> on at dusk.*

PHRASAL VERBS

turn (something) off	to stop something mechanical, such as a television, radio, fan, car, etc., from functioning *Could you turn off the air conditioner? It's freezing in here.*
turn (something) on	to cause something mechanical, such as a television, radio, fan, car, etc., to function *Turn on the VCR and we can watch the video.*
turn out	to come to an event, such as a performance, lecture, etc. *I was pleased that so many people turned out for the lecture last night.*
turn in	to go to sleep, or to give something to someone *It's already midnight! Time for me to turn in./Don't forget to turn in your homework at the end of class.*

IDIOMS

to turn a situation around	to do something to improve a situation in which things are not going well *Our company was failing, but when our new boss stepped in, she really turned the situation around.*
to turn over a new leaf	to begin to live in a new way, especially when you had been making some mistakes in your life *My son had been hanging around the wrong kids at school last year, but now that he's involved in theater, he's turned over a new leaf.*
to turn out to be	to become *He's turned out to be such a nice guy! I remember how he used to bully us when we were little.*

RELATED WORDS

turnaround (n.)	a complete change in a situation, usually from bad to good
turncoat (n.)	a person who goes from supporting one side of an argument to supporting the other
turning point (n.)	a moment in which a major change occurs, often in one's life
turn-on (n.)	something that excites you, especially sexually
turnout (n.)	the number of people that attend an event
turnover (n.)	a sweet pie-like pastry, or the amount of hiring and firing that goes on in a place of work

* Note that the form "will be being turned" is rarely used. To convey a future progressive passive, use the present progressive passive.

Verb Chart

wait

	ACTIVE	PASSIVE
Infinitive	to wait	to be waited
Past Infinitive	to have waited	to have been waited
Past Participle	waited	been waited
Present Participle	waiting	being waited

ACTIVE

	I	you/we/they	he/she/it

SIMPLE PRESENT	**SIMPLE PAST**	**SIMPLE FUTURE**
wait	waited	will wait
wait	waited	will wait
waits	waited	will wait

PRESENT PROGRESSIVE	**PAST PROGRESSIVE**	**FUTURE PROGRESSIVE**
am waiting	was waiting	will be waiting
are waiting	were waiting	will be waiting
is waiting	was waiting	will be waiting

PRESENT PERFECT	**PAST PERFECT**	**FUTURE PERFECT**
have waited	had waited	will have waited
have waited	had waited	will have waited
has waited	had waited	will have waited

PRESENT PERFECT PROGRESSIVE	**PAST PERFECT PROGRESSIVE**	**FUTURE PERFECT PROGRESSIVE**
have been waiting	had been waiting	will have been waiting
have been waiting	had been waiting	will have been waiting
has been waiting	had been waiting	will have been waiting

EXAMPLES:

I'm an artist, but I also wait tables.

How long have you been waiting for the doctor?

He had waited for the letter for days before he went to the post office to file a complaint.

PASSIVE

SIMPLE PRESENT	**SIMPLE PAST**	**SIMPLE FUTURE**
am waited	was waited	will be waited
are waited	were waited	will be waited
is waited	was waited	will be waited

PRESENT PROGRESSIVE	**PAST PROGRESSIVE**	**FUTURE PROGRESSIVE***
am being waited	was being waited	will be being waited*
are being waited	were being waited	will be being waited*
is being waited	was being waited	will be being waited*

PRESENT PERFECT	**PAST PERFECT**	**FUTURE PERFECT**
have been waited	had been waited	will have been waited
have been waited	had been waited	will have been waited
has been waited	had been waited	will have been waited

EXAMPLES:

The gifts were being waited for with great anticipation.

He has been waited on since day one of their marriage.

The kids were from a wealthy family and had been waited on hand and foot.

PRINCIPAL CONDITIONALS

PRESENT	**PRESENT PROGRESSIVE**	**PRESENT PASSIVE**
would wait	would be waiting	would be waited
would wait	would be waiting	would be waited
would wait	would be waiting	would be waited

PAST	**PAST PROGRESSIVE**	**PAST PASSIVE**
would have waited	would have been waiting	would have been waited
would have waited	would have been waiting	would have been waited
would have waited	would have been waiting	would have been waited

EXAMPLES:

We would wait for you, but we have to get home and relieve the baby-sitter.

I'm sure they would have waited if you had asked.

wait

Important Forms in Use

IF/THEN CONDITIONALS

	IF ...	...THEN	EXAMPLE
Real Present/ Future	wait/waits	simple present	*If I <u>wait</u> for the bus on this corner, I usually run into Marian.*
		will + base form	*If she <u>waits</u> for him to ask her, they'll never get married.*
Unreal Present/ Future	waited	would + base form	*If we <u>waited</u> any longer, we would miss the movie.*
Unreal Past	had waited	would have + past participle	*If she <u>had waited</u> for me, I would have had a ride home.*

SUBJUNCTIVE

ACTIVE	wait	*It is important that the patients <u>wait</u> in the waiting room until they have been called.*
PASSIVE	be waited	*It is essential that we <u>be waited</u> on by an experienced waiter.*

PHRASAL VERBS

wait on (someone)
: to serve someone, especially in a restaurant
If we can't get anyone to wait on us here, let's go to the restaurant across the street.

wait (something) out
: to be patient until something, such as a storm, has passed
I know it's pouring now, but let's wait it out. I'm sure it will stop shortly.

wait up
: to remain awake until something specific happens, such as someone comes home or you get some news
When the girls got home from the party, their father was waiting up for them. / Let's not go to bed now. Let's wait up to hear who won the election.

IDIOMS

to be waiting in the wings
: to remain in the background in hopes that your services will be needed sometime in the future
He told her he'd be waiting in the wings in case she ever grew apart from her current boyfriend.

to wait on someone hand and foot
: to do everything for someone else so that he or she doesn't have to do anything
It's disgusting how Harriet's boyfriend waits on her hand and foot. He has no self-respect.

to wait in vain
: to wait for something that never comes or never happens
I'm afraid you're waiting in vain. The doctor will not be able to see you today without an appointment.

can't wait
: to be excited about something that is going to happen in the future
I can't wait for vacation. We're going to Hawaii.

RELATED WORDS

waiting room (n.)
: a room in which one can pass time until a doctor's appointment, the departure of a train or plane, etc.

waiter (n.)
: a server in a restaurant

* Note that the form "will be being waited" is rarely used. To convey a future progressive passive, use the present progressive passive.

walk

	ACTIVE	PASSIVE
Infinitive	to walk	to be walked
Past Infinitive	to have walked	to have been walked
Past Participle	walked	been walked
Present Participle	walking	being walked

ACTIVE

I
you/we/they
he/she/it

SIMPLE PRESENT	SIMPLE PAST	SIMPLE FUTURE
walk	walked	will walk
walk	walked	will walk
walks	walked	will walk

PRESENT PROGRESSIVE	PAST PROGRESSIVE	FUTURE PROGRESSIVE
am walking	was walking	will be walking
are walking	were walking	will be walking
is walking	was walking	will be walking

PRESENT PERFECT	PAST PERFECT	FUTURE PERFECT
have walked	had walked	will have walked
have walked	had walked	will have walked
has walked	had walked	will have walked

PRESENT PERFECT PROGRESSIVE	PAST PERFECT PROGRESSIVE	FUTURE PERFECT PROGRESSIVE
have been walking	had been walking	will have been walking
have been walking	had been walking	will have been walking
has been walking	had been walking	will have been walking

EXAMPLES:

Are you walking to school or are you taking a bus?

We will have walked miles if we don't catch the bus soon.

He has been walking out of rehearsals for years now. Don't think anything of it.

PASSIVE

SIMPLE PRESENT	SIMPLE PAST	SIMPLE FUTURE
am walked	was walked	will be walked
are walked	were walked	will be walked
is walked	was walked	will be walked

PRESENT PROGRESSIVE	PAST PROGRESSIVE	FUTURE PROGRESSIVE*
am being walked	was being walked	will be being walked*
are being walked	were being walked	will be being walked*
is being walked	was being walked	will be being walked*

PRESENT PERFECT	PAST PERFECT	FUTURE PERFECT
have been walked	had been walked	will have been walked
have been walked	had been walked	will have been walked
has been walked	had been walked	will have been walked

EXAMPLES:

The dogs were walked by my next-door neighbor while I was out of town.

The batter was walked after the pitcher threw him four balls.

PRINCIPAL CONDITIONALS

PRESENT	PRESENT PROGRESSIVE	PRESENT PASSIVE
would walk	would be walking	would be walked
would walk	would be walking	would be walked
would walk	would be walking	would be walked

PAST	PAST PROGRESSIVE	PAST PASSIVE
would have walked	would have been walking	would have been walked
would have walked	would have been walking	would have been walked
would have walked	would have been walking	would have been walked

EXAMPLES:

I would walk but I'm not wearing comfortable shoes.

We would have walked if we had had time.

walk

Important Forms in Use

IF/THEN CONDITIONALS

	IF...	...THEN	EXAMPLE
Real Present/ Future	walk/walks	simple present	If I *walk* more than three blocks in these shoes, I get blisters.
		will + base form	If she *walks* a mile a day, she'll lose weight little by little.
Unreal Present/ Future	walked	would + base form	If we *walked* more instead of driving, we would be healthier.
Unreal Past	had walked	would have + past participle	If they *had walked*, they would have gotten here faster than by driving in this traffic.

SUBJUNCTIVE

ACTIVE	walk	It is important that the kids *walk* home along the supervised route.
PASSIVE	be walked	It is essential that the dogs *be walked* before you go to bed.

PHRASAL VERBS

walk away with	to win an award in a way that no one expects *A complete unknown walked away with the men's singles title in the U.S. Open.*
walk in	to enter a room unexpectedly *They never imagined that I would walk in while they were having dinner.*
walk into	to unexpectedly become involved in an often complicated or delicate situation *I walked into a very tense situation at work when I got back from vacation.*
walk off	to leave a person or people you were with abruptly, usually when you are angry *We were having a perfectly normal conversation, but when I mentioned the work he still owed me, he walked off.*

IDIOMS

to walk a tightrope	to be in a situation that could turn bad with any slight mistake *They've made a peace agreement, but both sides are walking a tightrope.*
Go take a walk!	an expression that is said to someone when you are rejecting what he or she has offered (informal) *You want me to pay one thousand dollars for that piece of junk? Go take a walk!*
to walk the walk	to do what is expected of you in a certain situation *If you want to work in the mayor's office, you have to walk the walk.*
to get your walking papers	to be fired *Did you hear that Jim got his walking papers at the end of the workday yesterday?*
to walk the earth	to be willing to do anything *Nicholas is really in love with his wife. He would walk the earth for her.*

RELATED WORDS

walker (n.)	a person who likes to walk or walks a lot, or a Zimmer frame
walking stick (n.)	a solid piece of wood that is used when hiking to help keep balance

Verb Chart

---

* Note that the form "will be being walked" is rarely used. To convey a future progressive passive, use the present progressive passive.

waste

	ACTIVE	PASSIVE
Infinitive	to waste	to be wasted
Past Infinitive	to have wasted	to have been wasted
Past Participle	wasted	been wasted
Present Participle	wasting	being wasted

ACTIVE

I
you/we/they
he/she/it

SIMPLE PRESENT	SIMPLE PAST	SIMPLE FUTURE
waste	wasted	will waste
waste	wasted	will waste
wastes	wasted	will waste

PRESENT PROGRESSIVE	PAST PROGRESSIVE	FUTURE PROGRESSIVE
am wasting	was wasting	will be wasting
are wasting	were wasting	will be wasting
is wasting	was wasting	will be wasting

PRESENT PERFECT	PAST PERFECT	FUTURE PERFECT
have wasted	had wasted	will have wasted
have wasted	had wasted	will have wasted
has wasted	had wasted	will have wasted

PRESENT PERFECT PROGRESSIVE	PAST PERFECT PROGRESSIVE	FUTURE PERFECT PROGRESSIVE
have been wasting	had been wasting	will have been wasting
have been wasting	had been wasting	will have been wasting
has been wasting	had been wasting	will have been wasting

EXAMPLES:
Take all of the food in the bowl. Don't waste it.

He'll waste away if he doesn't eat something!

She had wasted the chance to be an assistant to a top executive by showing up late for the interview.

PASSIVE

SIMPLE PRESENT	SIMPLE PAST	SIMPLE FUTURE
am wasted	was wasted	will be wasted
are wasted	were wasted	will be wasted
is wasted	was wasted	will be wasted

PRESENT PROGRESSIVE	PAST PROGRESSIVE	FUTURE PROGRESSIVE*
am being wasted	was being wasted	will be being wasted*
are being wasted	were being wasted	will be being wasted*
is being wasted	was being wasted	will be being wasted*

PRESENT PERFECT	PAST PERFECT	FUTURE PERFECT
have been wasted	had been wasted	will have been wasted
have been wasted	had been wasted	will have been wasted
has been wasted	had been wasted	will have been wasted

EXAMPLES:
A lot of food in this country is wasted.

If you give me all of that fruit, it will be wasted. I can't eat it all.

A lot of time had been wasted in trying to convince the famous author to speak at the anniversary celebration.

PRINCIPAL CONDITIONALS

PRESENT	PRESENT PROGRESSIVE	PRESENT PASSIVE
would waste	would be wasting	would be wasted
would waste	would be wasting	would be wasted
would waste	would be wasting	would be wasted

PAST	PAST PROGRESSIVE	PAST PASSIVE
would have wasted	would have been wasting	would have been wasted
would have wasted	would have been wasting	would have been wasted
would have wasted	would have been wasting	would have been wasted

EXAMPLES:
I would waste a lot of time if I worked at home because of all of the distractions.

If you had spent the money on a ticket for me, it would have been wasted. You know I don't like foreign films.

waste

Important Forms in Use

IF/THEN CONDITIONALS

	IF ...	... THEN	EXAMPLE
Real Present/ Future	waste/wastes	simple present	*If I waste a lot of time during the day, I have to work at night.*
		will + base form	*If Sarah wastes another perfectly good opportunity to speak with her boss, I'll be very disappointed.*
Unreal Present/ Future	wasted	would + base form	*If we wasted as much money this year as we did last year, we would have to file for bankruptcy.*
Unreal Past	had wasted	would have + past participle	*If you had wasted another minute looking for your hat, you would have missed your train.*

SUBJUNCTIVE

ACTIVE	waste	*We insist that you not waste another minute cleaning up and get outside to enjoy the beautiful day.*
PASSIVE	be wasted	*It is important that another opportunity like this one not be wasted.*

PHRASAL VERBS

waste away	to become very thin or to lose vitality, often due to illness *After her illness she just wasted away.*

IDIOMS

to lay waste to something	to destroy something *The budget cuts laid waste to all of the work that our organization did helping homeless people to get off the streets.*
to waste your breath	to vainly try to convince someone of something *Don't waste your breath! I'm not taking you to the mall today.*
to not waste words	to say what you have to say in as few words as possible *I wouldn't say that he's shy, but he certainly doesn't waste words.*
to be wasted on someone	to be unappreciated or misunderstood by someone *The finer points of his argument were wasted on me because I didn't have the background knowledge to understand them fully.*

RELATED WORDS

waste not, want not (exp.)	an expression used to advise someone not to use too much of something because it might be needed in the future
wasted (adj.)	very drunk, or not used
waste (n.)	what remains after the useful part of something has been used

* Note that the form "will be being wasted" is rarely used. To convey a future progressive passive, use the present progressive passive.

Verb Chart

watch

	ACTIVE	PASSIVE
Infinitive	to watch	to be watched
Past Infinitive	to have watched	to have been watched
Past Participle	watched	been watched
Present Participle	watching	being watched

ACTIVE

	I	you/we/they	he/she/it

SIMPLE PRESENT	SIMPLE PAST	SIMPLE FUTURE
watch	watched	will watch
watch	watched	will watch
watches	watched	will watch

PRESENT PROGRESSIVE	PAST PROGRESSIVE	FUTURE PROGRESSIVE
am watching	was watching	will be watching
are watching	were watching	will be watching
is watching	was watching	will be watching

PRESENT PERFECT	PAST PERFECT	FUTURE PERFECT
have watched	had watched	will have watched
have watched	had watched	will have watched
has watched	had watched	will have watched

PRESENT PERFECT PROGRESSIVE	PAST PERFECT PROGRESSIVE	FUTURE PERFECT PROGRESSIVE
have been watching	had been watching	will have been watching
have been watching	had been watching	will have been watching
has been watching	had been watching	will have been watching

EXAMPLES:
We watch a lot of TV every evening. *The next-door neighbors are watching our house for the next two weeks while we're in Aruba.* *They will have watched all of the James Bond movies after they see the one on TV tonight.*

PASSIVE

SIMPLE PRESENT	SIMPLE PAST	SIMPLE FUTURE
am watched	was watched	will be watched
are watched	were watched	will be watched
is watched	was watched	will be watched

PRESENT PROGRESSIVE	PAST PROGRESSIVE	FUTURE PROGRESSIVE*
am being watched	was being watched	will be being watched*
are being watched	were being watched	will be being watched*
is being watched	was being watched	will be being watched*

PRESENT PERFECT	PAST PERFECT	FUTURE PERFECT
have been watched	had been watched	will have been watched
have been watched	had been watched	will have been watched
has been watched	had been watched	will have been watched

EXAMPLES:
The children are being watched by their grandparents. *The Oscars will be watched by the largest audience ever this year.*

PRINCIPAL CONDITIONALS

PRESENT	PRESENT PROGRESSIVE	PRESENT PASSIVE
would watch	would be watching	would be watched
would watch	would be watching	would be watched
would watch	would be watching	would be watched

PAST	PAST PROGRESSIVE	PAST PASSIVE
would have watched	would have been watching	would have been watched
would have watched	would have been watching	would have been watched
would have watched	would have been watching	would have been watched

EXAMPLES:
We would be watching the Olympics but we don't have cable. *She would've watched out for you if she had known you were coming.*

watch

Important Forms in Use

IF/THEN CONDITIONALS

	IF ...	... THEN	EXAMPLE
Real Present/ Future	watch/watches	simple present	*If my son <u>watches</u> a violent movie, he gets angry and depressed.*
		will + base form	*If I <u>watch</u> your dog this weekend, will you watch mine next weekend?*
Unreal Present/ Future	watched	would + base form	*If we <u>watched</u> over them more carefully, they wouldn't get into trouble all the time.*
Unreal Past	had watched	would have + past participle	*If I <u>hadn't watched</u> him play, I wouldn't have believed how good he was.*

SUBJUNCTIVE

ACTIVE	watch	*It is important that passengers <u>watch</u> the emergency instruction video.*
PASSIVE	be watched	*He suggested that film <u>be watched</u> as many times as necessary until we had a feeling for the director's style.*

PHRASAL VERBS

watch for (someone or something)	to be on the lookout for someone or something *Watch for Jim. He's supposed to be here any minute.*
watch out for (someone or something)	to be careful of someone or something that could be dangerous *Watch out for Paul. He'll do anything to get what he wants.*
watch over (someone or something)	to take care of someone or something *Can you watch over my house while I'm on vacation?*

IDIOMS

a watched pot never boils	an expression that means that if you have too many expectations, you may not get what you want *Elizabeth can't think about anything except meeting someone. I always tell her that a watched pot never boils.*
to watch your back	to be careful of some danger that my come up on you by surprise *You want to trust everyone, but unfortunately in this job you have to watch your back.*
to watch your step	to do something carefully, especially when dealing with a person who may get angry easily *My coworkers warned me to watch my step around the general manager.*

RELATED WORDS

watch (n.)	a small clock that you can carry with you
watchdog (n.)	a dog that guards a house or other property
watchmaker (n.)	a person whose job is putting together watches
watchtower (n.)	a place from which a large property can be guarded

* Note that the form "will be being watched" is rarely used. To convey a future progressive passive, use the present progressive passive.

Verb Chart

wear

	ACTIVE	PASSIVE
Infinitive	to wear	to be worn
Past Infinitive	to have worn	to have been worn
Past Participle	worn	been worn
Present Participle	wearing	being worn

ACTIVE

I
you/we/they
he/she/it

SIMPLE PRESENT	SIMPLE PAST	SIMPLE FUTURE
wear	wore	will wear
wear	wore	will wear
wears	wore	will wear

PRESENT PROGRESSIVE	PAST PROGRESSIVE	FUTURE PROGRESSIVE
am wearing	was wearing	will be wearing
are wearing	were wearing	will be wearing
is wearing	was wearing	will be wearing

PRESENT PERFECT	PAST PERFECT	FUTURE PERFECT
have worn	had worn	will have worn
have worn	had worn	will have worn
has worn	had worn	will have worn

PRESENT PERFECT PROGRESSIVE	PAST PERFECT PROGRESSIVE	FUTURE PERFECT PROGRESSIVE
have been wearing	had been wearing	will have been wearing
have been wearing	had been wearing	will have been wearing
has been wearing	had been wearing	will have been wearing

EXAMPLES:

Who wears the pants in this family?

I will wear my new coat tonight so that you can see it.

His jokes had been wearing thin.

PASSIVE

SIMPLE PRESENT	SIMPLE PAST	SIMPLE FUTURE
am worn	was worn	will be worn
are worn	were worn	will be worn
is worn	was worn	will be worn

PRESENT PROGRESSIVE	PAST PROGRESSIVE	FUTURE PROGRESSIVE*
am being worn	was being worn	will be being worn*
are being worn	were being worn	will be being worn*
is being worn	was being worn	will be being worn*

PRESENT PERFECT	PAST PERFECT	FUTURE PERFECT
have been worn	had been worn	will have been worn
have been worn	had been worn	will have been worn
has been worn	had been worn	will have been worn

EXAMPLES:

I was shocked to see that my clothes were being worn by somebody I didn't know.

The designer's dress is being worn by the woman on the left.

The shoes had never been worn before.

PRINCIPAL CONDITIONALS

PRESENT	PRESENT PROGRESSIVE	PRESENT PASSIVE
would wear	would be wearing	would be worn
would wear	would be wearing	would be worn
would wear	would be wearing	would be worn

PAST	PAST PROGRESSIVE	PAST PASSIVE
would have worn	would have been wearing	would have been worn
would have worn	would have been wearing	would have been worn
would have worn	would have been wearing	would have been worn

EXAMPLES:

I would have worn something nicer if I had known other people were going to dress up.

What would you wear if you were me?

wear

Important Forms in Use

IF/THEN CONDITIONALS

	IF . . .	. . . THEN	EXAMPLE
Real Present/ Future	wear/wears	simple present	*If I <u>wear</u> that dress, everyone looks at me funny.*
		will + base form	*If she <u>wears</u> that, she'll never get the job.*
Unreal Present/ Future	wore	would + base form	*If we <u>wore</u> it out, we would buy a new one.*
Unreal Past	had worn	would have + past participle	*If I <u>had worn</u> my T-shirt today, we would have looked like twins.*

SUBJUNCTIVE

ACTIVE	wear	*It is important that you <u>wear</u> a suit and tie to the interview.*
PASSIVE	be worn	*It is essential that dark clothing <u>be worn</u> at a funeral.*

PHRASAL VERBS

wear away	to erode, to disappear gradually *The walkway along the beach wore away after many years.*
wear (someone) down	to lower somebody's resistance by putting on a lot of pressure *He finally lent us the car after we wore him down by pleading and making a million promises.*
wear (something) in	to use something until it fits comfortably, usually used with shoes *The new shoes are a little stiff but I'm wearing them in.*
wear (something) out	to begin to lose usefulness after long or hard use *My favorite jeans are beginning to wear out.*

IDIOMS

to wear your heart on your sleeve	to show emotions openly *Don't mind Frank. He always wears his heart on his sleeve.*
to wear the pants	to be in control in a household *You can do whatever you want when you go to college, but don't forget who wears the pants at home.*
to wear thin	to become tiresome, boring, or annoying *His jokes quickly began to wear thin.*

RELATED WORDS

wash-and-wear (adj.)	clothing made of a certain material that does not need to be ironed
wear and tear (n.)	damage or wear that can be expected through normal use

* Note that the form "will be being worn" is rarely used. To convey a future progressive passive, use the present progressive passive.

Verb Chart

work

	ACTIVE	PASSIVE
Infinitive	to work	to be worked
Past Infinitive	to have worked	to have been worked
Past Participle	worked	been worked
Present Participle	working	being worked

ACTIVE

I
you/we/they
he/she/it

SIMPLE PRESENT	SIMPLE PAST	SIMPLE FUTURE
work	worked	will work
work	worked	will work
works	worked	will work

PRESENT PROGRESSIVE	PAST PROGRESSIVE	FUTURE PROGRESSIVE
am working	was working	will be working
are working	were working	will be working
is working	was working	will be working

PRESENT PERFECT	PAST PERFECT	FUTURE PERFECT
have worked	had worked	will have worked
have worked	had worked	will have worked
has worked	had worked	will have worked

PRESENT PERFECT PROGRESSIVE	PAST PERFECT PROGRESSIVE	FUTURE PERFECT PROGRESSIVE
have been working	had been working	will have been working
have been working	had been working	will have been working
has been working	had been working	will have been working

EXAMPLES:
We are working in the same building, and so we often meet for lunch.

Ron worked on that case, so ask him if you have any questions.

I wasn't working when I moved to L.A., so I had a lot of time to explore the city.

PASSIVE

SIMPLE PRESENT	SIMPLE PAST	SIMPLE FUTURE
am worked	was worked	will be worked
are worked	were worked	will be worked
is worked	was worked	will be worked

PRESENT PROGRESSIVE	PAST PROGRESSIVE	FUTURE PROGRESSIVE*
am being worked	was being worked	will be being worked*
are being worked	were being worked	will be being worked*
is being worked	was being worked	will be being worked*

PRESENT PERFECT	PAST PERFECT	FUTURE PERFECT
have been worked	had been worked	will have been worked
have been worked	had been worked	will have been worked
has been worked	had been worked	will have been worked

EXAMPLES:
Can this character be worked into the movie somehow?

The crowd was worked up by the arrival of the headlining band.

The problems exist, but they are currently being worked through.

PRINCIPAL CONDITIONALS

PRESENT	PRESENT PROGRESSIVE	PRESENT PASSIVE
would work	would be working	would be worked
would work	would be working	would be worked
would work	would be working	would be worked

PAST	PAST PROGRESSIVE	PAST PASSIVE
would have worked	would have been working	would have been worked
would have worked	would have been working	would have been worked
would have worked	would have been working	would have been worked

EXAMPLES:
My client would work on your project if he weren't currently involved elsewhere.

You would have worked with her better than I was able to.

This scene would have been worked through ages ago if the script had been ready.

work

Important Forms in Use

IF/THEN CONDITIONALS

	IF . . .	. . . THEN	EXAMPLE
Real Present/ Future	work/works	simple present	*If I <u>work</u> late, my husband picks me up at the train station.*
		will + base form	*If you <u>work</u> out the details, we'll sign the contract this afternoon.*
Unreal Present/ Future	worked	would + base form	*If we <u>worked</u> together, we could get done in half the time.*
Unreal Past	had worked	would have + past participle	*If she <u>had worked</u> harder on the project, she would have gotten an A.*

SUBJUNCTIVE

ACTIVE	work	*We suggest that the crew work at reasonable hours.*
PASSIVE	be worked	*They requested that the details <u>be worked</u> out ahead of time.*

PHRASAL VERBS

work (something) out	to solve a problem *They weren't getting along, but they worked out their disagreements.*
work up	to develop or build *Henry worked up the courage to enroll in a skydiving program.*
work (something) in	to fit something into a schedule *I know we have a lot to talk about today, but can we work in a discussion of the new regulations?*

IDIOMS

to be worked up	to be upset, worried, or agitated about something *My mother got all worked up when I told her I wanted to drop out of school.*
to be in working order	to be functioning well *You can move in whenever you're ready. Everything seems to be in working order.*
to have your work cut out for you	to have a great deal of work to do *Sally's got her work cut out for her. She's going to be working and studying full time.*

RELATED WORDS

workhorse (n.)	a person who can work for long periods of time without getting tired
workaholic (n.)	a person who works too many hours in the week, who is addicted to work
workers' compensation (n.)	money that the government provides a worker who cannot work due to a work-related injury
workout (n.)	an exercise routine
work of art (n.)	a piece of art, such as a painting or a photograph

* Note that the form "will be being worked" is rarely used. To convey a future progressive passive, use the present progressive passive.

Verb Chart

write

	ACTIVE	PASSIVE
Infinitive	to write	to be written
Past Infinitive	to have written	to have been written
Past Participle	written	been written
Present Participle	writing	being written

ACTIVE

	I	you/we/they	he/she/it

SIMPLE PRESENT
write
write
writes

SIMPLE PAST
wrote
wrote
wrote

SIMPLE FUTURE
will write
will write
will write

PRESENT PROGRESSIVE
am writing
are writing
is writing

PAST PROGRESSIVE
was writing
were writing
was writing

FUTURE PROGRESSIVE
will be writing
will be writing
will be writing

PRESENT PERFECT
have written
have written
has written

PAST PERFECT
had written
had written
had written

FUTURE PERFECT
will have written
will have written
will have written

PRESENT PERFECT PROGRESSIVE
have been writing
have been writing
has been writing

PAST PERFECT PROGRESSIVE
had been writing
had been writing
had been writing

FUTURE PERFECT PROGRESSIVE
will have been writing
will have been writing
will have been writing

EXAMPLES:
We wrote so many essays this week that I don't want to write anymore.

Will you write a letter to the landlord?

They had written to the company but they hadn't heard anything.

PASSIVE

SIMPLE PRESENT
am written
are written
is written

SIMPLE PAST
was written
were written
was written

SIMPLE FUTURE
will be written
will be written
will be written

PRESENT PROGRESSIVE
am being written
are being written
is being written

PAST PROGRESSIVE
was being written
were being written
was being written

FUTURE PROGRESSIVE*
will be being written*
will be being written*
will be being written*

PRESENT PERFECT
have been written
have been written
has been written

PAST PERFECT
had been written
had been written
had been written

FUTURE PERFECT
will have been written
will have been written
will have been written

EXAMPLES:
The book was written by a young woman.

The rules had been written down carefully.

The letter is being written as we speak.

PRINCIPAL CONDITIONALS

PRESENT
would write
would write
would write

PRESENT PROGRESSIVE
would be writing
would be writing
would be writing

PRESENT PASSIVE
would be written
would be written
would be written

PAST
would have written
would have written
would have written

PAST PROGRESSIVE
would have been writing
would have been writing
would have been writing

PAST PASSIVE
would have been written
would have been written
would have been written

EXAMPLES:
Would you write down exactly what you want me to say when I call him?

We would have written if we had had your address.

write

Important Forms in Use

IF/THEN CONDITIONALS

	IF ...	... THEN	EXAMPLE
Real Present/ Future	write/writes	simple present	*If I <u>write</u> him an e-mail, he doesn't respond.*
		will + base form	*If she <u>writes</u> me, I'll write her back.*
Unreal Present/ Future	wrote	would + base form	*If I <u>wrote</u> every day, I'd have a better chance of finishing my novel this year.*
Unreal Past	had written	would have + past participle	*If I <u>had written</u> my dissertation, I would have gotten my Ph.D.*

SUBJUNCTIVE

ACTIVE	write	*It is important that your parent <u>write</u> a letter excusing you from the class.*
PASSIVE	be written	*It is essential that the rules <u>be written</u> down clearly.*

PHRASAL VERBS

write (something) down	to put something on paper *Write down my telephone number so you don't forget it.*
write (someone or something) off	to reject someone or something *At first I thought I really liked Tom, but after what he did, I wrote him off.*
write (something) out	to record something in detail *When I am given an essay topic, I always jot down some notes and then write them out.*
write (someone) up	to officially make a record of something wrong or illegal that someone has done *My boss wrote me up when I refused to follow his orders.*

IDIOMS

to be written all over your face	to be obvious from someone's expression *Disappointment was written all over her face.*
to write your own ticket	to be able to choose exactly what you want to do or where you want to go *She was such a good basketball player that she could write her own ticket when she looked for a college to go to.*

RELATED WORDS

writer's block (n.)	a situation in which a writer is unable to write
tax write-off (n.)	an expenditure that you can claim on your tax forms and thereby pay fewer taxes
writer (n.)	a person whose profession is writing

* Note that the form "will be being written" is rarely used. To convey a future progressive passive, use the present progressive passive.

Verb Chart

Part II
ENGLISH VERBS IN ACTION

1. Present Simple

A.

Let's start with the present simple tense. The present simple tense is the verb tense that you will use to talk about things that are done on a regular basis. We could say that these are activities that are routines or habits. The present simple tense is also used to talk about things that are always true, and even sometimes in reference to things that will happen in the future. For example, *"I always call my mother on Sunday"* is a routine, and *"It usually snows here in December"* is something that is a true statement. *"The train leaves at 3:00"* is an example of the present simple being used to talk about the future.

In the present simple tense, there is only one "conjugation" (with the exception of the verb *to be*). You will always use the base form of the verb (the infinitive minus "*to*"), except for the third person singular, *he, she,* and *it.* The third person singular requires an -*s*, (in some exceptional cases an -*es*, or an -*ies*) to be added to the end of the verb.

In section B, we will look at a few spelling rules that will help you to learn which verbs are irregular and require an -*es* or an -*ies*.

For now, let's take a look at the regular verb *work*.

> *I work*
> *I **work** at the café on the corner.*
>
> *he/she/it works*
> *Jim **works** from nine to five on Tuesdays and Thursdays.*
> *She **works** in the laboratory.*
> *Look at the watch. It **works** but it is losing time.*
>
> *you/we/they work*
> *We **work** when the baby is sleeping.*
> *You **work** very well together.*
> *They **work** best when they have had a chance to get some fresh air.*

Note once again that for all forms (*I, you, we, they*) we simply use the base form of the verb, and only the *he, she,* and *it* forms require an -*s* to be added.

B.

Now let's look at a few exceptions to the rule of -*s* in 3rd person singular.

1. Verbs ending in *s, ss, sh, ch, x*

For these verbs, you will have to add an -*es* instead of a simple -*s*. Some examples: *kiss, pass, wash, wish, watch, latch, box, tax,* etc.

Take a look at a few examples of sentences in the third person singular.

> *My mother **kisses** me goodbye every morning when*
> *   I leave for school.*
> *He usually **watches** TV after eating dinner.*
> *My next-door neighbor **washes** his new car every evening.*

Note that most of the examples are routines or activities that happen repeatedly.

2. Verbs *go* and *do*

You will also have to add *-es* to *go* and *do* if you are using the third person singular form in the present simple.

> David **goes** to work by subway.
> My daughter **does** her homework every afternoon before dinner.
> The sun **goes** up and the sun **goes** down.

3. Verbs ending in consonant + *y*

For verbs ending in a consonant + *y* you can learn a simple rule. You will have to drop the *-y* and add *-ies*. Some examples of verbs that end with a consonant + *y* are: *study, try, carry, apply, rely, hurry,* and *worry*.

> Pedro **studies** English on Tuesdays and Thursdays.
> My sister **carries** a briefcase to work every day.
> Because the student **applies** herself, she is able to meet the
>   requirements of the course.
> If she **hurries**, she will get here on time.

Note that you will use this same rule when making plurals for nouns that end in *-y*.

Be sure not to apply this rule to verbs ending in a vowel + *y*. Unlike the above verbs, verbs ending with a vowel + *y* are not considered irregular. You will simply add an *-s*, as you would with any regular verb.

> Martin **enjoys** working at the bank.
> Frank always **stays** at the same hotel when he goes to Miami.
> Jim **plays** saxophone with a quartet at a bar in Harlem.

4. Verb *to have*

A final exception is the verb *to have*, which becomes *has* in the third person present and present perfect.

> He **has** a lot of work to do.
> She **has** never been to France.

C.

1. **Answer each question as indicated. Don't forget to add *-s, -es,* or *-ies* for the third person.**

> EXAMPLE: *Where does he live? (in Chicago)*
>
> He **lives** in Chicago.

> 1. *How often do you go to the gym? (three times a week)*
> 2. *Where does he work? (at the local community college)*
> 3. *What does she want to study in college? (biology)*
> 4. *How often does it rain? (once a week)*
> 5. *What do they usually do on the weekends? (visit their relatives)*

2. The following sentences are about "*you.*" Change the pronoun in each case to "*she.*" Don't forget to change the verb as well.

> EXAMPLE: *You work in a bank, and like it very much.*
>
> *She **works** in a bank, and **likes** it very much.*
>
> 1. *Now that you go to college, you have to study on the weekends.*
> 2. *You worry all the time; you need to relax.*
> 3. *When you visit me, you always stay until 5:00.*
> 4. *You never carry your groceries.*
> 5. *You do a lot of work but then watch TV in the evening to relax.*

D. Answer Key

1.
1. *I **go** to the gym three times a week.*
2. *He **works** at the local community college.*
3. *She **wants** to study biology in college.*
4. *It **rains** once a week.*
5. *They usually **visit** their relatives on the weekends.*

2.
1. *Now that she **goes** to college, she **has** to study on the weekends.*
2. *She **worries** all the time; she **needs** to relax.*
3. *When she **visits** me, she always **stays** until 5:00.*
4. *She never **carries** her groceries.*
5. *She **does** a lot of work but then **watches** TV in the evening to relax.*

2. Auxiliaries

It is essential that every student of English understand how auxiliaries are used. You will use them to form questions and negatives, as well as certain tenses, aspects, and voices. Following is an overview of all auxiliaries. More specific information can be found in the lessons that follow.

A. Do/does/did

1. Present and past tense

In the present and past tense, you will use *do, does,* or *did* to make questions and form the negative. For the negative, add *not (don't, doesn't, didn't)*. For the third person (*he, she,* and *it*), use *does*.

> *Helen **likes** ice cream.*
> negative   *Helen **doesn't like** ice cream.*
> question   ***Does** Helen **like** ice cream?*

For all other forms (*I, you, we, they*), use *do*.

> *You **work** at a bank.*
> negative   *You **don't work** at a bank.*
> question   ***Do** you **work** at a bank?*

For all forms in the past tense, use *did*.

> *They **knew** the answer.*
> negative   *They **didn't know** the answer.*
> question   ***Did** they **know** the answer?*

Note that *do, does,* and *did (don't, doesn't, didn't)* reflect whether or not a subject is third person (*he, she, it*) and if a verb is in the past tense. Therefore, the main verb will always be in the base form (without *-s,* or any past tense marker).

> *Sarah **doesn't want** to join us.* (not *doesn't wants*)
> *The boys **didn't take** their ball.* (not *didn't **took***)

2. Question words

Use question words (*where, what, when, how, who,* etc.) before the auxiliary verb.

> ***Where** do you live?*
> ***What** do you do?*
> ***How often** does she take the subway?*

B. Other Auxiliary Verbs

1. The verb *to be*

The verb *to be* when used in progressive and passive sentences also acts as an auxiliary verb.

To form a question, invert the subject and the verb. For negatives, add *not* to the verb *to be*. Do not use *do, does,* or *did* when you use the verb *to be*.

Progressive
*I **am living** in New York.*

| negative | *I'm **not living** in New York.* |
| question | ***Am** I **living** in New York?* |

Passive
*My shoes **were made** in China.*

| negative | *My shoes **weren't made** in China.* |
| question | ***Were** my shoes **made** in China?* |

(See lesson 3.)

2. Have/has/had

Have, has, and *had* are auxiliary verbs used to form the perfect tenses. Use *have/has* for present perfect both in statements and questions. Use *had* to form the past perfect. Add *not* for questions.

Present Perfect
*Mr. Knight **has been** the principal for many years.*

| negative | *Mr. Knight **hasn't been** the principal for many years.* |
| question | ***Has** Mr. Knight **been** the principal for many years?* |

Past Perfect
*We **had finished** dinner by 8:00.*

| negative | *We **hadn't finished** dinner by 8:00.* |
| question | ***Had** we **finished** dinner by 8:00?* |

3. Modal verbs

The modal verbs are also auxiliary verbs. For questions, invert the subject and the verb. For negatives, add *not*. The verb following the modal verb is always in the base form.

*I **can come** with you.*

| negative | *I **can't come** with you.* |
| question | ***Can** I **come** with you?* |

(See lesson 31 for more about modal verbs.)

4. Question words

Use question words with any of the above auxiliary verbs.

__What__ can I bring to the meeting?
__How long__ have you lived in Seattle?
__Where__ are you going?
__When__ was your car tuned up last?

C.

1. Below you have answers that are missing questions. Form the question based on the answer. Use the question word that is given to begin your question.

    EXAMPLE: *They study English on Mondays.*

    When do they study English?

    1. *She never goes to the beach. (How often . . .)*
    2. *I am talking on the phone with Michelle. (Who . . .)*
    3. *He always has dinner at a restaurant near his home. (Where . . .)*
    4. *They are watching TV. (What . . .)*
    5. *It rains a lot in the spring. (When . . .)*

2. Some of the following sentences are affirmative, and some negative. Change them from affirmative to negative, or negative to affirmative.

    EXAMPLE: *We travel a lot.*

    We don't travel a lot.

    1. *My sister listens to music, and I enjoy reading.*
    2. *He is listening to the radio.*
    3. *My son needs help with his homework.*
    4. *The traffic light changes very quickly.*
    5. *Taxes were raised by the mayor.*

D. Answer Key

1. 1. ***How often does** she **go** to the beach?*
    2. ***Who are** you **talking** on the phone with?*
    3. ***Where does** he (usually) **have** dinner?*
    4. ***What are** they **doing**?*
    5. ***When does** it **rain** a lot?*

2. 1. *My sister **doesn't listen** to music, and I **don't enjoy** reading.*
    2. *He **isn't listening** to the radio.*
    3. *My son **doesn't need** help with his homework.*
    4. *The traffic light **doesn't change** very quickly.*
    5. *Taxes **weren't raised** by the mayor.*

3. The Verb *to Be*

A.

The verb *to be* is the only verb for which you will have to learn several conjugations in the present and the past. In the present tense there are three forms of the verb: *am, is,* and *are*. In the past, there are two forms of the verb: *was,* and *were*. The verb *to be* is used in present, past and future tenses.

	PRESENT	PAST
I	*am*	*was*
He/she/it	*is*	*was*
We/you/they	*are*	*were*

Present participle: *being*
Past participle: *been*

All verbs in the present tense can be contracted. (*I'm/He's/She's/It's/We're/They're/You're*). Let's look at a few examples of the verb *to be* using the past and present forms.

	PRESENT	PAST
I	*I'm going to bed early tonight.*	*I was very happy when I found my keys.*
He/she/it	*He is always late.*	*It was very hot last week.*
	She's arriving at 7:00.	*She was at home last night.*
We/you/they	*You're early!*	*You were early yesterday.*
	We are never here on Tuesdays.	*We were living in New York at the time.*
	They are coming soon.	*They were the last ones to arrive.*

Add *not* to make a negative. A contraction is often used.

PRESENT	PAST
I'm not	*wasn't*
he/she/it's not or *isn't*	*wasn't*
we/you/they're not or *aren't*	*weren't*

Here are some examples of negative sentences in past and present.

I
I'm not working tomorrow.
I wasn't worried.

He/she/it
She**'s not** here. (She **isn't** here.)
He **wasn't** happy with his scores.

You/we/they
They**'re not** coming. (They **aren't** coming.)
You **weren't** early yesterday.

To make a question, invert the subject and the verb.

He is listening to music.
question   **Is he** listening to music?

They are here.
question   **Are they** here?

A question word can be added before the verb *to be*.

How late are you working tomorrow?
When are they coming?
Etc.

B.

Let's look at when *to be* is needed to form certain verb tenses.

1.   Present simple and past simple
To be is used in the present simple and past simple if followed by an adjective or noun.

He **is a handsome man.**
The children **are happy** in their new school.
We **weren't surprised** when they came.

2.   Present progressive and past progressive
For present progressive and past progressive, use the auxiliary verb *to be* +
the *-ing* form of the main verb.

I **am taking** a course at the local community college.
Elise **isn't coming.** She has to take care of her cat.
My boss **wasn't listening** when I told him about the money we
   lost.

3.   Present or past perfect progressive
There is also a progressive form of the present or past perfect. You will use
have/has/had and the past participle of the verb *to be: been,* followed by a
verb + *ing*.

I **have been missing** you lately.
We **have been living** in New York for 3 years.
They **had been planning** to come, but couldn't.

D. Answer Key

1. 1. *been*
   2. *aren't*
   3. *were*
   4. *wasn't*
   5. *been*

2. 1. *will be*
   2. *have been*
   3. *is*
   4. *weren't*
   5. *were*

4. *There + to be*

Use *to be* with the subject *there* in the present, past, perfect or future to describe the presence of something.

> *There is* a lot of noise in the city.
>
> *There were* too many problems in our department last year. Let's start fresh.
>
> *There will be* a storm soon.
>
> *There have been* a lot of accidents at that intersection.
>
> *There had been* an explosion before the fire started.

5. Passive

The verb *to be* is also essential in forming the passive in all tenses. (See lessons 16 and 17.) In a passive construction, you will always use the verb *to be* + the past participle of the main verb. Let's look at a few examples.

> *The animal is fed and washed by the trainer.* (present simple)
>
> *The movie is being shown again next week.* (present progressive)
>
> *Taxes were raised again this year.* (past)
>
> *The criminal has been apprehended.* (present perfect)
>
> *The test will be given in the auditorium.* (future)
>
> *The work has to be done by the time I return!* (infinitive)

C.

1. In the following sentences, the verb *to be* is missing. Supply the correct form of the verb *to be*. Use a negative as indicated.

    > EXAMPLE: *We _____ living in Austin, Texas right now.*
    >
    > are

    > 1. *I have _____ studying English for six months.*
    > 2. *There _____ enough forks for everyone.* (negative)
    > 3. *Last night, we _____ having dinner when you called.*
    > 4. *She _____ working when I stopped by.* (negative)
    > 5. *We have _____ thinking about moving to Connecticut.*

2. Decide which verb tense (present, present perfect, past, future) is needed and write it in the space provided. Use a negative as indicated.

    > EXAMPLE: *There _____ ten students here yesterday.*
    >
    > were

    > 1. *There _____ 50 people at the party tomorrow.*
    > 2. *There _____ a lot of thunderstorms in our area recently.*
    > 3. *"I'm thirsty." "There _____ some orange juice in the refrigerator. Help yourself."*
    > 4. *I went to the movies, but there _____ any tickets left.* (negative)
    > 5. *When I got to the fire, there _____ three fire trucks there already.*

4. Present Progressive

A.

1. Formation

In order to form the present progressive tense, you will use the present tense of the verb *to be* and the *-ing* form of the main verb. Remember how the verb *to be* is conjugated:

> *I am (I'm)*
> *he/she/it is (he's/she's/it's)*
> *we/you/they are (we're/you're/they're)*

Now let's look at some examples of the verb *to be* with the *-ing* form of the main verb.

> *I*
> *I'm **having** breakfast right now.*
>
> *He/she/it*
> *He's **living** with me.*
> *It's **baking** in the oven at the moment.*
>
> *You/we/they*
> *You're **listening** to music.*
> *The bells **are ringing**.*

To make a question, invert the order of the subject and the verb *to be*. (See lesson 2.)

> ***Are you having** breakfast right now?*
> ***Is he living** with you?*

To express a negative, use *not*. (See lesson 2.)

> *I'm **not talking** to you.*
> *She's **not** (she **isn't**) **working** right now.*
> *The bells **aren't ringing**.*

2. Spelling changes in the *-ing* form

In most cases, you will form the progressive by simply adding *-ing* to the main verb: *going, walking, singing* etc. However, there are a few exceptions to this rule.

a. Verbs that end in *-e*

If there is an *-e* at the end of a verb, it should be dropped before you add the *-ing*. Verbs that end in *-e* are: *change, have, like, make, shake, take, hire,* etc.

> *When you called, I was **taking** a shower.*
> *He was **having** dinner when I got there.*
> *The car was **shaking** when I got on the highway.*

b. One syllable verbs ending in consonant/vowel/consonant

You should double the final consonant of a verb if it is one syllable and ends with these three letters: consonant, vowel, consonant.

cut	*cutting*
drop	*dropping*
hop	*hopping*
plan	*planning*
shop	*shopping*
sit	*sitting*
wrap	*wrapping*
tap	*tapping*

c. Two syllable verbs ending in consonant/vowel/consonant with a second syllable stress

If a verb is two syllables, ends in consonant/vowel/consonant, and the stress is on the second syllable, the last letter is also doubled.

forget	*forgetting*
begin	*beginning*
infer	*inferring*
refer	*referring*
prefer	*preferring*

d. Two syllable verbs ending in consonant/vowel/consonant with a first syllable stress

However, if the stress is on the first syllable, do not double the last letter; just add -*ing*.

happen	*happening*
open	*opening*
cover	*covering*
listen	*listening*
harden	*hardening*

B.

The present progressive tense is used when talking about things that are happening at the moment of speaking, as opposed to the present simple tense, which is used to talk about habitual activities.

> *You **are studying** English right now.*
> *It **is raining** right now.*

It can also describe activities that are true at the moment of speaking but continue.

> *We **are living** in Texas this year.*
> *She's **studying** at the community college for the next two months.*

Finally, the present progressive is sometimes used to talk about a future arrangement. (See Lesson 15.)

> I'm **having** lunch with Tom this afternoon.

C.
1. Use the subject and verb supplied to make a sentence in the present progressive.

    EXAMPLE: I/work

    I am working.

    1. I / study / mathematics at the university.
    2. He / sit / on the couch and / watch / TV.
    3. We / begin / to study more difficult verb tenses.
    4. They / make / dinner for me tonight.
    5. It / rain / right now.

2. Put the following verbs into the present progressive tense using the pronoun in parentheses. Use a negative as indicated.

    EXAMPLE: Where _____ ? (they, live)

    Where are they living?

    1. What _____? (they, do)
    2. Sorry, I can't talk now. _____ . (I, shop)
    3. When _____ ? (they, arrive)
    4. Be quiet. _____ to the radio. (she, listen)
    5. _____ a jacket. It must be warm outside. (he, wear, negative)

D. Answer Key
1. 1. I **am studying** mathematics at the university.
    2. He **is sitting** on the couch and **watching** TV.
    3. We **are beginning** to study more difficult verb tenses.
    4. They **are making** dinner for me tonight.
    5. It **is raining** right now.

2. 1. What **are they doing**?
    2. Sorry, I can't talk now. **I am shopping** (**I'm shopping**).
    3. When **are they arriving**?
    4. Be quiet. **She is listening** (**she's listening**) to the radio.
    5. **He is not wearing** (**he's not wearing**) a jacket. It must be warm outside.

Verbs in Action

5. Stative Verbs

A.

Some verbs are commonly not used in the progressive tenses. These verbs are called "stative verbs" because they usually describe states rather than activities. The most common stative verbs are:

know	*realize*	*suppose*
believe	*seem*	*belong*
understand	*remember*	*forget*
love	*hate*	*like*
need	*prefer*	*want*
smell	*see*	*hear*

Here are a few examples of sentences in which you would not use the progressive tense.

> *I know a lot about history. (not I am knowing)*
> *He believes in love at first sight.*
> *We prefer Mexican food.*
> *The dog belongs to me.*

These verbs are usually not progressive in the present, past or perfect tenses.

> *She has known him for months. (not She has been knowing)*
> *I've forgotten your name.*
> *We realized that we wouldn't make it in time.*
> *It seemed like rain.*

B.

There are situations in which you may use some of the verbs in a progressive tense, but with a change in meaning. Following are a few examples.

> *I see Jim right now. He's over there. (not I'm seeing Jim.)*
> *I am seeing Jim.* (meaning you are having a relationship with him.)
>
> *She understands a lot in English. (not She is understanding a lot in English.)*
> *She is understanding more and more every day.* (to show an increase in her ability)
>
> *Do you realize how long we have known each other? (not Are you realizing . . .)*
> *I am realizing that this isn't helping me.* (to show that the realization occurs over a period of time)

C.

1. Stative verb or present progressive? All of the following sentences are in the present progressive, but some contain stative verbs and should not be in the progressive tense. Determine whether the

2,000+ Essential English Verbs

sentence is correct or incorrect, and change those that are incorrect to the correct tense.

> EXAMPLE: *I am knowing my teacher very well.*
>
> *Incorrect. I **know** my teacher very well.*

1. *I am living in Chicago.*
2. *He is liking Japanese food very much.*
3. *The kids are needing new boots for winter.*
4. *He is owning a BMW.*
5. *Sally is traveling right now.*

2. Stative verb or present progressive? All of the following questions are in the present progressive, but some contain stative verbs and should not be in the progressive tense. Determine whether the question is correct or incorrect, and change those that are incorrect to the correct tense.

> EXAMPLE: *Are you knowing what time the train arrives?*
>
> *Incorrect. **Do** you **know** what time the train arrives?*

1. *Are you understanding the lesson we studied today?*
2. *What are you thinking of the music?*
3. *Is she liking Jim?*
4. *Are you working tonight?*
5. *What are you doing later?*

D. ANSWER KEY

1. 1. *Correct*
    2. *Incorrect; He **likes** Japanese food very much.*
    3. *Incorrect; The kids **need** new boots for winter.*
    4. *Incorrect; He **owns** a BMW.*
    5. *Correct*

2. 1. *Incorrect; **Do** you **understand** the lesson we studied today?*
    2. *Incorrect; What **do** you **think** of the music?*
    3. *Incorrect; **Does** she **like** Jim?*
    4. *Correct*
    5. *Correct*

Verbs in Action

6. Present Perfect

A.

The present perfect simple expresses events that start in the past and continue up to the present. It is formed using *have/has* + past participle. *"How long have you lived here?"* is an example of a question in the present perfect. The answer is *"I have lived here for six months."* You cannot use the past simple in this case, as it would indicate something that is finished. (See lesson 9 for further explanation.)

> *He/she/it*
> She **has visited** *several cities in the United States.*
> *"Has he ever been to Europe?" "Yes, he has."*
> *It hasn't rained here for three weeks.*

> *I/you/we/they*
> *"How long have you lived in New York?" "I have lived in New*
> *York for six years."*
> *You've played the guitar since you were young, haven't you?*
> *We have already eaten.*
> *They haven't arrived yet.*

Because this verb tense uses the past participle, it is important for you to learn this form for all verbs. The past participles of regular verbs end in *-ed*, just like the past tense. Irregular verbs, however, have various endings. Let's take a look at a partial list of past participles.

BASE FORM	PAST PARTICIPLE	BASE FORM	PAST PARTICIPLE
be	*been*	*make*	*made*
bring	*brought*	*run*	*run*
come	*come*	*say*	*said*
do	*done*	*sell*	*sold*
drive	*driven*	*sing*	*sung*
eat	*eaten*	*speak*	*spoken*
forget	*forgotten*	*steal*	*stolen*
get	*gotten*	*think*	*thought*
go	*gone*	*take*	*taken*
hide	*hidden*	*understand*	*understood*
know	*known*	*wear*	*worn*
leave	*left*	*write*	*written*

See the appendix for a more complete list, or refer to individual verb charts.

The contracted form of the subject and the auxiliary *have/has* is commonly used. It looks like this:

> *I've + p.p.*
> *I've been there before.*

> *He/she/it's + p.p.*
> *He's played at the Mercury Lounge.*

You/we/they've + p.p.
You've been *to Springfield, haven't you?*

Question formation is standard. Note that *have/has* is the auxiliary in this tense.

(Question Word) +	Auxiliary verb +	subject +	verb +	remaining words
How long	*has*	*she*	*studied*	*English?*
How many times	*have*	*you*	*been*	*there?*
	Have	*you*	*seen*	*David lately?*

The negative (*not*) is added to *have/has* and can be contracted (*haven't/hasn't*). *Never* can also be used in certain cases.

> *I* **haven't asked** *him yet.*
> **Hasn't** *she* **been** *there before?*
> *We* **have never seen** *her before.*

The auxiliary can be contracted with the subject, leaving *not* on its own, but this is not very colloquial and sounds old-fashioned in casual American conversation:

> *I've not been to France.*

However, with *never*, the auxiliary is often contracted with the subject:

> *They've never seen an Almodóvar film.*

B.

Now that you see how the present perfect is formed, let's look at some specific uses.

1. Using the present perfect with *how long/for/since*

We often use the present perfect to describe an activity that began at a specific point in the past and continues up to the present time. To ask the duration of or time frame for this occurrence, we use the question *how long*. For the response, you can express an amount of time using either *for* (to express the duration of an activity), or *since* (to express a specific starting point). Here are a few examples of questions and answers.

> *"How long have you lived in Chicago?" "I have lived in Chicago* **for** *2 years/***since** *2003."*
> *"How long has Helen studied English?" "She has studied English* **for** *10 years/***since** *she was a child."*
> *"How long have they worked there?" "They have worked there* **for** *several years/***since** *losing their jobs at the factory."*

Do not use the past tense to describe an activity that still continues, as in the above examples.

2. Using the present perfect with *ever* and *never*

The present perfect also allows us to discuss an activity that was completed in the past, but only if we are not concerned with the exact time of the occurrence. These questions often begin with "*Have you ever . . .*" or "*How many times have you . . . ?*"

> "*Have you ever traveled outside of the country?*" "*Yes, I have been to South America three times.*"
>
> "*Has John ever eaten sushi?*" "*No, he hasn't. There aren't any Japanese restaurants in his neighborhood.*" (He *has never eaten* sushi.)
>
> "*How many times have they come to visit you in Hawaii?*" "*They have never come here.*"
>
> "*What book can we buy Lola for her birthday? Has she read War and Peace?*" "*I don't think she has ever read anything by Tolstoy.*"

3. Using the present perfect with *yet/already*

Use *yet* for questions and negatives, and *already* for affirmative sentences.

> "*Have you finished dinner yet?*" "*No, not yet. Call me back in a few minutes.*"
> "*Have they gotten here yet?*" "*Yes, they have already arrived.*"
> "*Can I get a boarding pass?*" "*I'm sorry sir. You're plane has already taken off.*"

Note: The simple past tense can also be used with *yet* and *already* with little change in meaning.

4. Using the present perfect with *recently, lately, this week, this month, this year*

When the present perfect is used with *recently, this week*, etc., it emphasizes that the time period is not complete and the possibility that a certain activity may continue.

> It *has rained* a lot *this week*. (this week is not finished and it may rain more)
> We've *painted* the kitchen and the bathroom *today*. (today is not finished and we might paint more)
> John *has missed* a lot of work *lately*. (he might miss more)
> I *haven't heard* from them yet *this month*. (this month is not finished and you may hear from them)

Note: With words such as *recently, this week*, etc., the past and present perfect are often used interchangeably. Again, the present perfect emphasizes the unfinished nature of an activity. Look at how the past is used:

> We *painted* the bathroom and kitchen *today*. (We're not doing any more painting today!)

C.

1. Fill in the blank with the correct past participle.

> EXAMPLE: *Have you ever _____ snails? (eat)*
>
> *eaten*

1. *Have you _____ to her recently? (speak)*
2. *I'm sorry. I have _____ your name. (forget)*
3. *I would like to get in touch with Tom, but he hasn't _____ me with his address. (write)*
4. *Don't give Susan the keys. She has never _____ a car. (drive)*
5. *I can't believe he's not here. He has _____ about this event for two weeks. (know)*

2. Choose either *for* or *since* to correctly complete the following sentences.

> EXAMPLE: *I have worked here _____ two months*
>
> *for*

1. *I have lived in Chicago _____ three years.*
2. *He has worked in that restaurant _____ it opened.*
3. *We have played music together _____ we were children.*
4. *They have wanted to redo their kitchen _____ several years.*
5. *You have been a professor _____ many years, haven't you?*

D. Answer Key

1.
1. *spoken*
2. *forgotten*
3. *written*
4. *driven*
5. *known*

2.
1. *for*
2. *since*
3. *since*
4. *for*
5. *for*

7. Present Perfect Progressive

A.

The present perfect progressive can often be used interchangeably with the present perfect. It describes an activity that started in the past and continues up until the present. See part B for specific differences between the simple and progressive forms. To form this tense, use *have/has* + *been* + the main verb + *-ing*. Remember that *has* is used for the third person (*he, she, it*). Here are some examples.

> *"How long **have you been working** here?" "**I've been working** here for two months."*
> *"**Has she been enjoying** herself?" "Yes. It's a beautiful resort."*
> ***You've been seeing** him a lot lately.*
> ***They have been traveling** for six months now.*

For questions, invert the auxiliary (*have/has*) and the verb. For negatives, use *haven't* or *hasn't*.

> Question: *Where **has she been working** lately?*
> Negative: *She **hasn't been working**. She doesn't have a job.*

B.

In some cases, you will see a difference between the present perfect and the present perfect progressive. The progressive emphasizes the activity in progress:

> *"What **have you been doing**?"*
> *"John and I **have been painting** all afternoon." (emphasis on the activity)*
> *I've **been reading** that book all afternoon. (emphasis on the activity)*

The present perfect emphasizes the finished task.

> *"What **have** you **painted** so far?"*
> *"We**'ve painted** the living room and the dining room." (emphasis on what has been completed)*
> *I've **read** several books this summer. (emphasis on what has been completed)*

In other cases, we can use the present perfect progressive (like the present perfect simple) to explain how long something has been happening. This activity may still continue, or it may have recently stopped. You can use either the present perfect or the present perfect progressive without any change in meaning.

> *How long have you been studying English? (or How long have you studied English?)*
> *She has been working here **for** at least a year now/**since** last year." (or She's worked here . . .)*

Remember that *for* expresses the duration of an activity, and *since* refers to the specific starting point.

C.

1. Answer the questions using the present perfect progressive tense. Use *for* or *since* as needed, and use contractions.

> EXAMPLE: *How long have you been living in New York? (six years)*
>
> *I've been living in New York for six years.*

> 1. *How long has he been working in the library? (1979)*
> 2. *How long have we been waiting for him? (20 minutes)*
> 3. *How long has she been traveling? (six months)*
> 4. *How long have they been thinking about coming to visit? (we moved here)*
> 5. *How long has it been raining? (this morning)*

2. Change the following sentences to the progressive tense.

> EXAMPLE: *I've lived there for two years.*
>
> *I've been living there for two years.*

> 1. *We've had a lot of problems recently.*
> 2. *They've visited us a lot lately.*
> 3. *He's finished his project at school.*
> 4. *I haven't done the work.*
> 5. *It hasn't snowed very much recently.*

D. ANSWER KEY

1. 1. *He's been working in the library **since** 1979.*
   2. *We've been waiting for him **for** 20 minutes.*
   3. *She's been traveling **for** six months.*
   4. *They've been thinking about coming to visit **since** we moved here.*
   5. *It's been raining **since** this morning.*

2. 1. *We**'ve been having** a lot of problems recently.*
   2. *They**'ve been visiting** us a lot lately.*
   3. *He**'s been finishing** his project at school.*
   4. *I **haven't been doing** the work.*
   5. *It **hasn't been snowing** very much recently.*

8. Past Simple

A.

The past simple tense is used to describe an activity that happened at a specific time in the past and has been completed. For this reason, we often use time words that are related to the past: *ago* (*one year ago, one month ago, five minutes ago*), *last* (*last year, last night, last week*), *yesterday,* and so on. There are both regular and irregular past tense verbs. Regular past tense verbs are formed by adding an *-ed* to the base form. There are many irregular past tense verbs that you will have to learn.

Look at the following examples of regular past tense verbs.

> I **looked** at the movie schedule and **picked** one that I like.
> He **worked** last week but he's on vacation this week.
> We **talked** on the telephone but we **didn't decide** anything.
> They **helped** me and I **thanked** them.

Note that for the past tense, there is no change for third person (*he, she, it*). This also applies to negatives and questions.

Now let's look at irregular verbs in the past tense. Here is a short list of them with all three forms (base form, simple past, past participle). To see a complete list, look in the appendix.

BASE FORM	SIMPLE PAST	PAST PARTICIPLE
bring	brought	brought
choose	chose	chosen
do	did	done
drive	drove	driven
eat	ate	eaten
give	gave	given
go	went	gone
leave	left	left
see	saw	seen
sell	sold	sold
speak	spoke	spoken
take	took	taken
think	thought	thought
understand	understood	understood

Here are a few examples of sentences using the irregular past tense verbs.

> I **spoke** to him last Friday.
> He **chose** to go to the community college in the neighborhood.
> We **went** to California two weeks ago.

B.

For negatives, add *didn't* before the base form of the verb. (Remember that as the auxiliary (*didn't*) shows the past tense the main verb will be in the base form.) Here are some examples of affirmative and negative sentences.

Affirmative: I **wanted** to go.
Negative: I **didn't want** to go.

Affirmative: He **asked** me to come.
Negative: He **didn't ask** me to come.

Affirmative: He **studied** a lot yesterday.
Negative: He **didn't study** a lot yesterday.

Also use *did* or *didn't* for forming questions. You must invert the subject and the verb. Remember the word order in questions.

(Question word) + auxiliary verb + subject + main verb + remaining words

"What **did** you **do** last night?" "I watched a movie on TV."
"**Did** you **listen** to the radio this morning?" "Yes, but I didn't hear anything interesting."
"When **did** she **see** him?" "She saw him this morning."
"How **did** they **get** here?" "They took the bus."

C.

1. Complete each sentence with the correct form of the verb in the past tense.

   EXAMPLE: We _____ to the mountains last week. (go)

   went

   1. They _____ the train to Chicago. (take)
   2. We _____ a note for them. (leave)
   3. She _____ about the question. (think)
   4. You _____ the movie, didn't you? (like)
   5. I _____ the article well. (understand)

2. The following sentences are in the past tense. Make affirmative sentences negative, and negative sentences affirmative.

   EXAMPLE: He went to the mountains.

   He didn't go to the mountains.

   1. We enjoyed the play last night.
   2. She ate too much.
   3. He chose a tie to go with his suit.
   4. They didn't bring a bottle of wine.
   5. She didn't see him in concert.

D. ANSWER KEY

1. 1. *took*
2. *left*
3. *thought*
4. *liked*
5. *understood*

2. 1. *We didn't enjoy the play last night.*
2. *She didn't eat too much.*
3. *He didn't choose a tie to go with his suit.*
4. *They brought a bottle of wine.*
5. *She saw him in concert.*

9. Present Perfect or Past Simple?

A.

Sometimes you may be uncertain whether to use the present perfect tense or the past simple tense. Let's look at some differences between the tenses.

1. Finished action vs. no specific time

It is very important to remember that the past simple tense always expresses a finished action in the past, no matter whether it happened five minutes ago, five months ago, or five years ago. Use the present perfect when you refer to an experience when no specific time is mentioned.

> Present Perfect: *"**Have you ever been** to San Francisco?" "Yes, I **have been** to San Francisco."* (no specific time reference)
> Past tense: *"When **did you go** to San Francisco?" "I **went** last year."* (a specific past time referred to)

> Present Perfect: *"**Have you eaten** at the new restaurant?" "Yes, I **have**."* (no specific time reference)
> Past tense: *"When **did you eat** there?" "I **ate** there last week."* (a specific time in the past referred to)

2. How long?

Also, remember that the present perfect tense (simple or progressive) talks about how long something has been happening. This activity is still going on, or has just recently finished. Therefore, it is different from the past simple which always expresses a finished activity. Compare the following sentences.

> Present Perfect: *I **have worked** at a bank for five years.* (and you still work there)
> Past simple: *I **worked** at a bank for five years.* (but you don't work there anymore)

> Present Perfect: *I **have lived** in Russia for three years.* (and you still live there)
> Past simple: *I **lived** in Russia before I came to the U.S.* (but you don't live there anymore)

3. Unfinished time

Often, if we want to emphasize that a period of time is not finished (such as *this morning, this week, this year*), we will use the present perfect instead of the past.

> Present perfect: *"How many times **have you been** to the gym this week?"* (the week is not finished)
> Past tense: *"How many times **did you go** to the gym last week?"* (the week is finished)

(See lesson 6 for further explanation.)

B.

1. Complete the sentences below with the correct form of the verb: past simple or present perfect. Use a negative as indicated.

> EXAMPLE: *She _____ here for three years. (live)*
>
> *has lived*

1. *We _____ to the movies yesterday. (go)*
2. *Today is their anniversary; they _____ married for 10 years. (be)*
3. *He _____ since October. (work, negative)*
4. *You _____ the key, didn't you? (take)*
5. *I _____ three cups of coffee so far today. (have)*

2. Complete the sentences below with the correct auxiliary verb: *haven't/hasn't/didn't* or *have/has/did*. Use the clue in parentheses.

> EXAMPLE: *She _____ been there before.* (present perfect, negative)
>
> *hasn't*

1. *_____ you ever eaten snails?* (present perfect)
2. *She _____ ask him about the money yesterday.* (past simple, negative)
3. *How long _____ they lived in the country?* (present perfect)
4. *_____ they come to the lecture?* (past simple)
5. *When _____ you talk to her last?* (past simple)

C. ANSWER KEY

1. 1. *went*
2. *have been*
3. *hasn't worked*
4. *took*
5. *have had*

2. 1. *Have*
2. *didn't*
3. *have*
4. *Did*
5. *did*

10. Past Progressive

A.

We use the past progressive tense when we talk about an activity that was in progress in the past. You will use the verb *to be* in the past (*was/were*) as an auxiliary, along with the *-ing* form of the main verb. Sentences such as *"The children were playing"* and *"It was raining"* are in the past progressive. They are activities that did not occur in one moment and, therefore, are expressed using the past progressive tense. Let's look at a few more examples.

> *I*
> *I **was living** in San Salvador before I moved to New York.*
>
> *He/she/it*
> *Carolyn **was living** in Washington, D.C., from 1990 to 1993.*
> *It **was raining** when I left work yesterday.*
>
> *We/you/they*
> *We **were watching** TV when the lights went out.*
> *You **were working** yesterday, weren't you?*

For questions, invert the subject + auxiliary verb. (See lessons 2, 3, and 4.)

> *What **were you doing** here last night?*
> *Why **was he making** a phone call from the street when he has a*
>   *cell phone?*
> ***Were you expecting** me to wait for you?*

For negatives, add *not* to the auxiliary verb. Remember how to form *to be* in the past tense.

> *I wasn't*
> *I **wasn't listening**, but she was.*
>
> *He/she/it wasn't*
> *It **wasn't working** correctly.*
> *He **wasn't helping** and so I told him to go home.*
>
> *You/we/they weren't*
> *We **weren't living** in Chicago in 1995.*
> *They **weren't drinking** last night.*

B.

The past progressive can be used in several ways. Read the following paragraph, and notice the activities that were in progress when the narrator arrived at the park.

> *When I got to the park so many things **were happening**. The sun*
> ***was shining**, and several groups of children **were playing***
> *baseball. A man **was riding** his bicycle and his friend **was***

*jogging beside him. A woman and her young son **were having** a picnic.*

We also use the past progressive to find out what was happening around a specific time in the past. Questions and/or answers often refer to that specific time and the time surrounding it (*at or around 8:00, at or around 12:30, etc.*)

> *"What were you doing last night at 10:00?" "I was watching TV."*

Also, you will often see the past progressive and the past simple used together. In this case, an activity in progress (past progressive) is interrupted by an activity that happens at a specific moment (past simple).

> *We **were having** dinner last night when the phone **rang.***
> *The lights **went out** while the students **were taking** a test.*
> *While I **was driving** home last night, it **began** to rain.*

Finally, two activities may be in progress at the same time.

> *The kids **were playing** while their parents **were preparing** the picnic.*

For spelling rules with *-ing*, see lesson 4.

C.

1. **Complete the following sentences with the verb in the past progressive tense.**

   > EXAMPLE: *He _____ on the phone. (talk)*
   >
   > *was talking*
   >
   > 1. *We _____ in the park. (walk)*
   > 2. *She _____ him with his homework. (help)*
   > 3. *It _____ last night. (rain)*
   > 4. *They _____ to music. (listen)*
   > 5. *You _____ me a question. (ask)*

2. **Form a question in the past progressive using the clues given.**

   > EXAMPLE: *where/you/go*
   >
   > *Where were you going?*
   >
   > 1. *What/they/do?*
   > 2. *Where/she/live?*
   > 3. *Why/he/sing?*
   > 4. *How/you/travel?*
   > 5. *When/the movie/start?*

D. ANSWER KEY

1. 1. *were walking*
    2. *was helping*
    3. *was raining*
    4. *were listening*
    5. *were asking*

2. 1. *What were they doing?*
    2. *Where was she living?*
    3. *Why was he singing?*
    4. *How were you traveling?*
    5. *When was the movie starting?*

11. Past Perfect and Past Perfect Progressive

A.

1. Past perfect formation

To form the past perfect, you will use *had* + the past participle. Here are a few examples.

> I **had lived** in France for 10 years before I came to the United States.
> He **had never tried** mussels before he went to Belgium.
> When they got to the airport, the plane **had already left**.

In this tense, *had* is the auxiliary verb. To form a question, invert the subject and verb.

> What **had he done** to make them so angry?
> **Had you ever seen** the man before?

To form a negative, add *not* to the auxiliary. The contracted form is *hadn't*.

> He **hadn't noticed** the man sitting in the chair.
> We **hadn't been** there more than a minute when it started to rain.

Affirmative verbs can also be contracted.

> I'd
> He/she/it'd
> We/you/they'd
> **She'd heard** a lot about him before they met.

2. Past perfect progressive formation

Form the past perfect progressive using *had been* + verb + *-ing*.

> Earl **had been buying** lottery tickets for 17 years when he bought a winning ticket.
> We **had been studying** for hours when we decided to take a break.

B.

1. Order of events

We use past perfect to show the order in which things happened in the past. It often occurs in a sentence along with the past tense. An action using past perfect happened before an action in the simple past. The following sentences are examples.

> Before I met him, I **had heard** a lot about him.
> When I got to work, I found out that I **had missed** an important meeting.
> When I spoke to Hal, I found out that his wife **had had** a baby.

In contrast, if the past perfect is not used, the order of events is different. Compare the following sentences.

> *When I arrived at the party, my friend **had** already **left**.* (My friend had left *before* I arrived.)
> *When I arrived at the party, my friend **left**.* (My friend left *after* I got to the party.)

2. How long?

Both the past perfect and the past perfect progressive can be used to show how long an event or action was occurring in the past before something else occurred.

> *We **had lived** in France for seven years before moving to Spain.*
> *The cat **had been sleeping** for hours when I got home.*
> *I **had been working** for hours and was exhausted when I got home.*

The past perfect progressive can also be used to describe a general progressive occurrence in the past. The event or action is now completed, but at one point it was incomplete and continuous.

> *We **had been thinking** about moving to Paris.*
> *They **had been hoping** for a little boy.*

3. Past unreal conditionals

Both the past perfect and the past perfect progressive are used in the past unreal conditionals.

> *If she **had heard** the phone, she would've answered it.*
> *If they **had been living** here at the time, they would've come to the opening.*

C.

1. Use the clues given below to form a sentence in the past perfect.

> EXAMPLE: *The plane/already/left*
>
> *The plane had already left.*

1. *She/never/be/to London before*
2. *They/not/eat/yet*
3. *We/live/there for two months*
4. *I/just/wake up*
5. *He/already/leave*

2. Use either the past simple or the past perfect in the sentences below.

> EXAMPLE: *They hadn't begun to eat yet when we _____ (get) to the restaurant.*
>
> *got*
>
> 1. *She had lived there for two months before she _____ (find) a job.*
> 2. *They _____ (already/leave) when we got there.*
> 3. *Cynthia _____ (never/see) him before she met him last night.*
> 4. *We hadn't been to a musical before we _____ (see) "The Producers" last night.*
> 5. *They _____ (already/prepare) the dinner by the time we arrived.*

D. ANSWER KEY

1. 1. *She had never been to London before.*
   2. *They had not eaten yet.*
   3. *We had lived there for two months.*
   4. *I had just woken up.*
   5. *He had already left.*

2. 1. *found*
   2. *had already left*
   3. *had never seen*
   4. *saw*
   5. *had already prepared*

12. Using the Modal *Will*

To express a spontaneous decision, an offer, a promise or a prediction in the future, use *will*. For example, "*I'll help you with that,*" is an offer and "*I'll come with you,*" is a spontaneous decision. (For plans or arrangements in the future, use *be going to* or the present progressive.)

A contraction can be used for all forms.

I will	*I'll*
He/she/it will	*He/she/it'll*
You/we/they will	*You/we/they'll*

Will is a modal verb. That means that the verb that follows *will* is always in the base form. Also, there is no added *-s* for the third person *he, she,* and *it.* (See lesson 33.)

The negative of *will* is *will not* or *won't.*

> "*You **won't** believe what happened!*" "*Really? Tell me about it.*"

For a question, invert the subject and the auxiliary *will*.

> ***Will you** come with us?*
> *What **will you** do if you don't get the job?*

B.

Here are some more specific uses of *will*.

1. **Making predictions**
   > "*Do you think that Sophia **will come**?*" "*Yes. I'm sure she**'ll come**.*"
   > *There's a possibility that it **will be** cold this weekend. Take a sweater.*

2. **Making offers**
   > *You're not feeling well. I**'ll make** dinner tonight.*
   > "*The telephone is ringing.*" "*I**'ll get** it.*"

3. **Making requests**
   > "*Will you **help** me?*" "*Sure. No problem.*"
   > "*Will you **open** the door, please?*" "*Of course.*"

4. **Refusing**
   > *I hate spinach. I **won't eat** it!*

5. **Making promises, threats or warnings**
   > "*You can't watch TV now. You have homework to do.*" "*I promise I**'ll do** my homework after the show!*"
   > *If you don't turn in that essay, I**'ll fail** you.*

6. **Expressing Conditions** (see lesson 17)
   > *If we are late, we **won't be** able to see the movie.*
   > *If you come for dinner, I**'ll make** your favorite dessert .*

C.

1. *Will* has many uses. There are six described in the lesson above. Match each sentence below to one of the six uses above.

> EXAMPLE: *I'll get the door for you.*
>
> 2. Making offers.

> 1. *If you don't give me the money, I'll have to talk to your boss.*
> 2. *Will you help me with the dinner?*
> 3. *What do you think he will do?*
> 4. *I'll call him for you.*
> 5. *If you talk to him, will you ask him to call me?*

2. Make the following sentences affirmative if they are negative, or negative if they are affirmative.

> EXAMPLE: *We won't be there.*
>
> *We will be there.*

> 1. *I think he'll go.*
> 2. *I'm sure she'll help me with my problem.*
> 3. *They won't find out.*
> 4. *It won't rain tomorrow.*
> 5. *They'll be there early.*

D. ANSWER KEY

1. 1. *5. Making threats/6. Expressing conditions*
   2. *3. Making requests*
   3. *1. Making predictions*
   4. *2. Making offers*
   5. *3. Making requests/6. Expressing conditions*

2. 1. *I think he **won't go**.*
   2. *I'm sure she **won't help** me with my problem.*
   3. *They'**ll find out**.*
   4. *It **will rain** tomorrow.*
   5. *They **won't be** there early.*

13. Future Progressive

A.

The future progressive tense allows us to talk about an activity that will be in progress at a certain time in the future. It is, like all progressive tenses, formed with the verb *to be* and the *-ing* form of the main verb. With *will* it will look like this: *will be* + main verb + *-ing*.

Let's see how it looks.

> *"What **will you be doing** tomorrow night at 8:00?"*
> *"I**'ll be working**. I have to work late tomorrow night."*

The negative is formed by adding *not* to *will*. To form a question invert the subject and the auxiliary *will*.

> *"What **will you be doing** in 10 years?"*
> *"I **won't be living** in this tiny apartment!"*

Remember that *will* is a modal verb and follows all of the rules for modals (see lesson 31). The verb following *will* is always in the base form. Also, there is no added *-s* for the third person *he, she,* and *it*.

B.

1. Answer the following questions according to your own thoughts about your life in the future. Use complete sentences.
   1. *Where will you be living in ten years?*
   2. *Where will you be working next year?*
   3. *What time will you be arriving home tonight?*
   4. *What will you be doing tomorrow night at 6:00?*
   5. *What will you be doing at this time next year?*

2. Make each of the following sentences negative.
   1. *I'll be studying English next year.*
   2. *He'll be arriving at 7:00.*
   3. *We'll be working.*
   4. *They'll be traveling.*
   5. *It'll be raining all night.*

C. ANSWER KEY

1. *1–5 Answers will vary*

2. 1. *I won't be studying English next year.*
   2. *He won't be arriving at 7:00.*
   3. *We won't be working.*
   4. *They won't be traveling.*
   5. *It won't be raining all night.*

Verbs in Action

14. Future Perfect and Future Perfect Progressive

A.

The future perfect tense allows us to talk about something that will be completed by or before a certain time in the future. It is formed by using *will have* + past participle. Remember that modal verbs (like *will*) are always followed by the base form of the verb—in this case, *have*.

> Call back after lunchtime. We **will have finished** by then.
> She **will have finished** her degree by the year 2008.

To form a negative, add *not* to the auxiliary verb (*will*) and form questions by inverting the subject and the auxiliary verb.

> Don't count on getting the final draft tomorrow. She **won't have finished** by then.
> I'll come at 2:00. **Will you have gotten** the instructions by then?

B.

We can also use a progressive form in the perfect. Like all progressives, it is formed by using the verb *to be* and the *-ing* form of the main verb. It will look like this: *will have been* + verb + *-ing*. Remember that the verb *to be* will be in the past participle form, *been*.

> If she works until midnight, she **will have been working** on that project for twelve hours.
> Can you believe that by next month we **will have been living** in our house for ten years?

C.

1. Complete the sentence with the correct form of the verb. The verb form will depend on whether the tense is future perfect or future perfect progressive.

> EXAMPLE: *She will have _____ here two years. (work)*
>
> *worked* (future perfect)

1. *They will have _____ two movies by 10:00. (watch)*
2. *He will have been _____ for one year in May. (travel)*
3. *You will have _____ me for three years at the end of this semester. (know)*
4. *We will have been _____ for 10 hours at 8:00. (work)*
5. *She will have _____ hundreds of books before she retires. (write)*

2. Each of the following sentences has a mistake. Find it and correct it.

> EXAMPLE: *She will has studied there two months.*
>
> *She will **have** studied there two months.*
>
> 1. *What she will have done by the end of the day?*
> 2. *We will have work for a long time.*
> 3. *It's too late. The plane will have leave by the time we get there.*
> 4. *You will had finished by 2:00, won't you?*
> 5. *She will have had dinner?*

D. ANSWER KEY

1. 1. *watched*
2. *traveling*
3. *known*
4. *working*
5. *written*

2. 1. *What **will she** have done by the end of the day?* (reverse the subject and auxiliary verb)
2. *We will have **worked** for a long time.* (use the past participle)
3. *It's too late. The plane will have **left** by the time we get there.* (past participle is required)
4. *You will **have** finished by 2:00, won't you?* (always use the base form after a modal)
5. ***Will she** have had dinner?* (invert the subject and auxiliary verb in questions)

Verbs in Action

15. Other Future Tenses

A.

In the last three lessons, we have looked at how to use the verb *will*. Now let's look at some other ways to express the future. Specifically, how can we talk about future arrangements and plans? We cannot use *will*, but there are several other ways of doing so.

1. Future with *to be going to*

The *going to* future is one way to talk about plans or decisions that you have made before the moment of speaking. To form the *going to* future you will use *to be* (am/is/are) + *going to* + main verb (base form). Here are a few examples.

> **I'm going to invite** the Garcias over for dinner.
> **She's going to help** me on the project.
> **We're going to build** a new house near the river.
> **They're going to call** him about the job tomorrow.

Add *not* to form a negative.

> A: "I'm **not going to** come with you."
> B: "Why not? I thought you liked parties."
> A: "Charlie **isn't going to** be there and so I'd rather not go."

To form questions, invert the subject and the auxiliary verb.

> What **are you going to do** tonight?

You will also see that *going to* is used for predictions, when there is evidence that something is going to happen.

> The sky is really dark. It's **going to rain**.
> Her acting was excellent. She's **going to win** an Oscar.

2. Present progressive for future

We can also use the present progressive for the future (see lesson 4 for formation). It is very similar to *going to* in use, but focuses more on specific arrangements that we have made.

> Harold and Maude **are taking** a cruise this summer. We should do
>   that next year.
> I'm **having** lunch with Carolyn tomorrow. Do you want to join us?
> Helen **is baby-sitting** from 6:00 to 8:00 tomorrow and then she's
>   **coming over** to watch a movie.

However, the difference is slight—present progressive and *going to* futures can often be interchanged.

> She's **baby-sitting** tomorrow. or   She's **going to baby-sit**
>   tomorrow.
>
> She's **coming over** to watch   or   She's **going to come**
>   a movie.   **over** to watch a movie.

3. Present simple for future

Finally, the present simple can also be used to indicate a future event. Usually it refers to a fixed time or schedule in the future. Look at the following sentences.

> *The train **leaves** at 3:54 this afternoon.*
> *The gym **opens** at 7:00 tomorrow morning.*
> *The movie **begins** early; we should go.*

B.

1. Complete the future plans below by using *be going to*, present progressive or present simple as indicated.

> EXAMPLE: *She/work/on Monday* (present progressive)
>
> *She is working on Monday.*

> 1. *He/have dinner with Jim/tomorrow (be going to)*
> 2. *We/play tennis/at the gym (present progressive)*
> 3. *They/be/at the party on Saturday (be going to)*
> 4. *She/have/a birthday party this weekend (present progressive)*
> 5. *The movie/start/at 7:40 (present simple)*

2. There is a mistake in each sentence below. Find the mistake and correct it.

> 1. *You are taking a vacation this summer?*
> 2. *She will have a party next week.*
> 3. *The train don't leave until 5:00.*
> 4. *We not going to come with you.*
> 5. *The store open at 10:00.*

D. ANSWER KEY

1.
1. *He is going to have dinner with Jim tomorrow.*
2. *We are playing tennis at the gym.*
3. *They are going to be at the party on Saturday.*
4. *She is having a birthday party this weekend.*
5. *The movie starts at 7:40.*

2.
1. ***Are you** taking a vacation this summer?* (invert the subject and auxiliary verb in questions)
2. *She **is having/is going to have** a party next week.* (the present progressive and *to be + going to* are both preferable to *will* for plans or arrangements)
3. *The train **doesn't** leave until 5:00.* (don't forget the third person form)
4. *We **are** not going to come with you.* (you must have the verb *to be +going to*)
5. *The store **opens** at 10:00.* (don't forget the third person -s)

16. Passive Voice: Form

A.

In English, we contrast two voices: the active and the passive. In the active voice, the subject of the sentence (the agent) is active or causes the action of the sentence. In the passive voice, the object of the active sentence becomes the subject.

> Active sentence: Shakespeare **wrote** Hamlet.
> Passive sentence: Hamlet **was written** by Shakespeare.

The "*by*" phrase *(by Shakespeare)* tells who or what did the action, and is often unnecessary.

Let's look at how to form the passive, and in the next lesson we'll look at when this tense is used.

The passive tense will always be formed using the verb *to be* (in any tense) + past participle. The most common are listed here.

> Present simple passive
> *I **am required** to wear a uniform at work.*
>
> Present progressive passive
> *My watch **is being fixed** at the shop down the street.*
>
> Present perfect passive
> *His TV **has been fixed** several times, but it still doesn't work.*
>
> Past simple passive
> *Three men **were arrested** in connection to the robbery.*
>
> Past progressive passive
> *I felt like I **was being followed**.*
>
> Past perfect passive
> *By the time we arrived, the work **had been done**.*
>
> Future simple passive
> *Your shirt **will be cleaned** by Tuesday.*
>
> Future perfect passive
> *"Is your group finished preparing the presentation?" "Not quite, but I'm sure that most of the work **will have been finished** by the end of the day."*
>
> Passive infinitive
> *I don't want **to be held** responsible for this mistake.*
>
> Passive gerund
> *He doesn't enjoy **being given** so much responsibility at work.*
> *Their house, built in a valley, was in danger of **being hit** by a tornado.*

Modals – Present passive
*This problem **can be fixed.***
*Smoking **should be banned** in bars and restaurants.*

Modals – Past passive
*It **should have been banned** years ago.*

B.

It is very common in spoken English to hear the passive formed with the verb *get* in place of *be*. Look at the following constructions:

> *I **got stung** by a bee.*
> *He **got called** for jury duty.*
> *Your application **will get rejected** if you haven't filled in all the*
> *correct information.*

This is not normally used in formal written English, but you will hear this in everyday conversation. See the appendix for a list of the most common verbs used with the auxiliary *get.*

C.

1. Change the following sentences from active voice to passive voice. Do not use a "*by*" phrase if it is unnecessary.

    > EXAMPLE: *He broke the window.*
    >
    > *The window was broken.*

    1. *The driver drove her to the station.*
    2. *Someone made his shoes in China.*
    3. *The mayor has to raise taxes.*
    4. *The school should have given the test on Tuesday.*
    5. *They are fixing my watch.*

2. Use *should* and one of the verbs below to complete the following passive sentences.

    > EXAMPLE: *The kids _____ at 2:00.*
    >
    > *The kids **should be picked up** at 2:00.*

    pick up   take   handle   send   recycle   finish

    1. *Resumes _____ to the personnel department.*
    2. *The medicine _____ three times a day with meals.*
    3. *The work _____ by this Friday.*
    4. *Paper, glass, and metal _____.*
    5. *This package is fragile. It _____ with care.*

Verbs in Action

D. ANSWER KEY

1. 1. *She was driven to the station.*

2. *His shoes were made in China.*

3. *Taxes have to be raised.*

4. *The test should have been given on Tuesday.*

5. *My watch is being fixed.*

2. 1. *should be sent*

2. *should be taken*

3. *should be finished*

4. *should be recycled*

5. *should be handled*

17. Passive Voice: Usage

A.

Sentences in the active and the passive voice can have similar meanings. The passive voice, however, is used when emphasis is placed on the object of the active sentence, rather than on the subject (the agent). The passive is commonly used in the situations listed below:

1. The agent is unknown or not important

*Our house **was built** in the 1920s.*   (We don't know who built it.)

2. The agent is obvious

*The man **was arrested**.*   (It's obvious that the police arrested the man. It's not necessary to say *by the police*.)

*His car **was made** in Germany.*   (It's clear that the employees of the factory made his car. We don't need mention them.)

3. To take responsibility away from what or who did the action

*Your documents **have been misplaced**.*   (Even if we know who misplaced the documents, we avoid blaming them by using the passive voice.)

B.

You can mention the agent in a passive sentence by using a *"by" phrase*. A *"by"* phrase is commonly used when new information is introduced or you specifically want to highlight the agent of the passive sentence.

*The book we read in class was written **by a famous politician**.*
*The building was designed **by the architect Frank Gehry**.*

C.

1. Look at the sentences below and identify whether they are passive or active.

EXAMPLE: *My watch was made in Switzerland.*

passive

1. *He is woken up every day by the bells.*
2. *Your call is being transferred.*
3. *They will work on it tomorrow.*
4. *The wallet was left on the table.*
5. *You have been to so many places.*

2. Use a verb in the passive voice (past tense) to complete the sentences below.

> EXAMPLE: *The short story _____ by a well-known author.*
>
> *was translated*
>
> translate   find   write   steal   arrest   ask

1. *The man _____ when the police found out that he was driving under the influence.*
2. *The stolen cars _____ in a nearby town.*
3. *My wallet _____ while I was riding the bus yesterday.*
4. *After causing a disturbance at the concert, the kids _____ to leave.*
5. *My favorite novel _____ by J. D. Salinger.*

D. ANSWER KEY

1.
1. *passive*
2. *passive*
3. *active*
4. *passive*
5. *active*

2.
1. *was arrested*
2. *were found*
3. *was stolen*
4. *were asked*
5. *was written*

18. Real Conditional: Present and Future

A.
1. Zero conditional

CONDITION	RESULT
If + present simple,	*(then)* present simple

*If you **heat** water, it **boils**.*
*If she **eats** seafood, she **gets** sick.*

Note that *if* can be replaced by *when* or *whenever*.

2. First conditional

CONDITION	RESULT
If + present simple,	*will* + base form of the verb

If you make dinner, I will come.
If you do that again, she'll be very angry.

Questions are formed by inverting the subject and the auxiliary verb.

What will you do if you can't find your keys?
How do you manage if you don't earn enough money?

You can put a negative (*not*) in the condition or the result clause, or both.

*If my husband **doesn't** work in the summer, he usually spends hours in the garden.*
*If I **can't** find my keys, I'll call the locksmith.*
*If I help him, then he **won't** need Cindy's help.*

B.
Now let's look at how these conditionals are used.

1. Zero conditional
The zero conditional sets up a possible condition and a definite result.

*If she **eats** seafood, she **gets** sick.*

That is, every time she eats seafood (a possible occurrence), she gets sick (the definite result).

2. First conditional
The first conditional sets up a possible condition and a probable result.

If it rains tomorrow, we won't go to the beach.

It might rain tomorrow (a possible occurrence) and in that case, we will not go to the beach (the probable result).

Notes:
a. *Will* is a modal verb, but almost any other modal or modal-like verb can be used in a first conditional sentence (*can, must, should, have to*, etc.)

*If you **come** early on Tuesday, you **can** help me set up the tables and chairs.*

*If Natalie **stays** late at school, she **should** call home to let her parents know.*

*If he **fails** the test, he **has to** sign up for summer school.*

b. *Will* can be replaced by another future tense such as *going to*.

*If he eats all of that food, he**'s going to get** sick.*

c. In all conditional sentences, the two clauses (condition and result) can be inverted. In written English, you don't need to use a comma.

*You **can help** me set up the tables and chairs **if** you **come** early on Tuesday.*

C.

1. Complete the sentences with the correct form of the verb. Use negative as indicated (neg.).

1. *If you _____ (stay) at that hotel, you will regret it.*
2. *If he _____(have, neg.) enough money, I will lend him some.*
3. *If they _____ (try), I'm sure they can do it.*
4. *He'll be late if he (leave, neg.) _____ right now.*
5. *If they _____ (talk, neg.) about it, they will never solve their problems.*

2. Match the following conditions to their logical result.

1. *If you stay in the sun too long,*   a. *you should see a doctor.*
2. *When he works so much,*   b. *she has trouble waking up.*
3. *If they don't buy it now,*   c. *you will get burned.*
4. *If she doesn't drink coffee,*   d. *he doesn't have time for anything else.*

5. *If you get sick,*   e. *the prices will go up.*

D. ANSWER KEY

1. 1. *stay*
    2. *doesn't have*
    3. *try*
    4. *doesn't leave*
    5. *don't talk*

2. 1. *c.*
    2. *d.*
    3. *e.*
    4. *b.*
    5. *a.*

19. Unreal Conditional: Present and Future

A.
Second Conditional

CONDITION	RESULT
If + past tense	*would/could* + base form of the verb

*If we **won** the lottery, we **could travel** around the world.*
*If I **saw** a ghost, I **would scream**!*

Questions invert the subject and the auxiliary verb (*would/could*) in the result clause.

*What **would you** do if you found a wallet on the street?*

And you can use a negative in the condition or the result clause.

*If I **didn't call** my parents every weekend, they would be upset.*
*If he invited me to his party, I **wouldn't go**.*

Note that for all conditional sentences, the two clauses (condition and result) can be inverted. If you put the result before the condition, you don't need to use a comma in written English.

I would be upset if you didn't call me.

The verb *to be* in the condition clause is often changed to *were* for all forms (*I, you, he, she, it, you, we,* and *they*).

*If I **were** you, I wouldn't do it.*
*If she **were** older, she could go into the bar.*

Contractions with *would* are used in the result clause.

I'd

He/she/it'd

We/you/they'd

I'd come if she called.
We'd go if they asked.

B.
Now let's look at how we use the second conditional.

The second conditional expresses an unreal condition, and an imagined result. The condition is unreal because it is improbable or impossible.

*If Patrick **earned** enough money this year, he **would buy** a car.*

The condition is improbable because we know that it is unlikely that Patrick will earn enough money.

*If I **were** an animal, I **would be** a bird.*

Here the condition is impossible because the speaker is not an animal. The second conditional also is useful when giving advice.

> If I **were** you, I **would take** the job.
> I **wouldn't buy** the house if I **were** them.

C.

1. Complete the sentences with the correct form of the verb. Use past tense for unreal conditionals (lesson 19) and *will* for real conditionals (lesson 18). Use the negative as indicated (neg.).

    EXAMPLE: *If I _____ you, I would go.*

    were

    1. *If he _____ (have) enough time, he would take a night class.*
    2. *If it _____ (rain) tomorrow, we're not going to the beach.*
    3. *If my little sister _____ (bother, neg.) me so much, I wouldn't mind sharing a room with her.*
    4. *If she _____ (let) you borrow her car, we can go to Philadelphia tomorrow.*
    5. *If they _____ (be) smarter, they would buy instead of renting.*

2. In the following unreal conditionals, either the condition or the result is incomplete. Use either the **past tense** or **would/could + base form** to complete each sentence. Use negative as indicated.
    1. *We _____ (take) the train if we had enough time.*
    2. *If she were older, she _____ (go) on her own.*
    3. *My brother would fix your car if he _____ (be, neg.) on vacation.*
    4. *If this house _____ (have) a backyard, it would be perfect.*
    5. *If you _____ (behave, neg.) so badly, our class would be much better.*

D. ANSWER KEY

1. 1. *had*
    2. *rains*
    3. *didn't bother*
    4. *lets*
    5. *were*

2. 1. *would take*
    2. *would go*
    3. *weren't*
    4. *had*
    5. *didn't behave*

20. Unreal Conditional: Past; Mixed Conditionals

A.

The unreal past conditional is formed by using the past perfect and *would* + the present perfect. It looks like this:

CONDITION	RESULT
If + past perfect,	*would/could* + *have* + past participle (*would* + present perfect)

> If Tim **had had** time, he **would've visited** us last summer.
> If **we'd known** about discount, we **would've bought** our blender at Macy's.

As you can see in the examples above, you can use contractions in both the condition (*I'd, you'd, he'd, she'd, we'd, they'd*) and the result clause (*would've/wouldn't have*).

Questions invert the subject and the auxiliary verb (*would*) in the result clause.

> What **would you** have done if you had failed the test?

And you can use a negative in the condition or the result clause.

> If you **hadn't** reminded her about the robbery, she **wouldn't** have gotten so upset.
> If he had remembered the passports, we **wouldn't** have missed our flight.

Note that for all conditional sentences, the two clauses (condition and result) can be inverted.

> I would have been upset if you hadn't called me.
> I wouldn't have gone if he had invited me to his party.

B.

This conditional expresses an unreal condition and an imagined result in the past. Let's say you arrived at work late this morning because you forgot to set your alarm last night.

> If you **had set** your alarm last night, you **wouldn't have been** late for work.

Both the condition (*if you had set your alarm clock*) and the result (*you wouldn't have been late for work*) happen in the past. They are called *unreal* because they are impossible—they describe a situation in the past that did not happen.

> If I'**d known** you were feeling sick, I **would've canceled** the meeting. (but I didn't know, and I didn't cancel the meeting)

> If she **hadn't studied** so hard, she **wouldn't have gotten** into
> Harvard. (but she did study very hard, and she did get into
> Harvard)

1. Mixed conditionals

You might find that in some cases, you will use a past condition and a present result (of an unreal conditional). That is, you're looking at the present result of an unreal condition. Here are two examples.

> If you **hadn't come** home so late last night, I **wouldn't be** so
> angry right now. (but you did, and the result is I am angry
> now)
> If I **hadn't drunk** so much last night, I **wouldn't have** such a
> terrible hangover today. (but I did drink too much, and I have
> a hangover now)

C.

1. The following sentences are unreal past conditionals. Complete them with the appropriate verb forms for the condition clause or the result clause.

> EXAMPLE: I _____ (call) you if I had had your number.
>
> would have called

1. What would you have done if she _____? (come)
2. If they _____ (eaten, neg.) at Bodega Joe's, they wouldn't have gotten sick.
3. The actress _____ (win) an Oscar if she had taken the part in the movie.
4. If John _____ (study, neg.) Russian, he wouldn't have been able to translate for them.
5. Kathleen _____ (look for) another job if her boss hadn't given her a raise.

2. Match the following conditions to their logical result in the following mixed conditionals.

1. If she had taken more courses in education,	a. he wouldn't be so tired.
2. If Tom hadn't eaten so much,	b. I could get my money back.
3. If I hadn't lost my receipt,	c. she would be a better teacher.
4. If you had put your keys away,	d. they wouldn't be so angry now.
5. If we had notified them last week,	e. you wouldn't be looking for them now.

D. ANSWER KEY

1. 1. *had come*
   2. *hadn't eaten*
   3. *would have won*
   4. *hadn't studied*
   5. *would have looked for*

2. 1. c
   2. a
   3. b
   4. e
   5. d

21. Infinitives

A.

Infinitives (*to* + base form) have simple, progressive, and perfect forms, in both passive and active voice. Let's look at the different forms an infinitive can take.

The plain infinitive is made up of *to* + base form of the verb.

> *She liked **to swim** more than she liked **to do** other sports.*

The progressive infinitive is made up of *to be* + verb + *-ing*.

> *She seems **to be enjoying** her new job.*

The perfect infinitive is made up of *to have* + past participle.

> *Jim would like **to have been** there, but he couldn't go.*
> *They seem **to have understood** what we were saying.*
> *She appears **to have accepted** the bad news surprisingly well.*

The perfect progressive infinitive uses *to have been* + verb + *-ing*.

> *We seem **to have been driving** around in circles.*
> *She seems **to have been doing** a good job so far.*

The passive infinitive is *to be* + the past participle of the verb.

> *He wanted **to be recognized** for all of the work that he did.*

The passive perfect infinitive is *to* + *have been* + the past participle.

> *He seems **to have been delayed** by traffic.*

B.

You will find the infinitive used in several ways.

1. Verbs followed by an infinitive

Many verbs are followed by an infinitive. You will need to learn which verbs these are. A few examples are: *agree, attempt, offer, fail, need, seem, forget, would like* and *promise*. (See Lesson 27.) Let's look at a few example sentences.

> *He agreed **to meet** me at 12:00 but then he didn't come.*
> *She needs **to be picked up** after school.*
> *We fail **to see** the humor in this prank.*
> *She promised **not to do** it again.*
> *They seem **to have been** upset, but we don't know why.*

Notice the negative (*not*) comes before the infinitive.

2. Verb + object + infinitive

Other verbs are followed by an object and then an infinitive. Some examples are: *want, need, tell, ask, would like, expect, order, warn,* and *teach*. (See lesson 28.)

*The teacher **asked us to be** quiet.*
*My mother **would like me to come** straight home today.*
*She **told us not to tell** anyone.*
*We **warned them to be careful** when crossing the street.*

3. Infinitives of purpose

An infinitive can tell us why or for what purpose something is done. You can use the simple infinitive, or *in order to*. Here are some examples.

> ***To make** the food taste better, the chef adds butter and salt.* (or ***In order to make** the food taste better . . .*)
> *He's going to San Francisco **to look** for a job.*
> *He needs something **to cut** the grass.*
> *She brought me some flowers **to make** me feel better.*
> *"Why did he call you?" "**To make** plans for tomorrow night."*

4. Infinitive after question words

The infinitive can follow question words (*who/m, what, where, when, why, how*) after certain verbs: *know, tell, find out, remind, remember, ask, explain, understand,* etc.

> *Do you know **how to swim**?*
> *He doesn't understand **what to do**.*
> *Can Sally tell us **when to lock** the doors?*
> *I'll have to find out **whom to contact** about the power outage.*
> *Did he remind you **where to leave** the contract?*

5. Infinitive after certain adjectives

Use the infinitive after certain adjectives, such as *impossible, dangerous, safe, hard, interesting, exciting, better, worse,* etc.

> *Is it **safe to swim** here?*
> *He's **impossible to understand**.*
> *This room is **hard to work** in. There's not enough light.*
> *It's **interesting to know** that so many people speak Spanish in New York City.*
> *Is it **better to love** or **to be loved**?*

6. *too* + adjective + infinitive

You can also use the infinitive after *too* + an adjective.

> *She's **too young to drink**.*
> *It's **too far to walk**. Let's take the bus.*
> *This dish is **too hot to eat**. Let's wait until it cools down.*
> *I have **too much to do**. I can't go to the concert.*
> *Put your son down. He is **too old to be carried**.*

C.

1. The infinitive takes many forms. Follow the cues to form the infinitive correctly in the following sentences.

> 1. *He wanted* _____ *(go).* (plain infinitive)
> 2. *He would like* _____ *(be) there.* (perfect infinitive)
> 3. *They appear* _____ *(have) a good time.* (progressive infinitive)
> 4. *She wants* _____ *(get) a degree in biology.* (plain infinitive)
> 5. *We asked* _____ *(pick up) last.* (passive infinitive)

2. Respond to your friend's suggestion for an activity by using the clues in parentheses.

> EXAMPLE: *Let's go outside! (It's too cold . . .)*
>
> *It's too cold to go outside.*

> 1. *Let's play tennis! (It's too hot . . .)*
> 2. *Let's go out tonight! (He's too tired . . .)*
> 3. *Let's go to a bar! (She's too young . . .)*
> 4. *Let's do the work here. (It's too dark . . .)*
> 5. *Let's walk. (It's too far . . .)*

D. ANSWER KEY

1.   1. *to go*
   2. *to have been*
   3. *to be having*
   4. *to get*
   5. *to be picked up*

2.   1. *It's too hot to play tennis.*
   2. *He's too tired to go out tonight.*
   3. *She's too young to go to a bar.*
   4. *It's too dark to do the work in here.*
   5. *It's too far to walk.*

22. *-ing* Forms of the Verb: Present and Perfect Participles and Gerunds

A.

The *-ing* form of the verb is used both as a gerund (a noun) and as a present or perfect participle.

1. Formation of gerunds and participles

Both gerunds and participles are formed by adding *-ing* to the verb. There is a present and a perfect form.

present	*Living in London was a wonderful experience.*
perfect	*Having lived in London, Jon was the perfect person to be a liaison between the New York office and the London office.*

2. Spelling changes

a. For most *-ing* verbs, simply add *-ing* without any spelling changes.

> *He is **working** in Argentina.*

However, some verbs require spelling changes.

b. For verbs that end in *-e*, drop the *-e* before adding *-ing*.

> *He was **living** overseas.*

c. Double the final consonant in words that end with these three letters: *consonant, vowel, consonant.*

> *He is always **forgetting** about our Tuesday afternoon meetings.*

Note: In the preceding case, if the stress in a two syllable word is on the first syllable, the final letter is not doubled. (*happening, opening,* etc.)

(See lesson 4 for a more complete explanation.)

B.

Let's look at how gerunds and participles are used in sentences.

1. Gerunds

a. A gerund can be used as the subject of a sentence or as the object of certain verbs (see lesson 29 for a more complete explanation of verbs + gerunds).

> *I enjoy **swimming**.*
> ***Smoking** is a dangerous habit.*
> ***Traveling** around Europe is something I have always wanted to do.*

Being left alone in a strange place is not my idea of fun.

*We couldn't understand his not **wanting** to go.*

b. A gerund follows an *adjective + preposition* combination.

*We're **interested in learning** about the Aztecs before our trip to South America.*

*Our organization is **dedicated to solving** environmental problems.*

(See appendixes for a more complete listing of common adjective + preposition combinations.)

c. A gerund follows a *verb + preposition* combination.

*He **left** the table **without finishing** his meal.*

*Do you ever **think about moving** to another country?*

(See appendixes for a more complete listing of common verb + preposition combinations.)

2. Participles

The *-ing* form at other times is a participle. Here are some specific cases in which you will see the *-ing* participle used.

a. Progressive tenses

The *-ing* participle is used in all progressive verb tenses, active and passive.

*The kids **are watching** TV.*

*The game **was being watched** with great interest by the players on the bench.*

*She **would have been watching** her son more carefully if she had known how dangerous the jungle gym was.*

b. *-ing* clauses

A sentence with two clauses can begin with a participle clause. In this case, the subject must be the same in both clauses.

***Feeling** bad about refusing her offer, he called to apologize.*

(Because he was feeling bad about refusing her offer, he called to apologize.)

*While **working** overtime, he doesn't have to worry about money.*

(Because he is working overtime, he . . .)

An *-ing* clause in the perfect tense indicates that the action happened before the action in the main clause.

***Having taken** two weeks off in the summer, Sally had no vacation days left during the winter.*

***Having finished** his presentation, he left the room.*

c. Adjective clauses

You can use an -ing clause to describe someone or something. It marks an omission of *who is/was, that is/was,* or *which is/was.*

> *Who is the woman **sitting** on the bench?*
> *The lawyer **representing** the plaintiff has just entered the courtroom.*
> *The CD **playing** now is one of my favorites.*

(See also lesson 23 for adjective clauses with past participles.)

d. Sensory verbs

After sensory verbs, you can use an -ing participle. The word order will be *sensory* verb + object + -ing form of the verb. Some examples of sensory verbs are: *hear, feel, smell, taste, notice, observe,* and *watch.*

> *I **saw** Doug **running** out of the house.*
> *She **felt** someone **watching** her.*
> *When we walked into the house, we **smelled** something **burning.***
> *They **heard** him **walking** across the bridge, but they couldn't see him.*

C.

1. Change the bolded verb in the sentences below so that it is in the progressive form.

> EXAMPLE: *They **live** in London.*
>
> *They **are living** in London.*

> 1. *By the year 2050, we **will eat** all of our meals in the form of pills.*
> 2. *The Smiths **lived** in California before they moved to Texas.*
> 3. *The kids **were watched** by a strange man sitting on a bench in the park.*
> 4. *By the time I'm 65 years old, I **will have worked** at the agency for thirty years.*
> 5. *I **would have talked** more last night if I had felt better.*

2. Complete the sentences below by conjugating the verbs correctly. Use the sensory verb in the past tense and the -ing form of the verb. Make a question as indicated by a question mark (?).

> EXAMPLE: *I/see/him/run/out of the house*
>
> *I saw him running out of the house.*

> 1. *we/hear/someone/talk/in the next room*
> 2. *I/feel/something/crawl/on my leg*
> 3. *you/see/someone/enter/the house/?*
> 4. *they/notice/something/unusual/happen/next door*
> 5. *he/watch/the children/leave/the school*

D. ANSWER KEY

1. 1. *will be eating*
   2. *were living.*
   3. *were being watched*
   4. *will have been working*
   5. *would have been talking*

2. 1. *We heard someone talking in the next room.*
   2. *I felt something crawling on my leg.*
   3. *Did you see someone entering the house?*
   4. *They noticed something unusual happening next door.*
   5. *He watched the children leaving the school.*

23. Past Participles

A.

The past participle of regular verbs will always be formed by adding -*ed*, but irregular verbs have several different endings. Note that there are some common patterns for irregular endings. Keep in mind that in the following examples you will see the base form, the past, and the past participle.

	BASE FORM	PAST SIMPLE	PAST PARTICIPLE
1. -*i* to -*o* to -*en*			
	drive	*drove*	*driven*
	ride	*rode*	*ridden*
	write	*wrote*	*written*
2. -*ght* verbs			
	think	*thought*	*thought*
	catch	*caught*	*caught*
	buy	*bought*	*bought*
	seek	*sought*	*sought*
3. -*i* to -*a* to -*u*			
	drink	*drank*	*drunk*
	sing	*sang*	*sung*
	swim	*swam*	*swum*
4. verbs with no change			
	cut	*cut*	*cut*
	put	*put*	*put*
	bet	*bet*	*bet*
5. base form and participle the same			
	become	*became*	*become*
	run	*ran*	*run*
	come	*came*	*come*

Not all verbs follow these patterns, most notably the verb *to be* (see lesson 3). See the appendixes for a complete listing of irregular past participles.

B.

You will use the past participles to form certain verb tenses and in clauses.

1. Present and past perfect

The past participle follows the auxiliary (*have/has/had*) in the present and past perfect tense.

> She **hasn't** always **lived** here.
> They **haven't tasted** the caviar yet.
> He **had been** there before, but he **hadn't seen** the sculpture by Rodin.

Verbs in Action

There is also a perfect infinitive in the active and passive voice:

> *He is known **to have been** an excellent doctor.*
> *She would have preferred not **to have been recognized**.*

2. Passive voice

All verbs in the passive voice are formed using *to be* + the past participle.

> *The movie **was being screened** on the following Friday.*
> *If nothing goes wrong, she **will be offered** the position.*
> *She said that she wanted **to be left alone**.*

(See lessons 16 and 17 for more about the passive voice.)

3. Adjective clauses

Adjective clauses with the past participle have a passive meaning. The omission of *who is/was, that is/was,* or *which is/was* is notable. Look at the following examples.

> *The car **driven** by the two women veered off the road.* (The car that *was driven* by . . .)
> *The tree **cut down** by the loggers was a 200-year-old redwood.* (The tree that *was cut down* by . . .)

Compare to adjective clauses with the present participle, which have an active meaning.

> *The man **leaning** on the tree is the trainer.* (The man *who is leaning* . . .)

(See lesson 22.)

C.

1. Complete the sentences below using the correct form of the past participle.

> EXAMPLE: *They have _____ (take) a lot a trips lately.*
>
> *taken*

> 1. *Have you _____ (see) the new Batman movie?*
> 2. *That author has _____ (write) many books.*
> 3. *The new styles have _____ (catch) on quickly.*
> 4. *He seems to have _____ (think) a lot of your artwork.*
> 5. *The reporter had _____ (refuse) to disclose the name of her source.*

2. Use the correct form of the past participle in the following passive sentences.

> EXAMPLE: *My watch will have been _____ (fix) by 12:00.*
>
> *fixed*
>
> 1. *The movie was being _____ (show) when the lights went out.*
> 2. *The door had been _____ (leave) open, and the thief walked right in.*
> 3. *You will be _____ (ask) to leave if you cannot follow our rules.*
> 4. *The medicine has to be _____ (take) with food.*
> 5. *The children are being _____ (look) after by their grandparents.*

D. ANSWER KEY

1. 1. *seen*
    2. *written*
    3. *caught*
    4. *thought*
    5. *refused*

2. 1. *shown*
    2. *left*
    3. *asked*
    4. *taken*
    5. *looked*

24. Reported Speech

In reported speech, a direct statement, "*I can't make it to the party,*" is restated in the past tense, "*She said that she couldn't make it to the party.*" We use it when we want to "report" what someone else has said.

1. One tense back

Reported speech is usually used to talk about something in the past, so the verbs in the direct quotation are changed so that they are "one tense back." That is:

present	becomes	past
present perfect	becomes	past perfect
past	becomes	past perfect (or past)
will	becomes	*would*
can	becomes	*could*

Let's look at some examples.

> Direct statement: I **enjoy** working at the bank.
> Reported Speech: Martin said (that) he **enjoyed** working at the bank.

> Direct statement: I **will help** you on Sunday.
> Reported Speech: Susan said (that) she **would help** me on Sunday.

> Direct statement: Galina **has been living** in New York for six years.
> Reported Speech: He said (that) Galina **had been living** in New York for six years.

> Direct statement: Robert **went** to the store.
> Reported Speech: My mom said (that) Robert **had gone (went)** to the store.

Note that the word *that* is optional in all cases.

2. Situations that are still true

If the direct quotation is still true at the moment that it is being reported, it is not necessary to follow the rule "one tense back." For example, if Martin (see above) still enjoys working at the bank, then we don't need to change *enjoys* to *enjoyed*. If Susan is still going to help you on Sunday (and Sunday has not passed), we don't need to change *will* to *would*, etc.

> Martin said (that) he enjoys working in the bank.
> Susan said (that) she will help me on Sunday.

However, the "one tense back" rule can always be followed and be grammatically correct.

B.

1. *Say* and *tell*

There are important differences in the way that *say* and *tell* are used in reported speech. Most importantly, *tell* must be followed by an object.

> He **told me** (that) he was going to be late.
> He **said** (that) he was going to be late. (no object)

2. Reporting requests and commands

When we are commanding, ordering, or asking someone to do something, we use the infinitive. In reported speech, the word order will look like this:

> Subject + Verb + Object + (*not*) Infinitive

Common verbs are *ask, tell, want, warn, would like, persuade, convince,* and *expect.* Study the following examples:

> *I wanted him to buy the groceries after work.*
> *My mother told me to come home at 10:00.*
> *His wife asked him (not) to put the car away.*
> *The students convinced the teacher to go on a fieldtrip to*
> *Philadelphia.*

C.

1. The following sentences are in direct speech. Rewrite them in reported speech. Use "*she said*" for each answer. Make sure to use the "one tense back" rule, and change pronouns if necessary.

> EXAMPLE: *I like him.*
>
> *She said that she liked him.*

> 1. *He can't come.*
> 2. *They won't eat at that restaurant.*
> 3. *I don't like my new haircut.*
> 4. *You should take the Q train to my house.*
> 5. *He has never been to San Francisco.*

2. The following sentences are requests or orders. Using the verb in parentheses, report the request or order. Make sure to use verb + object + infinitive. Use *he* as the subject and *me* as the object.

> EXAMPLE: *Buy a loaf of bread. (ask)*
>
> *He asked me to buy a loaf of bread.*

> 1. *Don't come home late. (warn)*
> 2. *Take a sweater. (tell)*
> 3. *Come to the movies! (persuade)*
> 4. *Please bring a bag of ice. (would like)*
> 5. *Don't buy it. (convince)*

D. ANSWER KEY

1. 1. *She said (that) he couldn't come.*
2. *She said (that) they wouldn't eat at that restaurant.*
3. *She said (that) she didn't like her new haircut.*
4. *She said (that) I should take the Q train to her house.*
5. *She said (that) he had never been to San Francisco.*

2. 1. *He warned me not to come home late.*
2. *He told me to take a sweater.*
3. *He persuaded me to come to the movies.*
4. *He would like me to bring a bag of ice.*
5. *He convinced me not to buy it.*

25. Reported Questions and Embedded Questions

A.

When questions are reported, the verb usually moves one tense back. (See the previous lesson for further explanation.) *"How old **are** you?"* is a direct question. *"She asked me how old I **was**"* is a reported question. The question is now a statement, which means that the subject/verb order is not inverted, nor are the auxiliaries *do/does/did* used.

1. Information questions

*How old **are** you?*	*She asked me how old I **was**.*
*Where **is** he from?*	*She wanted to know where he **was** from.*
*What **did** he **do**?*	*She asked him what he **had done**/ what he **did**.*
*Where **have** you **been living**?*	*She wanted to know where I **had been living**.*
*How long **had** they **waited**?*	*She asked us how long they **had waited**.*

2. Yes/no questions

Use *if* or *whether* for reported *yes/no* questions (questions that can be answered with a *yes* or *no*).

Do you like it?	*She asked me **if** I liked it.*
Did he come?	*They asked her **whether** he had come/came.*

You can also use *whether or not.*

Did you enjoy yourself?
*He wanted to know **whether or not** I had enjoyed myself.*

B.

An embedded question is a question within another question or sentence. It follows the same rules as reported questions, but can be preceded by a variety of phrases, such as *Can you tell me, Do you know, I'm wondering*, etc. In addition, the verb tense does not change.

1. Information questions

Where is Broadway?	**Can you tell me where** *Broadway is?*
When is it going to rain tomorrow?	**I'm wondering when** *it's going to rain tomorrow.*

2. Yes/no questions

Use *if* or *whether* for embedded yes/no questions.

Can I bring my daughter?	*Do you know **if** I can bring my daughter?*
Does the cake need more time?	*I can't tell **whether** the cake needs more time.*

The expression *whether or not* can also be used.

> *Do you know **whether or not** you'll feel like going out tonight?*

Note: Do not invert the subject and verb in the embedded question.

> *Can you tell me where Broadway **is**?* (not *where **is** Broadway*)
> *I'm wondering when it**'s** going to rain.* (not *when **is it** going to rain*)

3. Outer questions or statements

Remember that an embedded question can be within either another question or a statement. Notice the verbs in these outer questions or statements: *know, wonder, ask, tell, think,* etc.

Common phrases that front an embedded question:

> *I don't know*
> *I wonder/I'm wondering*   + *if/whether*/question word
> *I can't tell*
> *I'd like to know*
> etc.

Common questions that front an embedded question:

> *Can you tell me*
> *Did you ask*
> *Do you ever wonder*   + *if/whether*/question word
> *Do you know*
> *Do you think*   + clause (without *if/whether*/question word)

Remember to put a period after a statement, and a question mark after a question. Note that any subject could be used in the above statements and questions.

C.

1. Use *if* or *whether* to report the following *yes/no* questions. Use *she asked me* in each reported question.

> EXAMPLE: *Does she like ice cream?*
>
> *She asked me if/whether she liked ice cream.*

1. *Will you be ready at 12:00?*
2. *Does she call often?*
3. *Did they listen to the program?*
4. *Were you home last weekend?*
5. *Is it raining?*

2. Report the following questions using the question word given. Use "*He wanted to know*" for each answer.

> EXAMPLE: *What time is it?*
>
> *He wanted to know what time it was.*

1. *Where are you going?*
2. *What will they think?*
3. *When did the accident occur?*
4. *How do you feel?*
5. *How long has she been writing?*

3. You and a classmate need to buy a gift for your friend's birthday and are trying to find out some information about him. Begin each embedded question with the words in parentheses.

> EXAMPLE: *Does he like music? (Do you think . . .)*
>
> *Do you think that he likes music?*

1. *Is he into sports? (I wonder if . . .)*
2. *Does he read a lot? (Do you know whether . . .)*
3. *Has he traveled a lot? (Do you know if . . .)*
4. *How often does he listen to music? (I'm wondering . . .)*
5. *Would he like to come with us? (We'd like to know whether or not . . .)*

D. ANSWER KEY

1.
  1. *She asked me if/whether I would be ready at 12:00.*
  2. *She asked me if/whether she called often.*
  3. *She asked me if/whether they listened/had listened to the program.*
  4. *She asked me if/whether I was/had been home last weekend.*
  5. *She asked me if/whether it was raining.*

2.
  1. *He wanted to know where I was going.*
  2. *He wanted to know what they would think.*
  3. *He wanted to know when the accident occurred/had occurred.*
  4. *He wanted to know how I felt.*
  5. *He wanted to know how long she had been writing.*

3.
  1. *I wonder if he is into sports.*
  2. *Do you know whether he reads a lot?*
  3. *Do you know if he has traveled a lot?*
  4. *I'm wondering how often he listens to music.*
  5. *We'd like to know whether or not he would like to come with us.*

Verbs in Action

26. Verb + Infinitive

A.

When a verb is followed by another verb, the second verb will either be an infinitive (*to* + base form) or a gerund (verb + *-ing*). Certain verbs can be followed only by one or the other, although in some cases, either is grammatically correct. In this lesson we will look at the verbs that are followed by infinitives. Look at these examples.

> *I'd **like to go** to the movies tonight.*
> *My family **agreed to celebrate** the holidays at my house this*
> *   year.*

When the verbs listed below are followed by another verb, the second verb will always be an infinitive:

would like	*expect*	*dare*
want	*decide*	*learn (how)*
appear	*refuse*	*afford*
arrange	*plan*	*pretend*
agree	*ask*	*seem*
try	*forget*	*offer*
manage	*mean*	*threaten*
hope	*intend*	*fail*
choose	*tend*	*attempt*

Here are some examples of these verbs in sentences, followed by an infinitive. As you will notice, the first verb can be in any tense and the second verb remains in the infinitive form.

> *I can't go out tonight. I **plan to finish** this by the time I go to bed.*
> *She **refuses to help** even though I have asked her several times.*
> *She **has failed to win** the title again.*
> *We **agreed to meet** at 12:00.*
> ***Did** she **expect to win** this year?*
> *She **didn't intend to harm** the plants, but the pesticide was too*
> *   strong.*

Note that in question formation the verb + infinitive structure remains intact.

> *Would you like **to save** your work?*
> *Has she ever refused **to participate** before?*

The first verb can be negated, or *not* can come before the infinitive.

> *She **didn't decide** to come*   or   *She decided **not** to come to the*
> *   to the meeting.*   *meeting.*
> *The **didn't intend** to hurt*   or   *They intended **not** to hurt you.*
> *   you.*

There are also progressive, perfect, and passive forms of the infinitive. (See lesson 21 for more on the infinitive in different tenses.)

*They **expect to be leaving** around 1:00 tomorrow.*
*He **seems to have worked** (to have been working) a lot this year*
considering his good grades.
*She **refuses to be helped** even though she's having trouble.*
*He **doesn't seem to have been affected** by the loss.*

B.

1. Complete the following sentences by using one of the given verbs
in the infinitive form.

EXAMPLE: *The students agreed _____ to study for the test.*

to meet

to leave   to contact   to finish   to arrest   to host   to meet

1. *Who knows if it will really happen, but the workers have agreed*
_____ the project by Friday.
2. *The city is hoping _____ the 2012 Olympics.*
3. *Even though the landlord threatened to have her evicted, the*
woman refused _____ her apartment.
4. *The policeman threatened _____ them if they didn't move their car.*
5. *The secretary attempted _____ the patient to advise him of a*
cancellation.

2. Complete the following sentences by using one of the given verbs
in an appropriate present or past tense.

EXAMPLE: *The taxi driver _____ to receive a large tip for*
carrying my bags

expected

promise   seem   offer   refuse   expect   pretend

1. *It was so nice of my next-door neighbor to _____ to watch my*
children while I was shopping.
2. *The two cats _____ to be getting along better today.*
3. *They _____ not to have heard me when I called them.*
4. *I lent John my car but only after he _____ to be careful.*
5. *Even though she would have preferred it, the doctor _____ to let*
her go home yesterday.

C. ANSWER KEY

1. 1. *to finish*
    2. *to host*
    3. *to leave*
    4. *to arrest*
    5. *to contact*

2. 1. *offer*
    2. *seem*
    3. *pretended*
    4. *promised/had promised*
    5. *refused*

27. Verb + Object + Infinitive

For certain verbs, an object follows the verb and precedes the infinitive. The object can be a noun or a pronoun. A more complete explanation of how each verb is used follows in part B.

advise	allow	ask*
cause	challenge	convince
encourage	expect*	forbid
force	get	help*
invite	order	permit
persuade	require	remind
teach	tell	urge
warn	want*	

> Terry **convinced his mother to take** a vacation.
> My mother **taught me to play** the piano.
> **Did** you **warn him not to drink** the coffee until it cooled down?

Recall the object pronouns that you can use to replace a noun:

SUBJECT	OBJECT
I	me
you	you
he	him
she	her
it	it
we	us
they	them

Questions follow standard structure. Invert the auxiliary and the subject. The *verb, object,* and *infinitive* order remains intact.

> **Did** Stan **encourage his daughter to go** to camp?
> **Do** they **want him to answer**?
> **Would** you **like the waiter to bring** the check?

For negatives, the first verb can be negated (follow standard rules for negation) or *not* can precede the infinitive.

He **didn't** tell us to go.	or	He told us **not** to go.
I **won't** expect you to arrive before 8:00.	or	I will expect you **not** to arrive before 8:00.

B.
1. Object and infinitive
The following verbs from the above list are followed by an object and infinitive.

tell	expect	warn
remind	persuade	convince
urge	teach	require

permit	order	allow
encourage		

> The security guard got tired of **reminding customers to pick up** their bags from the coat check.
>
> My teachers **encouraged me to study** organic chemistry.
>
> The counselor wished she could **persuade more high-schoolers not to drop out** of school.

2. Object and infinitive, or infinitive

However, the verbs that are marked by an asterisk (*) can be followed by an object and infinitive, or simply by an infinitive.

expect	help
would like	need
want	ask

> I expect **you** to be serious and set a good example.
>
> He needs **someone** to give him a hand around the house.
>
> We asked **them** to turn up the music when they played a song that we liked.
>
> I would like **him** not to be so aggressive.

Compare the above sentences to the one below in which the verb is not followed by an object.

> I **expect to have** a good year.
>
> I **need to speak** to the manager.

(See lesson 27.)

3. Passive structure for verb + object + infinitive

When any of the verbs listed in this lesson are used in the passive voice, the object becomes the subject of the sentence. Therefore, the object position is lost. (The subject may or may not be included in a *"by"* phrase.)

> Active: My parents **allowed me to stay out** late when I was a child.
>
> Passive: I **was allowed to stay out** late when I was a child (by my parents).

Here are a few more examples of passive sentences.

> You were told repeatedly to finish the work by Tuesday!
>
> The students aren't permitted to leave the campus during the lunch break.
>
> She has been persuaded to stay.

Note that an adverb can precede the infinitive (as with *repeatedly* in the above example) in all infinitive forms.

> The clerk reminded her manager constantly to call her by her first name.

C.

1. Use the cues given below to make sentences using verb + object + infinitive.

> EXAMPLE:"*Take your change,*"*said the clerk. (remind/customer)*
>
> *The clerk reminded the customer to take his change.*

1. *"Please come!" said my friend. (persuade/me)*
2. *"Watch out for the car!" said the man. (warn/the boy)*
3. *"You can go out tonight," said the mother. (allow/her son)*
4. *You may take two suitcases on the flight. (permit/us) (The airline . . .)*
5. *"The students will have to turn in three essays during the semester," said the teacher. (require/them)*

2. Make the following sentences passive. Don't include "by" phrases. Be careful to use the same verb tense.

> EXAMPLE: *The teacher allowed me to take extra time to finish my test. (I . . .)*
>
> *I was allowed to take extra time to finish my test.*

1. *He urged me to speak to the police immediately. (I . . .)*
2. *The coach will convince the boys to end the game early. (The boys . . .)*
3. *The police have ordered the driver to step out of his car. (The driver . . .)*
4. *The bartender was asking the men to leave. (The men . . .)*
5. *My parents had taught me to respect the elderly. (I . . .)*

D. ANSWER KEY

1. 1. *My friend persuaded me to come.*
   2. *The man warned the boy to watch out for the car.*
   3. *The mother allowed her son to go out tonight.*
   4. *The airline permitted us to take two suitcases on the flight.*
   5. *The teacher required them to turn in three essays during the semester.*

2. 1. *I was urged to speak to the police immediately.*
   2. *The boys will be convinced to end the game early.*
   3. *The driver has been ordered to step out of his car.*
   4. *The men were being asked to leave.*
   5. *I had been taught to respect the elderly.*

Verbs in Action

28. Verb + Gerund

When a verb is followed by another verb, the second verb will either be an infinitive (*to* + base form) or a gerund (verb + *-ing*). In this lesson we will look at the verbs that are followed by gerunds.

admit	*advise*	*appreciate*
avoid	*can't help*	*consider*
continue	*delay*	*deny*
detest	*discuss*	*dislike*
enjoy	*escape*	*explain*
feel like	*finish*	*forgive*
give up	*hate*	*imagine*
keep	*loathe*	*mention*
mind	*miss*	*postpone*
prevent	*prohibit*	*propose*
quit	*recommend*	*regret*
resent	*risk*	*suggest*
support	*tolerate*	*understand*

We **enjoy snorkeling**, but **don't like scuba diving**.
He **considered quitting** his job.
They **have discussed relocating** to a new neighborhood.

Questions follow the standard structure. Invert the subject and the auxiliary verb, while the verb + gerund word order remains intact.

Do you **like studying** here?
What would he **suggest doing** if he were here?

To form negative sentences, you can either negate the first verb (follow standard rules for negation) or place *not* before the gerund.

He **didn't mention going** to the party.	or	He **mentioned not going** to the party and going out for dinner instead.
They **won't appreciate our staying** for so long.	or	They **will appreciate our not staying** for so long.

In the last example above, a possessive pronoun follows the verb and precedes the gerund. Any possessive pronoun can be used.

I	*my*
You	*your*
He	*his*
She	*her*
It	*its*
We	*our*
They	*their*

Look at a few more examples to get a better understanding.

*He **considered my working** for him, but not very seriously.*
*We **minded their taking up** so much space, but didn't say anything.*

In everyday speech, you may also hear an object pronoun used in place of the possessive pronoun. In strict or formal English, this is still considered incorrect.

B.

Let's look at some different groupings of verbs that are followed by gerunds.

1. Like or dislike

In general, verbs that express *like* or *dislike* are followed by a gerund. The verbs with an asterisk can also be followed by an infinitive. (See lesson 29)

appreciate	hate*
enjoy	dislike
like*	loathe
love*	
prefer*	can't stand*

Here are a few examples.

*"Do you **like swimming** or **jogging** to get exercise?" "I **prefer swimming**."*
*I **can't stand waiting** in line. Let's go to another club.*
*My mother **loves taking care of** her grandchildren.*

2. Other verbs + gerund

In the list below, you will find more common verbs that are followed by the gerund.

avoid	delay	finish
keep (on)	postpone	put off
quit	stop	consider
discuss	mind	mention
suggest		

*Would you **mind stopping** at the grocery store on the way home?*
*He **quit playing** guitar when he graduated from college.*
*Carolyn **suggested going** to the Mermaid Parade, but we didn't have time.*
*They **didn't mention being** upset. Are you sure they were?*
*The couple **considered not having** children until they were older.*

3. *Go* + gerund

Often, if a physical activity is involved, the structure *go* + gerund is common.
We go jogging on Tuesdays and Thursdays.
    Other activities that can be combined with *go* are:

Go	swimming
	running
	shopping
	walking
	bike riding
	hiking
	snorkeling
	skiing
	sightseeing
	clubbing (informal)
	drinking (informal)

etc.

The following examples show the above expressions in use.

> "Did you **go snorkeling** while you were on vacation?" "No, but we
> went swimming every day."
>
> "Do you want to **go hiking** this weekend? I want to try out my
> new boots."
>
> "Where are you going? I thought we were **going shopping** this
> afternoon."

C.

1. Choose the correct verb to complete the following sentences. Use a gerund.

> EXAMPLE: *We appreciate _____ in such a beautiful area*
>
> *living*
>
> live   sightsee   shop   bring up   look for   relax   see

1. *Has he considered _____ a new job?*
2. *Will they appreciate _____ me if I stop by later?*
3. *On their day off, the girls went _____ for hours.*
4. *John really dislikes _____ on vacation. He prefers _____ on the beach.*
5. *I saw her, but she avoided _____ the unpleasant subject.*

2. Complete the following sentences with one of the verbs given. Remember to put the verb in the correct verb tense with the third person -*s* if necessary.

> EXAMPLE: *She _____ going to the dentist.*
>
> *hates*
>
> hate   go   mention   mind   quit   delay

1. *Don't _____ my winning the lottery. I don't want everyone to know.*
2. *She _____ smoking on her 30th birthday.*
3. *They _____ starting the race repeatedly because of the rain.*
4. *Would you _____ closing the window? It's freezing in here.*
5. *We _____ running almost every day this week. That's great!*

D. ANSWER KEY

1.
   1. *looking for*
   2. *seeing*
   3. *shopping*
   4. *sightseeing/relaxing*
   5. *bringing up*

2.
   1. *mention*
   2. *quit*
   3. *have delayed/delayed*
   4. *mind*
   5. *have gone*

29. Gerund or Infinitive?

A.

In this lesson we will look at verbs that can be followed by either a gerund or an infinitive. Some verbs can be followed by either one with no change in meaning. For others the meaning of the sentence changes depending on whether the gerund or the infinitive is used.

1. No change in meaning

The following verbs do not change meaning whether followed by gerund or infinitive.

begin   start   continue   hate   like   love   can't stand

*I begin **working** at 8:00.*	or	*I begin **to work** at 8:00.*
*He continued **sleeping**.*	or	*He continued **to sleep**.*
*She hates **doing** laundry.*	or	*She hates **to do** laundry.*
*We like **driving**.*	or	*We like **to drive**.*
*They love **winning**.*	or	*They love **to win**.*

2. Change in meaning

Some verbs have a significant change in meaning depending on whether you use the gerund or the infinitive.

forget   remember   regret   try

Forget/remember + gerund	(forget/remember something that happened in the past)
Forget/remember + infinitive	(forget/remember to do something)

*I'll never **forget meeting** her the first time.*
*I **forgot to send** the letter.*
*I **remember talking** to her but I can't remember what she said.*
*I'll **remember to pick** up the cake. Don't worry!*

Regret + gerund	(regret something you did in the past)
Regret + infinitive	(regret something done at the present time)

*She will always **regret dropping** out of school.*
*We **regret to inform** you that we cannot raise your credit limit.*

Try + gerund	(a suggestion)
Try + infinitive	(attempt to do something)

*You lost your voice? **Try drinking** tea with lemon and honey.*
*He **tried to open** the window but it was impossible.*

B.

1. Gerund or infinitive? The following verbs require either a gerund or an infinitive when followed by another verb (only one option is correct). Look back at lessons 28 and 29 to remember which verbs require a gerund and which require an infinitive.

    EXAMPLE: *He appreciates* _____ *(hear) from her every once in a while.*

    hearing

    1. *The Washingtons can't afford* _____ *(take) a vacation this year.*
    2. *When I leave the room, I would like you to keep on* _____ *(work) on your essays.*
    3. *We arranged* _____ *(see) the apartment at 12:00.*
    4. *How old were you when you learned how* _____ *(ride) a bicycle?*
    5. *Have they finished* _____ *(repair) your car yet?*

2. The following sentences require either a gerund or an infinitive. Both are grammatically correct, but only one logically completes the sentence. Use the context to decide which one is appropriate.

    EXAMPLE: *He always regretted (to leave/leaving) the big city for a small town.*

    leaving

    1. *He will try (to make/making) it to the meeting, but he has an earlier obligation.*
    2. *You forgot (to take/taking) the cake out of the oven? I knew I should've set the timer.*
    3. *Do you remember (to travel/traveling) in England? That was one of my favorite trips.*
    4. *We regret (to notify/notifying) you of the loss of your documents.*
    5. *If you want to get the job you should try (to rewrite/rewriting) your resume.*

C. ANSWER KEY

1. 1. *to take*
    2. *working*
    3. *to see*
    4. *to ride*
    5. *repairing*

2. 1. *to make*
    2. *to take*
    3. *traveling*
    4. *to notify*
    5. *rewriting*

Verbs in Action

30. Modal Verbs

A.

The modal verbs are auxiliary verbs. That is, they are always combined with a main verb.

> We **should** make dinner. It's late.
> They **will** be arriving any minute.

The modal auxiliaries are:

can	*could*	*will*
would	*shall*	*should*
may	*might*	*must*

B.

There are certain rules characteristic of all modal verbs. It will help to get an understanding of how all modals function before we look at their meaning.

1. Modals do not have endings to indicate form, such as person or tense. That means that there are no *-s*, *-ed*, or *-ing* endings.
   > He **can** come with us. (do not add *-s* to the verb)

2. Modals are auxiliary verbs; they are always combined with another verb. That verb will always be in base form (the infinitive without *to—go, drive, see*, etc.).
   > We must **help** them. (*help* is in the base form)

   The exception to this rule is when the modal is used as the short answer to a question.

   > Will you help them?   Yes, we will.

3. To make a modal negative, add *not* to the modal. Sometimes there is a contracted form.
   > You **should not** do that.   or   You **shouldn't** do that.
   > They **must not** be late.   or   They **mustn't** be late.

4. For questions, invert the subject and the modal verb.
   > **Will he** come?
   > **Can he** answer the question?

   (Note: Never use *do, does,* or *did* to form negatives or questions.)

5. There is a progressive form for modals, which is modal + *be* + verb + *-ing*.
   > You **must be thinking** of someone else.

6. The modals have a perfect form: modal + *have* + past participle.
   > He **should have been** here by now.

7. Most modal auxiliaries have more than one use. Take *can*, for example.

*I **can't** do it. (can expresses ability)*
***Can** you help me? (can expresses a request)*
*Ticket holders **can** enter through any gate. (can expresses*
permission)

C.

1. Complete the following sentences with a verb that logically follows the modal verb.

> EXAMPLE: *I could _____ a bike when I was young.*
>
> *ride*
>
> ride   rain   show up   take   find   travel
> 1. *We should _____ some flowers when we go to her concert.*
> 2. *The trains are running slowly. They may _____ late for the meeting.*
> 3. *It's overcast this morning. Do you think it will _____*
> 4. *If a won a million dollars, I would _____ around the world.*
> 5. *I can't work with him. You had better _____ someone else to do the job.*

2. Each sentence below has a mistake in the use of the verb. Correct each mistake.

> EXAMPLE: *He can to cook.*
>
> *He can cook. (do not use "to" after a modal)*

1. *I can found out the answer.*
2. *We will be take the train to the airport.*
3. *He should has come earlier.*
4. *They must to complete the forms.*
5. *We may had a problem.*

D. ANSWER KEY

1. 1. *take*
   2. *show up*
   3. *rain*
   4. *travel*
   5. *find*

2. 1. *I can find out the answer.* (a modal is always followed by a verb in the base form)
   2. *We will take/be taking the train to the airport.* (use either the base form or *be* + *-ing* form)
   3. *He should have come earlier.* (a modal is always followed by a verb in the base form, even if it is the perfect form: *have* + past participle)
   4. *They must complete the forms.* (do not use *to* after a modal verb except *ought to*)
   5. *We may have/have had a problem.* (a modal is always followed by a verb in the base form, not the past)

31. Modal and Modal-Like Verbs of Obligation, No Obligation and Prohibition

A.

In this lesson, we will look at modal verbs, and other modal-like verbs, that express obligation, no obligation and prohibition. We will include some verbs that are not modals, but whose uses and meanings are very similar to those of modals. It is important to see how these verbs function alongside the modals.

First, let's look at the verbs that express obligation.

1. Obligation

FUNCTION	PRESENT TENSE	PAST TENSE
OBLIGATION	*must*	*had to*
	has/have to	*had to*
	has/have got to	*had to*

> Use *have to, have got to,* and *must* to express obligation.
> *I can't go out tonight; I **have got to** do my homework.*
> *He **has to** be at the theater at 7:15 tonight.*
> *We **must** go visit your aunt in the hospital.*

Must is generally stronger than *have to,* and is often used for rules and regulations.

> *All cell phones **must** be turned off during the performance.*
> *Passengers **must** show their passports upon boarding the aircraft.*

Note the past tense of *must* is *had to.*

> *I **must** do this work tonight. I've been putting it off for weeks!*
> *I **had to** do that work last night. I'd been putting it off for weeks!*

Note that *have to* follows all rules for regular verbs. The following questions show that *have to* can be used in any verb tense or even with another modal.

> *"**Do you have to** wear a uniform at work?" "No. I just **have to** dress formally."* (present tense)
> *How long **have you had** to listen to the party next door?* (present perfect)
> ***Will you have to bring** your own tent when you go camping?* (with a modal)

Have got to is commonly used in the contracted form.

> *I've*
> *he's, she's, it's*   *got to*
> *you've, we've, they've*

*We've **got to** go. It's almost three and our flight leaves at five.*
*He's **got to** help me with the dinner. I can't do it myself.*

Have got to is rarely used in a question or negative form.

2. No obligation

FUNCTION	PRESENT TENSE	PAST TENSE
NO OBLIGATION	*don't/doesn't have to*	*didn't have to*
	don't/doesn't need to	*didn't need to*
	needn't	

Don't have to and *don't need to* are modal-like verbs that signify that it is not necessary to do something. They can be used interchangeably with only slight change in meaning. Look at these examples.

*You **don't have to** get here so early tomorrow. (or you **don't need to** . . .)*
*He **didn't have to** get me a gift for my birthday. That was very sweet. (or he **didn't need to** . . .)*
*You **needn't bring** anything. We're all set.*
*I **don't have to** go to class on Monday because it's a federal holiday.*

Note: *Don't have to* and *mustn't* have very different meanings. *Don't have to* means that something is not necessary; *mustn't* expresses prohibition. See below.

3. Prohibition

FUNCTION	PRESENT TENSE	PAST TENSE
PROHIBITION	must not (mustn't)	
	cannot (can't)	couldn't
	am not/isn't/aren't	wasn't/weren't
	allowed to	allowed to

These verbs express something that you are *restricted or prohibited* from doing. Again, *must not* expresses stronger prohibition.

*You **must not** arrive late to the test. If you do, you **will not be allowed to** take it.*
*Students **must not** leave the classroom until all papers have been collected.*

Cannot—more commonly abbreviated as *can't*—expresses prohibition in more common, everyday situations.

*You **can't** take that. It's not yours.*

Verbs in Action

Not allowed to implies a rule of prohibition.

> I**'m not allowed to** *stay out after 10:00.* (my parents don't allow me)
>
> *Smoking* **is not allowed** *in the hotel lobby.* (a hotel rule)

For the past tense, use *wasn't/weren't allowed to* or *couldn't.*

> *As a child, I* **wasn't allowed to** *go to school by myself.*
>
> *Also, I* **couldn't** *talk on the phone for hours because my mother didn't let me.*

Be allowed to and *can* are used in affirmative sentences to express permission. See lesson 34 for more on permission.

> *You* **can** *take my car, but only if you're really careful.*
>
> *You* **are allowed to** *smoke on the terrace.*

B.

1. **You are trying to find out information about your friend's new job. For each statement below, use the same modal or modal-like verb to form a logical question.**

    > EXAMPLE: *No, He doesn't have to wear a uniform.*
    >
    > *Does he have to wear a uniform?*

    > 1. *Yes, he* **has to** *work on Sundays.*
    > 2. *Yes, he's* **allowed to** *make personal phone calls.*
    > 3. *Yes, he* **can** *leave the building during lunch break.*
    > 4. *No, he* **doesn't need to** *take more than one subway to get to work.*
    > 5. *No, he* **won't have to** *ask for vacation time.*

2. **Complete the sentences with the most logical modal of obligation, no obligation, permission, or prohibition from the list below.**

    > EXAMPLE: *We* _____ *forget to take our passports.*
    >
    > *must not*

    > must not   allowed to   needn't   have to   had to   can
    >
    > 1. *In that coffee shop, you* _____ *get one free refill.*
    > 2. *He* _____ *arrive so early next time. There's nothing to do until later.*
    > 3. *They don't* _____ *carry all of the boxes themselves. We can help.*
    > 4. *You are* _____ *to smoke in the kitchen but not in the other rooms.*
    > 5. *She didn't come because she* _____ *work.*

C. ANSWER KEY

1. 1. *Does he have to work on Sundays?*
    2. *Is he allowed to make personal phone calls?*

3. *Can he leave the building during the lunch break?*
4. *Does he need to take more than one subway to get to work?*
5. *Will he have to ask for vacation time?*

2. 1. *can*
2. *needn't*
3. *have to*
4. *allowed to*
5. *had to*

32. Advice: Modals and the Second Conditional

A.

1. Advice

Let's look now at two different ways to offer advice.

FUNCTION	PRESENT TENSE	PAST TENSE
ADVICE	should (not)	should (not) + have + past participle
	ought to	ought to have
	had better (not)	

You **should** get some rest.
He **had better** come on time today.

Should and *ought to* are used interchangeably. However, *ought to* will rarely be used in the negative, or for forming questions. Use *should* instead. Let's look at a few examples.

That's the third cigarette he's smoked since we got here. He **shouldn't smoke** so much.
"**Should I take** a sweater?" "I think you should. It's supposed to be cold."
He **ought to** visit his grandmother more. She's alone too much of the time.

Had better is used for stronger or more urgent advice.

You'**d better leave** right now if you don't want to miss your flight!
She'**d better not** let him see her kissing his best friend!

Had better is usually used in the contracted form and has no past.

I'd	better	
He'd, she'd, it'd	better	pay the bill before they turn off the phone.
We'd, you'd, they'd	better	

The perfect form of *should* and *ought to* adds *have* + past participle. It expresses advice in the past, or regret that you have about something you did or didn't do. The contraction (*should've*) is commonly used.

I was so sick last week. I **should've gone** to the doctor. (but I didn't go)
You **shouldn't have said** that. Now your teacher is angry with you. (but you did say that)
Should we **have called** earlier?
He **ought to have warned** them before he showed up so late at night.

Note that *ought*, unlike other modals, is always followed by *to* before the base form of the verb.

2. Second conditional to offer advice

You can also use a second conditional to give advice. This is a common way to tell somebody what you think is a good idea, or what you would do if you were in his or her position. Use the condition clause *If I were you*.

> **If I were you**, I wouldn't consider it.

In informal contexts, you can use *were* or *was* in the condition clause.

> **If I was you**, I'd ask before you use the CD player.

And you can use *would* or *wouldn't* in the result clause.

> You look exhausted. If I were you, I **would** get some rest and I **wouldn't** stay up so late at night.

See lesson 19 for more about second conditionals.

B.

1. **Match the following problems with the logical advice in the next column.**

> EXAMPLE: *I need to lose weight.*
>
> *You should get more exercise.*

1. *I feel sick.*	*a. You should look for a new job.*
2. *I don't earn enough money.*	*b. You ought to stop drinking coffee.*
3. *My apartment is too small.*	*c. If I were you, I would see a doctor.*
4. *I feel very stressed out.*	*d. You'd better call your accountant.*
5. *My taxes are due tomorrow.*	*e. You ought to contact my landlord.*

2. **Use the cues given to express a regret. Use the perfect form of the verb.**

> EXAMPLE: *I _____ (should/see) a doctor.*
>
> *should have seen*

1. *He'll never get the job. He _____ (should/send) his resume in long ago.*
2. *She lost her job. She _____ (should/not/be) late so many times.*
3. *They had an accident. The driver _____ (should/drive) more carefully.*
4. *The food is spoiled. We _____ (ought to/eat) it yesterday.*
5. *My bike was stolen. I _____ (should/buy) a better lock.*

C. ANSWER KEY

1. 1. *c*
    2. *a*
    3. *e*
    4. *b*
    5. *d*

2. 1. *should have sent*
    2. *shouldn't have been*
    3. *should have driven*
    4. *ought to have eaten*
    5. *should have bought*

33. Modals of Possibility and Certainty

A.

We use modals of possibility and certainty when we believe something to be true, but we cannot verify it with 100 percent certainty. There are degrees of possibility and certainty, as you can see below in the chart.

1. 99% certain

PRESENT	PAST
must	*must have* + past participle

*The kids have been playing outside for hours. They **must be** hungry.*

*He's late. He **must have had** a problem.*

2. 50% certain

PRESENT	PAST
may (not)	*may (not)*
might (not)	*might (not)(have* + past participle)
could	*could*

*"Who's at the door?" "It **might be** the mailman."*

*"Who do you think called at midnight last night?" "It **may have been** a wrong number."*

3. 99% certain (negative)

PRESENT	PAST
must not	*must not*
can't	*can't (have* + past participle)
couldn't	*couldn't*

*"Do you know why he didn't come to the concert?" "He **must not be** interested in opera."*

*"Did Tim write this letter?" "He **can't/couldn't have written** it. That's not his hand writing."*

Note: There is a progressive form both for the past and present. Use the modal verb + *be* + verb + *-ing*.

*He must **be/have been working** late.*

*He may **be/have been picking up** some things for dinner.*

B.

1. Write a sentence that expresses probability using the cues provided.

EXAMPLE: *Do you think we will be on time? (may) We . . .*

We may be on time.

1. *Do you think he's married? (must) He . . .*
2. *Do you think he is studying music? (may) He . . .*
3. *Do you think they are coming tonight? (may not) They . . .*
4. *Do you think she has a demanding job? (must) She . . .*
5. *Do you think there will be enough food? (might not) There . . .*

2. **The following statements of possibility and certainty are all in the present. Put them into the past.**

> EXAMPLE: *He must have a lot of money.*
>
> *must have had*

1. *She may be working hard.*
2. *They must look terrible after the long trip.*
3. *We couldn't be in the right place.*
4. *Her mother might feel upset about the news.*
5. *The doctor could be wrong in his diagnosis.*

D. ANSWER KEY

1.
1. *He must be married.*
2. *He may be studying music.*
3. *They may not be coming tonight.*
4. *She must have a demanding job.*
5. *There might not be enough food.*

2.
1. *may have been working*
2. *must have looked*
3. *couldn't have been*
4. *might have felt*
5. *could have been*

34. Other Modals

A.

In this lesson, we will look at modals that express ability, requests, offers, permission, and suggestions. Study the charts and examples below to get a better idea of how the modals *can, could, would,* and *may* are used. Remember that some modal verbs have more than one meaning. This means that you may have seen these verbs in the previous lessons, only to find them listed below in one or more places.

1. Ability

PRESENT	PAST
can	*could*
(am/is/are able to)	*(was/were able to)*

2. Requests/offers

PRESENT	PAST
can	-
could	-
would	-
may	-

3. Permission

PRESENT	PAST
can	-
may	-

4. Suggestions/unrealized possibility

PRESENT	PAST
could	*could have* + past participle

B.

Study the following examples of each group of modal verbs.

1. Ability

> *"**Can** you **cook**?" "No, but I'd like to learn how."*
> *I **could speak** French when I was a child, but I'm afraid I've forgotten everything I knew.*

You cannot use two modal verbs together. However, if you want to express ability in combination with another modal (for example, the future *will/would*), use *be able to.*

> *She **won't be able to come** to the meeting.*
> *If he spoke better English, he **would be able to get** a job as a secretary.*

2. Requests and offers

a. Polite requests

Use *would you, could you,* or *can you* to make an imperative sound more polite.

*"**Can you** give it to me?"*	*"Of course."*
*"**Could you** do that for me?"*	*"Certainly."*
*"**Would you** open the door for me please?"*	*"No problem."*

b. Offers

Use *may* or *can* when you want to offer to do something for someone. *May* is more formal than *can*.

> ***Can I** make you some lunch?*
> ***May I** help you?*

3. Permission

Use the following modals for asking (*may, can, could*) and giving permission (*may, can*). *May* is very formal, and *could* sounds slightly more polite than *can.*

> ***May I** go to the bathroom?*
> *"**Can we** come in?"*
> *"**Could I** borrow your pen?"*

4. Suggestions/unrealized possibility

Use *could* to make suggestions.

> *"I want to take my brother out this weekend. Do you have any suggestions?" "You **could take** him to a jazz club in the city."*
> *If he doesn't have a job, he **could check** with the personnel department here.*

The perfect form *could have* is used to express a suggestion that was possible in the past, but that wasn't done. Look at the following examples to get a better idea of how this modal is used.

> *Why did you fly to Washington, D.C.? You **could have taken** the train.* (you had the possibility of taking the train but you didn't)
> *He stayed in a hotel? He **could've stayed** with me.* (he had the possibility of staying with me but he didn't)

There is also a progressive form in the present and perfect.

> *You **could be helping** me out instead of just standing there!*
> *Why was he working at such a small firm? He **could've been working** at any of the biggest firms in the country.*

Note that you will often see the contracted form of *could have (could've)* used.

C.

1. Each sentence below uses a modal verb. Choose another verb from the list that completes the following sentences logically.

    EXAMPLE: *We could _____ at the Purity Diner or Snooky's tonight.*

    eat

    eat call communicate lend use type

    1. *Could you _____ me some money? I don't get paid until Thursday.*
    2. *I studied French, but I can barely _____ with anyone.*
    3. *I know you're not very good with the computer. Can I _____ that document for you?*
    4. *I'm going to a party. Can I _____ the car tonight?*
    5. *"Where should I stay when I go to Barcelona?" "You could _____ my friend Pedro if you don't want to stay in a hotel."*

2. The following sentences explain what was done. Show the unrealized possibility by using the perfect form (*could have*). Replace the object in boldface type with the object in parentheses.

    EXAMPLE: *He stayed at a hotel. (with me)*

    He could've stayed with me.

    1. *We took **an airplane**. (the train)*
    2. *They ate **pizza**. (fish)*
    3. *She studies **medicine**. (music)*
    4. *You were living in **the suburbs**. (the city)*
    5. *I **drove** to the party. (walk)*

D. ANSWER KEY

1. 1. *lend*
    2. *communicate*
    3. *type*
    4. *use*
    5. *call*

2. 1. *We could've taken the train.*
    2. *They could've eaten fish.*
    3. *She could've studied music.*
    4. *You could've been living in the city.*
    5. *I could've walked to the party.*

Verbs in Action

35. Phrasal Verbs

A.

There are many verbs in English that can be combined with prepositions (or adverbs acting as prepositions) to give the verbs new meanings. These are called phrasal verbs. The adverb or preposition that follows the verb is called a particle. Surprisingly, the meaning of a phrasal verb may not be transparent from the verb and the particle used in the combination. For example, you can *run out of* a room, which literally means to leave quickly. However, to *run out of gas* on the highway means to exhaust your supplies of gasoline. Phrasal verbs are commonly used in English in both formal and informal speech and writing. It is important for you to be able to understand them and begin to incorporate them into your language little by little.

Let's look at some rules that apply to all phrasal verbs before we look at specific examples of each kind.

1. Three main categories

Phrasal verbs can be grouped into three main categories: separable, inseparable, and intransitive. Separable and inseparable phrasal verbs take an object. Intransitive phrasal verbs do not.

a. Separable phrasal verbs

For separable phrasal verbs, the verb and particle can be split. That means that the object can be come between the verb and the particle, or after the particle. If the object is a pronoun (me, you, him, her, it, us, them), then it must come between the verb and its preposition. In the following example, *look over* is the phrasal verb, and *the manuscript* is the object. Notice the difference between the three sentences below.

> She **looked over the manuscript**. (object after the verb)
> She **looked the manuscript over**. (object between verb and particle)
> She **looked it over**. (object pronoun between verb and preposition)

b. Inseparable phrasal verbs

An inseparable phrasal verb also takes an object, but the object must follow the phrasal verb in all cases. In the following example, *look after* is the phrasal verb. *My cat* is the object in the first sentence and *her* is the object pronoun in the second.

> I need to find someone to **look after my cat** while I'm on vacation.
> My mother is elderly and can't be left alone. Can you **look after her** while I go to the store?

c. Intransitive phrasal verbs

Some phrasal verbs do not take an object. Here are a few examples.

*We don't earn a lot of money, but we **get by**.*
*The plane **took off** ten minutes ago.*

2. Meaning

A phrasal verb often has a meaning that does not correlate to the specific verb and particle combination. Therefore, it can be difficult to guess the meaning of the verb unless you have context to help you.

get over	recover
look over	check carefully
get by	manage with less than what you would like

Also, some phrasal verbs may have more than one meaning, as in the example of *take off*.

*He **took off** his jacket.* (remove)
*The plane **took off**.* (leave the ground)
*I'm **taking off**.* (to leave quickly)
*The new product really **took off**.* (to have a lot of success)

In the above examples, the first use of *take off* is a separable phrasal verb. The next three are intransitive. Another example of a phrasal verb with different meanings is *stand up*.

*I **stood up** because I had to go to the bathroom.* (to move from a seated to a standing position)
*My date **stood me up** last night.* (to not appear when you have planned to meet someone)

As with *take off, stand up* also can be a separable phrasal verb or an intransitive phrasal verb with a change in meaning.

3. Formation

Phrasal verbs follow all conventions of regular verbs. Use *do/does/did* to form questions and negatives. Check the past tense and past participle of irregular verbs. Use *have/has/had* for the perfect. Add the verb *be* + *-ing* to form the progressive. Also, phrasal verbs have both active and passive forms.

*__Did__ the plane **take off** on time?*
*I **haven't stood up** for hours.*
*John **is filling out** the application.*

Verbs in Action

B.

1. The following are separable phrasal verbs. Determine the object pronoun for the underlined object, and change the sentence by placing the object pronoun between the verb and the particle.

    EXAMPLE: *He took off his jacket.*

    He took it off.

    1. *She figured out the answer.*
    2. *The students looked up the word in the dictionary.*
    3. *Last week I turned in the application.*
    4. *He tried on the shoes in the shoe store.*
    5. *Susan invited over my husband and me.*

2. The following are inseparable phrasal verbs. Change the object to an object pronoun. The pronoun must follow the phrasal verb.

    EXAMPLE: *The store ran out of oranges.*

    The store ran out of them.

    1. *We were looking for Susan.*
    2. *I ran into Sam last night.*
    3. *We're looking forward to the movie.*
    4. *Ben doesn't get along with the cats.*
    5. *She looks up to her father.*

C. ANSWER KEY

1.
1. *She figured it out.*
2. *The students looked it up in the dictionary.*
3. *Last week I turned it in.*
4. *He tried them on in the shoe store.*
5. *Susan invited us over.*

2.
1. *We were looking for her.*
2. *I ran into him last night.*
3. *We're looking forward to it.*
4. *Ben doesn't get along with them.*
5. *She looks up to him.*

36. Separable Phrasal Verbs

In this lesson, we will look at some common separable phrasal verbs and their meanings. Remember that a separable phrasal verb is one in which the verb (*take*) and the particle (*off*) can be separated by the object. Look at the three different sentences below to see where the object and object pronoun occur.

> The man *took off his jacket*. (object follows the verb)
> The man *took his jacket off*. (object between verb and particle)
> The man *took it off*. (object pronoun between the verb and the particle.)

Remember that if you replace an object with a pronoun (me, him, her, it, you, us, them), then the pronoun must come between the verb and the particle.

Let's look at some verbs and their meanings. For the following verbs, (s.t./s.o.) indicates that "something" or "someone" (the object) can be placed between the verb and the particle.

figure (s.t.) out:	to understand or deduce something after thinking about it *Did you **figure out the answer**? No, I haven't **figured it out**.*
look (s.t.) up:	to find out the meaning of something by looking in a reference book such as a dictionary or encyclopedia *Did you **look up the definition** in the dictionary? Yes, I **looked it up**.*
make (s.t.) up:	to invent a story to entertain or deceive *Did she **make up that excuse** so she wouldn't have to see me? No, she didn't **make it up**.*
turn (s.t./s.o.) in:	to hand over someone or something to those who asked for it *Did John **turn in the criminal** to the police? Yes, he **turned him in**.*
try (s.t.) on:	to put something on to see if it fits *Do you want to **try on this dress**? No, I don't want to **try it on**.*
call (s.t.) off:	to cancel an event or meeting, etc. *Did Anita **call off the engagement**? No, Richard **called it off**.*

close (s.t.) down:	to close an establishment such as a restaurant or a shop *Have they **closed down our favorite restaurant**? Yes, they've **closed it down**.*
drop (s.t./s.o.) off:	to take something or someone and leave it/them in another place, usually in a car *Can we **drop off Lester** on the way home? Yes, we can **drop him off**.*
fill (s.t.) in/out:	to enter the required information into a form, application, etc. *Did I **fill in the form** correctly? Yes, you **filled it in** just fine.*
give (s.t.) up:	to stop doing something, to quit *Should we **give up chocolate** for Lent? Let's not **give it up**.*
let (s.o.) down:	to be unable to fulfill expectations that someone else has for you, to disappoint *Did we **let down Anastasia** when we told her we weren't coming? No, we didn't **let her down**.*
pick (s.t./s.o.) up:	to collect something that has been prepared for you at the laundry, a store, etc., or to collect someone from a specific place in a car or by some other means or transportation *Can you **pick up the dry-cleaning** on your way home? Yes, I can **pick it up**.*
rule (s.t./s.o.) out:	to eliminate a possibility *Don't **rule out going to Las Vegas on our honeymoon**. Don't worry; I haven't **ruled it out**.*
turn (s.t./s.o.) down:	to reject a proposal *Did you **turn down your boss's offer**? No, I didn't **turn it down**.*
throw (s.t) away:	to put something into the garbage *Will you ever **throw away that old chair**? No, I'll never **throw it away**.*

A few separable phrasal verbs are only used with the object—usually an object pronoun—between the verb and the preposition:

stand (s.o.) up:	to not appear when you have planned to meet someone *He **stood her up** on prom night.*
talk (s.o.) into/out of:	to convince someone to do/not do something after some persuasion *You've **talked me into** seeing the new Scorsese movie.*

B.

1. Phrasal verbs with *back*

Phrasal verbs with the particle *back* (*take back, put back*, etc.) have the meaning of the verb plus "return." If you *take something back,* you return it to the store where you purchased it. If you *put something back,* you return it to where you got it (off a shelf or from a closet, for example). Let's look at a few more examples.

> *Jane called. You should **call** her **back**.* (return her phone call)
> *You still have my book. When are you going to **give** it **back**?*
>   (return the book)
> *Liz is still out. What time did she say she would **get back**?* (return to where you are)

Here is a list of verbs that can be used with back.

> *come back* (intransitive)
> *call (s.o.) back*
> *give (s.t.) back*
> *get back* (intransitive)
> *go back* (intransitive)
> *pay (s.o.) back*
> *put (s.t.) back*
> *take (s.t.) back*
> *write (s.o) back*

With the exception of *come back, get back,* and *go back* which do not take an object (int.), these verbs are all separable.

C.

1. Complete the following sentence logically with a phrasal verb from the list below. Don't forget to change the form of the verb as needed.

> EXAMPLE: Yesterday, we _____ the possibility of going to Sweden for vacation.
>
> *ruled out*

Make sure to put the verb in the correct form.

> rule out   figure out   make up   look up   talk into   give up
>
> 1. *If you don't know the meaning of a word, _____ it _____ in the dictionary.*
> 2. *I smoked for seven years but last year I _____ it _____.*
> 3. *Even though we studied the problem for hours, we couldn't _____ the answer.*
> 4. *I knew she was _____ an excuse when she said her cat had died.*
> 5. *I didn't want to go out, but my roommate _____ me _____ it.*

2. Use the appropriate particle to complete the following sentences.

> EXAMPLE: *He tried _____ the sweater.*
>
> *on*
>
> 1. *Because of the rain, they called _____ the concert.*
> 2. *We picked him _____ from school and dropped him _____ at his house.*
> 3. *John filled _____ the paperwork for his new job.*
> 4. *I submitted the proposal, but they turned it _____.*
> 5. *We could've gotten a free ticket, but I had thrown _____ the boarding passes.*

D. ANSWER KEY

1. 1. *look up*
    2. *gave up*
    3. *figure out*
    4. *making up*
    5. *talked into*

2. 1. *off*
    2. *up/off*
    3. *in/out*
    4. *down*
    5. *out*

37. Inseparable Phrasal Verbs

A.

In this lesson, we will look at inseparable phrasal verbs. These are verbs that also take an object (as with separable phrasal verbs), but in which the verb and the particle cannot be separated. Therefore, the object must follow the particle. For example, in the sentence *I ran into Matthew yesterday on the subway*, the verb (*ran*) and the particle (*into*) must come together. Look at a few more examples.

> He **came down with a terrible cold**.
> My aunt **went out with him** for two months but the relationship didn't last.
> Vacation starts next week. I'm **looking forward to it**.

break up (with)*:	to end a romantic relationship with someone *My sister **broke up with** her boyfriend last weekend.*
look for:	to attempt to find something or someone *Can you help us **look for** the car keys?*
look forward to:	to feel excitement about something that will happen in the future *We're **looking forward to** coming to visit you this summer.*
run into:	to meet someone by chance, or to collide with someone or something *I **ran into** her at the library last Saturday.*
get along (with)*:	to have a good relationship with *Does Ramit **get along with** Samir?*
catch up (with)*:	to be at the same place as another person in terms of work, abilities, position, etc. after having fallen behind *Frank nearly **caught up with** Ahmed in the last mile of the marathon.*
come down with:	to get a sickness such as a cold or the flu *John feels like he's **coming down with** the flu.*

count/depend/rely on:	to trust another person to be there for you when you need them *You can **count on** me to finish the project in time.*
deal with:	to handle a person, problem or situation, in some cases with the implication that it will be difficult *You just relax; I'll **deal with** it.*
drop out (of)*:	to withdraw from something for which you have signed up, such as school, or a group activity (a chorus, sports team), without completing it *I **dropped out** of medical school when I found out I wasn't good at biology.*
get over:	to recover *Sharon still hasn't **gotten over** her jet lag.*
go out with:	to have a romantic relationship with another person *Who's she **going out with** these days?*
look up to:	to respect or admire someone *I really **look up to** my grandmother. She inspires me in so many ways.*
look down on:	to consider someone to be inferior, or to treat someone as if they were inferior to you *This world would be a better place if fewer people **looked down on** people who have less money than they do.*
put up with:	to tolerate a person or situation, often even though you are not happy with it *How do you **put up with** all of this noise?*
wind/end up:	to end in a certain state, or doing a certain activity, after a series of events *Did you **end up** going to Alya's birthday party last weekend?*

* Without the final particle, these phrasal verbs have the same meaning, but become intransitive.

B.

1. Phrasal verbs with *get* related to transportation

The following phrasal verbs with *get* involve entering or exiting vehicles or places.

get on:	to board a large vehicle, such as an airplane, bus, train, or boat, or to mount a bicycle, motorcycle, or large animal, such as a horse *We didn't realize that we had forgotten our bathing suits until we had **gotten on** the plane.*
get off:	to exit a large vehicle, such as an airplane, bus, train, or boat, or to dismount a bicycle, motorcycle, or large animal, such as a horse ***Get off** the bus at 72nd street.*
get in/into:	to enter a smaller vehicle, such as a car, truck, or van, or to enter a place, such as a room, building, or bed *It's starting to rain! **Get in** the car and we'll wait it out there.*
get out (of):	to exit a smaller vehicle, such as a car, truck, or van, or to exit a place, such as a room, building, or bed *I'll have to **get out of** the car to reach the ticket booth.*

C.

1. Complete the following sentence logically with a phrasal verb from the lists above. Make sure to put the verb in the correct form.

EXAMPLE: *She _____ her cold quickly.*

got over

1. *Why didn't you come yesterday? I thought I could _____ you!*
2. *Terri _____ one of her old college friends yesterday.*
3. *Would you say that Martin Luther King Jr. is someone that you _____ and respect?*
4. *My mother doesn't _____ my new boyfriend. They don't even talk to each other.*
5. *Last week I _____ a terrible cold.*

2. Use the appropriate particle or particles to complete the following sentences.

> EXAMPLE: *She got _____ the car and started the engine.*
>
> *in/into*

> 1. *Can you deal _____ the customers while I do the cleaning up?*
> 2. *How long has she been going _____ him?*
> 3. *I can't put _____ this mess any longer! We need to straighten up.*
> 4. *Naomi got _____ the horse easily, but she didn't know how to get _____.*
> 5. *It's tempting to drop _____ school when all of your friends already have jobs.*

D. ANSWER KEY

1.
1. *count on*
2. *ran into*
3. *look up to*
4. *get along with*
5. *came down with*

2.
1. *with*
2. *out with*
3. *up with*
4. *on/off*
5. *out of*

38. Intransitive Phrasal Verbs

Finally, we have a group of phrasal verbs with no object following them: the intransitives. Some of the phrasal verbs below actually can take an object if a second particle is added:

John and I broke up.
*John broke up **with** me.*

break down:	to stop working, usually something mechanical such as a car *The car **broke down** on the way to the wedding.*
break up:	to end a romantic relationship *I just heard that Joe and Sam **broke up**! That's so sad!*
catch on:	to gain popularity *I love this trend for natural hair and makeup, but do you really think it'll **catch on**?*
check in:	to register for something previously arranged such as a stay at a hotel or an airplane flight *We have to **check in** before we go through security.*
clear up:	to become clear, often used in relation to weather and sickness/infection *It's really **clearing up** out there; I don't think we'll need our umbrellas.*
come back:	to return *Do you think they'll ever **come back**?*
fall through:	to not work out as expected (usually a plan, agreement or other arrangement) *We were supposed to get out of town this weekend, but our plans **fell through**.*
get up:	to rise from bed *Time to **get up**! No more lollygagging!*
get back:	to return *When they **get back**, we'll all go out for ice cream.*
go back:	to return *They realized they were driving in circles, so they just **went back**.*

Verbs in Action

give up:	to admit defeat
	*We **give up**! How many politicians does it take to screw in a light bulb?*
grow up:	to move from childhood to adulthood
	*He **grew up** so fast; I wish he could have been a little boy forever.*
look out:	to be careful
	***Look out**! There's a big hole in the sidewalk!*
show up:	to appear
	*We were a bit worried when you didn't **show up**.*
show off:	to behave in such a way as to call excessive attention to something you have or something which you have done
	*He always drives that fancy car around town; he really likes to **show off**.*
stand up:	to move from a sitting to a standing position
	***Stand up** so I can see how tall you've gotten!*
take over:	to assume control
	*Jane will be **taking over** while I'm on vacation.*
take off:	to leave the ground (such as an airplane), to leave quickly, to increase
	*We should really **take off**; it's getting late.*
wake up:	to awaken after sleeping
	*I was still tired when I **woke up**.*

B.

1. Complete the following sentences with a phrasal verb from the list above. Change the form of the verb as necessary.

EXAMPLE: *My plane _____ six hours late yesterday.*

took off

1. *I know he lives in Michigan now, but where did he _____?*
2. *"Why does he always wear those fancy clothes?" "I guess he likes to _____."*

3. *I was late to work because my car _____ .*
4. *It was raining this morning but it has _____ since then.*
5. *After working for hours on the crossword puzzle, Bill _____ .*

2. **Use the appropriate preposition to complete the following sentences.**

EXAMPLE: *She went _____ to the gym to pick up the bag she forgot.*

back

1. *Did you find out why Hank never showed _____ last night?*
2. *After my boss was fired, the assistant director took _____ .*
3. *We were hoping to go to California for vacation but our plans fell _____ .*
4. *What time do we have to check _____ at the airport?*
5. *Diego and Frida broke _____ after a long relationship.*

C. ANSWER KEY

1. 1. *grow up*
   2. *show off*
   3. *broke down*
   4. *cleared up*
   5. *gave up*

2. 1. *up*
   2. *over*
   3. *through*
   4. *in*
   5. *up*

39. *Make* and *Do*

The verbs *make* and *do* are commonly mistaken by second language speakers. In this lesson we will look at their uses and try to help you to avoid this confusion.

A.

The verb *make* is used:

1. to mean "create," "produce," or "build"

    > He's going **to make** a table for the kitchen.
    > They **made** the clothing by hand.
    > He **made** a sculpture out of clay.
    > Can you **make** a fire?
    > The law **was made** in 1909.

2. to mean "cook"

    > Have you **made** dinner yet?
    > Your next door neighbor **made** those delicious desserts.

3. to mean "force" or "cause to be" (use *make* + object + base form)

    > My parents **made me study** medicine even though I wanted to be a musician.
    > Don't **make us do** it again!
    > His behavior **made us feel** uncomfortable.

4. to mean "earn" or "achieve"

    > Doctors **make** a lot of money.
    > They **made** important strides in their research.

5. to mean "become" or "be"

    > She'll **make** a great doctor someday.
    > Jim **would've made** a great baseball player if he hadn't suffered that injury.

6. to mean "catch"

    > We just **made** the train! It was about to leave the station when we got there.

7. with "sense" to mean "to be reasonable"

    > That idea **makes sense**.

B.

The verb *do* is used:

1. to mean "perform" or "execute"

    > We **did** our homework before going to bed.
    > They **did** the job in a short amount of time.

2. with tasks or chores

do   *the laundry*
                                  the shopping
                                  the vacuuming
                                  the dishes

etc.

*"**Did** you **do the shopping**?" "No, I'll **do** it later."*
*I see he **didn't do the dishes**.*
*Someone else will have **to do the laundry** because I did it last time.*

3. to describe performance

*They **did** a good job.*
*The entire class **did** poorly on the exam.*
*She **did** the right thing by calling the police.*
*She was ill but now she's **doing** better.*

4. to talk about occupation or work

*What **do** you **do** for a living?*
*They're **redoing** their house.*

C.

1. Complete the following sentences with either *make* or *do* in the correct form.

EXAMPLE: *We _____ our homework last night*

did

1. *Did you _____ the laundry this morning?*
2. *I don't know how much money he _____ at his current job.*
3. *My parents _____ me study science even though I didn't like it.*
4. *They are _____ their own house.*
5. *Do you think we _____ the right thing when we bought the car?*

2. Change the following sentences from affirmative to negative, or from negative to affirmative.

EXAMPLE: *He didn't make a lot of money.*

He made a lot of money.

1. *The students did a good job.*
2. *I haven't made dinner.*
3. *She made it impossible to work together.*
4. *They aren't making two bedrooms.*
5. *She does her homework before going to bed.*

Verbs in Action

D. ANSWER KEY

1. 1. *do*
    2. *makes*
    3. *made*
    4. *making*
    5. *did*

2. 1. *The students **didn't do** a good job.*
    2. *I **have** made dinner.*
    3. *She **didn't** make it impossible to work together.*
    4. *The **are** making two bedrooms.*
    5. *She **doesn't** do her homework before going to bed.*

40. *Used to, Would, Be Used to*, and *Get Used To*

Used to, would, be used to, and *get used to* are often confused. Their use and structure are distinct even though they may appear to be the same. Let's look at each individually.

A.

1. *Used to* + base form

Used to is strictly used in the past tense. You will use it when you want to describe a state in the past that no longer exists, or an activity that you did habitually in the past that you no longer do. Look at these examples.

> We **used to go** to the beach every summer, but now I prefer going to the mountains.
> Sam **used to have** long hair, but he cut it when he got a new job.
> I **used to enjoy** watching horror movies when I was a kid.
> That chair **used to be** over in that corner, didn't it?

Used to has a negative (*didn't use to* or *never used to*) and a question form (*Did/Didn't you use to . . .?*). Note that the past tense suffix *-d* disappears in both cases, with the use of *did*.

> **Didn't he use to** live in this neighborhood?
> I **didn't use to** like vanilla ice cream, but now I do.

2. *Would* + base form

Would is a modal verb that can be used to express an activity that you did habitually in the past, but that is no longer done (just as *used to*). However, it can not describe a state in the past. (For example, do not say, *Sam would have long hair.*)

Following are some examples.

> I **would** always **ask** him to join us but he never did, so I don't ask anymore.
> When we got to our summer cottage, we **would have to** turn on the water and the electricity before we could go in.

A verb in the simple past can be used in any of the above sentences, although the repetition of the activity in the past is not emphasized as strongly.

B.

1. *Be used to* + noun/*-ing*

Be used to describes an activity that you are accustomed to doing. It differs from *used to* because it is used in the present tense (or any tense for that matter) and *used to* is not. Also, it is followed by either a noun or an *-ing* form of the verb (and not the base form).

> I **am used to living** in a big city now. (I am accustomed to it.)

He **is used to working** by himself these days.
We **are used to** our new dog.

You can use *be used to* also in the past, though you may not hear it as often in this tense.

When I lived in France, I **was used to buying** bread every
morning from the boulangerie.
We **were used to living** in a small apartment but we enjoy
having a larger home.

If you want to express *be used to* in a progressive or perfect form, use *get used to* (see below).

2. *Get used to* + noun/-*ing*

Get used to also expresses something you are accustomed to or accustomed to doing, but it expresses the process of becoming accustomed to it. It is used in the progressive and perfect forms instead of *be used to*.

I **am getting used to** my new job. (I am not accustomed to it,
but soon will be)
He **hasn't gotten used to** living here yet. (he is not accustomed
to it yet)

The past tense shows that the process of getting accustomed to something is complete.

We **got used to** the noise in New York, but it wasn't easy.

You can also use a modal with *get used to*.

We **will get used to** the new time zone in a couple of days.
I'm not happy, but I **must get used to** our new situation!

C.

1. The following are all activities that you did in the past but that you no longer do. Rewrite the clause in boldface type using *used to*. Some sentences are negative.

EXAMPLE: *I work in a bank, but before I was a teacher.*

I used to be a teacher.

1. *I live in London, but before **I lived in Rome.***
2. *I am a serious student now, but before **I wasn't a serious student.***
3. *I don't listen to rock music now, but **I did listen to it when I was younger.***
4. *I read the paper every morning, but before **I didn't read the paper.***
5. *I don't have any pets, but **I had a dog when I was a child.***

2. Complete the following sentences with either *used to, would, be used to,* or *get used to.*

> EXAMPLE: I _____ live in St. Louis.
>
> *used to*
>
> 1. *I live in a building of musicians, so I _____ hearing people practice their instruments by now.*
> 2. *What was the hardest thing for you to _____ doing now that you have a child?*
> 3. *When we were little, Alice and Irene _____ come for the Saturday evening concerts.*
> 4. *"I know it's December, but I _____ wearing a winter coat yet. Have you?" "Yes, I have."*
> 5. *I _____ sharing a room with my big sister and now I can't _____ having the room to myself.*

D. ANSWER KEY

1. 1. *I used to live in Rome.*
   2. *I didn't use to be a serious student.*
   3. *I used to listen to rock music.*
   4. *I didn't use to read the paper.*
   5. *I used to have a dog.*

2. 1. *am used to/have gotten used to*
   2. *get used to*
   3. *used to/would*
   4. *haven't gotten used to*
   5. *was used to/get used to*

APPENDIXES

Past Tense Forms and Past Participles of Irregular Verbs

BASE FORM	PAST TENSE	PAST PARTICIPLE
arise	arose	arisen
be	was/were	been
bear	bore	borne/born
beat	beat	beat
become	became	become
begin	began	begun
bend	bent	bent
bet	bet	bet
bid	bid	bid
bide	bode/bided	bided
bind	bound	bound
bite	bit	bitten/bit
bleed	bled	bled
blow	blew	blown
break	broke	broken
breed	bred	bred
bring	brought	brought
build	built	built
burst	burst	burst
buy	bought	bought
cast	cast	cast
catch	caught	caught
choose	chose	chosen
cling	clung	clung
come	came	come
cost	cost	cost
creep	crept	crept
cut	cut	cut
deal	dealt	dealt
dig	dug	dug
dive	dive/dove	dived
do	did	done
draw	drew	drawn
dream	dreamed/dreamt	dreamed/dreamt
drink	drank	drunk
drive	drove	driven
eat	ate	eaten
fall	fell	fallen
feed	fed	fed
feel	felt	felt
fight	fought	fought
find	found	found
fit	fit	fit
flee	fled	fled
fling	flung	flung
fly	flew	flown
forbid	forbade	forbidden
forecast	forecast	forecast
forget	forgot	forgotten
forgive	forgave	forgiven
forgo	forwent	forgone
forsake	forsook	forsaken
freeze	froze	frozen

BASE FORM	PAST TENSE	PAST PARTICIPLE
get	got	gotten/got
give	gave	given
go	went	gone
grind	ground	ground
grow	grew	grown
hang	hung	hung
have	had	had
hear	heard	heard
hide	hid	hidden
hit	hit	hit
hold	held	held
hurt	hurt	hurt
keep	kept	kept
kneel	kneeled/knelt	kneeled/knelt
knit	knitted/knit	knitted/knit
know	knew	known
lay	laid	laid
lead	led	led
leap	leaped/leapt	leaped/leapt
learn	learned/learnt	learned/learnt
leave	left	left
lend	lent	lent
let	let	let
lie	lay	lain
light	lit	lit
lose	lost	lost
make	made	made
mean	meant	meant
meet	met	met
mishear	misheard	misheard
mislay	mislaid	mislaid
mislead	misled	misled
misspeak	misspoke	misspoken
mistook	mistake	mistaken
misunderstand	misunderstood	misunderstood
mow	mowed	mown
offset	offset	offset
outdo	outdid	outdone
outgrow	outgrew	outgrown
outshoot	outshot	outshot
overcome	overcame	overcame
overeat	overate	overeaten
overhear	overheard	overheard
overlay	overlaid	overlaid
override	overrode	overridden
overrun	overran	overrun
oversee	oversaw	overseen
overshoot	overshot	overshot
oversleep	overslept	overslept
overtake	overtook	overtaken
overthrow	overthrew	overthrown
partake	partook	partaken
pay	paid	paid
plead	pleaded/pled	pleaded/pled
prepay	prepaid	prepaid

2,000+ Essential English Verbs

BASE FORM	PAST TENSE	PAST PARTICIPLE
put	put	put
quit	quit	quit
read	read	read
rebuild	rebuilt	rebuilt
redo	redid	redone
remake	remade	remade
repay	repaid	repaid
reread	reread	reread
retell	retold	retold
rethink	rethought	rethought
rewrite	rewrote	rewritten
rid	rid	rid
ride	rode	ridden
ring	rang	rung
rise	rose	risen
run	ran	run
say	said	said
see	saw	seen
seek	sought	sought
sell	sold	sold
send	sent	sent
set	set	set
sew	sewed	sewn/sewed
shake	shook	shaken
shed	shed	shed
shine	shone/shined	shone/shined
shoot	shot	shot
show	showed	shown/showed
shred	shredded/shred	shredded/shred
shrink	shrank/shrunk	shrunk
shut	shut	shut
sing	sang	sung
sink	sank	sunk
sit	sat	sat
sleep	slept	slept
slide	slid	slid
sling	slung	slung
slink	slunk/slinked	slunk/slinked
slit	slit	slit
smell	smelled/smelt	smelled/smelt
sneak	sneaked/snuck	sneaked/snuck
speak	spoke	spoken
speed	sped/speeded	sped/speeded
spell	spelled/spelt	spelled/spelt
spend	spent	spent
spill	spilled/spilt	spilled/spilt
spin	spun	spun
spit	spit/spat	spit/spat
split	split	split
spoil	spoiled/spoilt	spoiled/spoilt
spread	spread	spread
spring	sprang/sprung	sprung
stand	stood	stood
steal	stole	stolen
stick	stuck	stuck

BASE FORM	PAST TENSE	PAST PARTICIPLE
sting	stung	stung
stink	stank/stunk	stunk
stride	strode	stridden
strike	struck	struck
string	strung	strung
strive	strove/strived	striven/strived
swear	swore	sworn
sweat	sweat/sweated	sweat/sweated
sweep	swept	swept
swim	swam	swum
swing	swung	swung
take	took	taken
teach	taught	taught
tear	tore	torn
tell	told	told
think	thought	thought
throw	threw	thrown
thrust	thrust	thrust
tread	trod/treaded	trodden/trod
typecast	typecast	typecast
unbend	unbent	unbent
undergo	underwent	undergone
underlie	underlay	underlain
undersell	undersold	undersold
understand	understood	understood
undertake	undertook	undertaken
undo	undid	undone
unwind	unwound	unwound
upset	upset	upset
wake	woke/waked	woken/waked
wear	wore	worn
weave	wove/weaved	woven/weaved
wed	wed/wedded	wed/wedded
weep	wept	wept
wet	wet	wet
win	won	won
wind	wound	wound
withdraw	withdrew	withdrawn
withhold	withheld	withheld
withstand	withstood	withstood
wring	wrung	wrung
write	wrote	written

Verbs Followed by a Preposition

admit to
advise against
agree with
apologize for
approve of
argue with/about
believe in
blame for
care about/for
choose between/among
consist of
count upon/on
deal with
depend upon/on
dream of/about
excel in/at
feel like
fight for
forgive for
made from

hope for
insist upon/on
introduce to
keep from
object to
participate in
plan on
prevent from
prohibit from
rely upon/on
resort to
stare at
stop from
subscribe to
succeed in
talk about
thank for
think about/of
wonder about

Adjectives Followed by a Preposition + a Verb in Gerund Form

be accustomed to
be afraid of
be angry at/with
be annoyed with
be ashamed of
be awful at
be bored with/by
be capable of
be comfortable with
be committed to
be composed of
be content with
be convinced of
be curious about
be dedicated to
be different from
be disappointed in/with
be done with
be envious of
be equipped with
be excited by
be familiar with
be fond of
be frightened by
be good at
be grateful to/for

be guilty of
be innocent of
be interested in
be jealous of
be known for
be limited to
be located in
be made of
be nervous about
be opposed to
be pleased with
be prepared for
be proud of
be ready for
be related to
be responsible for
be satisfied with
be scared of
be shocked by/at
be sorry for/about
be tired of
be unhappy about
be upset with
be used to
be worried about

Verbs Followed by a Gerund

admit
advise
appreciate
avoid

can't help
consider
continue
delay

deny	mind
detest	miss
discuss	postpone
dislike	prevent
enjoy	prohibit
escape	propose
explain	quit
feel like	recommend
finish	regret
forgive	resent
give up	risk
hate	suggest
imagine	support
keep	tolerate
loathe	understand
mention	

Verbs Followed by an Infinitive

afford	manage
agree	mean
appear	need
arrange	neglect
ask	offer
attempt	pay
can't wait	plan
choose	pretend
dare	refuse
decide	request
deserve	seem
expect	struggle
fail	swear
forget	tend
grow	threaten
help	try
hesitate	volunteer
hope	wait
hurry	want
intend	wish
learn (how)	would like

Verbs Followed by a Gerund or an Infinitive

begin	love
can't stand	prefer
continue	remember*
forget*	start
hate	stop*
like	try (*)

Verbs Followed by an Object and an Infinitive

advise	challenge
allow	convince
ask*	encourage
cause	expect*

---

* can also be followed by an infinitive without an object

forbid
force
get
help*
invite
order
permit
persuade

require
remind
teach
tell
urge
warn
want*

Adjectives Followed by an Infinitive

admit to
advise against
agree with
apologize for
approve of
argue with/about
believe in
blame for
care about/for
choose between/among
consist of
count upon/on
deal with
depend upon/on
dream of/about
excel in/at
feel like
fight for
forgive for
made from

hope for
insist upon/on
introduce to
keep from
object to
participate in
plan on
prevent from
prohibit from
rely upon/on
resort to
stare at
stop from
subscribe to
succeed in
talk about
thank for
think about/of
wonder about

Verbs That Can Take *Get* as the Auxiliary Verb in the Passive

get asked
get awoken
get beaten
get bitten
get built
get broken
get called
get canned
get canceled
get chosen
get divorced
get driven
get fed
get fired
get hired

get hurt
get infected
get left
get lost
get married
get paid
get rejected
get scratched
get shaken
get stolen
get stung
get swept
get taken
get upset
get written

---

* these verbs can be followed by either gerund or infinitive but the meaning will change